Applications in Basic Marketing
Clippings from the Popular Business Press

2004-2005 Edition

William D. Perreault, Jr.
University of North Carolina

and

E. Jerome McCarthy
Michigan State University

 **McGraw-Hill Irwin**

Boston   Burr Ridge, IL   Dubuque, IA   Madison, WI   New York   San Francisco   St. Louis
Bangkok   Bogotá   Caracas   Kuala Lumpur   Lisbon   London   Madrid   Mexico City
Milan   Montreal   New Delhi   Santiago   Seoul   Singapore   Sydney   Taipei   Toronto

McGraw-Hill
Irwin

APPLICATIONS IN BASIC MARKETING:
CLIPPINGS FROM THE POPULAR BUSINESS PRESS 2004-2005 EDITION

Published by McGraw-Hill/Irwin, a business unit of The McGraw-Hill Companies, Inc., 1221 Avenue of the Americas, New York, NY, 10020. Copyright © 2005 by The McGraw-Hill Companies, Inc. All rights reserved. No part of this publication may be reproduced or distributed in any form or by any means, or stored in a database or retrieval system, without the prior written consent of The McGraw-Hill Companies, Inc., including, but not limited to, in any network or other electronic storage or transmission, or broadcast for distance learning.

Some ancillaries, including electronic and print components, may not be available to customers outside the United States.

This book is printed on acid-free paper.

1 2 3 4 5 6 7 8 9 0 QPD/QPD 0 9 8 7 6 5 4 3 2

ISBN   0-07-286470-2
ISSN   1099-5579

Publisher: *John E. Biernat*
Executive editor: *Linda Schreiber*
Coordinating editor: *Lin Davis*
Managing developmental editor: *Nancy Barbour*
Marketing manager: *Danial Silverburg*
Media producer: *Craig Atkins*
Senior project manager: *Christine A. Vaughan*
Manager, new book production: *Heather D. Burbridge*
Director of design: *Keith J. McPherson*
Lead supplement producer: *Cathy Tepper*
Senior digital content specialist: *Brian Nacik*
Compositor: *Electronic Publishing Services, Inc., TN*
Printer: *Quebecor World Dubuque, Inc.*

www.mhhe.com

Preface

This is the fifteenth annual edition of *Applications in Basic Marketing*. We developed this set of marketing "clippings" from popular business publications to accompany our texts—*Basic Marketing* and *Essentials of Marketing.* All of these clippings report interesting case studies and current issues that relate to topics covered in our texts and in the first marketing course. We will continue to publish a new edition of this book *every year.* That means that we can include the most current and interesting clippings. Each new copy of our texts will come shrink-wrapped with a free copy of the newest (annual) edition of this book. However, it can also be ordered from the publisher separately for use in other courses or with other texts.

Our objective is for this book to provide a flexible and helpful set of teaching and learning materials. We have included clippings (articles) on a wide variety of topics. The clippings deal with consumer products and business products, goods and services, new developments in marketing as well as traditional issues, and large well-known companies as well as new, small ones. They cover important issues related to marketing strategy planning for both domestic and global markets. The readings can be used for independent study, as a basis for class assignments, or as a focus of in-class discussions. Some instructors might want to assign all of the clippings, but we have provided an ample selection so that it is easy to focus on a subset which is especially relevant to specific learning/teaching objectives. A separate set of teaching notes discusses points related to each article. We have put special emphasis on selecting short, highly readable articles—ones which can be read and understood in 10 or 15 minutes—so that they can be used in combination with other readings and assignments for the course. For example, they might be used in combination with assignments from *Basic Marketing,* exercises from the *Learning Aid for Use with Basic Marketing,* or *The Marketing Game!* micro-computer strategy simulation.

All of the articles are reproduced here in basically the same style and format as they originally appeared. This gives the reader a better sense of the popular business publications from which they are drawn, and stimulates an interest in ongoing learning beyond the time frame for a specific course.

We have added this component to our complete set of **P**rofessional **L**earning **U**nits **S**ystems (our **P.L.U.S.**) to provide even more alternatives for effective teaching and learning in the first marketing course. It has been an interesting job to research and select the readings for this new book, and we hope that our readers find it of value in developing a better understanding of the opportunities and challenges of marketing in our contemporary society.

William D. Perreault, Jr. and E. Jerome McCarthy

Acknowledgments

We would like to thank all of the publications that have granted us permission to reprint the articles in this book. Similarly, we value and appreciate the work and skill of the many writers who prepared the original materials.

Lin Davis played an important role in this project. She helped us research thousands of different publications to sort down to the final set, and she also contributed many fine ideas on how best to organize the selections that appear here.

The ideas for this book evolved from and built on previous editions of *Readings and Cases in Basic Marketing*. John F. Grashof and Andrew A. Brogowicz were coauthors of that book. We gratefully recognize the expertise and creativity that they shared over the years on that project. Their fine ideas carry forward here and have had a profound effect on our thinking in selecting articles that will meet the needs of marketing instructors and students alike.

We would also like to thank the many marketing professors and students whose input have helped shape the concept of this book. Their ideas—shared in personal conversations, in focus group interviews, and in responses to marketing research surveys—helped us to clearly define the needs that this book should meet.

Finally, we would like to thank the people at McGraw-Hill/Irwin, our publisher, who have helped turn this idea into a reality. We are grateful for their commitment to making these materials widely available.

W.D.P. and E.J.M.

Contents

Getting Information for Marketing Decisions

Product

Place

Promotion

Price

Marketing Strategies: Planning, Implementation and Control

Ethical Marketing in a Consumer-Oriented World: Appraisal and Challenges

Marketing's Value to Consumers, Firms, and Society

Making High-Tech Play Less Work

To Broaden Appeal, Toy Designers Try a New Formula: Digital but Not Daunting

BY MICHEL MARRIOTT

In the late 1990's, as personal computers were becoming as common in many American households as televisions and cordless phones, the toy industry quickly embraced technologies like microprocessors, optical sensors and audio synthesizers. But some parents complained that child's play was becoming anything but. Toys and games, they said, were becoming too difficult to set up, charge up and play.

This year, toymakers are increasingly seizing on a strategy embraced already by their consumer electronics counterparts: use smarter technology to make products as simple and easy to enjoy as marbles and jump ropes. This shift in the $31.9 billion toy industry (including the $11.2 billion video-game sector) will be evident at the 101st Annual American International Toy Fair, which opens on Sunday in New York.

"In a mature industry, manufacturers are looking for that specific edge that will get their products chosen over someone else's," said Michael Redmond, a senior industry analyst for the NPD Group. Incorporating sophisticated but easy-to-use technology into toys and children's games is more and more important in gaining an edge, he said—particularly given a 3 percent decline in toy sales (excluding games) last year in the United States.

The results of that strategy will soon be apparent on retail shelves. Expect to see plush animals and toy action figures that sing or respond directly to television programs without any need for special transceivers and tangles of wire; a video game whose main character seamlessly responds to thousands of words and phrases spoken by players; and a hybrid game system from Japan that lets players wield real tennis rackets and baseball bats against virtual opponents on their TV sets.

This crop of toys and games, which should begin appearing as early as this spring, uses technology to lower barriers that may have made some playthings almost too complicated, too geeky, for average consumers. Toy and game makers say that consumers want the learning curve to be little more than a speed bump.

"Right out of the package the technology adds to the play value," said Thomas P. Conley, president of the Toy Industry Association, which represents 85 percent of the toymakers in the United States. "What we've got to remember is that all of this is trying to enhance the play value for the child, so the child can enjoy the toy longer."

Mr. Conley said that at least 70 percent of the toys being shown at this year's Toy Fair use microchips. "That number grows every single year," he added. "The chip technology keeps getting better and better, so the toys are able to do more and have more features and still come in at those magic price points that retailers like."

For example, Thinkway is expanding the wildly popular cyberworld of Neopets with a line of interactive Neopet toys that are not only voice-activated but are also engineered to detect a player's mood and respond like a real pet. Bandai America has its own interactive doll, Berry Talkin' Apple Dumplin', that says more than 60 words and phrases but "learns" to recombine them in new ways the more a child talks to the doll. And LeapFrog is introducing technology-enhanced learning toys that incorporate functions like handwriting recognition and software that enables children to enter their homework problems into a hand-held device and get help by way of improved microprocessing.

Advanced microchip technology is also permitting some familiar devices to act more toylike as their makers reach for younger consumers.

YOUR BIDDING In the action-adventure game Lifeline, players will direct the character Rio, left, by speaking aloud rather than using a controller or buttons. Rio can understand 5,000 words and about 100,000 phrases.

The latest product from Wildseed, a software company based in Kirkland, Wash., that makes interactive accessories for cell-phones, is a line of shells that snap on and off special wireless phones from Wildseed that are expected to cost less than $100. The shells, called SmartSkins, contain a microchip that personalizes a phone, instantly loading it with digital music, video clips, pictures, wallpaper, games, special ring tones and more without the need for lengthy downloads or tedious typing on tiny wireless handset keypads. The shells are expected to cost $25 to $50.

"Technology for technology's sake? The typical parent sees through that," said Kevin Curran, general manager of Fisher-Price Friends, which produces toys based on characters like Elmo on "Sesame Street" and Blue from "Blue's Clues." "You really have to tap into children's play patterns. If the technology doesn't reinforce the play pattern, then it becomes superfluous."

At Toy Fair—an event open only to the industry, with more than 1,500 toy and children's entertainment companies unveiling their latest products—Fisher-Price is showing, among other products, InteracTV. Mr. Curran describes it as a $40 "learning platform" that lets children play and learn with television characters through special DVDs and a simple remote-control panel.

The brightly colored plastic panel uses infrared sensors and touch-screen technology that wirelessly "speaks" to any standard DVD player with the touch of a child's finger—even if the child does not point the panel at the DVD player.

Children as young as 3 can use InteracTV to play along, answering questions and solving problems, with familiar television characters like Dora the Explorer and SpongeBob SquarePants, Mr. Curran said.

A child watching Dora on everyday television could shout answers to questions posed on the air. But with a DVD made for InteracTV, the child can enter answers and get immediate feedback in the characters' voices.

The lightweight control panel can store multiple remote-control codes that let children use it with a number of different DVD players, including one at home, and perhaps another in the car or at a grandparent's house, Mr. Curran added.

In another effort to capitalize on children's viewing habits, Mattel Entertainment is releasing a new Barbie DVD and videotape, the fourth in a series for the fashion-doll-turned-thespian, with a computer-animated Barbie starring in "The Princess and the Pauper."

The production's innovation will take place not on the screen, however, but in the living room. One of the characters, a sweet-natured cat named Serafina, will be sold as a

(Cont.)

$40 plush toy stuffed with digital technology that will let it move (wag its tail and purr, for instance) and sing along with parts of the story when prompted by the video.

Julia Jensen, a spokeswoman for Mattel, said that a watermark technology sends signals from the film to the toy cat through a wireless transmitter that looks like a small jewelry box.

"Consumers are not interested in the complex side of any of this," Ms. Jensen said. "We've talked to mothers and know that as they see everything around them getting easier to use, they want their children's toys as easy and seamless, too."

In the same vein, Mattel and Warner Brothers Animation have teamed up to produce a series of Batman toys—a hand-held communicator, action figure and Batmobile—that will use a wireless technology called video-encoded invisible light to respond to minute pixel changes embedded in a new animated television series.

The series, "The Batman," which is to begin in the fall on Kids' WB and the Cartoon Network, is based on the comic-book legend who morphed into a TV and a movie hero but will feature a younger version of the character, with sleeker, more high-tech gizmos than those seen even in the movies, Warner executives said.

Jim Wagner, senior vice president for marketing at Mattel, said the wireless signals would be undetectable to viewers, but not to the Mattel toys made to sense and respond to them.

Mr. Wagner said that the Batmobile, for instance, the most expensive of the interactive toys at $52, can be prompted to turn on its lights, deploy its fins and make sounds as if its motor is running, all by receiving signals from the television screen.

Even video games, long since harnessed to the family television set, are getting a make-it-easier makeover.

Next month, Konami Digital Entertainment America plans to release Lifeline, developed by Sony Computer Entertainment Japan for the Sony PlayStation 2 console. Konami spokesmen say the game is the first fully voice-activated action-adventure video game.

Most of the action is controlled by a player speaking through a headset to a virtual woman named Rio, a survivor of a mysterious explosion aboard a space station hotel orbiting the earth. Rio can understand 5,000 words and about 100,000 phrases, said Robert Goff, a Konami product manager.

The game, already a major hit in Japan, appeals to hard-core gamers, said Mr. Goff, but also to those intimidated by a video game

YES, ROBIN? A hand-held communicator from Mattel and Warner Brothers Animation, part of a new series of Batman toys, will use wireless technology to respond to onscreen cues in a new animated TV series that starts this fall. The cues are relayed by minute pixel changes.

pad's array of buttons. "It's a pretty hard thing to learn," he said of a game controller, although "many of us have grown up with it."

Lifeline's voice recognition virtually eliminates the need for a game controller as players direct Rio through the ruined space station, solving problems and fighting menacing creatures.

In a typical sequence, a player directs Rio to enter a guest room to search for clues to explain the fates of its missing inhabitants. After a player tells Rio to retrieve and open a book there, the character soon comes under attack by a swarm of creepy aliens.

When the player shouts, "Shoot, head!" Rio fires her weapon at the creature's head. "Dodge to the right!" and she complies. "Shoot stomach!" and Rio does.

"It's a more intuitive way to interact with someone," Mr. Goff said of controlling action by telling a character what to do with a voice command rather than using a joystick, buttons and triggers. "Imagine voice activation coming in to football video games. You could call audibles, call man-to-man, zone defenses. Every game could benefit."

Game designers at the SSD Company in Kusatsu, Japan, had a similar thought but took a different route in eliminating the game controller from its video games, its engineers said recently. Their solution is XaviX (pronounced ZAH-vicks), a game system that marries conventional video game technology with toy baseballs, bats, tennis rackets and bowling balls embedded with wireless sensors.

Someone playing a XaviX game—tennis, for instance—inserts the game cartridge into an $80 XaviX set-top box connected to a television set. Rather than a game controller, the player picks up a special toy racket, squares off in front of the television and swings, smacking a virtual ball that reacts almost like a real one on the screen. The virtual spectators cheer, depending on the level of play; the score is kept; and the real human players often work up a real sweat, said Andre Job, vice president for marketing at the TSC Group, which helped develop XaviX for the American market.

"I think the key thing for kids and adults, no matter the form of entertainment, is that they want simplicity," Mr. Job said. "They want to spend their time playing and enjoying the experience instead of spending enormous amounts of time with complexities, wondering how a thing works."

Southwest Airlines: The Hottest Thing in the Sky

Through change at the top, through 9/11, in a lousy industry, it keeps winning Most Admired kudos. How? ■ *Andy Serwer*

It's a little strange how some folks still think about the airline business. There are the big players, they'll tell you, like Delta, United, and American. And then you have the smaller fish. The low-cost carriers, led by that wacky Southwest Airlines, which they mention almost as an afterthought.

Now, hang on a minute. Let's look at those "industry leaders" and ask: Big like how? Well, United parent UAL filed the largest bankruptcy in aviation history ($25 billion in assets) in December 2002. That's big. American is weighted down with nearly $18 billion of debt on its books. That's pretty big. And finally, the three large airlines lost a total of some $5.8 billion last year. That's big too.

Now let's look at Southwest Airlines. Last year the company earned $442 million—more than all the other U.S. airlines combined. Its market capitalization of $11.7 billion is bigger than that of all its competitors combined, too. And last May, for the first time, Southwest boarded more domestic customers than any other airline, according to the Department of Transportation. Sure, the majors still have more revenue—Southwest, with about $6 billion in sales in 2003, ranks only No. 7 in that department—and they have more planes and carry more passengers when you include their overseas routes. And yes, some analysts question whether Southwest's amazing growth trajectory can continue. But, bottom line: Is there any question which company is the leader of this industry?

No wonder Southwest has landed in the top ten of FORTUNE's Most Admired Companies in each of the past six years—a distinction shared only by Berkshire Hathaway, General Electric, and Microsoft. Its accomplishments would be estimable in any industry. (Southwest was the nation's best-performing stock from 1972 through 2002, according to *Money* magazine, up a gravity-defying 26% per year.) But that Southwest has achieved this measure of success

in the snakebit airline biz is nothing short of astonishing. What's more, Southwest has sustained that success—and its grip on the top ten list—even nearly three years after its eccentric founder, Herb Kelleher, stepped down as CEO (he's still chairman) and after a swarm of upstart airlines, from JetBlue to Ted, have tried to horn in on its formula.

To figure out how, you could do worse than go back to the airline's conception. Southwest famously began 33 years ago when Kelleher (a lawyer by training) and a partner drew up a business plan on a cocktail napkin. Through decades of battling the big airlines, Southwest hasn't really changed its original formula. It enters markets in which traditional airlines hold sway and then blasts them with much lower fares. Southwest flies "point to point" (city to city), ignoring the hub-and-spoke model of most other airlines. It flies only 737s. It serves no meals, only snacks (peanuts, mostly). It charges no fees to change same-fare tickets. It has no assigned seats. It has no electronic entertainment on its planes, relying instead on relentlessly fun flight attendants to amuse passengers.

That formula has so far proved unbeatable. Consider Southwest's success against just one old-line competitor: US Airways. According to analysis by Michael Roach, an industry consultant with Unisys R2A, a division of the technology company, when Southwest entered the San Francisco—Southern California markets in the late '80s, US Air had a 58% market share in those routes. By the mid-'90s, Southwest had driven US Air completely out of them. In the early '90s, Southwest entered Baltimore Washington International Airport (BWI), where US Air had a significant hub; now US Air is down to 4.9% of the traffic at BWI, while Southwest ranks No. 1 with a 47% share.

While it's hard for Southwest to play the underdog these days—and it certainly isn't sneaking up on anybody anymore—it's still the industry maverick. No matter what its

competitors say or do, no company walks the talk quite like Southwest. It's iconoclastic, quirky, and sometimes just plain bizarre. Southwest has so much insouciance, in fact, that it has allowed itself to become the sub-

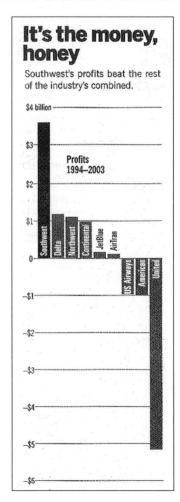

It's the money, honey

Southwest's profits beat the rest of the industry's combined.

Profits 1994–2003

ject of a reality TV show on cable channel A&E called *Airline.* ("We all have our baggage" is the tagline.) The cameras follow Southwest employees—who don't always come across as sugar and spice—as they deal with all manner of crisis: Nasty, staggering drunks. Passengers who stink like Limburger cheese. Chicago thunderstorms. (And yes, the show has been successful enough that A&E wants to renew for next season.) Hard to imagine most admired company Wal-Mart subjecting itself to that kind of scrutiny!

If competitors are trying so hard to copy Southwest, why in the names of Orville and Wilbur Wright haven't they been able to duplicate its success? "Because they don't get it," says Southwest's idiosyncratic president and COO Colleen Barrett. "What we do is very simple, but it's not simplistic. We really do everything with passion. We scream at each other and we hug each other." There's no question that the other airlines practice the screaming part. They haven't been so good at the hugging.

Barrett, a 59-year-old Vermont-born grandmother with a long, gray ponytail, has been with the company since the beginning. In fact, she started as Herb Kelleher's legal secretary. Kelleher, 72, is one of the most unusual businessmen in our country's history. He has some of the best people skills on earth. He is also a walking paradox. As brilliant as he is batty, Kelleher is half P.T. Barnum, half Will Rogers, half Clarence Darrow, and half Jack Welch. (Yes, that adds up to two men—but if you drank as much Wild Turkey and smoked as many cigarettes as Kelleher does, you'd be seeing double too.) Despite battling prostate cancer five years ago and turning over the CEO reins to his longtime protégé Jim Parker in August 2001, Kelleher is still intimately involved in the company, handling critical government affairs, scheduling, aircraft purchasing, and strategic planning. The public face of Southwest Airlines, however, now belongs to Parker and Barrett.

To truly understand why this company continues to be such a hit with customers, you have to go behind the wall and take a look. Pay a visit to Southwest's headquarters just off Love Field in Dallas, and you'll probably think you've wandered onto the set of *Pee-wee's Playhouse.* The walls are festooned with more than ten thousand picture frames—no exaggeration—containing photos of employees' pets, of Herb dressed like Elvis or in drag, of stewardesses in miniskirts, of Southwest planes gnawing on competitors' aircraft. Then there are the teddy bears, and jars of pickled hot peppers, and pink flamingos. There is cigarette smoking, and lots of chuckling, and nary a necktie to be seen.

"To me, it's comfortable," says Barrett, who as the ultimate keeper of the culture sits at a desk with a burning scented candle surrounded by the densest zone of bric-a-brac. "This is an open scrapbook. We aren't uptight. We celebrate everything. It's like a fraternity, a sorority, a reunion. We are having a *party!*" she says, throwing up her hands. I ask Barrett how much her annual picture-frame budget is. "Oh, I couldn't tell you that," she says. "Let's just say that I first gave out the framing work to this hippie fella, and now he has a business with 13 employees."

Okay, but come on. This is a serious business, right? So how does Southwest reconcile this insanity—studied though much of it is—with the fact that it flies 5.5 million people through the air each month? (Southwest—knock on Kelleher's head—has never had a fatal crash.) "Yes, our culture is almost like a religion," says company CFO Gary Kelly, "but it's a dichotomy. In many ways we are conservative. Financially, for instance." Indeed, Southwest is the only airline that maintains an investment-grade rating on its debt—a remarkable accomplishment in that business. And keeping a hawk's eye on costs is just as much a part of the company's culture as its silliness.

Yet lately, even though the airline still has some of the lowest expenses in the industry, costs have been climbing at Southwest. A key metric used in the business is cost per available seat mile (CASM), and in 1995 Southwest's CASM was 7.07 cents. Today it is up to 7.60 cents. One reason: Fuel prices have risen significantly since then. Another reason: higher compensation. "Southwest's pilots have been getting greedy," says industry consultant Roach. "They seem to think that because they work at the best airline in the business, they should get paid the most."

But let's put the cost creep in context. The big carriers all have CASMs of between 9 cents and 13 cents, and they haven't been closing the gap on Southwest. In other words, their costs are increasing at the same rate. (True, JetBlue has been able to achieve costs below Southwest's, but its have also been climbing recently—which in part explains why JetBlue's once highflying stock is off some 50% from its peak.) And Southwest management is working hard to keep a lid on costs. For instance, late last year the company announced it was closing down three call centers to save money—more than $20 million annually—as more of its customers make reservations online. "We are not satisfied with these inflationary trends," says Southwest CEO Jim Parker dryly and determinedly.

Follow the leader

The low-cost copycats aren't copying Southwest as closely as you might think.

	Founded	Fleet	Hubs	Unions	Assigned seats	Ticket-change fees	Food	In-flight entertainment
Southwest	1971	Boeing 737s	No	Yes	No	No	Snacks only	Wisecracking flight attendants
AirTran	1993	Varied	Yes	Yes	Yes	$50	Snacks only	Nothing right now
JetBlue	2000	Airbus A320s[1]	No	No	Yes	$25	Snacks only	DirecTV at each seat
Song	2003	Boeing 757s	No	Pilots only	Yes	$25	Meals for sale	Satellite TV at each seat; pay-per-view movies; videogames
Ted	2004	Airbus A320s	Yes	Yes	Yes	$100	Meals for sale	Nothing special

[1]Will add 100 Embraer 190s in 2005.

(Cont.)

Keeping costs under control and keeping its culture alive: These are huge challenges for Southwest as it moves from upstart to prime-time player. The company now has 34,000 employees and flies to 58 cities (59 when it opens up in Philadelphia in May). Las Vegas, with 185 daily departures, has become Southwest's most-served airport. It has a fleet of almost 400 jets, with hundreds more on order (which will be painted deep "canyon blue," replacing the carrier's familiar brown and red). That's big.

So what about it, Herb Kelleher? Is the company losing its soul, as some critics have said? "No," says Kelleher, puffing on an early-morning Merit Ultra Light. (I opt for a PayDay candy bar, which he keeps in a jar on his desk—"because I drink," he says.) "It'd better not be, because I'm not going to be around forever," he laughs. "Listen, we have an incredible esprit de corps here. It's like the Marine Corps. The intangibles have always been more important than the tangibles. Plus we run this company to prepare ourselves for the bad times, which always come in the business."

Of course, the airline industry is just now emerging from the absolute worst of bad times—9/11 and its aftermath. While the rest of the industry laid off thousands of people and lost more than $22 billion over the past three years, Southwest didn't furlough a single employee and remained in the black every quarter. In fact, it has kept its string of profitable years alive at 31 straight. That's because, unlike its competitors, Southwest has wide enough margins to take a hit.

Even though Southwest has mostly flown above the storm clouds during the past few years, the world has changed dramatically for this business and this company. In Jet-Blue and AirTran, Southwest faces a couple of strong, innovative, low-cost competitors (see table). Orlando-based AirTran has been growing fast, operating primarily out of its Atlanta hub—yes, a hub. JetBlue and its high-profile CEO, David Neeleman (who once worked at Southwest), have managed to generate a huge amount of buzz with their cool new Airbus A320s outfitted with DirecTV at every seat (great for kids!). Though Jet-Blue is still much smaller than Southwest—it has some 50 aircraft and a hundred more on order—and doesn't yet directly compete with any of Southwest's routes, this newbie has definitely caught Jim Parker's attention. For instance: "We have looked and are looking at in-flight entertainment," Parker says. "Right now it just costs too much."

Delta's Song and United's Ted—the low-cost airline-within-an- airline concepts—provide Southwest with another set of challenges. Or do they? Already Song has delayed a planned expansion of its cross-continental routes. As for Ted, it's too early to tell—but its parent, UAL, which is still in Chapter 11, obviously has huge issues. (Read: very high costs.) While some see Song and Ted as parental saviors, Susan Donofrio of Deutsche Bank Securities is less sanguine. "Song and Ted aren't real, viable competitors to Southwest," she says. "They are Band-Aid fixes. The mainline carriers have to address their fundamental cost issues."

As for Kelleher, he's content merely to say, "I've seen this movie before." Perhaps left unsaid is, "And it doesn't end well." Indeed, a recent report of Donofrio's contains a list of 13 low-cost carriers that have filed for bankruptcy since 1991—and that's not counting Kiwi twice and Midway three times!

Meanwhile, Kelleher and Parker continue to do what they do best: take aim at the big guys. On May 9, Southwest will enter Phila-delphia, a stronghold of beleaguered US Air, which emerged from bankruptcy last year. To Kelleher, the City of Brotherly Love holds special significance. "I grew up in New Jersey," he says, eyes ablaze. "Philadelphia was my city. I bought my first suit there. Went to my first dance there." More to the point, the Philadelphia market is overpriced and underserved, Kelleher says, a problem that Southwest is going to "cure." With a metro-politan-area population of more than seven million, "it is the nation's eighth-largest city, but its airport is only the 18th busiest," Parker points out. Overall, industry consultant Roach expects that Southwest's fares—one-way to Providence for as low as $29, to Orlando for $79—will be 25% to 75% lower than US Air's. Some say US Air's very survival is at stake. "We're not going to run away and hide," says a US Air spokesman. "We will be a vigorous competitor to Southwest in Phila-delphia on every route they fly."

High-stakes jousting with the majors. Squeezing every nickel. All the while keeping the fun level cranked up to the max. That's how Southwest does business. No question, it's a tricky and singular model. And no question it all begins with Herb Kelleher. So what happens when Kelleher finally does depart from the company? Roach of Unisys puts it thus: "I never thought of Southwest as just the Herb Kelleher show. I look at it like Christianity or Islam. It was started by one guy, but it sure keeps on going." Much to the chagrin of its competitors. And much to the delight of its employees, customers, and shareholders.

What's Wrong With This Printer?

Believe it or not, it's too solid. So Hewlett-Packard spent $1 billion to replace it with new machines that won't hold a person's weight. But they sell for less—and can squash rivals.
■ *by Noshua Watson*

The bet-the-company project that came to be known within Hewlett-Packard as the Big Bang started out with a whimper. And with grumbles and complaints that it shouldn't and couldn't be done. That was how the printer engineers who gathered for a kickoff meeting in Vancouver, Wash., three years ago reacted to the mandate laid down by their boss, Vyomesh Joshi. The mandate was to build a $49 printer—one $30 cheaper than HP's least expensive model at the time. Making a cheap printer was not itself an earthshaking proposition, but how Joshi intended to go about it certainly was. He didn't want just one low-end model; he wanted the engineers to conjure an entire new line of more than 50 consumer products—inkjet printers, digital cameras, "all in one" printer/fax/copier/scanners, and more. He wanted the engineers to ignore the models then being sold and start from scratch.

He wanted HP to be able to introduce the entire product line in one fell swoop. And he wanted to take it from concept to store shelves in less than three years—18 months faster than HP had ever accomplished a product launch.

The designers in the conference room that day, however, weren't in a history-making frame of mind. They were justifiably proud of the high-quality printers they'd been building, and if high quality meant higher prices, so what? Quality was what HP was known for.

To explode their complacency and focus their attention on the real need to build a frugal machine, manager Tom Alexander finally grabbed an HP printer and set it on the conference room floor. Then he stood on it, all 200 pounds of him. The point behind his grandstanding? Customers aren't going to use printers as step stools, so don't add costs by building them strong enough to withstand the

weight of a grown man. Instead, design them to fit in the kitchen and print nice pictures.

Alexander's Stand helped open the way to a project that was audacity itself. Manufacturers often dream about reengineering an entire key product line, but few actually dare try. The risk is enormous not only because of the direct capital expense, but also because the market moves on. While the manufacturer is tied up getting the new line out the door, customers stray and competitors pounce.

With Joshi's Big Bang, the $47-billion-a-year company (before its merger with Compaq) was betting more than $1 billion: $125 million for R&D, $900 million for manufacturing, and $200 million for marketing. More important, HP was gambling its crown jewel. Printers, ink, and related products accounted for 43% of HP's sales and 65% of HP's profits. If the new product line stalled or flopped when it debuted, it would sap HP's strength and very likely hammer the stock.

The gamble didn't scare Joshi, 48. The greater risk, he felt, was to maintain the status quo. HP had gained preeminence in the printer market by relying on the "waterfall" or "cascade" method of product development. Engineers would design a printer, put it on the market at a high price, and then gradually tweak the design to reduce the manufacturing cost. Meanwhile they'd also work on developing the next-generation machine. When the new generation eventually hit the shelves, HP would lower the prices on the old machines. The waterfall method worked: It put the emphasis where HP was strongest—on its superior engineering and allowed it to dominate the inkjet-printer market during the 1990s. But in late 1997, HP got a shock when competitor Lexmark introduced the first inkjet printer to sell for less than $100. By mid-1999

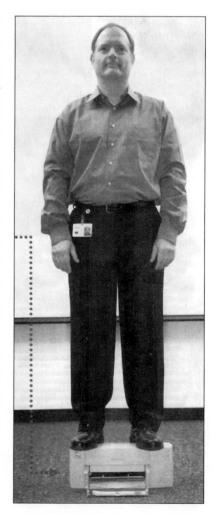

(Cont.)

Lexmark had doubled its market share to 14%, according to market researcher ARS. The price pressure was on.

Joshi predicted that HP's low-end printer business would slowly but surely erode unless HP abandoned the waterfall practice and went head-to-head with Lexmark on price. That meant the cost of making printers had to come down—way down.

When Joshi came to that conclusion in 1999, he was not yet in charge of the printing group, and CEO Carly Fiorina was new to the company, having come from Lucent just four months before. The head of the printing group, Carolyn Ticknor, then Joshi's boss, saw the urgency in his proposal and pushed for the massive capital investment. Other division heads objected—it was a risk they felt HP could not afford—but Joshi and Ticknor prevailed. Convinced that the imaging business would be a high-growth area and merited a billion-dollar investment, Fiorina overrode the objections, cut the check, and gave Joshi free rein.

Joshi's cost-cutting concept was this: He wanted his engineers to build 14 inkjet printers and seven all-in-ones using two new, cost-efficient platforms while he squeezed productivity from every link in the supply chain. The printer platforms consist of the main chassis and printer carriage on which the plastic casing and output trays rest. The Malibu mechanism was developed for high-performance, top-of-the-line models like the 7350 and the 5550 that start at $150. But the key to the Big Bang's low-end strategy was the Crossbow platform, a design that taxed the Vancouver engineers' ingenuity.

In developing the Crossbow line, HP engineers had to count pennies for the first time. To make money on low-end printers, HP would have to make more than a million Crossbows a month. At that volume, each additional cent in unit manufacturing costs adds up quickly. For three months the engineers brought design after design to management only to be told that it wasn't cheap enough. And the heat was on: The old waterfall cycle had taken about four years. "We wanted to do it in less than three years," says Joshi, "because Lexmark was already there."

Finding the solution, the designers finally realized, depended on a kind of printer-engineer Zen. To clear their minds, they began to conceive of the printer not as a complex mechanism but rather as an empty box. It was perfectly light and inexpensive but would get heavier and

The engineers brought design after design to management only to be told that it wasn't cheap enough.

costlier with every new feature. The object of the exercise was to think simply, adding only what the customer would absolutely need. Suddenly bells and whistles like the ability to print on glossy paper or card stock seemed easy to live without.

But frugality had its limits. One of the fiercest debates broke out over the power switch. Technically there is no need for an on-off switch, since a PC can turn on a printer automatically, and installing a manual switch adds about $1 per machine in cost. The engineers thought they had hit on easy savings until the marketing department got wind of it. The marketers argued that the average customer wouldn't understand how the printer could turn on and off without a power button and would become frustrated looking for it. The power switch stayed.

While the Vancouver engineers were perfecting the Crossbow mechanism and case designs, engineers in Corvallis, Ore., were racing to overhaul the most technologically complex part of the printer: the cartridge. "If a printer is a car, the cartridge is the engine and the gas tank," says Keith Bartlett, a cartridge group vice president. HP's intellectual-property stronghold in cartridges is formidable: Each cartridge is supported by nearly 100 patent applications, and in their

own extension of Moore's law, HP's engineers have succeeded in doubling the number of ink drops per second every 18 months.

The little jewel boxes are also big money. For every printer on a store shelf, HP makes ten to 20 cartridges. Some go in the printers, and the rest go to retail stores as replacements, where they sell for between $20 and $35 each. A customer spends more on cartridges over time than on the printer itself. Not surprisingly, cartridges and other supplies account for half of the imaging group's revenues and a higher percentage of its profits.

Because of the high volumes, savings on the manufacturing cost of the cartridges would be even more significant than savings on the printer itself. The cartridge engineers shaved off "nickels and dimes," says Bartlett, by using thinner plastic on the cartridge casings and covering the top with a paper label rather than a plastic cap.

The biggest savings were to be found by altering the cartridge's engine head, the most important part of the inkjet system. The head consists of a silicon plate perforated by ink nozzles and glued to a piece of flexible plastic embedded with metal circuits. The flexible plastic wraps around the bottom of the cartridge, which skims back and forth above the paper's surface. When it's printing at full speed and top quality, the nozzles fire eight to ten million drops of ink a second.

The more ink-shooting nozzles on the engine head, the better the printing speed and quality. But engine heads are cut from pricey silicon wafers. The HP engineers' challenge was to make the heads smaller, thus using less silicon, without sacrificing the number of nozzles. In the end they managed to shrink the engine head to half its original size and still squeeze 30% more nozzles onto it by making each nozzle narrower. (They also refined the ink.)

By early 2001 Joshi, now head of the imaging and printing group, was ready to move the new line into the plants. To guard its cartridge-making secrets, HP designs and manufactures the little boxes almost entirely in-house, at a design and fabrication facility in Corvallis and high-volume manufacturing plants in Ireland, Singapore, and Puerto Rico. Printers, meanwhile, are farmed out to contract manufacturers in Southeast Asia, China, and Mexico.

HP's contract factory owners were in for a big surprise. After test runs were complete, Joshi wanted to increase production from zero to

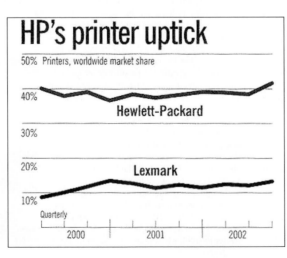

HP's printer uptick

50% Printers, worldwide market share

40%

Hewlett-Packard

30%

20%

Lexmark

10%

Quarterly

2000   2001   2002

(Cont.)

one million units a month within three months, ten times faster than any previous ramp-up for an HP product. To support the huge volume, HP's manufacturers would have to build factories, and do it faster than ever. Under the old system, engineers would design the production line in the U.S. to get out the kinks before sending the plant blueprints overseas. That process typically took about 18 months. But under the pressure of the Big Bang, Joshi gave them only one year. To speed up building the plants, engineers passed along tooling specifications to the factories before the printer designs were final. There wasn't a minute to lose, and everyone felt it. Paul Speer, who supervises the Vancouver engineers, recalls debating alternatives in his cubicle with two program managers when the fire alarm went off. Sent out into a rainstorm, Speer and his staffers huddled behind a passenger van in the parking lot to continue their discussion.

Building printers from just two platforms—the Malibu and the Crossbow—made the production line more efficient. Before the Big Bang, HP had built printers using multiple platforms, and the production line had to shut down and retool when switching from one platform to the other. Now several different models could be built from the Crossbow alone. The line could run continuously, splitting into smaller lines to finish off different products. The Crossbow printer's compact dimensions doubled the number that HP could pack on a shipping pallet, saving shipping costs. Even a 20-year veteran like Speer was awed by the millions of machines spilling from the production lines by early 2002. "I walked into a factory in Singapore and looked all the way down the line to the curvature of the earth," he claims. "All I could see were Crossbow printers."

Back home, HP's marketing department was

To support the huge volume, HP's suppliers would have to build new plants, and build them faster than ever.

preparing to sell this sea of Crossbows. The timing couldn't have been worse. HP's merger with Compaq had just been announced. The tech sector was in a slump. Still, the marketers knew they had to go all-out to make sure Big Bang wasn't a bust. After mailing one million direct-mail "magalogs" and outfitting three tractor-trailers with HP products and demos to tour the U.S., the company invited major retailers, including Circuit City, Office Max, and Best Buy, to Cupertino, Calif., for product demos. The retailers were hesitant to commit to buying the Big Bang line. HP was making a lot of demands: It wanted better displays, with all its new printers lined up together in a single aisle. At the same time, HP had disappointed many retailers by failing to keep them stocked with its old products. Without a guarantee that the new machines would be in the stores on time, the retailers wouldn't advertise the Big Bang printers in their Sunday circulars.

HP marketers promised to supply more than 8,000 stores by July 28, 2002. To make that date, the printers would have to be shipped from Asia in May or June at the latest. Most of the factories kept to the schedule, but by June it was apparent that thousands of printers weren't going to make it onto ships because of manufacturing problems in Singapore. Rather than jeopardize its relationships with retailers, HP paid a huge sum to transport tens of thousands of printers from Southeast Asia

by air. By July 28, HP had put more than one million printers on store shelves.

Joshi had been waiting for that moment for three years. Despite the economic slump in general—and the tech slump in particular—he was optimistic. "I was extremely confident," Joshi says. "I felt like a proud parent." In the next few months the market justified his pride. In a year when overall printer sales fell 10%, HP's printer sales increased by 3% between June and December. Shipments of color inkjet printers to stores grew by 18%. Joshi was particularly pleased by the results in the high-margin all-in-one market: After the Big Bang, HP took 20 percentage points of market share—most of it from Lexmark—to grab nearly 70% of the market. In June, Joshi had promised Wall Street that his $20 billion business would grow 10%, with 12% to 15% margins. In the fourth quarter his results made analysts purr—record revenues of $5.6 billion, representing 12% year-over-year sales growth. His margins: 16.5%.

Joshi's lieutenants now brag that he wants a Big Bang every year. "We're improving our cost structure all over HP," says Larry Lesley, senior vice president in the imaging and printing group. "This isn't an endgame; it's an ongoing philosophy." Leveraging its new competitive advantage, HP plans to launch new products in June and to continue to make the existing Big Bang line faster and better. As John Solomon, printer category manager, summarizes the success of the new line, "It's much cheaper to make, much better in terms of image quality and speed, and it's half the size." But success does have its price: "Of course, you can no longer stand on it."

"What's Wrong with This Printer?," *Fortune,* Feb 17, 2003, p. 12OC–12OH.

Selling Cellphones with Mixed Messages

By Gabriel Kahn

In China, a special karaoke-enabled cellphone plays music and scrolls lyrics while you sing into the mouthpiece. A phone in South Korea allows you to download video clips and exchange them with friends. And in the U.S., there's a phone from Verizon Wireless that lets users play games.

These devices are all made by **Motorola Inc.**—and they also happen to be practically the same phone, known as the T720 in the U.S. and the V730 elsewhere. The thing that separates them is Motorola's multipronged sales strategy, which targets different markets with different phone features.

The mixed message reflects a new trend sweeping the same $60 billion cellphone industry. At the moment when technological standards for cellphones are becoming more universal, marketing campaigns for the phones are becoming more local. Giants such as Motorola of Schaumburg, Ill., **Siemens** AG of Germany and Sony Ericsson Mobile Communications Ltd., a venture of **Sony** Corp. of Japan and **Telefon AB L.M. Ericsson** of Sweden, once rolled out ads globally; now, they tailor their messages to different audiences.

Driving the change is the evolution of the cellphone itself, from phone to fashion item and now to a vehicle for content, such as music, news or games. And content is extremely local.

"The industry is moving from a device-centric approach to an experience-centric approach, and that is making it a lot more local," says Brian Holmes, Motorola's Asia Pacific marketing manager.

So, for example, Motorola opted to play up the karaoke capability of the V730 in China. A special China ad campaign designed by **WPP Group** PLC's Ogilvy & Mather depicts a latter-stage Elvis impersonator crooning into a V730 mounted atop a microphone stand. The specially designed phone, which comes preloaded with two songs, was born of an alliance with Chinese cellular operator **China Unicom.**

Karaoke would seem a natural selling point for South Korea, too, where amateur singing is a popular pasttime. But Motorola's research in South Korea showed that karaoke took a backseat to other functions, such as downloading video clips from soccer matches.

For people like Mr. Holmes, brought up in a design-based culture that emphasized sleeker cellphones, the shift to content means he has to move even faster than he did when he was following the latest fashion trends. "It means our product is radically changing by the minute," he says.

So is the research. "In the '90s, you could just have a focus group with a few phone owners, and the discussion was who had the smallest phone," says Pasi Jarvenpaa, **Nokia** Corp.'s Asia Pacific director of marketing for mobile phones. "The scope is now much broader and the answers a lot less obvious. We now look for a psychographic orientation, such as people who are open to change."

The shift in cellphone marketing tactics also can be seen in the demise of ad campaigns that touted just technology—even as the phones themselves continue to become more sophisticated. Instead of throwing around acronyms for the latest messaging technologies, "now we put a lot of focus on what's on the street and what's in the stores," says Philip Vanhoutte, London-based vice president for marketing of Sony Ericsson.

That change in focus is forcing companies to rejigger more than just marketing. The cellular division of Siemens strengthened its marketing and research operations in Asia so that it can now feed back local consumer insights to headquarters in Germany while a new phone is still in the planning stage. More input upfront means less retooling later on, says Mark McCallum, vice president for product and marketing for mobile phones.

In both Europe and Asia, Siemens is targeting the same group for its C55 phone: the "social-centric set," a mostly teenage, female audience focused on friends and dating. But based on its research it has two distinct marketing plans. In Europe, it is promoting the phone's ability to record sounds and play them back or send them to friends. In Asia, it is shipping the same phones with special luminescent covers that glow in the dark, which emphasizes the phones' romantic or "puppy love" feature, says Mr. McCallum.

Advertising

To get their messages across, more and more nonprofit organizations are going commercial.

By Nat Ives

With an ad in Parade magazine on Sunday, the American Heart Association will begin its first-ever paid advertising campaign, a $36 million, three-year effort to raise awareness of heart disease and stroke. The group hopes that writing checks will help deliver its message more effectively compared with donated advertising, which often translates into "far from prime time."

With the decision to go commercial, the heart association becomes the latest prominent nonprofit group to buy both media time and creative services. The American Cancer Society made the same decision four years ago and now spends $10 million to $12 million a year on ads.

Research suggests that charitable groups overall have increased their ad outlays recently. Spending by charities increased to $576.5 million in 2003, from $497.7 million in 2002, a gain of 15.8 percent, according to Nielsen Monitor-Plus. By comparison, overall ad spending climbed to $99.7 billion last year from $94.9 billion in 2002, up 5.1 percent.

Nonprofits and advocacy groups face many of the same challenges that confront corporate advertisers, marketing experts said, citing the deluge of come-ons directed at ever-more-splintered audiences.

"It's been common for charities to get donated advertising in the past," said Stephen M. Adler, chief executive at JAMI Charity Brands in New York, which helps match nonprofit groups with corporate benefactors. "But what's happening now is charities are having a harder time reaching their target audience."

Jerry Della Femina, chairman at Della Femina Rothschild Jeary & Partners in New York, said counting on donated time and space had become a bigger gamble than before. "Public service announcements basically are unfortunately the beggars of the advertising industry," he said. "The networks put them on at 3:30 in the morning, somewhere between guys selling you knives and guys selling you dumpling makers."

Specialists in issues and advocacy advertising at the Seattle office of DDB Worldwide, part of the **Omnicom** Group, say that they, too, have seen changing demands from their nonprofit clients.

"Increasingly, nonprofits are getting more sophisticated," said Candy Cox, managing part-

ner. "They want to play in the very best media in order to communicate their messages."

At the Advertising Council in New York, which facilitates public service campaigns that use donated services and media, executives acknowledged the limits of donated time but said that many groups had few other options.

"From time to time, some organizations decide to make an investment in paid campaigns to complement their public service campaigns," said Peggy Conlon, president and chief executive at the Ad Council. "It's a perfectly good strategy, but year after year, the donated-media, public-service-advertising model really is the best for nonprofits."

The heart association's decision to open its purse stemmed from research revealing a decline in brand awareness, said Claire Bassett, a board member at the association in Dallas. "Everywhere from California to the Northeast to Omaha, Neb., by and large everyone said we have to raise the awareness," Ms. Bassett said.

So the group conducted a review for its first agency of record, selecting Campbell-Ewald in Warren, Mich., to create a paid campaign that would include print and broadcast elements directed at both English and Spanish speakers. It bought time on network shows like "60 Minutes" and "Everybody Loves Raymond," programs that would be nearly out of the question for public service announcements surviving on donated time.

The association also bought time on cable networks including A&E, Discovery Health and Lifetime. In addition to Parade, print ads will appear in publications including Essence, Ladies' Home Journal, Oprah and Reader's Digest.

Planning the media buy was in some ways more clear-cut than striking the right tone with the content, which is intended to remind consumers that heart disease affects not only men but also women and children, said Jeff Scott, president for integrated account services at Campbell-Ewald, part of the **Interpublic Group** of Companies.

"We took a look at depicting a world in which the American Heart Association didn't exist," Mr. Scott said, describing images of an emergency room filled with poorly trained staff and little or no equipment. "That was potentially alienating," he said.

Instead, the campaign emphasizes real families that have faced heart disease. One

ad reads, "Heart disease affects three kinds of people. Children. Women. Men." A somber couple is shown in front of an small empty chair. "John Godleski died of heart disease," the ad continues. "He was just 2 years old."

All elements of the campaign encourage consumers to visit the association's Web site or call a special number to take a "Learn and Live Health Quiz." The level of participation in the quiz will help measure the effort's effectiveness, Mr. Scott said.

The heart association did not retain a big-name corporate sponsor to defray costs because it wanted to control the message as completely as possible at this point, but executives did not rule out future corporate involvement.

Outsiders pointed to partnerships between nonprofits and companies as a major source of financing in the future.

For nonprofits with possibly controversial messages to spread, paying for advertising is often the only way to gain wide distribution. That was the case with a new campaign against job discrimination from the Gill Foundation, a group that advocates lesbian, gay, bisexual and transgender rights.

"With free media, the best way to get on the air is to make a spot that won't offend anybody," said Eric Gutierrez, associate creative director at DDB Seattle, which created the campaign. "When you're making a spot about something like gay rights, you're probably going to offend somebody."

Like the heart association work, the Gill Foundation commercials portrays real people, in this case gay Americans who had not previously disclosed their sexual orientation at work, but publicly reveal their orientation in the spots.

One print ad reads, "For gays and lesbians, America is 14 states that recognize our right to live free from job discrimination, and 36 states that don't."

It is still possible for public service campaigns to receive exposure in desirable times and venues. An Ad Council study of its campaigns from 1999 through 2002 found that only 30 percent of its public service announcements appeared during the overnight hours.

Then there was a spot appearing during the Super Bowl pregame show this year that raised awareness of H.I.V. But that spot, also created by DDB Seattle, had a little help: the clients behind it were the Henry J. Kaiser Family Foundation and **Viacom**, owner of CBS, which broadcast the game.

Microsoft Hopes People See SPOTs When Glancing At Watches

New Data-Enabled Timepieces

· · · · · · · · · · · · · ·

Two companies start selling wristwatches that will bring news, other info—for fee.

· · · · · · · · · · · · · ·

By Patrick Seitz
Investor's Business Daily

Microsoft Corp. thinks your wristwatch should do more than tell the time. It also should give you the news, weather, traffic, sports and stock prices, plus send you instant messages and Outlook calendar reminders.

The debut last month of watches using Microsoft's smart personal objects technology, or SPOT, and its service for bringing content to those objects, called MSN Direct, marks the company's first foray into what it calls "glanceable" displays.

Using new MSN Direct-powered watches from Fossil Inc. and Suunto, people can glance at data that's important to them during meetings, business lunches and other places where a cell phone, pager or handheld computer would be obtrusive or rude.

"We're very excited about the watch and its potential," said Doug Kramp, Fossil's senior vice president of consumer technology. "Technology is really merging with fashion for the first time. On the wrist you basically have oceanfront property in terms of accessibility, convenience and discreetness."

The MSN Direct watches from Fossil and Suunto let users customize the data they receive wirelessly. The watches cost from $179 to $300. The MSN Direct service is available in the 100 largest U.S. cities and costs $9.95 a month, or $59 a year. That cost is likely to be the biggest challenge to adoption of the technology, says Matt Rosoff, an analyst with independent research firm Directions on Microsoft.

"Most consumers won't be willing to pay $10 a month for the kind of information that's available on MSN Direct," Rosoff said. "It seems a little pricey for what you get."

He says Microsoft is still mulling price. If sales are low, the Redmond, Wash., company could cut prices, he says.

Microsoft also needs to show that the service will be updated with new features and channels of information, Rosoff says. Among the channels yet to roll out are traffic, sports, movie show times and restaurant recommendations.

With the annual payment plan, MSN Direct comes to less than $5 a month. "That's a couple of lattes," Fossil's Kramp said. Plus, the service will only get better, he says.

The notion of paying a fee for data delivered to your watch is new to most people and will take time to sink in, says Bill Mitchell, corporate vice president of Microsoft's mobile platforms unit.

Another challenge is to get people used to the idea of having to recharge their watches like cell phones every few days, Mitchell says. Consumers also have to take the time to personalize their watches online from their PCs, he says.

Coverage area is another potential drawback. The service is delivered over FM subcarrier bandwidth in the top 100 metropolitan markets, but coverage in the suburbs can be spotty. In Chicago, for example, coverage misses large portions of the prosperous north and west suburbs.

The MSN Direct watches are bigger than most watches, but compare in size to many designer watches. The size is comparable to watches Fossil makes under license for the Diesel, Armani and DKNY brands, Kramp says.

"Big is in fashion now, so this is pretty consistent with a lot of the watches we're selling," he said.

Suunto opted to make its first MSN watches thicker and heavier than Fossil's SPOT watches by adding a bigger battery. Suunto claims to get double Fossil's battery life from its rechargeable lithium ion battery, about five or six days, says Suunto President Dan Colliander.

Suunto sees a good fit with the SPOT watches and its sports instruments. Suunto

SPOT On

Two companies last month came out with the first watches that use Microsoft's SPOT technology, which lets the watches receive such data as stock quotes, news and weather forecasts

9:30a 11/5
56°F
Currently
Seattle
SUUNTO

Suunto N3 smart wristwatch with MSN Direct service

A Dick Tracy brand Fossil Wrist Net watch with MSN Direct service

(Cont.)

sells watches with such features as integrated satellite navigation, heart rate monitors, altimeters and barometers. It targets divers, bikers, hikers, climbers, golfers and other active lifestyles with its products.

"We expect this will significantly increase our user base in the U.S. and allow people a nice way to understand what Suunto is about," Colliander said. "This brings us different types of users, perhaps more of the sports enthusiasts who sit on their couch and watch sports rather than the ones who are actively participating."

Besides news and other services, the SPOT watches display accurate time. The MSN Direct service references an atomic clock as its standard and broadcasts this time to SPOT watches over the local FM radio waves.

The MSN Direct business will be "minuscule" to Microsoft for the foreseeable future, Rosoff says. But he says it's important for several reasons.

First, the devices are another attempt by Microsoft to extend the reach of its software beyond personal computers. With the SPOT watches, Microsoft has shown that its software can run in small-memory, low-power devices and offer competition to Sun Microsystems Inc.'s Java software. Microsoft wants to use its SPOT technology and MSN Direct service in a host of devices, such as key chains, traveling alarm clocks and refrigerator magnets.

Also, the FM subcarrier network that Microsoft has built out—it had to put some equipment at FM towers—with local radio stations could conceivably be put to other uses, Rosoff says. Delivering traffic and other information to in-dash car receivers is one possibility, he says.

Microsoft sees the MSN Direct watches as being like TV sets and will continue to improve the programming they can receive, Mitchell says. He expects refinements in location-based data such as weather and traffic in the months ahead.

Microsoft has lots of bandwidth to broadcast data to its subscribers. A typical radio station can deliver about 125 megabytes of such content a day, he says.

Dangerous Terrain

As ATVs Take Off in Sales, Deaths and Injuries Mount

Motorcycle-Like Vehicles Fall Into Regulatory Void; Industry Split on Rules

Jessica Adams's Brief Ride

By John J. Fialka

MORGANTOWN, W.Va. — The last time Jessica Adams's mother saw her alive, she was spread-eagle on a gravel embankment along a rural road here. Jessica looked like she was sleeping, but her neck was broken. By the time she arrived at the hospital, she was dead.

Jessica, a petite 13-year-old, and another girl, age 14, had borrowed an adult-size all-terrain vehicle and sped off down a paved road to a nearby Boy Scout camp. Witnesses saw Jessica sitting behind the driver. Police say she died after the ATV veered out of control, climbed a 5-foot embankment and hit a tree.

Sales of ATVs—the four-wheel, motorcycle-like vehicles made to navigate rough terrain at speeds as high as 70 mph—climbed 89% between 1997 and 2002. In 2002, the latest year for which figures are available, manufacturers say they sold 825,000 ATVs in the U.S., exceeding sales of small pickup trucks. Kawasaki Motors Corp., Honda Motor Co., Arctic Cat Inc., Polaris Industries Inc., Yamaha Motor Corp. and other ATV makers that previously focused on selling snowmobiles say they've found a juicier market in ATVs.

But as ATV sales have expanded to more than $3 billion a year, so have deaths and injuries, particularly among children. According to the federal Consumer Product Safety Commission, Jessica was one of 357 people to die in ATV crashes in 2002, up 67% from 1997. Serious injuries more than doubled in the same period, with 113,900 riders hurt in 2002.

Since 1992, a third of the injured have been under 16, and children under 12 have accounted for 14% of deaths. ATV injuries are 12 times as likely to be fatal to children as bicycle accidents, says the National Safe Kids Campaign, a nonprofit that tracks childhood deaths.

Judging the relative danger of ATVs is tricky. There were more deaths and injuries on ATVs than on snowmobiles or personal watercraft in 2002. ATV use results in more injuries per vehicle than cars, though there are more deaths per vehicle in cars. A more meaningful measure might be deaths and injuries per mile traveled, but those figures aren't available for ATVs, snowmobiles or personal watercraft. Cars travel many more miles than the other vehicles.

When problems first cropped up with ATVs in the 1980s, federal regulators prodded the industry to stop making three-wheel versions. But today, their four-wheel cousins operate in a virtual regulatory void. Unlike cars, trucks and motorcycles, they aren't subject to regulation by the National Highway Traffic Safety Administration because they're not designed for highway use. The CPSC is investigating allegations of safety problems but hasn't found any evidence of improper design. Since the agency only regulates products, not their potential misuse, the agency's chairman says states are in a better position to deal with ATV accidents.

Yet state regulation is minimal. Only 10 states require that ATV drivers have a driver's license. While 27 states set a minimum age for ATV drivers, two-thirds allow 12-year-old drivers and, in Utah, 8-year-olds are legal. Only 20 states require riders to wear helmets. Thirty-four bar most uses of ATVs on paved roads, but those laws are frequently ignored. In West Virginia, with the nation's highest ATV-related per capita death rate, legislators have debated rules for seven years without passing any.

With little pressure from the government, the industry has had internal fights over how much to regulate itself, if at all. Alarmed by increased deaths and injuries and concerned about potential liability, manufacturers have proposed laws in West Virginia, Pennsylvania and other states that would require riders to wear helmets, bar ATVs from paved roads, prohibit passengers on ATVs, and keep children under 16 off adult-size vehicles. The industry "really has a comprehensive plan in place and states are implementing pieces of that in varying degrees," says Tim Buche, president of the Specialty Vehicle Institute of America in Irvine, Calif., which represents ATV makers.

But ATV makers have encountered resistance from some dealers who favor allowing passengers on ATVs and want to open more paved roads to the vehicles. Meanwhile, consumer advocates criticize manufacturers' proposals as being designed merely to shift responsibility from companies to consumers and state law-enforcement authorities. These advocates prefer a federal ban on sales of ATVs for use by kids under 16.

"Self-regulation by the ATV industry has led to larger and faster ATVs and more children being killed and injured," says Rachel Weintraub, an attorney for the Consumer Federation of America in Washington.

Manufacturers also are resisting some state regulation. In Maine, for example, legislators are preparing to address ATV safety and trespassing problems. The industry has countered with less-stringent proposals. "Industry is more focused on this than they have been in a long time," says Paul Jaques, head of an ATV task force appointed by Maine's governor. "They recognize that if somebody doesn't do something about these things, this whole thing's going to blow up."

The first ATV was a small, motorized tricycle developed by a Honda engineer around 1970. The machines were first popular among farmers, foresters and others who put them to

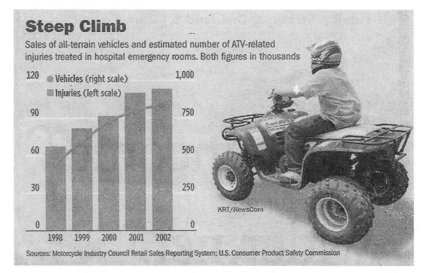

Steep Climb

Sales of all-terrain vehicles and estimated number of ATV-related injuries treated in hospital emergency rooms. Both figures in thousands

Vehicles (right scale)
Injuries (left scale)

KRT/NewsCom

Sources: Motorcycle Industry Council Retail Sales Reporting System; U.S. Consumer Product Safety Commission

(Cont.)

work. Recreational users began to boost U.S. sales in the 1980s.

But the three-wheel vehicles were difficult to handle, especially for untrained drivers. After more than 260 ATV users died in accidents in 1987, the CPSC sued the five largest manufacturers, asking a federal court to halt production and sales because ATVs were "imminently dangerous consumer products."

The manufacturers, who had already planned to switch to four-wheel vehicles, agreed to stop production of three-wheelers. They also agreed to stress more prominently warnings that are now bolted onto today's vehicles. The warning labels say drivers should wear helmets; passengers shouldn't be allowed; the vehicles are hard to steer on paved roads because the low-inflated balloon tires are made to grip uneven terrain; and children under 16 should ride only smaller, less-powerful machines under parental supervision.

Four-wheel ATVs, which are more stable, soon grew more popular than their predecessors, especially with recreational users. Sales over the last 10 years have increased five-fold, and 70% of users now ride ATVs as a "family recreational activity," according to the ATV manufacturers group.

In recent years, the industry has rolled out hot-rod-like "high performance" ATVs capable of higher speeds and quicker acceleration. Marketing pitches revel in speed and power. In sales brochures for its Predator ATV line, Polaris says "survival of the fittest is the rule . . . And like all dominant beasts, Predator continues to evolve. That's a good thing. Because out here, you're either Predator or you're prey." The line includes adult models and smaller versions built for children as young as 6.

A Yamaha brochure for one of its less-powerful models says, "The whole point of the ATV movement is to get out there and experience Mother Nature; the pace at which you experience it is, of course, entirely up to you. Tear along when the mood strikes you."

Manufacturers say they don't market adult-size models to youngsters. In brochures, the industry shows family groups wearing goggles and helmets, with parents supervising children, who ride smaller machines. "Riding an ATV is an exercise in responsibility," says a Honda brochure.

However, children often use adult-size ATVs. Jeff DeVol, a dealer in Parkersburg, W. Va., says he and his salesmen tell customers that children can't safely handle adult-size machines, which cost $3,000 to $6,000 apiece, and urge parents to buy child-size models, which run as high as $3,000. But some buyers don't believe him, he says, and many can't afford more than one machine. Buyers sometimes fib about the recipient and get a "household ATV" that winds up being used by teens, he says.

The Consumer Federation and several medical and environmental groups have petitioned the CPSC to ban the sale of adult-size ATVs for use by children under 16. Ms. Weintraub of the Consumer Federation says the ban would enable the agency to fine or bring criminal charges against manufacturers who don't police dealers. It would also send "a powerful message to parents," she says.

The CPSC has the power to impose a ban or order vehicles redesigned if it finds they pose substantial harm, says Hal Stratton, the commission's Republican chairman. But, after months of research and public hearings in West Virginia, New Mexico and Alaska, the agency hasn't found design flaws so much as "behavior problems" in how people ride, he says.

Even consumer advocates haven't cited design flaws in ATVs. And because the CPSC regulates products, not how people use them, it may not be able to act, Mr. Stratton says. However, agency staffers haven't completed their investigation or decided what could be done. One possibility is suggesting model legislation to states, Mr. Stratton says.

West Virginia's experience suggests why state regulation is piecemeal or nonexistent. The rural, mountainous state is one of six with no ATV regulations. It counts about 200,000 of the vehicles, or about one for every nine persons.

The number of deaths and injuries among young people "is an epidemic in terms of what we previously experienced," says Jim Helmkamp, an epidemiologist for the Center for Rural Emergency Medicine at West Virginia University. Since 1990, West Virginia has averaged 15 ATV deaths per year, at least 35% of them on paved roads. Last year, there were 27, the center says. Mr. Helmkamp has conducted studies showing that states with helmet-use and other regulations have lower death and injury rates.

Julian Bailes, head of the neurosurgery department at West Virginia University Hospital, where Jessica Adams was pronounced dead, says the hospital's emergency staff has seen 238 ATV-related injuries and deaths over the last decade. About a third of the victims were under 18 and 80% weren't wearing helmets, he says.

"What stands out is the stupidity of some of these accidents," he says. The worst involve parents carrying young children as passengers. The kids are "almost always thrown off and sometimes the vehicle rolls over on them."

But efforts to regulate ATV use, including that by children, have gone nowhere. "The local bubba wants to ride on the roads," says Leff Moore, lobbyist for West Virginia's Recreational Vehicle Association, a group of 14 dealers who have been pushing the manufacturers' proposed legislation since 1996. It would codify into law the warnings already bolted onto vehicles, requiring helmet use

and barring children under 16 from riding on adult-size ATVs.

The legislation has never gotten close to a decisive vote, largely because of opposition by a splinter group of ATV dealers led by Mr. DeVol, the Parkersburg dealer. He says safety problems have less to do with the vehicles than with the people who use them. "My customers tell me that if the law results in a blanket statement that ATVs are prohibited from all paved roads in the state, basically you're making criminals out of them," he says.

Each year, Mr. DeVol's group has succeeded in persuading enough lawmakers to oppose the manufacturers' favored legislation. The group's lobbyist, Sam Love, says he makes a practice of reminding legislators how many of their constituents use ATVs. "When you have 200,000-plus people in the state, this is something legislators need to know before they enact restrictive legislation."

Last year, as the bill moved through the Senate, Mr. Love persuaded lawmakers to add an amendment that would have explicitly opened 20,000 miles of rural roads—many of them paved—to ATVs. (Currently, West Virginia law is ambiguous about whether ATVs are legal on paved roads.)

At that point, the manufacturers pulled their support, killing the bill. Mr. Moore, the industry lobbyist, says encouraging ATV users to use more paved roads could raise the state's "body count" and spur federal regulators to take more drastic steps.

Last month, the ATV manufacturers prodded West Virginia legislators with an open letter published in local newspapers demanding that the stalemate finally be broken. Now Democratic Gov. Bob Wise is trying to broker a compromise between the opposing dealer groups that would impose safety education, helmets and a no-passenger rule on children under 18.

As state police and Jessica's family have pieced together her Sept. 30, 2002, accident, the seventh-grade honor student had just finished supper and done her homework. It was around 6 p.m. She went for a walk in "Healthy Heights," the trailer park where she lived. Cynthia Lefever, her mother, says she felt little reason for concern. "She was very health and safety conscious," Ms. Lefever says.

Jessica went down the street to see a fellow seventh-grader, who wasn't home. But his 17-year-old brother rolled out the family ATV, a 2002 Honda Rancher that showroom dealers say is capable of speeds up to 50 mph. A spokesman for American Honda Motor Co. says Jessica's death was a "tragedy" beyond the manufacturer's control. "We try to make vehicles as safe as possible, but it requires supervision of the parents as well," he says.

Ms. Lefever says Jessica had never shown much interest in the machines. But another friend, a 14-year-old girl, jumped on the driver's seat and Jessica climbed on behind.

(Cont.)

An hour later, someone heard moaning coming from the nearby woods. It was the 14-year-old, who had been thrown off. She suffered a punctured lung and bruised ribs. Jessica was lying quietly nearby.

Jessica's friends fashioned a tribute of her stuffed toys and favorite candy next to the tree the ATV struck. Mr. Helmkamp, of the state's Center for Rural Emergency Medi-cine, is preparing a more lasting memorial: a video describing her death that he hopes to distribute among state schools. "This was an event that could have been prevented," he says.

Meanwhile, teenagers in Jessica's neigh-borhood still get out to joyride. Jessica's mother can hear them revving their ATV engines at night. Sometimes she sees them collecting at a nearby gas station, compar-ing their shiny machines. "A lot of them are boys," she says. "They think they're invin-cible."

Finding Target Market
Opportunities

Hot Starbucks To Go

It's a new American institution. Its stores are everywhere. Doubters say it can't get much bigger. But Howard Schultz is setting up his company for more growth—in coffee and beyond. ■ *Andy Serwer*

I'm in Seattle, talking with the father of the richest man in the world, who is speaking eloquently about a remarkably successful younger man who lives right here in his hometown. Yes, the speaker is Bill Gates the elder, but no, he's not talking about his son the Microsoft guy. Gates is telling me about Howard Schultz, the man who built the Starbucks coffee company. Gates, before he retired, was lead partner of the biggest law firm in town, Preston Gates, and he just happened to be Schultz's attorney when Schultz was nothing more than an ambitious East Coast transplant with a jones for coffee. "A lawyer's eyes start to sparkle when he sees a person like Howard come in with a plan like Starbucks," recalls Gates. "Howard has an ability that isn't widespread. He is very directed and dogged, and a very decent person too. Howard Schultz is an incredible story."

That from a man who knows incredible stories.

Schultz, of course, has now created an American institution. Starbucks today is possibly the most dynamic new brand and retailer to be conceived over the past two decades. The company's stores—over 7,500 and counting—are everywhere from Omaha to Osaka to Oman. That's a blessing for the company's millions of latte-dependent customers but something of a challenge for Schultz and his team because it raises the saturation question. If Starbucks is already everywhere, how can it keep growing so fast?

"We are in the second inning of a nine-inning game," Howard Schultz says. "We are just beginning to tap into all sorts of new markets, new customers, and new products." Many of Schultz's ideas about how to achieve these are unconventional—like refusing to franchise—but that's the Starbucks way, and millions of us seem to love it. We stream into Starbucks to buy coffee for $1.75 that we used to pay 50 cents for. We drop into our local Starbucks to read on plush couches. We lug in our laptops and hold meetings, and we buy gifts and music there. We load money onto the company's stored-value cards. How unusual a set of customer experiences is that?

Behind the counter and at headquarters,

Starbucks is an unusual company too. It strives to mix capitalism with social responsibility. It gives all its employees who work more than 20 hours a week stock options and health-care benefits. It doesn't advertise on TV. And it funds breakneck expansion through its own cash flow, not by selling stock or debt.

Right now Starbucks is growing at an eye-popping rate. Its revenues continue to climb at above 20% a year. Same-store sales (that is, sales at stores open more than a year) rose at an 11% clip in November and December, the best showing in over a decade. Starbucks stock was up 56% last year—and 3,028% since its 1992 IPO--and is now hitting all-time highs. (The stock, as always, is priced sky-high on a P/E basis.) If you think Starbucks is everywhere now, don't be surprised to see even more stores in places like Winslow, Ariz., and Warsaw, Poland.

To achieve that kind of omnipresence, Schultz is building his company for bigness—hiring a new management team, constructing huge coffee-roasting plants, and helping coffee growers improve their crops to meet Starbucks' exacting standards and insatiable demand. Last year the company bought Seattle Coffee Co., a chain of lower-priced coffee shops, and it plans to expand the business to $1 billion in annual revenue. Starbucks will open dozens of stores in France starting this month. And in the U.S. it plans on opening more stores with drive-thru windows this year. Altogether, the company says, it will open 1,300 new stores worldwide in 2004.

"I consider Howard Schultz to be a kind of genius," says former Senator Bill Bradley, now an Allen & Co. banker, who joined the Starbucks board last June. As a New York Knick, Bradley was a boyhood idol of Schultz's. (Today Schultz is the lead owner of the NBA Seattle SuperSonics.) "Howard is consumed with his vision of Starbucks," Bradley says. "That means showing the good that a corporation can do for its workers, shareholders, and customers."

Today Schultz, 50, is a genial, self-effacing type, over six feet tall, lanky, and trim, with shiny white teeth. His expression when

speaking with people is generally either empathic or collaborative. His accent doesn't reflect his Brooklyn roots, and his vocabulary is like a college professor's, filled with words like "empowerment" and "visual cues."

"He's happiest in his stores" is something you hear over and over about Schultz. And why not? Starbucks is a pretty darn nice place to hang out. During my recent visit with Schultz in Seattle, he really wanted to show me the store at 23rd and Jackson, located in a low-income, minority neighborhood. And so we drove over in his Porsche Cayenne SUV. (He's not *that* understated.) We park, walk in, and order coffee. "After we put this store in, all these other national companies came in," he says, pointing to a Hollywood Video store and a Walgreens across the way. Employees and customers greet Schultz, though some are more interested in chatting about the Sonics than about the Christmas Blend.

"Starbucks has become what I call the third place," says Schultz, seated and sipping one of his five or so daily cups of company product (usually black). "The first place is home. The second place is work. We are the place in between. It's a place to feel comfort. A place to feel safe. A place to feel like you belong." Schultz says he's trying to create something that never really existed in the U.S.: café life, for centuries a hallmark of Continental society. Schultz points to the British pub, too, as a close cousin of his third place, and notes that a Barnes & Noble has some of the same characteristics. Whether or not you buy his concept, it is unassailable that the number of people visiting Starbucks—25 million people each week—is impressive.

Four years ago Schultz stepped aside as CEO to become the Starbucks chairman and chief strategist, much like his counterpart across town at Microsoft. He gave the CEO job to Orin Smith, a decade his senior, who had joined the company in 1990. Why did Schultz do it? "Because Orin deserved the job," Schultz says simply. The move freed Schultz from routine tasks like budget meetings and let Smith focus on critical matters such as driving same-store

(Cont.)

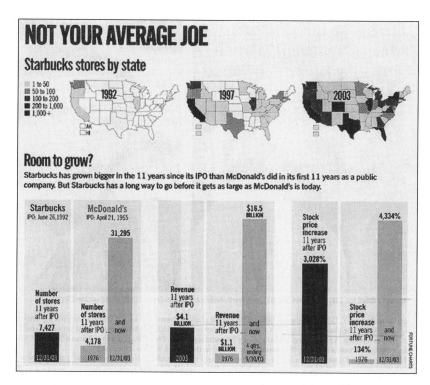

NOT YOUR AVERAGE JOE

Starbucks stores by state

- 1 to 50
- 50 to 100
- 100 to 200
- 200 to 1,000
- 1,000+

1992   1997   2003

Room to grow?

Starbucks has grown bigger in the 11 years since its IPO than McDonald's did in its first 11 years as a public company. But Starbucks has a long way to go before it gets as large as McDonald's is today.

Starbucks IPO: June 26, 1992
McDonald's IPO: April 21, 1965

Number of stores 11 years after IPO — 7,427 (12/31/03)
Number of stores 11 years after IPO — 4,178 (1976) — and now 31,295 (12/31/03)

Revenue 11 years after IPO — $1.1 BILLION (1976) — and now $4.1 BILLION (2003)
Revenue 11 years after IPO — $16.5 BILLION (4 qtrs. ending 9/30/03)

Stock price increase 11 years after IPO — 3,028% (12/31/03)
Stock price increase 11 years after IPO — 134% (1976) — and now 4,334% (12/31/03)

FORTUNE CHARTS

---

sales. At first, Smith says, only yuppies went to Starbucks. But now, with no special marketing at all, "we are bringing in a much wider demographic than we thought possible—older people, younger people, people of different ethnic backgrounds." It just seems as though the word is out. "Starbucks understands that Americans want to trade up," says Jeff Brotman, co-founder of Costco and an old friend of Schultz's. "They are aspirational, and Starbucks is a part of that very powerful force in our society. That's why I am so convinced Starbucks has even more legs than we ever expected."

Smith also says the company is now selling drinks all through the day and night—some stores are open 24 hours—thanks to new specialty drinks like teas and Frappuccinos, and during all seasons of the year too (think holiday peppermint mochas). "Our new automatic espresso machines are making our service faster than ever, and our merchandising has never been stronger," Smith says. The focus on same-store sales doesn't mean Starbucks is ignoring expansion. "We are able to open stores in places we never thought possible," Smith explains, citing Starbucks outlets run as a joint venture with Magic Johnson in inner-city neighborhoods and ones in smallish towns like Temple, Texas.

One trick Starbucks hasn't pulled out

of the bag recently—at least not in the past three years—is to raise prices, though it probably could without customers' batting an eye. Why do customers pay $3.50 for a latte? The short answer is that they think it's worth it. But what are they getting? Some of the finest coffee available commercially. Custom preparation. (How many retailers could put up with "I'll have a grande low-fat triple-shot half-caf white-chocolate mocha, extra hot, easy on the whipped cream. And I'm in a rush.") Then there's the Starbucks ambiance. The music. The comfy velvety chairs. The smells. The hissing steam. "We aren't in the coffee business, serving people. We are in the people business, serving coffee," Schultz says.

Howard Schultz grew up on some of Brooklyn's meaner streets. He was raised in a cramped apartment in the Bayview public housing

"We're in the second inning of a nine-inning game. We are just beginning to tap into all sorts of new markets, customers, and products."

project in Canarsie, where he shared a tiny bedroom with his brother and sister. If you go there today, especially at night, you get a feeling for just how grim and scary the place is. The grounds of the project are deserted and dirty, and huge jets roar in low on their way to J.F.K. Airport. Inside, the halls are dark and narrow. You hear sounds coming through the walls, and nasty cooking smells fill your nostrils. It's not that different from the way it was when Howard was growing up—not terrifying, but tough in a *West Side Story* kind of way. Jewish families like Howard's living side by side with Italians, Irish, and African Americans. Kids playing ball, fighting, and flirting. You figured out where to fit in and tried to stay out of harm's way.

Howard was kind of shy around girls, but he was a natural leader and a consummate playground rat. Stickball, basketball, slapball, skully, football, baseball, punchball—he'd play them all, day and night. Howard would be the captain and pick the teams. He'd bring in all the kids, make them feel included, make them a part of the team. He'd draw up the plays and make everyone compete like hell. Later in the day he'd take them on a subway ride all the way to Yankee Stadium in the Bronx to see Mickey Mantle. He'd buy bleacher tickets and then sneak them down to the expensive seats. And for a time the kids would feel as if they had escaped the projects, and that they were part of something bigger than Bayview. "It shaped my character," says Schultz. "But I always wanted to escape. I always wanted to improve my standing."

Schultz frequently tells a story about coming home one day as a boy to find his father, Fred—who worked a variety of blue-collar jobs to keep his family going—laid up on the couch with a broken ankle. His father couldn't work. He lost his job, and he had no medical benefits. The family's tight finances became even tighter. "I will never forget that episode," says Schultz. "I never want that to happen to our employees." That's why thousands of part-time Starbucks workers have full medical benefits.

Howard's ticket out of Brooklyn was football. "He wasn't a great athlete," says Canarsie's current football coach, Michael Camardese, who played on the junior varsity when Howard was quarterback. "But he was very hard-working and smart. The team was pretty bad back then, and Howard was constantly being chased out of the pocket." Howard landed a scholarship to play football for the Wildcats of Northern Michigan University, and he became the first member of his family to go to college. Northern Michigan, in the town of Marquette on Lake Superior on the state's Upper Peninsula, has to be one of the coldest campuses in America, but at least Howard was out of Canarsie.

His football career was a washout, so Howard focused on his studies. After graduation he took a position as a Xerox salesman in New York, then a plum job for a young man with student loans to repay. Soon after, Schultz moved over to Hammarplast, an importer of Swedish kitchenware. Schultz noticed that one of his customers, a little coffee company in Seattle, had a brisk order pattern for some of his coffeemakers. Schultz went out to investigate. And that's how Howard Schultz walked into the Starbucks Coffee, Tea, and Spice store in Seattle's Pike Place Market. Immediately, he knew he wanted to work at the company the rest of his life.

Why? Here he was, a successful New York City executive who had already made it out of the projects. And as for Starbucks, it wasn't much of anything at the time. The company had been founded in 1971 by a couple of local coffee aficionados, Gerald Baldwin, Gordon Bowker, and Zev Siegl, who were disciples of Peet's Coffee in Berkeley. When Howard came calling, the company had just four stores. And it sold only beans, not drinks. "I walked into the market and into the store. There was something incredibly special," Schultz says. "The aroma. The authenticity. But it also felt like a rough diamond. It was something I felt I could polish into a jewel."

Schultz desperately wanted in, but the owners weren't easily convinced. Why would they want a slick East Coast salesman? Schultz's family was unsure too. In his book, *Pour Your Heart Into It*, Schultz describes what was going through his mind: "Taking a job at Starbucks would mean giving up that $75,000-a-year job, the prestige, the car, and the co-op, and for what? . . . My mother was especially concerned."

In 1982, Schultz got his wish and joined Starbucks as director of retail operations and marketing. He began by selling coffee to restaurants and coffeehouses in Seattle, which back then was far from the bastion of urban hipness that it has become. Only a decade earlier, someone had erected the infamous WILL THE LAST PERSON TO LEAVE SEATTLE PLEASE TURN OFF THE LIGHTS billboard, after huge Boeing layoffs. The city was still in a funk, and it would be years before Kurt Cobain's screaming genius and Nora Ephron's cinematic confection *Sleepless in Seattle* helped revive it. Schultz toiled away in Seattle's damp chill, reporting to a couple of owners who weren't really interested in making Starbucks big—which is exactly what Schultz wanted to do.

"Starbucks understands that Americans want to trade up. That's why I'm so convinced that Starbucks has even more legs."

Just a year after joining Starbucks, Schultz was traveling to Milan and walked into an espresso bar. Right away he knew he could bring the concept to the U.S. "There was nothing like this in America," he says. "It was an extension of people's front porch. It was an emotional experience. I believed intuitively we could do it. I felt it in my bones."

But Starbucks' owners wouldn't really give it a try. So Schultz left the company in 1985 to start a small chain of espresso bars called Il Giornale in Seattle and Vancouver. Two years later Starbucks' owners wanted to sell the company. Schultz raised $3.8 million from local investors to buy them out, negotiating the deal with Bill Gates the elder. (Gates bought some stock at that point, which hardly seems fair considering the success of his son's venture.) Finally, Schultz was in charge of his dream.

Out at Starbucks' roasting plant 15 miles southeast of downtown Seattle, in the shadow of Mount Rainier, there's a blown-up black-and-white photograph of the company's operations back in the early 1980s. What you see is a small-time operation, a handful of employees watching over coffee roasters amid piles of burlap sacks of beans. It's an amazingly far cry in an impossibly short period of time. Today Starbucks is a sleek, fast-growing beast with more than $4 billion in annual sales. It made $268 million in profits last year. Starbucks' profit margins are lower than those of McDonald's and others in the fast-food or restaurant businesses, partly because it has higher salaries and benefit costs since it doesn't franchise. To Schultz that is simply the price you pay for doing business his way, and it is nonnegotiable. Declining to franchise is a hugely important part of the Starbucks formula. "I look at franchising as a way of accessing capital, and I will never make the tradeoff between cheap money and losing control over our stores," says Schultz.

Starbucks has over $300 million of cash on its balance sheet and next to zero long-term debt—even with all those new-store openings. It is so conservatively run that the company could be accused of being over-capitalized. Its return on equity is only around 12% or 13%, and the stock pays no dividend. "We are keeping our powder dry," says CFO Michael Casey. "This position gives us flexibility if we were to make an acquisition."

The company is growing so fast that it has just completed its third and fourth state-of-the-art roasting facilities, in Nevada and Amsterdam. Even if the company's growth slows by half, to 12% or so, Starbucks could be doing $7 billion in sales in five years. Which is why Schultz has added a whole new team of executives, from companies like Wal-Mart, Dell, and PepsiCo. "I wanted to bring in people who had experience working at $10 billion companies," he says.

One such hire is Jim Donald, a press-the-flesh type who is head of Starbucks' core North America business and some say heir apparent to Orin Smith as CEO. Donald was a manager at Safeway and Albertson's, and spent five years at Wal-Mart running its food operations—"I was the last guy Sam [Walton] hired" before he died, Donald says. As Starbucks grows, its margins are bound to

(Cont.)

shrink, and Schultz says he values Donald's "ability to operate in a low-margin environment."

Even as it grows, Starbucks isn't likely to lose its touchy-feely quality, which comes directly from Schultz and gives the company a cultlike zeal. Starbucks employees sometimes sound almost Maoist, as in, "Well, I read in Howard's book . . ." Schultz says, "The most important thing I ever did was give our partners [employees] bean stock," meaning Starbucks stock options. "That's what sets us apart and gives a higher-quality employee, an employee that cares more."

Schultz cares too. At 5 A.M. on July 7, 1997, Schultz and his family were asleep at his house in East Hampton, N.Y., when the phone rang. Three Starbucks employees had been murdered in a botched robbery in Washington, D.C. "I was stunned. Catatonic," says Schultz. He chartered a plane and arrived in D.C. before nine that morning. He took charge of the scene and stayed for a week, visiting the store, working with the police, meeting with the victims' families, attending the funerals. Ultimately Schultz decided that all future profits from the store would go to organizations working for victims' rights and violence prevention. Schultz dedicated his book to the three employees. "You cannot do better in a crisis than he did in that instance," says Washington Post CEO Don Graham. "He went way beyond the normal bounds."

As Starbucks stretches and grows, it is making itself felt in all manner of businesses besides coffee. It has a dreamy line of coffee ice cream, and a ready-to-drink coffee beverage business it runs with PepsiCo. Now it is moving further afield to tap into the brand equity it has built.

As crazy as it sounds, music has become one of Starbucks' zingiest brand extensions. Music at Starbucks began when a store manager named Timothy Jones made tapes for his store, which proved so popular that the company licensed compilations for sale. "I had to get talked into this one," says Schultz. "But then I began to understand that our customers looked to Starbucks as a kind of editor. It was like, 'We trust you. Help us choose.'" In 1999, Schultz bought Hear Music of Cambridge, Mass., run by Don MacKinnon, who was putting together albums of cool music, both old and new, that wasn't getting played on the radio. Since then Hear has released about 100 albums and sold about five million CDs, including the Artist Choice series,

"I had to get talked into [selling music]. But I began to understand that customers look to Starbucks as a kind of editor."

in which performers like the Rolling Stones and Ray Charles pick their favorite tracks by other artists.

In financial services, Starbucks has recently teamed up with Bank One to offer the Starbucks Card Duetto Visa, so named because it's a two-in-one product that is both a stored-value card and a traditional credit card. Customers get points at Starbucks for using the Visa. "We could have partnered with any number of retailers, but Starbucks really is on the cutting edge of this," says Bank One CEO Jamie Dimon at the rollout of the Duetto at a Starbucks in downtown Manhattan.

There are limits to how far Starbucks can go here. The company tried its hand in publishing, teaming up with Time Inc. (publisher of FORTUNE) to roll out a magazine called Joe, which flopped. Schultz still keeps a rack of Joe issues in his office "as a reminder." Another embarrassing foray came in 1999, when Schultz declared Starbucks an Internet company and the stock fell 15% in one day. "I got caught up in it," Schultz admits.

Today, 22 years after joining Starbucks and molding it in his image, Howard Schultz is a very rich man. He controls more than 18 million shares of Starbucks worth some $600 million. Schultz was also an early investor in eBay and owns tens of millions of dollars of that stock as well. His net worth is said to be in excess of $1 billion. Guarded about his personal life, Schultz lives with his wife, Sheri, and their teenage son and daughter in a 6,300-square-foot, three-bedroom home—with Rothkos and Kiefers on the walls—in a gated community overlooking Lake Washington. At night you can hear his son shooting baskets at their backyard hoop.

Basketball is Schultz's other hometown pursuit. Three years ago he and a group of other local businessmen bought the Sonics for some $200 million. Sit with Schultz in the front row at center court, and you see the truly competitive and, well, passionate, side of him. Call him a slightly more mellow ver-

sion of Mark Cuban. Slightly. "Fuck! That was a bad shot," he says. (Like so many others, what Schultz has discovered about the NBA is that success in business does not necessarily translate into wins on the hardwood.)

So it's a good, rich life, and a long way from Canarsie. The big question for Schultz is whether Starbucks can keep it up. There are those on Wall Street who say that Starbucks' game is almost over. With all those thousands of stores—more than 1,400 in California, another 1,000 in Asia, and 168 in Manhattan—there must be no more room to grow. And yet there are reasons to think that Starbucks has years, perhaps even decades, to go before it taps out its growth. Eventually, Schultz suggests, his company will have in the neighborhood of 25,000 stores. (McDonald's, by the way, has more than 30,000 stores.) Starbucks could expand even faster than it does, but it governs its growth to make sure it can maintain quality—which is why it sees no need for national TV advertising, which Schultz believes would diminish the brand.

That's also one reason Starbucks is resisting the siren call of Bentonville, at least for now. "The guys from Wal-Mart wanted to talk business with us, and they told me to come down to Bentonville to talk," says North American chief Jim Donald. "I told 'em, 'It's a busy time right now, maybe in a little bit.' They called back and asked me again, and I said no. Finally I told them, 'If you guys want to talk so bad, come on up here to Seattle.' And they did!" But no agreement was reached, so naturally Wal-Mart is quietly trying out its own coffee bar concept, called Kicks Coffee Cafe, at a single Wal-Mart in Plano, Texas.

Spurn distribution through Wal-Mart? Now there's a company that goes its own way. But again, Howard Schultz's business has always been different, and perhaps for that reason frequently underestimated. Ten years ago a financial commentator called Starbucks "the short of the decade." It wasn't in the 1990s, and a third of the way into the next decade, it still isn't. Instead, Starbucks seems to be moving neatly from a startup to a blue chip, as Schultz's concept of a "third place" catches on. It's as American as Caramel Macchiato.

PC companies swoop into consumer electronics biz

Consumers win as turf war rages over TVs, cameras

By Michelle Kessler
USA TODAY

LAS VEGAS—The plush Wynn Las Vegas casino will have flat- panel TVs in every guest room when it opens in 2005.

But the 7,000 TVs won't be from leading consumer electronics makers, even though developer Steve Wynn contacted "Sony, Samsung—all of them."

Wynn is expected to announce today that he instead bought TVs from PC maker Gateway, which has been in the electronics business for only a year. Wynn liked Gateway's low prices and flexible designs.

That Sony is expected to lose a deal to Gateway shows how PC-focused companies are changing the consumer electronics industry. Hewlett-Packard, Apple Computer and Dell are plunging into consumer electronics as never before. They're hustling to boost revenue as their traditional businesses mature and to stake out territory as the long-awaited convergence of computing and digital entertainment occurs.

Their entry into new markets is expected to lead to lower prices, more choices for consumers and tougher days for companies pursuing consumer dollars. Although electronics giants such as Sony, Panasonic and Pioneer Electronics have the advantage of experience, they haven't faced significant new competitors in more than a decade. The shakeout "will make the PC battles of the past look like child's play," says Creative Strategies technology analyst Tim Bajarin.

The focus on consumer electronics has been building for months and is culminating at the giant Consumer Electronics Show in Las Vegas.

In a keynote speech Wednesday, Microsoft Chairman Bill Gates announced his company's latest foray into what has been an elusive market for the software giant: Microsoft software that more easily melds PCs and TVs. Other announcements: No. 1 chipmaker Intel, known for PC processors, is expected to announce plans to make chips for digital TVs. Printer maker Epson launched projection TVs.

But those are just the latest moves. In the past year, No. 1 PC maker Dell started selling digital music players and TVs. Hewlett-Packard launched a line of digital

cameras and is expected to get into TVs. Cisco Systems, No. 1 maker of Internet networking equipment, bought Linksys Group, which makes networking gear for homes and small offices. CEO John Chambers called the acquisition Cisco's biggest bet in years.

Luring the new big guns: higher-margin products such as pricey TVs and digital music players; fast-growth markets such as digital cameras and DVD players; and a play to make the previously work-focused PC the center of home entertainment.

Digital electronics, Gates says, are "a new opportunity." They are also a natural extension of PCs, says Gary Shapiro, CEO of the Consumer Electronics Association. In some ways, a digital TV is a closer cousin of a PC than of an analog TV. That's because digital technology turns precise bits of data into pictures and sound, while analog devices convert a less-precise stream of information. Apple's iPod digital music player, which accounts for 6% of its revenue, is basically a computer hard drive with music-playing software. Digital video recorders, such as TiVo, store TV programs on hard drives similar to those in computers.

"The technology of the PC industry has completely taken over consumer electronics," says venture capitalist Roger McNamee of Silver Lake Partners.

CATCHING THE DIGITAL WAVE

It may be harder for some electronics companies to shift to digital than it is for computer companies to get into electronics. But they have little choice. Digital photography is surpassing film, forcing companies such as Eastman Kodak to retool. Digital music sales are expected to reach $200 million this year, taking a chunk out of the CD market. While the U.S. PC market is expected to be worth $59 billion this year, the U.S. consumer electronics market could hit $101 billion.

The fate suffered by Sony's analog TV business illustrates how fast the shift is occurring. It has long been a cash cow because Sony could charge high prices for its finely tuned sets based on bulky cathode-ray-tube technology. But rivals such as Samsung and Sharp

(Cont.)

took the lead in recent years in digital flat-panel TVs. In April, Sony stunned investors with an almost $1 billion quarterly loss. The next quarter, its usually strong TV revenue fell 16%. Sony is now playing catch-up in flat-panel TVs and recently said it will cut 20,000 jobs. Sony isn't the only company feeling the impact of the new entrants, which are affecting:

▶ **Prices.** They're dropping fast for all kinds of products, from TVs to portable music players. "Consumers are the winners here," says Intel Vice President Louis Burns. Example: a 35% drop in price, to $532, for a popular flat-panel TV last year, according to the most recent data from researcher NPD Group.

Computer companies can keep prices low because they're used to running lean. PCs often have profit margins of 5% to 10%, compared with 20% or more for many consumer electronics products.

Gateway shocked the electronics industry in 2002 when it introduced its $2,999 flat-panel plasma TV. At the time, similar sets from electronics players cost about $5,000. "Dell and Gateway are setting the entry-level price point," says Pioneer Senior Vice President Russ Johnston. Pioneer, a leading TV maker, has tinkered with prices to compete and has boosted its advertising budget more than 250%, Johnston says.

Dell this year began offering a powerful digital music player for about $250, when similar players cost $300 or more. That helped spur more affordable high-end players, including Apple's $249 iPod Mini.

▶ **Time to market.** Digital cameras and other electronics are hitting the market faster than ever. One reason is that computer companies are accustomed to developing products quickly. Because computer technology changes fast, most companies refresh products every few months. They also move fast because parts are standardized, and products are quickly assembled in Asian factories. In contrast, electronics companies tend to refresh products just once a year and take longer to design and build.

Even so, electronics makers are trimming design times to keep up. Samsung recently designed a digital music player in four months, a process that once took a year. Pioneer and Panasonic say they're streamlining design to reduce time to market.

Consumer gizmos boom

Computer companies, trying to boost revenue, are plunging into consumer electronics.

U.S. wholesale revenue for consumer products is expected to rise again this year ...

$96.4 in billions $101.0

1 — estimate
Source: Consumer Electronics Association

... even as retail prices have fallen for products such as flat-panel TVs

Average price, 15-inch LCD TV[3]:

$665.04 $532.66

Gateway introduces its LCD TV   Dell introduces its TV

2 — Latest figure
3 — Most common model
Sources: NPD Group, companies

By Adrienne Lewis, USA TODAY

▶ **Distribution.** Products once sold only in electronics stores, such as Best Buy and Circuit City, are now sold in all kinds of places. Dell sells most of its TVs and music players online and via phone. Gateway runs its own chain of retail stores. That takes business from traditional retail chains, where most consumer electronics companies peddle their products, says electronics analyst Tom Edwards with NPD.

Electronics makers are responding by increasing their sales channels. Sony is more heavily promoting its five U.S. Sony Style retail stores and boosting its Web offerings. Philips Electronics recently struck a deal with Lane Home Furnishings to sell home entertainment systems in furniture stores. Samsung is running more than 40 online ad campaigns and a promotion with Time Warner Cable.

Still, the different ways to buy can confuse consumers, who are unable to make side-by-side comparisons of many products, Edwards says.

UNPREDICTABLE CONTEST

The computer companies won't necessarily come out on top. Some past forays into consumer electronics have been disasters. Intel made everything from digital cameras to toys in the late 1990s before shuttering the money-losing business in 2001. Gateway, Compaq and Dell made TV-like devices for surfing the Internet that also flopped. And Microsoft's TV set-top boxes never took off.

The PC-focused companies are also accustomed to customers who forgive buggy products. That doesn't work with consumer electronics. "The product has to work 24/7," says Rajeev Mishra, a director at Epson. "Customers won't wait while it reboots."

And the products have to be especially easy to use. That has caught some computer companies off guard. When Cisco bought Linksys, Cisco employees accustomed to handling major crises from technology experts were "unprepared to deal with the consumers when they started to call in," says Cisco Senior Vice President Charlie Giancarlo. Now, Cisco has better-trained staff to handle calls from consumers. The electronics business differs from big business networking gear "in almost every possible way," Giancarlo says. "But it represents a tremendous opportunity."

THE NET'S SECOND SUPERPOWER
China will soon be No. 1 in Web users. That will unleash a world of opportunity

For years, China's Kingsoft Corp. struggled to make money selling consumer software. Then last year, the company, based in the southern city of Zhuhai, shifted its focus to the Internet. In September, Kingsoft launched Sword Online, a rollicking game that lets players create their own characters, strike cyberalliances, and fight virtual attackers. The new business is taking off: In just six months, more than 1.7 million people have signed up, paying either $4.20 a month or $1.20 for 25 hours. Kingsoft expects the game's success to help it double revenues this year, to about $20 million, expand into other Asian markets, and become a world-class innovator in online gaming. "We want to be the pioneers," says Oliver Wang, Kingsoft's chief technology officer.

Such dreams may seem outsize, but Chinese dot-commers have good reason to think big. China's Internet is booming. More than 22 million newbies piled onto the Web last year, bringing the total number of Chinese online to 80 million. That makes China second only to the U.S. in Internet subscribers—and the Middle Kingdom won't be No. 2 for long. By 2006, it is expected to pass the U. S. with 153 million Chinese online, estimates investment bank Piper Jaffray & Co. The surge is being driven by several factors, including a strong economy that's letting people buy PCs and the opportunity the Net provides to skirt China's tight government censorship. "The Internet is growing like crazy here," says Craig Watts, managing director of Norson Telecom Consulting in Beijing.

HEADLONG RUSH
The expanding audience has set off a building spurt in recent months reminiscent of Silicon Valley in the late 1990s. Local businesses such as Kingsoft are moving onto the Net, staking a claim to the rich opportunities ahead. Foreign Web companies, including Yahoo! Inc. and eBay Inc., are making acquisitions to expand their operations in the country. And entrepreneurs from around the world are opening shop on China's Net. They range from Peggy Yu, a 38-year-old MBA from New York University who runs what she hopes will be the Amazon.com Inc. of China, to Li Ka-shing, the Hong Kong billionaire whose portal Tom Online Inc. plans to raise as much as $200 million in an initial public offering scheduled for this month.

Investors are just as gung-ho about the market. Sina Corp., the largest Net portal in China, has seen its shares surge eightfold over the past year, to $45. Numerous companies, such as Tom Online and wireless message service Linktone Ltd., are lining up to sell stock to a hungry public. Even venture capitalists are getting bolder. In February, business-to-business auction site Alibaba.com landed $82 million from Fidelity Investments, Softbank, and other venture players—the largest VC investment in a China Net company ever.

No question, China's Internet companies have lots of growing up to do. Add up the market caps of all the publicly traded players, and the total comes to less than $10 billion. That's one-quarter of an eBay, one-third a Yahoo. In most markets, the Chinese dot-coms are well behind rivals in the U. S., Japan, and Korea. And just as in the U. S., the boom probably will lead to excess, with some poorly conceived businesses imploding.

Still, look at what's happening from Zhuhai to Shanghai to Beijing, and you realize that the implications could be profound. So far, the Internet has been dominated by a single country—the U.S. Now, China has the potential to become the second major power of the Digital Age. By 2006, it is expected to have more people on the Net, more broadband subscribers, and more mobile-phone customers than any other nation on earth. "To have 300 million people in China use the Internet is a tiny issue," says Jack Ma, Alibaba's founder and CEO.

You won't need to speak Mandarin to surf the Web. But important innovations will emerge from the country, especially in markets such as Net services for mobile phones and online gaming. Foreign companies that want to be dominant Net players—think eBay and Amazon—will need to have a presence in China. And high-tech multinationals will have to consider China not just when they're selling products but also when they're designing them. Last fall, Nortel

China's Evolving Net
China's portals are expanding, and entrepreneurs are launching e-tailing, mobile, and gaming services. Here's a look:

THE ESTABLISHMENT			THE RISING STARS		
SINA The most popular portal, Sina has 95 million registered visitors. It has links with Korean companies for online gambling and Yahoo! for auctions.	**SOHU** It has become profitable by sending Internet content to its customers' cellular telephones in the form of short text messages.	**NETEASE** After a misstep with a serious accounting scandal, its ads, text messages, and games have made William Ding one of China's richest men.	**SHANDA** This gaming company just recruited the former head of Microsoft in China to be its president. It is planning to go public in an IPO this year.	**TOM ONLINE** The portal spin-off of Li Ka-shing's media group aims to raise as much as $200 million in an IPO. It focuses on cutting-edge wireless services.	**LINKTONE** The number of cell phone users who subscribe to Linktone for wireless games, cartoons, and horoscopes has shot up 73%, to 5.6 million in six months.
REVENUES: $114 million	**REVENUES:** $80 million	**REVENUES:** $65 million	**REVENUES:** $97 million*	**REVENUES:** $77 million	**REVENUES:** $17 million
PROFITS: $31 million	**PROFITS:** $26 million	**PROFITS:** $39 million	**PROFITS:** Not available	**PROFITS:** $20 million	**PROFITS:** $3.6 million

* Estimate

Data: BusinessWeek

(Cont.)

Networks Ltd. decided to invest $200 million in a research and development facility in Beijing to develop networking and wireless gear.

While sheer size is the obvious reason for China's growing Net influence, the policies of the Chinese government are just as important. Under President Hu Jintao, the Beijing government is carefully nurturing local companies to help them compete in the global marketplace. Not content with low-end manufacturing, Beijing is determined to turn China into a high-tech force that can rival the U.S., Japan, and others in innovation. Already, the government has used the billions it spends on networking gear to help China's Huawei Technologies Co. and ZTE Corp. become world-class rivals to Cisco Systems Inc. and Nortel. Huawei's exports doubled last year, to more than $1 billion, out of $3.8 billion in total sales.

That may be a sign of what's to come. Beijing is trying to set the standards for several key Web technologies that may let the country's manufacturers become significant players around the world. Take Wi-Fi, the wildly popular wireless technology. In December, Beijing mandated that a new Chinese encryption standard for Wi-Fi be used in all gear sold in the country after June 1. The move is necessary, officials say, to make Wi-Fi more secure. To comply with the rule, foreign companies have to share their product designs with one of the two dozen Chinese companies Beijing has designated as licensees of the standard. These companies will integrate the standard into the designs and then help produce the equipment.

"OMINOUS MOVE"

Howls of protest have come from American high-tech companies. Dennis Eaton, chairman of the Wi-Fi Alliance, says many of the trade group's members, which include Intel, Cisco, and Broadcom, are worried that they could lose their edge by disclosing chip designs and other intellectual property to potential Chinese rivals. He says some may even stop shipping Wi-Fi products to China this June. In early March, the Bush Administration wrote a letter protesting the mandate, and U.S. industry representatives vow to fight the policy, which they say violates World Trade Organization rules. "It's a very ominous move for the Chinese government to take," says Anne Stevenson-Yang, manag-

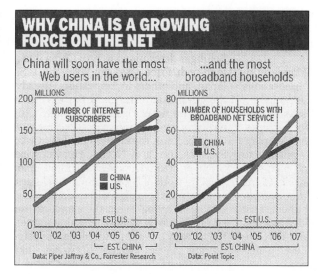

WHY CHINA IS A GROWING FORCE ON THE NET

China will soon have the most Web users in the world...

MILLIONS
NUMBER OF INTERNET SUBSCRIBERS
■ CHINA
■ U.S.
EST. U.S.
'01 '02 '03 '04 '05 '06 '07
└─ EST. CHINA ─┘
Data: Piper Jaffray & Co., Forrester Research

...and the most broadband households

MILLIONS
NUMBER OF HOUSEHOLDS WITH BROADBAND NET SERVICE
■ CHINA
■ U.S.
EST. U.S.
'01 '02 '03 '04 '05 '06 '07
└─ EST. CHINA ─┘
Data: Point Topic

ing director in Beijing for the U.S. Information Technology Office, a lobbying group for U.S. high-tech companies.

Even if the U.S. companies ultimately win in a WTO court, a legal battle still may be a losing proposition. A company such as Intel or Broadcom would have to forgo sales to China for years to prove their point. That's why Beijing's policies likely will help several Chinese tech companies follow in the footsteps of Huawei, becoming powerful enough to compete globally. Among those with the most potential are networking gear maker Harbour Networks Co. and chipmaker Semiconductor Manufacturing International Corp.

Focusing on the trade dispute, however, risks missing an important development in China's tech industry. Just as Beijing is trying to tip the scales for domestic manufacturers, local Net companies are coming up with promising innovations on their own. In part, that's because of the special characteristics of the Chinese market. As in the U.S., portals were the first Net companies to emerge in China. But the country's top three—Sina, Sohu, and NetEase—soon found that, unlike their American brethren, they could not rely on ad sales, since online advertising was scarce.

Instead, the companies in 2002 struck gold with paid messaging services. These are tailor-made for China, which has 286 million mobile-phone users, nearly double the number in the U.S. Through revenue-sharing deals with China's two state-owned cellular operators, the portals charge to send news updates, games, and online dating info to mobile phones. The services have evolved

far beyond simple text messages. Sohu even sends out color greeting cards with voice messages from basketball star Yao Ming. Multimedia services are expected to help push the market from $200 million in 2001 to $3 billion this year, estimates Lehman Brothers Inc.

Upstarts also are experimenting with a wide range of paid content. One runaway success has been virtual games, played either online or on mobile phones. In the case of games like Kingsoft's Sword Online, thousands of people compete against one another at the same time, taking on game identities and amassing special powers over weeks or months. China's online game market is expected to grow fivefold by 2007, to $809 million, says researcher IDC.

Certainly, China is playing catch-up in many Internet markets. E-commerce, for example, has been slow to develop because so few Chinese have credit cards and the mail is unreliable. But Yu is starting to make progress with Dangdang.com, a distinctly Chinese version of Amazon. Dangdang lets would-be buyers pay with money orders and even old-fashioned cash on delivery. To get packages to customers, Dangdang hired a fleet of delivery boys who zip around China's biggest cities on bicycles. Yu says more than 2 million customers have bought books, CDs, and DVDs from Dangdang, with an average order of about $10. "We have figured out the basics," she says.

There's little doubt that, as tens of thousands of Chinese go online for the first time every day, the country is changing. It's becoming a more attractive place for foreign companies to invest—and it's starting to show signs of indigenous innovation. "China is part of the leading edge," says Robert Mao, president and CEO for Nortel's Greater China operations. Just look to Kingsoft's Wang. He's working with next-generation technologies so that his company will be able to offer mobile-phone games that blend movies, voice, and data. With that kind of service and with the largest potential audience in the world, it's little wonder he's dreaming big.

By Bruce Einhorn in Zhuhai

Yes, Women Spend (And Saw and Sand)

BY FARA WARNER

MARIETTA, Ga.—Sheila Miller grips the black rubber handle of a circular saw, struggling to drive the blade through a tough piece of laminated wood flooring. Cheered on by her two daughters and three dozen women attending a Home Depot Do-It-Herself workshop here in late January, Ms. Miller finishes the job and shakily turns over the saw to Wendy Tijerina, the manager of the flooring department.

"I just moved into a new house, and there's a lot of things to be done," Ms. Miller, 42, said, noting that she had already completed some of the easier home-improvement tasks.

"But now I'm coming to the big tools," she added. "They are my biggest fear, but I'm not paying somebody to do something I can do myself."

Her determination to tackle the toughest tasks—like sanding and sealing a countertop in her kitchen—is no surprise to executives at **Home Depot,** which is based nearby, in Atlanta. More than two years ago, under its relatively new chief executive, Robert L. Nardelli, the company embarked on an 18-month study of all its shoppers, paying particular attention to women. Home Depot executives pored over consumer data, and, with the ideas they gathered, the company is spending more than $1 billion to renovate many of its 1,700 stores.

Home Depot's main rival, **Lowe's,** had already been marketing to women and had redesigned its stores to feature departments considered more appealing to them: lighting, accessories, paint and flooring. It even widened its aisles to help eliminate "butt brush," the uncomfortable contact that can occur as consumers navigate the aisles, and something that women particularly disliked, the company found.

"We're always looking to improve the stores, and many of the changes have made a real difference in the way women see Lowe's," said Julie Yenichek, a spokeswoman for the company.

The moves have paid off for Lowe's. And now Home Depot, too, appears to be reaping rewards from its effort. While Lowe's had consistently outperformed Home Depot for several years in same-store sales, those for stores open at least a year, Home Depot outpaced its rival in its fourth quarter. On Tuesday, Home Depot announced that its same-store sales for that quarter, which ended on Feb. 1, were up 7.6 percent over the period a year earlier. That compared with a gain of 7.3 percent at Lowe's in its quarter ended Jan. 30. Home Depot also had a 39 percent gain in its fourth-quarter profit, versus 28 percent at Lowe's.

Although Mr. Nardelli did not attribute all of Home Depot's gains to its marketing toward women, he did say during a conference call with reporters that the company's remodeled stores had outpaced others.

Home Depot found that women wanted clean and tidy stores—no pastels, please—that offered all the nuts and bolts of a home-improvement store and lots of information about how to do renovations.

Company executives say they think they have found a combination that plays well to a growing group of women: those who not only make the decisions about home improvement but also end up doing much of the work themselves.

By deciding to teach women about tools, rather than carrying tools specifically designed for women, Home Depot hopes to avoid offending its male consumers, especially the professional contractors who account for 35 percent of its $58 billion in annual sales. "We can't give up one gender just to please another one," said John Costello, the company's executive vice president for merchandising and marketing.

With the help of Shelley Nandkeolyar, a former Williams-Sonoma executive, Home Depot has also overhauled its catalog and its Web site to make them more appealing to women, offering decorating ideas alongside images of the tools needed for the projects. It has also increased its television sponsorship of renovation reality programs like "Trading Spaces," which are popular with women.

The Marietta store, in a former Kmart, shows the sometimes big, sometimes small changes that the company is making. To make the store feel less intimidating, Home Depot has made the shelves shorter—and beige instead of orange. (The bland color doesn't compete for attention when consumers are picking paint and flooring.) Aisle markers are like those in grocery stores, and maps help customers find products. And the polished concrete floors reflect light, making them less industrial-looking than those in older stores.

Other things have not changed. The tool corral—including a dozen saws bristling with sharp teeth and 50 different hammers hanging on an industrial Pegboard—has not been remodeled, but its shelves have been lowered slightly so the tools are easier to see. Lumber, drywall and insulation are still stacked in huge quantities near the checkout counters set aside for professional shoppers.

"If you make it too girlie, you're messing with the secret sauce of Home Depot," said Jason L. Feldman, the company's director of style, innovation and design. "Women told us, 'I want to shop where men shop for tools.'"

For years, executives at Home Depot said surveys had shown that even without doing anything to its stores, it had as many female shoppers as Lowe's.

Still, Home Depot has had a male-dominated image. "Women may have had the impression that they weren't welcome," said Mary Lou Quinlan, founder and chief executive of Just Ask a Woman, a research firm.

The company acknowledges the image problem. "Historically, we have overmarketed to men and undermarketed to women," said Mr. Costello, who faced a similar problem when he was at Sears, Roebuck. There, he helped create the "softer side of Sears" campaign to moderate the retailer's manly image as a seller of Craftsman tools. At Home Depot, Mr. Costello has revamped the company's advertising under a new tag line: "You can do it, we can help."

The encompassing nature of that message reflects the delicate balance the company is trying to strike. While Lowe's moved aggres-

Selling Improvements

Both Home Depot and Lowe's have intensified their marketing to women in an effort to increase sales.

Comparable-store sales change

■ THE HOME DEPOT
▨ LOWE'S

'94 '95 '96 '97 '98 '99 '00 '01 '02 '03
Fiscal years ended in January

Source: The companies

sively to market toward women, executives at Home Depot worried that any drastic change would upset men, its core customers, who might shun stores that felt too feminine.

Fortunately for Home Depot, it found that women held the same negative view of overly feminine stores—an opinion it discovered as it developed the Do-It-Herself workshops.

The sessions began several years ago as informal "ladies' nights" at a few stores around the country. Last year, the company decided to formalize the program and to offer the workshops on the same night every few months across the country. At first, company executives thought the workshops would deal primarily with advice on home decorating—painting techniques and color trends, for example. But they changed those ideas after polling potential participants.

"These women wanted to tackle the big things," said Anna Siefken, who oversees the national workshops. She said women had requested sessions on how to use power tools, install carpeting and perform basic plumbing tasks.

Now Home Depot sends e-mail messages to thousands of women before the sessions so the women can determine the topics.

"Many of them are repeat customers, so as they gain confidence doing one project, they want to move on to even bigger projects," Ms. Siefken said.

In its research, Home Depot also found that growing numbers of couples worked together on home-improvement projects. "I think some companies are still locked into a definition of the nuclear family where women's and men's roles are strictly defined," Mr. Costello said. "The reality is of an increasing partnership. Women are definitely equal partners in home renovations."

The company calls these people the "home perfectors." While they make up just 21 percent of Home Depot shoppers, they account for 46 percent of the spending, especially for projects like outdoor kitchens and home theaters.

The demographic trend was visible at a recent Do-It-Herself workshop in Marietta. A few men took their seats after snagging cookies from a table with a handwritten sign that said, "For the ladies' seminar." Jerry Piska, 47, wore a name tag with "Denise" on it—a little joke by his wife, Kathleen, he said.

"My wife is the one with all the mechanical genius, and I provide the muscle," Mr. Piska said. The couple did not have a specific home-renovation project in mind, but Kathleen Piska wanted to learn more about how to install laminated flooring and a new product called Legato Carpet Squares. The squares have been a hot seller ever since they showed up on "Trading Spaces."

"Women see Hildy do a project and they want to know how to do it themselves," said Ms. Siefken of Home Depot, referring to one of the show's decorators.

For many women at the workshops, learning about home renovation is about more than making their homes look good. It is also about doing something they once considered impossible.

"I started out with a little faux painting; I was so inexperienced," said Jencie Boland, 50. "Then I decided to renovate an entire room. I put up studs and Sheetrock. It was my biggest project. I was so tired, but so overjoyed that I could do it."

SAND, SUN AND SURGERY
Asian hospitals are luring more patients from around the world

Shaun Reese's Bum Knee had been nagging him for months. He had torn a ligament a couple of years earlier that never healed properly, and the pain was getting worse. But the 48-year-old building contractor from Wyoming didn't have health insurance, so he kept putting off dealing with the problem. Then a friend suggested he fly to Thailand for some sun—and a spot of surgery on the side.

After some investigation, Reese took the advice, and in January he hopped a plane for Bangkok's Bumrungrad Hospital, where he had arthroscopic knee surgery. Total cost: $5,000—half for the surgery and the rest for airfare and three weeks recuperating on the beach. Back home, he would have paid $6,500 for the operation alone. In Thailand, he says, "the people are super nice, and the facilities are nice and clean and convenient." So nice, clean, and convenient, in fact, that Reese says he may return next year for a hip replacement.

Welshman Cyril Parry's problem wasn't the cost of surgery. He had coverage from Britain's National Health Service but had been waiting more than four years for a hip replacement. As his pain increased, he decided to take matters into his own hands. Online, he found the Web site of the Apollo Hospital in Madras, India, and discovered that a doctor there had worked with a pioneer of hip-replacement surgery in Britain. "His credentials were impeccable," Parry says. Although his family thought he was daft, 59-year-old Parry flew to Madras in November and had the operation. Less than two weeks later, he was home. Total cost: $8,300, which he paid out of pocket. He is thrilled with the results. "I could not have gone anywhere better," says Parry. But he notes that, upon his return, "the nurses at the NHS gave me an attitude of near-hostility for going overseas for my operation."

FEARS OF AVIAN FLU

Those NHS nurses—and their counterparts elsewhere in the developed world—may have to shed their attitude. Parry and Reese are among a growing army of patients traveling to Asia for medical care. Thailand's private hospitals treated more than 308,000 patients from abroad in 2002, generating some $280 million in revenue, according to the Thai Private Hospital Assn. And the business is growing. While just around 10,000 international patients checked in to Indian hospitals for everything from hernias to heart surgery last year, health-care tourism in India could become a $1 billion business by 2012, according to a report by McKinsey & Co. and the Confederation of Indian Industry. And Singapore attracted 200,000 foreign patients in 2002 and aims to serve 1 million annually by 2010. Medical care "will be a global business." says C.E. Tan, marketing manager at Parkway Group Healthcare, a chain of hospitals in Singapore that treated 122,000 foreign patients last year.

One potential hitch in the global ambitions of Asian hospitals: The region is seen as a breeding ground for infectious disease. This year's avian flu outbreak will surely cause some would-be patients to check in to local hospitals rather than fly to Asia for treatment. Last year's SARS epidemic took a big bite out of business for many facilities in the region. Although Thailand had no reported cases of the disease, "SARS kicked us quite badly," says Ralf Krewer, marketing manager at the International Medical Center of Bangkok Hospital. "Nobody wanted to get on a plane." And many foreigners are concerned about the safety of the blood supply in developing nations, although officials say those worries are unfounded. The blood used in Thai hospitals is monitored "by the International Red Cross, and every blood-donor clinic is inspected," says Surapong Ambhanwong, a board member of the country's National Blood Donor center.

Cutting Costs
Fees for common surgical procedures requested by medical tourists

	THAILAND/INDIA	U.S.
Heart bypass	$8,000-15,000	$25,000-35,000
Hip replacement	$7,500-8,750	$25,000-35,000
Breast Augmentation	$2,000-2,500	$4,500-8,000
Lasik eye surgery	$1000-1650	$4,000-6,000
Nose job	$1,000-1,750	$4,000-12,000

Data: Bangkok General Hospital, American Society of Plastic Surgeons, Society of Thoracic Surgeons.

Those are real concerns. But on price alone, you don't have to be a brain surgeon to do the math. In India or Thailand, a heart bypass costs $8,000 to $15,000, cataract surgery $500 per eye, and a root canal $80 to $225 per tooth. Those prices are a fraction of what U.S. hospitals or dentists might charge. And in both countries, privately run hospitals often provide foreign patients with live video consultations before they arrive, a personal paramedic, airport transfers in either a limousine or ambulance, and a couple of weeks in a hotel to recuperate.

While people have long traveled to far-flung, exotic locales for nose jobs, tummy tucks, and breast enhancements, Thailand wants to woo foreigners in need of nonelective medical treatment. A key catalyst for private Thai hospitals was the financial crisis of 1997-98. With their own middle-class clientele devastated by the economic collapse, the hospitals started courting foreigners to help fill their empty wards. Last year, more than 150,000 international patients (including those seeking outpatient care) from 140 countries came to Bumrungrad, generating 20% of its $112 million in revenue. Now, Bumrungrad is reaching even further afield, with referral offices in Oman, Australia, and the Netherlands.

India has similar ambitions. Naresh Trehan, executive director of the Escorts Heart Institute & Research Centre Ltd. in New Delhi, in August led a mission to Britain to pitch the NHS the idea of sending patients to India for everything from reconstructive surgery to cancer treatment. The NHS says it's not interested, but Trehan says some private insurers are considering the proposal. Although India's public hospitals are often run-down and underequipped, Trehan is confident that private Indian facilities can hold their own in the global operating theater. "We stand tall with the rest of them in the world," says Trehan, who spent 20 years practicing as a cardiac surgeon in New York. "People's impression of India's health care is the 1940s and 1950s," he says. "But in recent years, high-end medicine there has "taken a quantum leap."

To ease the concerns of potential patients, some of these hospitals are pursuing accreditation from the same groups that oversee medical facilities in the U.S. and Britain. Escorts is accredited by the British Standards Institute. Both Escorts and the Apollo Group

(Cont.)

hospitals are seeking certification from the U.S.-based Joint Commission on Accreditation of Healthcare Organizations. Bumrungrad already has accreditation from the Joint Commission. "We are trying to position ourselves as the Mayo Clinic of Asia, to be known as a referral center in this part of the world for patients from all over the world," says Ruben Toral, Bumrungrad's director of international programs.

The facilities are spending big bucks to attract more paying clients from abroad. Bangkok Hospital is building a $7.7 million, 104-bed heart center to be reserved entirely for foreign patients. In December, Escorts inaugurated a $20 million, 170-bed cardiac wing. To keep their customers satisfied, the hospitals often look more like luxury spas than sick bays. Bangkok Hospital offers single

Affordable procedures, excellent doctors—and spa-like facilities

rooms only (with adjoining quarters for family members) and provides in-room Internet access. It serves four different cuisines—Thai, Japanese, and two Western selections—every night. Bumrungrad's soaring lobby features a Starbucks café, a soothing fountain, and dozens of comfortable armchairs where patients and guests can relax. "I would give this five stars," says Yvonne Wilmink, a native of the Netherlands who traveled from her home in

Sri Lanka for knee surgery.

True, even five-star hospitals aren't for everyone if they're thousands of miles from home. Those with decent health insurance will probably stay put for surgery. But Asian medical facilities are betting that for people in developing markets where health care is sub-par, or for those on long waiting lists, or for anyone with inadequate coverage at home, the trip might be just what the doctor ordered.

By Frederik Balfour in Bangkok and Manjeet Kripalani in Bombay, with Kerry Capell and Laura Cohn in London

Businesses deliver services to you
Small companies help workers get errands done

By Lorrie Grant
USA TODAY

It's a bad mix: working in the spread-out suburbs and trying to run an errand during the day.

Dan Domerofski knows firsthand. His days stuck behind a desk as a financial analyst meant relegating routine chores like car care to the weekend. But since getting laid off two years ago, he created an auto-service business to ease some everyday tasks for other suburb-based workers by coming to them.

EQ-Oil Changers in Dublin, Calif., provides on-worksite automotive oil and filter change services to employees at about a dozen companies in the area, such as Milpitas, Calif.-based LifeScan, which makes glucose testers.

"It's been easy getting businesses," says Domerofski, 29, speaking of dozens of oil changes a day, as well as replacement of windshield wiper blades and headlamps.

EQ is among a growing number of local businesses that have found a niche by bringing services to workplaces in the suburbs. The convenience helps compensate workers for the remote location as well as enhancing productivity. Others:

▶ **Body Techniques.** Based in Alameda, Calif., it makes convenience downright soothing by offering massages at workers' desks. Clients, including Netscape and Yahoo, can schedule service online.

"There are companies who have workers' compensation issues, too, and they use the massage to deal with that," says owner Austin Lund, 32, who had planned to become a chiropractor before launching the business six years ago. Lund has expanded the business by creating a network of therapists to service corporations outside the San Francisco Bay Area.

▶ **Cleaners 2U.** Founded in 1974, the family-owned dry cleaner in Reston, Va., grew to 10 locations throughout suburban Washington. But with corporations, including Internet portal America Online, moving into the area the decision was made in 1997 to add a delivery service with next-day turnaround.

"Around here, it's fast-paced, and people don't want to go to the dry cleaner every day, but they're going to the office every day," says manager Kevin Smith, 34, whose dad started the company as Village

Cleaners. "The office pickup is (growing faster) and in response we've closed all but three stores and added delivery trucks."

The service includes a garment bag with the customer's name on it for pickup and drop-off.

▶ **Unique Shoeshine.** Carlos Rodrigues was shining shoes at luxury-car dealerships in Westchester County, N.Y., as a perk for prospective buyers. One customer was an executive at the headquarters of soft-drink maker PepsiCo in Purchase, N.Y. One thing led to another and soon Rodrigues had set up an on-site stand at PepsiCo to do shines and repairs.

Contacts there led to more corporate business. A deal with nearby MasterCard came on the recommendation of a PepsiCo executive who had once worked for the credit card company.

At MasterCard, an executive mentioned the service to someone at the local office of investment banker Morgan Stanley, where Rodrigues now has a new contract.

"Women are big customers because they have more shoes, but in the summer when they wear sandals business goes down about 40%. So I offer five shoeshines for the price of four," says entrepreneur Rodrigues, 42.

In most instances, the local businesses were in the suburbs in some form before their corporate neighbors arrived.

Corporate relocations usher in so-called follow-on with the same demographic changes that also make development of hotels, restaurants, and homes necessary, says John Melaniphy III, vice president at real estate consultant Melaniphy & Associates.

That quickly expands the local merchant's sales in developing areas, Melaniphy says, but they must strike quickly to adapt their products—such as adding on-site services—before large retailers come in with offerings from pharmacy to photo development to movie rentals at drastically lowered prices.

"Customer service is how the local merchants will survive," Melaniphy says.

Entrepreneur Joe Semprevivo

Create A Niche—By making cookies a diabetic could love, he pleased himself first

. . . .

By Curt Schleier
Investor's Business Daily

Joe Semprevivo wasn't going to let a little thing like a potentially debilitating disease stop him from enjoying life.

Semprevivo, 32, was diagnosed with juvenile diabetes when he was nine years old. To make his life even tougher, his parents owned an ice cream shop in Deming, N.M. Every day after school, he'd go to the store, help his parents make ice cream and watch other people enjoy his work.

Finally, at age 12, he had enough.

"I went back to the mixing room one day after school and I made a batch of the first-ever sugar-free ice cream," Semprevivo said in a telephone interview.

At first, his parents were less than thrilled when he came running to the front of the store, "my face painted in strawberry ice cream." But when he explained what he'd done, they were as thrilled as young Joseph was.

There was just one problem. It tasted great, but "when we froze it, it came out like a block of ice." So Joseph's father, Larry, worked on the recipe until he came up with a good product.

But this was Joseph's product and he took charge. He knew that customers respond to the personal touch. So he decided to do some research, and went to supermarket freezers to check out the labels on other ice creams. Personalization, he figured, would make his product stand out. So he went with a "square label with a picture of me on it—to add personality to the product line." He even recalled what the label copy said:

"Hello. My name is Joseph Semprevivo. At 12 years old, I created this delicious, sugar-free ice cream for all diabetics and health-conscious consumers."

Semprevivo made sales calls and used every advantage at his disposal.

"I was 12 years old. The supermarket managers thought it was adorable. They waived their fees for using their freezers for me. They asked me, 'Don't you get an allowance?' I said, 'Only if I sell ice cream.'"

Going For Taste

Over the next three years, Semprevivo got his ice cream into about 75 outlets, but young Joseph wanted more. He wanted a snack he could take to school, so he could be just like the other kids. His parents, who used to own a restaurant, secretly worked on coming up with a tasty sugar-free cookie.

"I was at a friend's house. I was supposed to spend the night, but my father called me and asked me to come home. When I got there he gave me this cookie to eat, and I had tears in my eyes. It was the first cookie I'd eaten since I was 9 years old, and I wanted to share this cookie with everyone in the country."

The ice cream business had drawbacks. Once a customer's freezer broke, and Semprevivo lost 1,000 pints of ice cream that were in the store on consignment. Cookies, however, had a shelf life. The family decided to concentrate on what they could do well, while maintaining some control. Mom and Dad worked on developing more flavors—they developed eight in the first year—and young Joseph tried his hand at marketing.

He got a lot of rejections early on, but, he said, "We were persistent. We wouldn't stop."

Semprevivo built his market one store at a time. His strategy was to go from independent supermarkets to regional chains to national chains. "Not only did I make sales calls, but I did product demos. I opened up the product, handed it out and explained the health benefits of the cookies," he said.

They attended regional food and trade shows to meet buyers and got letters of recommendation from the managers of stores they were already in. Every option was considered, including shipping the cookies on consignment. "I told them, 'I'll ship you product. If it sells, you pay me.' And they did."

He also set up a marketing program with the National Diabetes Outreach, which allows the organization to raise funds by selling Joseph's Lite Cookies. Slowly the company built its presence. Semprevivo estimates that cracking Kroger, a large national chain, took eight years and "1,100 sales calls. Seriously. The buyers kept changing. They have nine regions. My first break after eight years was in Atlanta, Ga. I remember her name: Susan. She was a regional buyer, and she said, 'I'll take a chance with your cookies. I'll take them on.'"

Controlled Growth

Semprevivo's entrepreneurial ability was recognized by the federal government. In 1989, President Bush presented the then-17-year-old Semprevivo with the American Success Award in a Rose Garden ceremony. (When the White House called the company to inform Semprevivo of the award, a secretary hung up, convinced it was a prank.)

Semprevivo At A Glance

Born: 1971 in Cherry Hill, N.J.
Education: B.A in marketing and managerial leadership from New Mexico State University.
Achievements:
■ Co-founded Joseph's Lite Cookies in 1986 with his parents.
■ Helped the company become the producer of the top-selling sugar-free cookies in the Western Hemisphere. Sells his products in more than 100,000 stores in the U.S. alone.
■ Won the U.S. Exporting Award from the Department of Agriculture in 2003 for his products. Also won the Senate Productivity Award for excellence in production and efficiency in New Mexico in 1997 and the Quality Hero Award in 1995.

(Cont.)

Semprevivo's business is privately held, so it doesn't release financial figures. He does say, however, that since its inception in 1986, he has never seen less than 47% year-to-year growth. But growth has not been pell-mell.

He believes in what he calls controlled growth. "I'll never buy a piece of equipment or move into a larger plant based on one customer," he said. "That way, even if you lose a customer or he files for bankruptcy, you are still protected."

The company first moved from the original ice cream store into a 2,000-square-foot plant, then into a 7,000-square-foot facility. It's now housed in a 48,000-square-foot building in a large industrial park. His production line runs at least 20 hours a day—and sometimes more than that—to keep up with demand.

Part of the reason for the company's success, according to Semprevivo, is an insistence on strict attention to quality. There are five people on duty at any time the line is running who are empowered to shut everything down if they suspect something is wrong with the cookies—their taste, their texture, their color. They are the shift manager, the bagging manager, the assistant manager and the line manager.

The fifth is the quality control manager. His enviable job is to taste a cookie every five minutes and press an emergency button if there's anything he doesn't like. When that happens, "we throw it away," Semprevivo said.

Semprevivo's employees—he calls them team members—get fully paid health and dental insurance and a 401(k) plan. The company also offers them lifetime employment.

"My saying to all my team members is, 'As long as I have a job, you have a job.' It's a real morale booster," he said.

It's a concept he'd like to see spread to other companies. "I want to change the corporate culture as much as I can," he told the El Paso Times. "If a small company can do it, any company can do it."

"Entrepreneur Joe Semprevivo—Create a Niche—By making cookies a diabetic could love, he pleased himself first," *Investor's Business Daily,* February 24, 2004. Reprinted by permission.

This Is Not a Sports Car, It's a Marketing Vehicle

Ford counts on GT to transform the image of its entire product line

By: JEAN HALLIDAY

It won't hit showrooms until summer, but Ford Motor Co. is already getting amazing marketing mileage from the sleek Ford GT. The super-hot supercar has generated reams of publicity and turned Ford's affordable, conservative image on its ear—exactly the auto giant's intention.

The 500-horsepower, street-legal car generated a standing ovation from employees last year at its unveiling and has since received a plethora of coverage and endorsements in auto enthusiast titles. "We couldn't have written those articles any better ourselves," said Martin Collins, general marketing manager of the division.

Consider this rave from *Motor Trend:* "The GT is more than just a sports car. It's a high-speed, high-profile declaration that the Ford Motor Co. is once again out to take on the world's best."

It clearly won't be a money-maker. Ford plans to produce only 3,500 of the $139,995 GTs over two model years for the U.S. market. "We don't expect to lose money on GT," Chairman-CEO William Clay Ford Jr. told *Automotive News* last year, "but frankly none of us are going to retire on GT either."

Instead, the GT has a greater purpose, to "raise the image of all our other products," said Mr. Collins.

That's why Ford made a seemingly inefficient media buy for a low-volume car, spending a bundle to advertise the GT with 60-second spot in the second quarter of Super Bowl XXVIII. In the spot, from WPP Group's J. Walter Thompson, Detroit, the car careens around 15 turns on a track and hits speeds in excess of 140 mph as the voice-over asks, "In what gear do you realize that a car is everything it is supposed to be? In what gear do you know nothing can catch you? In what gear do you know it is the one?" A 30-second spot that aired in the pre-game show pictured the car on a turntable.

"We couldn't have written those articles any better ourselves"

A PLACE ON 'IDOL'

The 60-second spot, in fact, will air only up to 15 times, said Rich Stoddart, marketing communications manager of Ford division. The spots will run during the Ford Championship at Doral golf broadcast on NBC next month and the finals of "American Idol" in May on Fox, in which Ford Division is a sponsor. In another high-profile media buy, a print ad for the racer also appears in Time Inc.'s *Sports Illustrated* swimsuit issue.

The GT ads carry the tagline that says it all about Ford's strategy: "The pace car for an entire company."

Mr. Stoddart said the theme was chosen because the car was built by the same people at Ford who "share the same passion but work on high-volume cars, SUVs and trucks." Mr. Collins added the GT "puts a little bounce back into everybody's step" at Ford.

The car can indeed provide "internal morale and bragging rights within the company," said Jeff Brodoski, an analyst at J.D. Power & Associates, who projected Ford executives, Ford dealers and Ford suppliers would buy the majority of the GTs.

Whether Ford can translate the GT momentum into sales of other models is another question. The sports car's return in 2004 marks the start of a slew of new models from Ford, which is calling 2004 "the year of the car." The brand's car sales slipped in recent years after it shifted its main focus to pickups and sport utilities. Ford Motor is in the midst of a five-year revitalization plan after a combined $6.4 billion loss in 2001 and 2002. For 2003, Ford posted its first profit since 2000 with $495 million in net income globally.

'A BLIP'

The marketer will launch the updated Focus this spring, the all-new Five Hundred sedan this summer to replace

---

Not a moneymaker: Ford expects the new GT to lure potential buyers to dealers, but it will only produce 3,500 of the $139,995 over two model years.

(Cont.)

the Taurus, and the redone 2005 Mustang this fall.

While the GT, which Mr. Brodski called "an engineering accomplishment," is likely to generate traffic at Ford dealerships, it won't necessarily close a sale of other brands. GT "will pretty much be a blip on the radar screen," he predicted, noting it will be difficult to tie the GT to actual sales of other Ford Motor products.

Art Spinella, VP of auto consultancy CNW Marketing/ Research, said the GT doesn't match the generally conservative, loyal buyer of Ford models "because performance isn't typically what they're looking for." He said the best "halo" cars are used as building blocks for a brand and its positioning, which is why he said Chrysler Group's $30,000-plus Plymouth Prowler roadster was a misfit for that affordable brand in the 1990s. Neither Plymouth nor Prowler survived.

A BETTER IDEA

But Ford clearly thinks it has a better idea. When Bill Ford announced in a February 2002 press conference that the automaker would build the sports car, he indicated it would

The GT "puts a little bounce back into everybody's step" at Ford

be just the start of an image overhaul for the company. "Our revitalization plan is centered on new products. The company that delivers the best cars and trucks wins and we're going to win. I can't think of a better symbol of that winning attitude than the GT40." His announcement came in the wake of the automaker's $5 billion-plus loss in 2001 and thousands of pending layoffs.

The GT has a storied history at Ford. In the mid-1960s, Henry Ford II, then chairman, ordered the development of the original GT to compete against Ferrari in racing after the Italian carmaker turned down his offer to buy the company. The Ford GT shook the racing world when it won the Twenty-Four Hours of LeMans in 1966, '67 and '68.

The brand's current iteration is also inviting comparisons to Ferrari. A test driver (reported in the January *Car and Driver*) said that the GT can go from 0 to 60 mph in 3.3 seconds, besting the $193,000 Ferrari Challenge Stradale, which limped along at 4 seconds.

Evaluating Opportunities in the Changing Marketing Environment

Here's the Beef. So, Where's the Butcher?

BY CONSTANCE L. HAYS

Over the summer, a new Pathmark supermarket opened in a fast-growing corner of Staten Island. From the outside, it looks unremarkable. But inside, it holds the latest in supermarket meat—steaks and cutlets that are not merely someone's future meal, but byproducts of the industry's battle to keep up with Wal-Mart, its biggest rival.

There in the meat section are small white tubs holding pale pink pork chops, their profiles distinct beneath the layer of plastic that seals them off from the world. They, too, look unremarkable except that they were not prepared by the store's butcher. This is "case ready" meat, which differs from traditional supermarket fare in that it is delivered, with its cutting, packaging and labeling complete, to stores in a process that has grown rapidly in popularity among retailers in the last 18 months.

It has also brought controversy. Some of the meat is injected with a saline solution to keep it both good-looking and fresh, and some shoppers complain about the taste. Many of the steaks and chops sold at Wal-Mart note, on their packages, that they contain up to 12 percent liquid. Do they shrink on the grill? Yes, say people who have cooked them. Union leaders anxious to preserve jobs have called for regulations on case-ready meat to make shoppers more aware of what they are buying.

A saline treatment 'keeps the bloom on the meat,' Wal-Mart says.

The main difference between case-ready meat and store-handled meat is that the former is cut, trimmed, packaged and labeled at a plant, not in the back room of a supermarket. The shelf life of case-ready meat is said to be longer, because the package is "flushed" with gas, usually combinations of oxygen and carbon dioxide, to keep everything inside looking fresh. The saline treatment "keeps the bloom on the meat," as a spokesman for **Wal-Mart Stores** put it.

Since September 2001, Wal-Mart has sold only case-ready meat. The change followed a vote by workers at a Wal-Mart supercenter in Texas who voted to join the United Food and Commercial Workers, a unit of the A.F.L.-C.I.O.

Pathmark is the first supermarket chain in New York City to serve meat to shoppers this way, but New York may be the final frontier. In the last year, meat packers report a surge in orders for case-ready meat as supermarkets eagerly follow Wal-Mart's lead.

Chickens have been case-ready for decades; 25 years ago, they too were split and packaged inside the stores' back rooms. But case-ready meat is a newer development, the biggest revolution inside the meat department since 1961, when boxed beef replaced the hanging steer that had to be wheeled into the back room.

Various competitive concerns have pushed stores away from the meatcutters and toward case-ready meat. The entry of Wal-Mart, the retail giant based in Bentonville, Ark., into the grocery business has made all supermarkets eager to trim costs. In recent years, Wal-Mart has made its supercenters, which combine groceries with general merchandise, the cornerstone of its expansion, and will open at least 200 new ones this year on top of the 1,258 already doing business, said a company spokesman, Tom Williams.

There are no meatcutters in the Wal-Mart stores, and they are likely to disappear from supermarkets that switch to case-ready meat, said John Niccollai, president of Local 464-A of the United Food and Commercial Workers in New Jersey. But beyond that, he said, the union objects to the absence of information about the meat in stores that sell case-ready products.

"This will cost us jobs, so we have a vested interest," Mr. Niccollai said. "But there are also a great many concerns we have about case-ready meat. There are additives and preservatives put in it. A number of people are allergic to what they put in the meat." Spokeswomen for the Food Allergy Network and the American Dietetic Association said they could not confirm whether people were allergic to the substances in case-ready meat.

In the New Jersey Legislature, a bill is pending that would require stores to post signs notifying shoppers if more than half the meat they sell is case-ready. Mr. Niccollai said supermarkets were largely opposed to the legislation. "When we send our union agents into the stores and they talk with people, the people have no idea that this product they are buying was not cut and weighed and wrapped in the back room," he said.

The cost savings for Wal-Mart include the elimination of meatcutters in stores (the experienced ones typically earn $1,000 a week) as well as reduced waste and improved efficiency. "It flows really, really well," Mr. Williams said. "The biggest savings we realize is in the efficiency of handling the product and moving it. You have so much more control over what you're ordering and what you need." Most of Wal-Mart's meat comes from **Tyson Foods**, a large Arkansas-based processor that acquired IBP, a beef and pork processor, in 2001.

Other supermarkets that find themselves up against Wal-Mart are turning to the same technique.

"Business is really, really growing," said Michael Queen, chief executive of **Pennexx Foods**, a Philadelphia processor that supplies many supermarkets and is half owned by **Smithfield Foods.** Pennexx, with $60 million in sales this year, will probably triple its sales by next year, he said, as supermarkets, which he described as having "tremendous fear of Wal-Mart," seek to cut costs.

Of course, prepackaged meat costs more than the unadorned raw material. "You are paying for the product and the packaging and the labor," said Mark Greenberg, vice president of meat for **Wakefern Food,** a cooperative that runs ShopRite supermarkets and buys from Pennexx, among other suppliers.

Wal-Mart's ubiquity has pressured all supermarket chains, putting some in unusual difficulty. The **Great Atlantic and Pacific Tea** Company, owner of the Food Emporium and A.&P. chains, announced last month that it would be forced to examine ways of cutting costs to improve profits. "We are probably operating in one of the worst possible retailing environments," A.&P.'s chairman and chief executive, Christian W.E. Haub, said, alluding to "tough choices" that would have to be made later this year. A few months ago, **Albertson's,** another major supermarket chain, retreated from Houston and several other parts of Texas where it competed with Wal-Mart; **Kroger** and regional chains remain.

Some executives say that it is not Wal-Mart, but the need to satisfy customers, that has made them introduce case-ready meat. "Wal-Mart has done it for other reasons," Mr. Greenberg said. "Our position is, we are looking to determine what the customer is looking for."

(Cont.)

Shoppers have altered their buying patterns, he added, which means they may be browsing for ground chuck at 9 o'clock in the morning on a Sunday, instead of 4 o'clock on a Friday afternoon. If there is no butcher working at that morning hour, they might be disappointed. But with case-ready meat, the product will be there waiting for them.

"A lot of our stores are 24-hour stores, but the butchers aren't working 24 hours," he said. "We want to make sure that when the customer comes in, the full variety is there." In ShopRite's 200 stores around the Northeast, case-ready is available along with store-handled meat, he added.

Mr. Niccollai said wholesale prices for case-ready meat were as much as 25 percent higher than for store-packaged meat. "You're going to save money, they feel, in terms of labor because you are not paying meatcutters," he said. "If you eliminate that, you can operate for less money. But what are you doing to your operation?" He believes that customers will go elsewhere for meat.

That has not been true at the Pathmark in Staten Island. "In this store, it's all case-ready," said Art Whitney, Pathmark's regional manager, as he stood near the meat case. "Over all, the acceptance is very good." A few shoppers have complained, he said,

that the deep tubs take up too much room in their refrigerators, compared with the flat trays that chops and other kinds of meat used to come in.

Chris Cossean, who was checking out a cartful of groceries in the store, is not one of them. "I have no problem," she said. "They're fine."

Dueling Diapers

Think big companies can't innovate? Look how Kimberly-Clark and P&G are fighting over disposable training pants. ■ *Matthew Boyle*

The battle for your baby's bottom—a brutal slugfest that makes the Coke-Pepsi showdown look like a playground tussle—took an even nastier turn last year. Procter & Gamble's overhaul of its $4-billion-a-year Pampers product line sparked a knockdown, drag-out price war with the Huggies line from Kimberly Clark, P&G's archrival in the $19-billion-a-year global baby-care market. (The price war took such a toll on Kimberly-Clark that new CEO Thomas Falk said it was largely to blame for the company's depressed fourth-quarter earnings.) The most interesting fight between Kimberly-Clark and P&G is taking place on one specific front: disposable training pants.

Worn by toddlers while they're being potty trained, the elastic diapers are pulled up over the legs like ordinary underpants, rather than being fastened at the sides—and they're the fastest-growing, highest-margin diaper product around. Kimberly-Clark invented the category in 1989 with its Huggies Pull-Ups brand and has dominated it ever since. But in the past 12 months P&G's Pampers Easy Ups have come from nowhere to grab 15% of the $1 billion U.S. training-pants market, reducing Pull-Ups' share from more than 50% to 41%, according to year-end data from Information Resources in Chicago. (Private-label brands and other products like nighttime pants make up the rest of the category.) P&G's sudden success shows the power of product and marketing innovation even late in the game.

In the 1980s, as parenting experts such as Dr. T. Berry Brazelton began counseling parents not to rush the potty training process, Kimberly-Clark—long known for product innovation—sensed an opportunity. Delaying potty training meant that kids would increasingly be in nappies longer. So why not create an entirely new category of diaper: disposable training pants that protected against accidents but also let the growing child feel as though she were wearing underwear just like a big kid? To help give that feel, Kimberly-Clark developed a clothlike outer cover and a breathable nonwoven material called stretchbonded laminate. It also built new machines

to attach the sides of the pants, a step not required for regular diapers.

To help sell parents on the concept, Kimberly-Clark argued that "switching out of diapers and into training pants help[s] speed the potty training process along," a claim made on Parentstages.com, a parenting site sponsored by Kimberly-Clark. That assertion isn't endorsed by the American Academy of Pediatrics, though. Some doctors say that the products are unnecessary and may even delay or prolong potty training. (In 1961, 90% of children were potty trained by age 2 1/2; by 1997, only 22% were.) Training pants give diaper makers the opportunity "to sell into the market two or three years longer than before ... and triple the life cycle of that consumer," says Ryan Mathews, a consultant who follows retail trends.

Whether or not training pants were strictly necessary, they took off. A dozen years later demand is still growing at a 15%-a-year clip. And there's plenty of room to expand, since only about half of the nation's 3.5 million training-age toddlers—defined as kids 18 to 48 months—wear disposable training pants, according to Dudley Lehman, group president of Kimberly-Clark's infant and child care division. (Some parents choose cloth training pants, some keep their kids in regular diapers, and some intrepid souls go right to underwear.) Pull-Ups are big moneymakers too. Training pants are typically 35% more expensive per unit than regular diapers at retail, giving them margins north of 20%, an analyst estimates (neither company will disclose its diaper margins).

If training pants are such an attractive category, why didn't P&G enter the market sooner? Well, it did. Pampers Trainers launched in 1994. But a combination of poor design and high production costs conspired to do them in. The company quietly killed Trainers in 1996. While Kimberly-Clark gloated, Procter went back to the drawing board.

Three years later P&G unveiled a new training-pant design. It chose to introduce it in Japan, the Land of the Rising Pant, where pant-type diapers command about half the market. (One reason: Japanese kids are

changed while standing up.) P&G's product, called Pampers Suku-suku, looked and felt much more like underwear than Trainers had without sacrificing absorbency, according to P&G global baby-care president Deb Henretta. Its clothlike exterior was softer and, Henretta hoped, more appealing than that of Pull-Ups. The design held its own in Japan and convinced P&G that it was on to something.

P&G soon moved to test markets in Scandinavia and Greece; a full rollout of what it was now calling Easy Ups followed across Western Europe and Britain in 2001. Europe

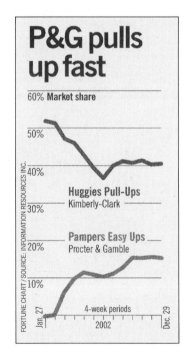

P&G pulls up fast

60% **Market share**

50%

40%

30%

20%

10%

Huggies Pull-Ups
Kimberly-Clark

Pampers Easy Ups
Procter & Gamble

4-week periods
Jan. 27   2002   Dec. 29

FORTUNE CHART/SOURCE: INFORMATION RESOURCES INC.

posed a special challenge, partly because kids there are toilet trained earlier. So P&G positioned Easy Ups as an extension of its premium diaper line rather than as a training pant. The strategy worked, and P&G says

(Cont.)

Easy Ups are now twice as popular as Pull-Ups in Western Europe. (Kimberly-Clark disputes this.) "They are a godsend!" says Kate Beard, a resident of Weston, 30 miles north of London, whose 3-year-old, Molly, wears Easy Ups at night.

The stage was finally set for Easy Ups' North American debut in February 2002. Kimberly-Clark execs, who had seen P&G try and fail in the U.S. market before, pooh-poohed Easy Ups' prospects. "Kimberly-Clark was trashtalking that P&G wouldn't even get a 7% share," says Tom Vierhile, executive editor of *Productscan Online,* which tracks the packaged-goods industry.

In fact, P&G got 7% in less than three months. That share has since more than doubled, thanks to a well-orchestrated attack on Pull-Ups' position. First, P&G threw buckets of advertising and marketing dollars into the Easy Ups launch. According to ad-spending tracker CMR in New York City, P&G spent $19 million on ads for Easy Ups in the first ten months of last year, more than the company spent on all other Pampers products

combined. Meanwhile, through aggressive couponing and other promotions, P&G cut the price on its training pants so that they cost only 15% more than regular diapers rather than 35% more. Shoppers buying Kimberly-Clark's Pull-Ups at Krogers would turn over their receipt to find a coupon for $4.50 off a jumbo package of Easy Ups, which usually sold for about $11.50. This wasn't exactly a new trick: "The easiest thing to do is to buy share by lowering the price," says Vierhile. And $40-billion-a-year P&G has much deeper pockets than $15 billion Kimberly-Clark.

On the production side, a new global manufacturing system (in which modular machinery can quickly be added to or removed from the diaper line) enabled P&G to release four product improvements to Easy Ups in just seven months. The upgrades included adding Elmo graphics, a thinner core, and a wetness indicator. Normally a single change could take a year or more. "That's stunning," says Bill Steele, an analyst at Banc of America Securities. "That should have their competitors worried."

Still, Kimberly-Clark insists it's not fazed. Lehman told *Advertising Age* last summer that "the jury's out" on Easy Ups' success, and he stands by that opinion. Kimberly-Clark has rolled out improvements to its Pull-Ups, making them 30% thinner and, more recently, adding refastenable sides. The company claims that consumers prefer its newest PullUps three to one over Easy Ups. And, Lehman boasts, it has the highest margins in the diaper industry.

Analyst Steele, for one, thinks Kimberly-Clark should worry: "If a 15% share doesn't indicate that P&G is here to stay, is Kimberly waiting for 40%?" he asks. "I was surprised that Kimberly didn't defend its position as aggressively as it should have. Perhaps they underestimated P&G." If Kimberly continues to do so, it will have quite a mess to clean up.

Latte Versus Latte

Starbucks, Dunkin' Donuts Seek Growth by Capturing Each Other's Customers

BY DEBORAH BALL AND SHIRLEY LEUNG

There's A new brew-haha in Latte-land.

For years, the product lines of the major U.S. brewed coffee sellers have been well defined. On the high end there is **Starbucks** Corp., with 5,439 locations in the U.S. During the past decade, the chain has made its expensive cappuccinos, frappuccinos, espressos and lattes part of the regular lexicon. On the other end, there is Dunkin' Donuts, which has 4,100 stores. Although concentrated in the Northeast, Dunkin' Donuts is the nation's largest seller of regular, nonflavored brewed coffee through fast-food outlets, with a 17% market share, compared with 15% for **McDonald's** Corp. and 6% for Starbucks, according to figures supplied by Dunkin' Donuts that the company said came from the market-research organization NPD Group.

Now, both companies are seeking to stir things up. Starbucks increasingly is looking for growth by opening stores in blue-collar communities where Dunkin' Donuts would typically dominate. Last month, when the Seattle coffee chain reported fiscal first-quarter earnings, executives gave much of the credit to its 10% jump in sales at stores open more than a year to this broadening demographic. Its coffee, explains Howard Schultz, Starbucks chairman and founder, is "an affordable luxury."

At the same time, Dunkin' Donuts, a unit of United Kingdom spirits group **Allied Domecq** PLC, wants to lure Starbucks's well-heeled customers with a new line of Italian brews that it claims it can deliver faster, cheaper and simpler.

"Espresso has become mainstream in America," says Jon L. Luther, chief executive of Allied Domecq's restaurant division, which also includes Baskin Robbins and Togo's. "And who does mainstream better than Dunkin' Donuts?" Its advertisements tout the same idea. One billboard reads: "Latte for Every Tom, Dick and Lucciano."

Last September, Dunkin' Donuts introduced its new cappuccinos and lattes in New England and is now launching the line in other stores in the U.S. A major ad blitz started in New York City last week. The company had expected the espresso products to represent 5% to 10% of store sales, and New Eng-

land stores are already inside that range.

On average, the new Dunkin' Donut drinks cost at least 20% less than Starbucks's offerings—and an espresso shot is just 99 cents, compared with $1.45 at Starbucks. The Dunkin' Donut drinks are labeled a no-nonsense "small," "medium" and "large" as opposed to Starbucks's "tall," "grande" and "venti." And Dunkin' Donuts has trained its staff to serve them quickly; the company worked with a Swiss manufacturer to develop equipment that makes a real espresso and fresh steamed milk in less than a minute.

"I can order a plain medium caramel latte and not deal with all that fancy stuff," says Kathleen Brown, a 30-year-old Boston lawyer who used to treat herself to a $4 Starbucks Caramel Macchiato but has switched to Dunkin' Donuts, where it costs much less.

To some Dunkin' Donuts regulars, though, the new sophistication is a little too much. Pat Kelly, a 26-year-old Boston police recruit who drinks Dunkin' Donuts coffee daily, refuses to try the new Dunkin' products (and never goes to Starbucks). The only guy in his group of police buddies who tried a Dunkin' latte got a razzing. "I'm not really a latte sort of guy," he says. "Those are yuppie drinks."

"I'm sure there are a number of folks who might be embarrassed" about buying a latte, Mr. Luther admits. "But espresso has gone mainstream, and for us to ignore it would be irresponsible."

So far, Starbucks's Mr. Schultz is taking a high-minded approach to the threat from his downscale competition. In an interview, he says he feels no pressure to lower the chain's famously high prices. "If Dunkin' Donuts is going to spend millions of dollars [in advertising] on coffee and espresso, that is really beneficial to Starbucks business," he says. "I wouldn't be surprised if our business goes up as a result."

Meanwhile, Starbucks, where regular drip coffee starts at $1.50 a cup, is pushing into Dunkin' Donuts' traditional territory. Mr.

Schultz says the idea that Starbucks could appeal to any income level came on a visit to a Chicago store several years ago. He noticed limousine drivers running in to pick up coffee for passengers. No surprise there. But he also saw a driver of a United Parcel Service truck running in, too. "I think he's going to make a delivery. No, he gets in line," recalls Mr. Schultz. "He has a 10-year-old thermos. He gets in line and asks, 'Can you fill up my thermos with two double lattes?'"

Starbucks formalized its march to open stores in low-income communities in 1998, establishing a partnership with former Los Angeles Lakers player Magic Johnson to open stores primarily in black and Hispanic communities. Mr. Johnson's **Johnson Development** Corp. operates theaters, T.G.I. Friday's restaurants and other retail businesses in urban areas.

To date, Johnson Development has opened 57 Starbucks, from New York's Harlem and Staten Island to Inglewood, Calif., with plans to open up 68 more over the next several years. Starbucks has already taken lessons learned from the Johnson partnership to apply them across the system, influencing the site selection of hundreds of other stores.

Sales at these Johnson stores mirror the robust performance of the rest of North America, which reported a 12% increase in same-store sales for January. These stores charge the same prices as any other Starbucks.

Marketing focuses on reaching out to local pastors and serving Starbucks at church coffee hours. "When you come into minority communities, church plays a very significant role," explains Ken Lombard, president of Johnson Development in Beverly Hills, Calif.

At a Starbucks that opened in the largely blue-collar South Side of Chicago, the upscale coffee house stands out among its neighbors: a check-cashing outfit, a Dunkin' Donuts, a McDonald's and JJ Fish & Chicken. So rare is a Starbucks in this locale that it's a popular first-date place, says store manager Monica Perez.

The price doesn't seem to be an issue. Last week, Jose Bahena, a 20-year-old Chicago metal shop foreman, plunked down $4.02 for a grande Frappuccino, the chain's signature creamy coffee drink. Mr. Bahena, who says he makes about $20,000 a year, comes to Starbucks four times a week. "It's so good," he says. "You have to pay for something good."

Grande Ambitions

Upscale drinks from Starbucks and Dunkin' Donuts are going foamy head to foamy head.

Dunkin' Donuts	Starbucks
Espresso Shot: 99 cents	Solo Espresso Shot: $1.45
Small Hazelnut Latte: $1.79	Tall Hazelnut Latte: $2.85
Medium Caramel Swirl Latte: $2.29	Grande Caramel Macchiato: $3.40
Large Mocha Swirl Latte: $2.69	Venti Caffe Mocha: $3.55

Source: the companies

A Debate on Web Phone Service

As Use Grows, How Will Government Handle Regulations?

BY MATT RICHTEL

Charles Davidson, a self-proclaimed gadget freak in Tallahassee, Fla., began using Internet-based telephone service last week. He can call anyone—not just the other 100,000 pioneers around the nation using such service, but any of the millions of people who use conventional telephones, like his parents in Elizabethton, Tenn.

But Mr. Davidson is more than an adventuresome consumer. As a member of the Florida Public Service Commission, he is a regulator who is eager to see Internet telephone service spread because he predicts it can make the nation's phone services less expensive and richer in features.

That is why Mr. Davidson wants the federal and state governments to let Internet-based phone service blossom, free from regulation, taxes and surcharges. Like a growing number of officials who advocate minimal oversight of the service—including Michael K. Powell, the chairman of the Federal Communications Commission—Mr. Davidson says Internet telephone service should be treated just like other unregulated Internet services, including e-mail messaging and Web surfing.

But unlike some proponents of deregulation, Mr. Davidson also has a nagging concern. Because Internet-based phone service rides over traditional telephone or cable lines, it will not work unless the conventional phone network is intact. The government has long regarded that network as a national asset akin to roads and highways, and it is a communications system whose reliability and virtual ubiquity make it the envy of most of the rest of the world. In fact, if users of Internet phones were not able to communicate with all the millions of people still plugged into the conventional telephone network, Internet telephone service would be little more than a hobbyist's experiment.

So Internet telephone service raises a public policy question: If the government does not continue to play a role in ensuring that the telephone network is reliable and universally available, does the nation risk losing a vital asset?

"It's a great question," Mr. Davidson said. "Do we, as a society, want to maintain a policy of 'always on'?"

Mr. Davidson, a former antitrust lawyer appointed to the Florida commission by the governor, Jeb Bush, a Republican, is still weighing his answer. But he says he tends to think that markets are more efficient than regulators—in other words, that laissez-faire can walk hand in hand with "always on."

Some of Mr. Davidson's counterparts in other states sound just as certain that only government referees can preserve the decades-old tradition of universal, reliable telephone service.

"If somebody doesn't regulate this, it's buyer beware," said Loretta Lynch, a member of the California Public Utilities Commission, who was appointed by the former governor, Gray Davis, a Democrat. Ms. Lynch, a lawyer, said the role of the telephone was too important to leave in the hands of market forces. "Telecommunications is essential to our democracy," she said. "It's essential, in fact, to keeping an informed populace."

If the issue were limited to the 100,000 or so customers currently using Internet-based telephones, the debate might remain largely theoretical. But the service seems on the verge of a takeoff.

The field's current leader is the **Vonage** Holdings Corporation, an Edison, N.J., company with about 80 percent of the market so far. Mr. Davidson is among its customers. Vonage estimates that it will have 250,000 customers by the end of 2004 and one million by 2006. **Time Warner** Cable, a unit of Time Warner Inc., and the **AT&T** Corporation have both announced major initiatives to roll out Internet-based phone service. The regional Bell company **Qwest Communications International** Inc. plans to offer Internet telephone service in its 14-state Rocky Mountain region as an alternative to conventional phone service. And every other major telecommunications provider has plans to introduce Internet-based service to take advantage of the technology's lower costs and the lack of regulation.

The F.C.C. has embarked on a series of public hearings around the country on whether and how to regulate Internet telephony. The agency's chairman, Mr. Powell, has said that his instinct is to subject telephone calls made using Internet technology to only minimal regulation in order to avoid costs and bureaucracy that he says would slow innovation and competition.

The public policy questions go to the heart of a social compact born in the 1930's. Then, the government granted regulated monopolies in individual markets to AT&T

Even among regulators, greatly divergent views about how to oversee telecommunications.

and other, smaller companies. In exchange, policy makers exacted a price: the telephone monopolies had to meet service quality standards and collect taxes and surcharges to support affordable, universal access even in rural or remote areas where free-market economics would not have made it cost-effective to string telephone wires.

Although AT&T's Bell System was split up in 1984, the existing four major telephone companies descending from it—**Verizon Communications,** the **BellSouth** Corporation, Qwest and **SBC Communications** Inc.—still face substantial regulation from the federal and state governments. Now, though, with the advent of Internet-based telephone service, as well as competition from wireless providers, there is growing momentum to rewrite 70 years of rules.

"The economic regulation was quid pro quo for giving it a monopoly," said Mr. Davidson of the rules governing the Bell companies. Now, he said, "there is no monopoly."

Mr. Davidson said he thought that competition from cable and wireless companies provided consumers an array of new choices. But among the various state and federal regulators who will weigh in

Michael K. Powell, the chairman of the Federal Communications Commission, has said that he supports minimal regulation of Internet phone services because he thinks the added costs and bureaucracy would slow innovation and competition

on the Internet-phone issue, there are many nuanced notions about how to proceed.

Some want to see state regulation eliminated; others want to see regulation streamlined but kept intact. Many want to retain guarantees of 911 service and universal service for low-income and rural residents, but they differ considerably on how to achieve those goals. Even within the National Association of Utility Regulators, an influential lobbying group of state regulators, some top officials have greatly divergent views about how to regulate telecommunications in the 21st century.

Not all industry executives agree, either, although most companies favor a significant rollback of regulations. One of the most unabashed supporters of Internet-based telephone service is Richard C. Notebaert, the chief executive of Qwest. Mr. Notebaert said Qwest, besides introducing Internet-based calling across its region, might even offer it nationwide.

Mr. Notebaert said that with Internet telephone service, he could save his customers 25 percent to 30 percent on their bills because they would not be required to pay the taxes and surcharges assessed to conventional phone service to support such things as phone service for low-income and rural residents. He said Internet-based service would enable his company to save "hundreds of millions" of dollars a year in costs associated with following regulatory requirements like tracking and reporting Qwest's customer service performance by various measures.

Mr. Notebaert acknowledged that moving to Internet telephone service would mean tradeoffs. "You're going to have to give things up to get 25 to 30 percent savings," Mr. Notebaert said. As to regulation, including universal service, he said, "I do not think it should be retained at all."

Some of the lower costs of Internet telephone service are a result of the underlying architecture. In the conventional telephone network, voice calls travel over a line that stretches from the home to a piece of phone company equipment called a circuit switch. The switch, and many others like it along the way, routes the call to its destination over local or long-distance networks. The switches can be expensive, as much as $10 million each, said John Hodulik, a telecommunications analyst with UBS Securities.

And adding to the costs is the fact that with conventional telephone service the line that carries the voice signal to and from homes is dedicated exclusively to one call at a time. With Internet-based calls, the information is broken down into small packets, so that the lines that carry the voice conversations can simultaneously transport many other packets of Internet traffic, like e-mail messages and World Wide Web pages. And

Internet calls do not require lots of expensive circuit switches, because each packet of data carries an address that helps it find its own way across the network.

Were telephone companies to build a network from scratch today, they likely would do so using the less expensive Internet architecture that has enabled start-up companies like Vonage to enter the market.

Vonage has invested a mere $12 million in technology, the company's chief execu-

---

Decades of rules are being revisited in light of advances in industry.

---

tive, Jeffrey A. Citron, said. That, he said, is a far cry from the $75 million to $100 million that some companies must spend to begin offering conventional telephone service. And Vonage spends only about $200 to set up each new customer, while a service provider selling conventional phone service might need to spend as much as $600 a customer, Mr. Citron said.

But some critics say a big reason Vonage and other Internet-based phone providers can cut costs is because they do not have to adhere to the same rules and regulations as the conventional telephone companies on whose local and national networks the Internet providers depend. Even an Internet telephony fan like Jeff Pulver, who was formerly on the Vonage board, acknowledged that a substantial amount of cost savings comes from avoiding the taxes, surcharges and access fees used to support the traditional phone network.

"Vonage benefits by not having to comply with those rules," he said. Mr. Pulver acknowledges that the Internet upstarts are practicing regulatory "arbitrage." But in his view the public policy response should be to deregulate all phone companies.

The fact that Vonage is not regulated and did not pay to build the national network may obscure the real cost of providing Internet-based phone service. Likewise, the cost to customers is not as low as it may seem. While consumers may pay less each month for Internet telephone service than for regular phone service, they cannot obtain the service unless they first have high-speed Internet access—on which they are likely to spend $40 to $70 a month. So the ability to use Internet phone service may actually require a total monthly outlay of $100 or more.

Those are table stakes far higher than the bare-bones "lifeline" conventional telephone service subsidized by the regulated industry's universal service fund, which can make basic dial tone and 911 service available to the poor or elderly for less than $10 a month in some states.

That is why policy makers like Ms. Lynch of the California resist the idea that Internet telephone service will lead to a telecommunications market so competitive that government regulation becomes unnecessary. She said that if conventional telephone companies like Qwest were allowed to avoid regulation by moving their business to Internet-based service, it would drain money from the universal service funds that have enabled low-income residents, as well as schools and libraries, to afford basic phone service.

"The pot of money used to make sure people can communicate will shrink," Ms. Lynch said. "It's a death spiral."

She also questions the premise that a competitive marketplace will satisfy consumer demands for reliable, affordable telecommunications. There are six major mobile phone companies, Ms. Lynch said, and despite vibrant competition, wireless service is still highly unreliable.

"Economic theory is not today's reality," Ms. Lynch said. "My job is not to hypothesize about Nirvana. My job is to deal with the realities today."

Mr. Davidson, in Florida, says he agrees that universal service is an important goal. But, he says he thinks the Internet phone technology should be allowed to mature before it is subjected to taxes and surcharges.

He also says he thinks that Internet-based telephone service providers should eventually be required to provide 911 service. But there, too, he would rather not force the issue just yet—in part because 911 service is difficult for Internet-based telephone services to accomplish.

Compared with traditional telephone calls, it is complicated to determine the precise location from which an Internet-based call has been placed, meaning that 911 operators would need to ask the caller to provide that information—even as the house is burning or the child is choking. Mr. Davidson said companies should have to disclose that shortcoming.

"The industry has a very clear obligation," Mr. Davidson said, "to let folks know that this isn't your father's 911."

But when asked when the industry would be mature enough to make 911 service mandatory, he showed his laissez-faire side. "I don't know," he said. "We should allow companies some time to get there."

For This Delicacy, Brand Recognition Is a Problem

BY NEIL MACFARQUHAR

BASRA, Iraq — The hundreds of packages of dates stacked on the cement factory floor and metal shelves of the venerable Al-Moosawi Company are remarkable for one curious absence.

The label does not mention they are Iraqi. The brand itself, "Dubai Dates," is misleading enough, but the name "United Arab Emirates" runs up one side of the package decorated with a drawing of a date bouquet.

Anyone handling the packages—and their predominantly Russian labels signal their ultimate destination—would have no idea they were grown around this southern port city.

That is the whole point, of course. Iraqis resort to subterfuge to avoid United Nations sanctions preventing exports of a product once viewed by the cognoscenti as more desirable than even the country's crude oil.

"Nobody wants to hear about anything called Iraqi dates, or for that matter about anything made in Iraq," lamented Fathi Atallah Raja, the Baghdad spokesman for the Iraqi Date Processing & Marketing Company, a semiprivate collective that handles all sales.

To a certain extent, the story of Iraq's dates mirrors the Iraqi experience since Saddam Hussein assumed control. What was once a thriving industry finds itself inexorably fading after 23 years filled with war, economic sanctions and a negligence driven by the pursuit of industrial development and other, more lethal projects.

Iraqis crow that the reputation of their dates was once such that Americans set sail with a whole shipload of date palm saplings to plant in California in the 1930's. Exports of the dates spanned the globe.

War wrought the first devastation. Millions of trees in what Iraq boasts was once the largest date forest in the world, on the Fao peninsula, just south of here, were either burned or felled by shrapnel during the raging battles of the 1980-88 war with Iran.

What were once majestic stands of palms are gone, replaced by a stunted, nightmarish landscape of decapitated trunks and blackened stumps. The former population of 16 million date palms around Basra is now estimated at 3 million.

The Persian Gulf war also took its toll, with a mysterious outbreak of disease afterward that some trace to depleted uranium shells.

Iraqi scientists identified the disease as a fungus, fusarium, that attacks the crown of the tree, causing it to topple and leaving the flaccid trunk weirdly twisted. It is known around here as Mad Palm Disease.

"The heart of the palm turns from white to black and it creates a bad smell," said Abbas Mahdi Jassim, director of the Center for the Study of Date Palms at the University of Basra. "We link it with the war because we didn't know this disease before."

The only way found to prevent the spread has been to fell the trees and burn them. Mr. Jassim, who earned a doctorate in horticulture from Kansas State University in 1988, is trying to regenerate tens of thousands of trees through tissue culture in test tubes. On several occasions, the chemically intensive process has attracted the attention of United Nations weapons inspectors trying to determine whether the medium in which the tiny sprouts grow might have a more sinister use.

Dates have long been a staple around the region's deserts—they are rich in minerals

War and disease have ravaged Basra's date industry.

and vitamins and last for months without refrigeration. The Koran includes no fewer than 18 mostly laudatory references to dates.

Sitting around the lunch table with a group of Iraqis talking about dates is vaguely reminiscent of, say, the French discussing cheese. The official date encyclopedia lists 627 varieties in Iraq, and everyone champions a favorite.

Great nostalgia for the finest Iraqi dates lingers throughout the Arab world. A Saudi household wishing to show a guest particular honor will bring out a basket of the exquisite Barhi variety, now cultivated there. Egyptians of a certain age, when hearing that a traveler is going to Iraq, will urge, "Bring back dates."

Growers in the Emirates and Saudi Arabia have bred millions of Iraqi date palms, becoming the main suppliers of the finer varieties that have all but disappeared in Iraq. Growers here sniff that others can never replicate the combination of conditions that give Iraqi dates their luscious, chewy quality.

"Sure other countries can grow the trees, but the dates of Basra have a special taste," boasted Sayid Abdel Rida al-Moosawi, the patriarch of the clan that founded Basra's first date processing factory in 1959.

Mr. Moosawi rails against what he calls American piracy in the gulf, stopping Iraqi products like dates—exports are now less than one-fifth what they were before the Iran-Iraq war.

He demurs on the subject of the bogus labels, however. "I seem to remember they are marked as made in Iraq," he said during an interview in the sprawling, turquoise-domed mosque that his family built in downtown Basra. "Besides, the Americans watch any ships moving from Iraq's territorial waters and they can confiscate the cargo whatever the trademark."

But Mr. Raja of the collective says Iraqis gamble on a variety of methods to evade the blockade, including phony labeling or shipping the dates on Iranian-flagged ships. (Similar methods have been used with oil.)

The United Nations bans all exports from Iraq except under the oil-for-food program.

A Western envoy in Baghdad acknowledged that the United Nations did not pay terribly close attention to contraband dates. It interdicts much of what leaves Iraq by sea, but the land borders are fairly porous, especially for products that are not exactly going to supply the secret wealth Iraq would need to develop weapons of mass destruction.

As with other fields where they excelled, Iraqis dream that after the sanctions are lifted and peace returns, they will reassert their domination of the market in fine dates.

"One day we will regain the same reputation, the same position," predicted Mr. Moosawi. "It will probably take 25 years to get back where it was."

Is Fat The Next Tobacco?

For BigFood, the supersizing of America is becoming a big headache ■ *Roger Parloff*

On August 3, 2000, the parody newspaper *The Onion* ran a joke article under the headline HERSHEY'S ORDERED TO PAY OBESE AMERICANS $135 BILLION. The hypothesized class-action lawsuit said that Hershey "knowingly and willfully" marketed to children "rich, fatty candy bars containing chocolate and other ingredients of negligible nutritional value," while "spiking" them with "peanuts, crisped rice, and caramel to increase consumer appeal."

Some joke. Last summer New York City attorney Sam Hirsch filed a strikingly similar suit—against McDonald's—on behalf of a class of obese and overweight children. He alleged that the fast-food chain "negligently, recklessly, carelessly and/or intentionally" markets to children food products that are "high in fat, salt, sugar, and cholesterol" while failing to warn of those ingredients' links to "obesity, diabetes, coronary heart disease, high blood pressure, strokes, elevated cholesterol intake, related cancers," and other conditions.

News of the lawsuit drew hoots of derision. But food industry executives aren't laughing—or shouldn't be. No matter what happens with Hirsch's suit, he has tapped into something very big. Seasoned lawyers from both sides of past mass-tort disputes agree that the years ahead hold serious tobacco-like litigation challenges for the food industry—challenges that extend beyond fast foods to snack foods, soft drinks, packaged foods, and dietary supplements. "The precedents, the ammo, the missiles are already there and waiting in a silo marked 'tobacco,'" says Victor Schwartz, general counsel of the American Tort Reform Association.

Junk food may not be addictive in the same way that tobacco is. But weight, once gained, is notoriously hard to lose, and childhood weight patterns strongly predict adult ones. Rates of overweight among small children—to whom junk-food companies aggressively market their products—have doubled since 1980; rates among adolescents have tripled.

In 1999 physicians began reporting an alarming rise in children of obesity-linked type 2 diabetes. Once an obese youngster develops diabetes, he or she will never get rid of it. That's a lot more irreversible than a smoking addiction.

Though many people recoil at the idea of obesity suits—eating habits are a matter of personal responsibility, they protest—the tobacco precedents show that such qualms can be overcome. Yes, most people know that eating a Big Mac isn't the same as eating a spinach salad, but most people knew that smoking was bad for them too. And yes, diet is only one risk factor out of many that contribute to obesity, but smoking is just one risk factor for diseases for which the tobacco companies were forced to fork over reimbursement to Medicaid. (The industry's share of the blame was statistically estimated and then divvied up among companies by market share.) The tobacco companies eventually agreed to pay $246 billion to the states, and juries are now ordering them to pay individual smokers eight-digit verdicts too.

By the Surgeon General's estimate, public-health costs attributable to overweight and obesity now come to about $117 billion a year—fast approaching the $140 billion stemming from smoking. Suing Big Food offers allures to contingency-fee lawyers that rival those of Big Tobacco, and the implications of that are pretty easy to foresee. While the food industry is not apt to be socked with anything like the penalties that hit tobacco, companies will face consumer-protection suits that might cost them many tens of millions of dollars and force them to significantly change marketing practices.

THE TRIGGERING EVENT OCCURRED in December 2001. That's when the Surgeon General, observing that about 300,000 deaths per year are now associated with overweight and obesity, warned that those conditions might soon cause as much preventable disease and death as smoking. The report prompted journalists to call John Banzhaf III, an antismoking activist and a

law professor at George Washington University School of Law, to see whether tobacco-style litigation might be in the offing. "I said, 'Well, no, there are important differences,'" Banzhaf recalls. But even as he talked, he began to change his mind.

Another key academic strategist in the tobacco wars, Northeastern University law professor Richard Daynard, was soon drawn into the fray. At a conference last April to discuss Marion Nestle's new book, *Food Politics,* he was asked to talk about possible obesity-related litigation. (Nestle, who chairs the nutrition department at New York University and whose name is pronounced NESSel, is not related to the founders of the food company.) Daynard, like Banzhaf, at first saw no analogy to tobacco. But as he read Nestle's book, he, too, began to change his mind.

Here's Nestle's argument. For at least the past 50 years public-health authorities have wanted to deliver a simple, urgent message to the American people: Eat less. They have been thwarted from doing so, however, by political pressure from the food industry. The meat industry alone spends millions a year on lobbying, apparently with great success. Instead of forthrightly saying, "Eat less red meat," government health authorities are forced to say, "Eat more lean meat." Food companies compound the confusion by advertising that their products can be "part of a balanced and nutritional diet," even though they know that their products are not typically consumed that way. Any food can theoretically be part of a balanced diet if you keep the portions tiny enough and eat lots of fruits, vegetables, and grains.

As Daynard well knew, advertising claims that are literally true, but misleading when viewed in a real-world context, can violate state consumer-protection laws. In some states, like California, plaintiffs can force companies to disgorge all profits attributable to advertising that employs such statements, and the plaintiff can win without having to prove that even a single individual was actually tricked by the statement.

The idea of bringing such suits against the food industry is not unprecedented. In 1983, for instance, the California supreme court greenlighted a suit brought by an advocacy group against General Foods over the way such breakfast cereals as Sugar Crisp and Cocoa Pebbles—which contain 38% to 50% sugar by weight—were being marketed to children. The plaintiffs argued that "although promoted and labeled as 'cereals,'" the products "are in fact more accurately described as sugar products, or candies." The court suggested that ads even implicitly claiming that such products were nutritious or healthful were plausible lawsuit targets. (After the ruling, the case settled.)

Last July, Daynard attended an informal meeting of lawyers and public-health advocates in Banzhaf's office in Washington. "The first question at John's meeting was, 'Is there a there there?'" Daynard recalls. "What persuaded us was, in a sense, the media. This thing is so radioactive in terms of media attention that cases will bring in other lawyers and bring in other cases."

Later that month a lawyer who'd never heard of Banzhaf or Daynard crashed their party. Sam Hirsch, who runs his own small practice in New York City, had become interested in food issues after an overweight associate referred to a burger as a "fat bomb." Though Hirsch, 54, had never brought a class action, he now filed two, one in Brooklyn and another in the Bronx. The suits, brought on behalf of classes of obese people, named McDonald's, Burger King, KFC, and Wendy's as defendants.

The press loved the story. The industry response was ferocious. The Coalition for Consumer Freedom, a trade group of restaurants and food and beverage suppliers (McDonald's is not a member), promptly took out aggressive full-page ads in newsmagazines. One showed a man's bloated, bare gut spilling over a belted waistline. The copy read: "Did you hear the one about the fat guy suing the restaurants? It's no joke."

For plaintiffs lawyers and nutrition activists, the Hirsch suit was a mixed blessing. Some worried that it was such a laughingstock that it might strengthen the forces pushing for tort reform. As a tool of public education, on the other hand, the Hirsch suit was a landmark. Even if the industry was winning the talk-show shout-fests, its arguments about personal responsibility sent a double-edged message, according to Daynard. "'If you're stupid enough to use our products, you deserve to get the diseases our products cause.' That's what it means if you deconstruct it," he says. "This sort of discussion is not good for the lawsuit, but it's very good for public health."

In August, Banzhaf invited Hirsch to the second meeting of his group. Afterward Hirsch decided not to pursue his two lawsuits, which had been filed on behalf of adults, and to bring instead a new class-action suit on behalf of obese children. He focused this suit on McDonald's alone. One prospective class member, 400-pound, 15-year-old Gregory Rhymes, who suffers from type 2 diabetes, stated in an affidavit that he has eaten at McDonald's "nearly every day" since he was 6. Neal Barnard, a doctor who heads a vegetarian advocacy group, submitted a declaration asserting that "the consumption of McDonald's products has significantly contributed to the development of [Rhymes's] obesity and diabetes."

McDonald's has mounted a spirited defense. "Every reasonable person understands what is in products such as hamburgers and fries," McDonald's lawyers argue in their papers, "as well as the consequences to one's waistline, and potentially to one's health, of excessively eating those foods over a prolonged period." The lawyers also warn that the plaintiffs' theories, if accepted, would usher in "an uncontrollable avalanche of litigation against other restaurants and food providers, as well as other industries (such as the pizza, ice cream, cheese, and cookie industries)." In a statement to FORTUNE, McDonald's said that it has long made nutritional information available to customers upon request. "Nutrition professionals say that McDonald's food can be and is a part of a healthy diet based on the sound nutrition principles of balance, variety, and moderation," the statement continues. McDonald's has asked a federal court in Manhattan to take the case away from the state court and then to dismiss it. The court has not yet ruled.

Targeting kids is the food industry's Achilles' heel, says plaintiffs lawyer John Coale, a veteran of tobacco and gun litigation. Fast food, snack food, and soft drink companies focus their marketing on children and adolescents through Saturday morning TV commercials; through cuddly characters like Ronald McDonald (the second most recognized figure among children after Santa Claus); through contracts to advertise and serve soft drinks and fast food in schools; and through ever-changing toys included in Happy Meals.

If misleading advertising can be linked to childhood disease, Coale says, "you've got yourself not only a lawsuit but a movement." Food industry insiders have already come forward to speak to Coale about disturbing marketing practices, he claims. "We're not bringing down the fastfood industry next Tuesday," he says, "but there are legitimate legal issues here."

HIRSCH'S CASE, SAY MANY PLAINTIFFS lawyers, is like the earliest tobacco and asbestos cases, which failed because the damning evidence had not yet come out. But once cases progress into the discovery stage, smoking-gun documents may begin to emerge, showing that the companies knew more than the general public about the impact that their products and advertising were having on children's health. Tort reform advocate Schwartz does not doubt this. "As discovery goes forward," Schwartz explains, "plaintiffs lawyers will be finding documents that, if held up in isolation, make it look like the industry had something to hide. That gives the case heft." Schwartz predicts that it will take about five years to reach that point.

Not everyone on the defense side is as fatalistic as Schwartz. Thomas Bezanson of New York's Chadbourne & Parke, who has defended tobacco, alcohol, and pharmaceutical companies, thinks that what happened to the tobacco industry was unique. "You had a very powerful attack made by the plaintiffs bar, the press, the politicians, and the state attorneys general," he says. "That only works if you are able to use all of those in a coordinated way to persuade society that the object of attack is some kind of pariah. I doubt that kind of attack can be lodged against food companies."

There is another important difference between tobacco and food. The tobacco industry "can't make a safe cigarette," says Banzhaf, "but fast-food companies can do almost everything we want without going broke. They can issue warnings, they can post fat and calorie content on menu boards, they can put more nutritious things on their menus. In fact, they already are." Last year, for instance, McDonald's reduced trans fatty acids in its fried foods and introduced low-fat yogurt and fruit roll-up desserts. A press release touts the yogurt as a "good source of calcium" and says that the fruit desserts provide 25% of the daily recommended value of vitamin C. "As a mom and registered dietician," a McDonald's staffer says in the release, "I know the importance of having this type of nutrient value in a snack food that kids enjoy."

Such gestures are themselves fraught with legal peril, however. Daynard mocks the McDonald's press release on its new healthy desserts, for instance: "We're talking about *desserts* to have *after their Happy Meals!*" protests Daynard. "The suggestion is that a really good mother would order *four* of them, right?"

If companies that produce high-calorie and high-fat foods are worried about future lawsuits, they aren't saying. PepsiCo, Cadbury

(Cont.)

Schweppes, and Kraft all declined to comment. Their trade group was less shy. "We advocate getting good messages to parents to help children develop good eating and exercise habits," says a spokesperson for the Grocery Manufacturers of America. "What we think is counterproductive is finger-pointing, reckless accusations, and lawsuits that won't make anyone any thinner." All the same, prudent food companies might do well to start scrutinizing their advertising and packaging, tweaking product lines, and, yes, squirreling away some reserves for potential judgments.

For at least one industry, though, the new spotlight on fat may be a glimmer of unaccustomed good news. Anecdotally, we've heard that smoking has helped a lot of people lose weight.

22

Who is minding the USA's food store?

Fruit, vegetables receive far less federal oversight than meat gets

By Anita Manning and Elizabeth Weise
USA TODAY

When shoppers fill their grocery carts, most assume that each of the foods they've chosen has been examined by an inspector employed by the government.

But the furor raised by the discovery last month of the first case of mad cow disease in the USA masks a truth about the nation's food supply: Meat is by far the most regulated and overseen item in the grocery cart; fruits and vegetables get only a fraction of the attention.

And yet federal health surveillance of food-borne diseases from 1993 to 1997 found 2,751 outbreaks. Those outbreaks totaled 12,537 individual cases involving fruits and vegetables, compared with 6,709 cases involving meat.

Industry critics are concerned that produce may be the Achilles' heel in the nation's food-safety network. There are no inspections of domestically grown produce unless there is a disease outbreak.

"In the last 10 years, the amount of produce crossing the borders has skyrocketed, but inspection hasn't," says Michael Hansen, a senior researcher for Consumers Union.

The Produce Marketing Association reports that imports of fresh produce increased from 13.8 billion pounds in 1993 to 20.2 billion pounds in 2000. Of that amount, the association says, the Food and Drug Administration inspects 2% to 3%.

A number of agencies have a specialty niche in the oversight of food, but the two major players are the U.S. Department of Agriculture and the FDA.

Both agencies are under fire by advocacy groups who say, in essence, that you can drive a truck through the loopholes in their inspection programs. Since a dairy cow was found to be infected with mad cow disease last month in Washington state, the USDA in particular has been fielding criticism that its front-line inspectors are not adequately trained.

In short, the nation's food safety is overseen by a partnership that critics say is flawed—and lopsided.

The Centers for Disease Control and Prevention estimates that 76 million people get sick, more than 300,000 are hospitalized and 5,000 die each year of diseases carried by all kinds of foods.

Though bad meat has long been considered the most dangerous item in the diet, the contamination of fruits and vegetables with deadly and antibiotic-resistant new bug strains such as E. coli O157:H7, salmonella and Listeria monocytogenes has brought them into the limelight—under which they're wilting.

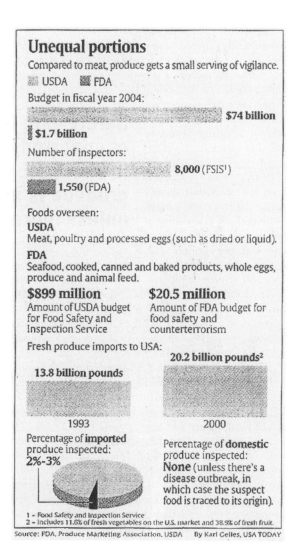

Unequal portions

Compared to meat, produce gets a small serving of vigilance.

▨ USDA ▨ FDA

Budget in fiscal year 2004:

$74 billion

$1.7 billion

Number of inspectors:

8,000 (FSIS[1])

1,550 (FDA)

Foods overseen:

USDA
Meat, poultry and processed eggs (such as dried or liquid).

FDA
Seafood, cooked, canned and baked products, whole eggs, produce and animal feed.

$899 million
Amount of USDA budget for Food Safety and Inspection Service

$20.5 million
Amount of FDA budget for food safety and counterterrorism

Fresh produce imports to USA:

13.8 billion pounds — 1993

20.2 billion pounds[2] — 2000

Percentage of **imported** produce inspected: 2%-3%

Percentage of **domestic** produce inspected: None (unless there's a disease outbreak, in which case the suspect food is traced to its origin).

1 - Food Safety and Inspection Service
2 - Includes 11.6% of fresh vegetables on the U.S. market and 38.9% of fresh fruit.

Source: FDA, Produce Marketing Association, USDA   By Karl Gelles, USA TODAY

(Cont.)

Perhaps the highest-profile recent case of bad vegetables involved imported green onions that caused a large outbreak of hepatitis A in a Chi-Chi's Mexican restaurant in western Pennsylvania. More than 550 people were infected last fall, and three died.

Through the late 1990s, multi-state outbreaks of food poisoning were traced to parasites called cyclospora in Guatemalan raspberries, to salmonella-infected sprouts and to E. coli-tainted lettuce and apple cider.

The problem, according to food-safety experts, is that the USDA gets the lion's share of federal food-safety dollars for overseeing meat, poultry and processed eggs, while the FDA gets a sliver of resources for overseeing everything else.

"Agriculture has three-quarters of the food-safety budget for a quarter of the food in the food supply. FDA has one-quarter for three-quarters of our food," says Marion Nestle, a professor of food science and nutrition at New York University and author of *Safe Food*.

Charles Benbrook, a consultant on food safety to Consumers Union and other groups, says he's concerned not only about germs on food but also high levels of pesticides used in developing countries to kill insects.

"FDA has acknowledged for years that there's no way their current system can detect any more than a small sample of the food that comes into the country with illegal residues, especially with the huge increase of imports of winter vegetables," he says.

The food oversight system began to decentralize many years ago. In 1906, Congress passed the Meat Inspection Act requiring that USDA inspectors, many of whom are veterinarians, inspect every live animal going into slaughter and every carcass.

A USDA Food Safety and Inspection Service inspector must be on site during operating hours at all 6,500 slaughterhouses and meat processing plants in the USA. Inspectors also monitor the meat line for signs of fecal matter and other problems.

Also in 1906, Congress created the Pure Food and Drugs Act. The USDA's Bureau of Chemistry was charged with sampling foods to check whether they were adulterated or misleadingly labeled. In 1930, the FDA was created within the Department of Health and Human Services, and responsibility for enforcing the Pure Food and Drugs Act moved to the new agency, splitting the nation's food-oversight system in two.

Years later, the result is that the FDA oversees seafood; cooked, canned and baked products; whole eggs; and produce, both imported and domestically grown. It also regulates what goes into animal feed and how it's labeled. And it does it with a lot less staff and money than the USDA.

The FDA's budget proposal for fiscal 2004 is $1.7 billion, including $20.5 million for food safety and counterterrorism. The USDA's budget proposal is $74 billion, including $899 million for the Food Safety and Inspection Service.

The FDA's authority and manpower have expanded as a result of counterterrorism efforts. About 1,550 inspectors are on the payroll; many are among the 900 new staffers, including lab technicians, hired in the past three years, says Robert Brackett, director of food safety in the FDA's Center for Food Safety and Applied Nutrition.

The USDA's Food Safety and Inspection Service, on the other hand, employs more than 8,000 inspectors across the country.

All the food in the USA minus meat and poultry is a lot of food for 1,550 inspectors, Brackett acknowledges. "We've had to become much more strategic, so we focus on those products with a higher risk, by their history or by their very nature," he says.

Of the cornucopia the FDA is in charge of, the most inspected part today is food imports. FDA employees are on duty at 90 of the USA's 317 official ports of entry, up from only 40 in past years , and a new cooperating agreement with the U.S. Customs Service allows customs agents to inspect food on behalf of FDA at ports where there is no FDA staffer.

Safety gap: Only 2% to 3% of imported fresh produce is checked. No domestic produce is inspected, unless there's an outbreak.

A GREATER PROBLEM

No amount of inspections makes up for the greater problem that food-safety advocates see with the agency: It presumes that all is well until something goes wrong.

The FDA does, in fact, require that all foods—domestic and imported—be "pure, wholesome, safe to eat and produced under sanitary conditions."

"The FDA operates a food-safety system in which the law says it is the company's responsibility to sell only safe food," says Carol Tucker Foreman, director of the Consumer Federation of America's Food Policy Institute.

(Cont.)

"The FDA assumes they meet that responsibility and only becomes actively engaged if they know there is a problem—and they usually know there is a problem because somebody got sick or there is a dead body."

In some cases, the FDA doesn't become aware of contamination until someone gets sick. An example is the imported green onions that caused a large outbreak of hepatitis A in a restaurant in western Pennsylvania last fall, infecting more than 550 people and causing three deaths.

All the USA's food, minus meat, poultry, is a lot for 1,550 inspectors.

"We'd normally pay more attention to fresh uncooked product," Brackett says, "but we had no reason to suspect those products would be contaminated until we did see an adverse event."

SPREADING THE BLAME

A similar charge—not having direct authority over the companies it oversees—also is frequently directed at the USDA.

While it's true that the USDA doesn't have the authority to force recalls or shut down plants, inspectors can withhold the agency's inspection stamp, making it impossible for the plant to process meat. Critics say that is a convoluted way of being in charge, but Garry McKee, administrator of the Food Safety and Inspection Service, counters that it works.

"We have the authority to remove our inspectors if there's a problem within the plant, so we can then really require the company to make changes that are necessary," he says. In 2003, the agency shut down more than 127 plants for violating their HCCP plans.

HCCP—Hazard Analysis and Critical Control Points—is a program used by the FDA and the USDA requiring each food production facility to identify the places where contamination or infection might occur

and then create systems that monitor those points to make sure it doesn't happen.

Now that mad cow has been found in the United States, USDA is adopting a tougher stance. The agency tests an estimated 25,000 cows out of 35 million slaughtered each year, which was considered a "statistically valid sample" in pre-mad-cow days.

In Europe, which has a long history with mad cow, all cows sent to slaughter older than 30 months are tested for the disease, which doesn't manifest until cattle are 3 to 4 years old. In Japan, every cow sent to slaughter is tested, regardless of age.

USDA Secretary Ann Veneman has pledged to enhance the nation's mad cow surveillance system and adopt a national animal identification system to enable the agency to react more quickly to food-borne outbreaks of all kinds. The agency also has said it will increase the number of cows tested to 40,000 per year.

SO WHAT'S NEXT?

Bringing the two agencies together has long been the holy grail of food-safety experts. The government's own General Accounting Office has issued numerous reports calling for the creation of a single agency to protect the food supply, but interagency turf wars have held that concept at bay.

FDA's Brackett cautions that while Americans may be hearing more about food-safety issues, "it's important to realize that food safety is broadening in terms of what we're looking for because of advances in science. We're finding more things that could be food-safety problems than may have existed 20 or 30 years ago."

Copyright 2004, *USA Today.* Reprinted with permission.

49

23

India Is Becoming Powerhouse; Growth Expanding Middle Class

Size, pace rival China's; English-speaking MBAs and gov't fuel takeoff.

. . . .

By Marilyn Alva
Investor's Business Daily

Move over, China. Here comes India. With a population of 1.1 billion, the second most populous nation after China is becoming the next emerging economic powerhouse.

Job growth in tech services is already fueling a rapidly growing consumer class much like China's economic miracle is minting a new yuppie class. Sales of autos, computers and cell phones are mushrooming.

More than 2 million cell phone connections are sold every month, making India the second fastest mobile phone market after China. And the mobile phone penetration rate is still below 3%. Car sales are tracking to hit 1 million a year by 2005, thanks in part to low interest rates.

If you follow the money, a lot of it seems to end up in India these days.

Foreign direct investment alone totaled $6 billion in 2003, says David Darst, chief investment strategist of Morgan Stanley's individual investors group. That compares with an average $2.5 billion a year from 1995 to 2002.

India's arrival as the developed world's biggest back office isn't the only reason it's coming on so strongly.

Robust growth in other sectors such as manufacturing, agriculture and consumer goods are fueling strong GDP growth—an estimated 8% this fiscal year, which ends in March. GDP might slow to 6.5% next year, but it's still among the top growth rates worldwide.

And this is just the start. A widely touted report by Goldman Sachs says India will eventually become the world's third largest economy after China and the U.S.

That might not happen for a few decades, but as Ashish Thadhani, senior vice

president at Brean Murray & Co., put it, "There is a sense that this is a very sustainable upswing."

Goldman Sachs says India's GDP growth starting in 2010 will equal and then surpass China's, which is now a sizzling 8% to 9%, but is expected to eventually slow. India's population also will likely pass China's.

India is still largely a nation of havenots. Average per-capita income is $500 a year. About 35% of the population live in poverty.

But because of its enormous population, India's growing middle class assumes formidable weight.

"Even if the middle class is just 5% or 10%, any percent of a billion is substantial," said Michel Leonard, chief economist of Aon Trade Credit, which maps risk for companies that want to do business in foreign countries.

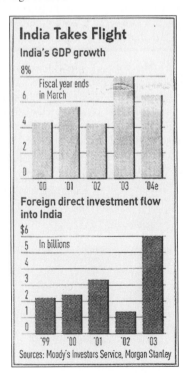

India Takes Flight

India's GDP growth

Fiscal year ends in March

'00 '01 '02 '03 '04e

Foreign direct investment flow into India

In billions

'99 '00 '01 '02 '03

Sources: Moody's Investors Service, Morgan Stanley

Government Reforms

Like China, India's government is making strides to improve creaky infrastructure and privatize government-dominated industries.

The government plans to soon sell off in an initial public offering about 10% of its oil and gas giant, Oil & Natural Gas Corp. The deal, valued at nearly $3 billion, would put it in the same ballpark as last year's biggest IPO: China Life Insurance Co.

"It would be a landmark offering," said Darst.

If demand is brisk, he says, it could lead to more government-sponsored IPOs.

In a recent report, he estimates the government owns $50 billion in listed holdings as well as stakes in several large unlisted concerns such as National Thermal Power Corp. and Life Insurance Corp. of India.

Foreign institutional investors own 17.5% of the top 50 Indian companies and 31% of the top 10, writes Darst. Capital inflow the last 12 months is 50% higher than any other 12-month period in India's history, he contends.

India's stock market rose about 80% in 2003. Some sectors with the best returns: auto, steel and financial services.

Of the hundreds of Indian public companies, only 10 trade in the U.S. via American depositary receipts (ADRs). But more are expected to list this year.

Indian ADRs include two banks, HDFC Bank Ltd. and ICICI Bank; a telecom services firm, Videsh Sanchar Nigram; and generic drug maker Dr. Reddy's Laboratories. Three are software outsourcers: Infosys Technologies Ltd., Satyam Computer Services Ltd. and Wipro Ltd.

India's foreign exchange reserves mushroomed $30 billion in the last year to $100 billion, leading Moody's Investors Service in late January to upgrade India's long-term foreign currency ratings to investment grade for the first time.

Insular India is giving rise to an open India. Over the last decade, India's unwieldy democratic government—with its socialist bent—has gradually loosened its

(Cont.)

grip over business and industry, easing regulations and opening its doors to foreign investors.

The government lowered import tariffs and granted tax breaks to outside investors.

Just recently, India agreed to ease foreign ownership limits in some sectors such as oil.

The government also is addressing infrastructure problems, such as poor roads and power outages. After the government decided last year to reform its power markets, foreign investors have been building several hydraulic electric plants.

New gas discoveries in the Bay of Bengal by India's Reliance Industries will likely help fuel what could be the world's largest power station, to be located in the poor northern state of Uttar Pradesh.

"Government efficiency and infrastructure in the last four years has gone from a level four to a level six on a scale of one to 10," said Partha Iyengar, vice president for Gartner India, based in Pune, India.

"Right now it's a good period to go into India," said Aon's Leonard. "People are making money in India. There are few people that have made money in China yet."

Morgan Stanley projects that leading Indian companies will post earnings growth of nearly 25% in fiscal 2004 end-

> "India has liberalized its trade before it's liberalized its capital markets. There's been some stock market reform, but buying and selling stocks is still archaic, about 20 years behind."
>
> **Mike Leonard,** *Aon Trade Credit*

ing in March, but slow to 14% in fiscal 2005. Darst cites slower industrial growth and a widening trade deficit.

Business process outsourcing is India's fastest growing industry. It's no secret that India's large pool of educated and English-speaking professionals make India the preferred low-cost outsourcing destination of American companies for an ever-expanding list of services, from call centers to strategic solutions.

Leonard says 90% of Aon's clients who want to outsource services consider India first. China, he says, is fourth on the list.

Despite the euphoria over India's prospects, some experts are starting to raise caution flags. They fear India's financial system won't be able to handle all the money that's flowing in.

"India has liberalized its trade before it's liberalized its capital markets," Leonard said.

He added, "There's been some stock market reform, but buying and selling stocks is still archaic, about 20 years behind."

Leonard notes the political situation is less volatile than in previous periods and that tension with Pakistan has recently eased. But those problems won't disappear.

He compares India to China, which opened it borders to foreign direct investment before it had liberalized its capital markets.

"(China) is trying to get its books in order and make it more appealing to investors," he said. "Whenever you have a liberalization, the banks are the last to go."

Economists believe India's banking system is in better shape than China's, especially in terms of non-performing loans and modernizing various transactional systems.

"This was an agricultural and cash-based economy," Darst said. "Large advances have been made with the deepening of the middle class."

"India Is Becoming PowerHouse; Growth Expanding Middle Class," *Investor's Business Daily,* February 13, 2004. Reprinted by permission.

24

HISPANIC NATION

Hispanics are an immigrant group like no other. Their huge numbers are challenging old assumptions about assimilation. Is America ready?

Maria Velazquez was born in a dingy hospital on the U.S.-Mexican border and has been straddling the two nations ever since. The 36-year-old daughter of a bracero, a Mexican migrant who tended California strawberry and lettuce fields in the 1960s, she spent her first nine years like a nomad, crossing the border with her family each summer to follow her father to work. Then her parents and their six children settled down in a Chicago barrio, where Maria learned English in the local public school and met Carlos Velazquez, who had immigrated from Mexico as a teenager. The two married in 1984, when Maria was 17, and relocated to nearby Cicero, Ill. Her parents returned to their homeland the next year with five younger kids.

The Velazquezes speak fluent English and cherish their middle-class foothold in America. Maria and Carlos each earn about $20,000 a year as a school administrator and a graveyard foreman, respectively, and they own a simple three-bedroom home. But they remain wedded to their native language and culture. Spanish is the language at home, even for their five boys, ages 6 to 18. The kids speak to each other and their friends in English flecked with "dude" and "man," but in Cicero, where 77% of the 86,000 residents are Hispanic, Spanish dominates.

The older boys snack at local *taquerías* when they don't eat at home, where Maria's cooking runs to dishes like chicken mole and enchiladas. The family reads and watches TV in Spanish and English. The eldest, Jesse, is a freshman at nearby Morton College and dreams of becoming a state trooper; his girlfriend is also Mexican-American. "It's important that they know where they're from, that they're connected to their roots," says

Maria, who bounced between Spanish and English while speaking to *BusinessWeek*. She tries to take the kids to visit her parents in the tiny Mexican town of Valle de Guadalupe at least once a year. "It gives them a good base to start from."

The Velazquezes, with their mixed cultural loyalties, are at the center of America's

---

"Mexicans working in the U.S. sent home about $13 billion last year, more than total foreign direct investment

---

new demographic bulge. Baby boomers, move over—the *bebé* boomers are coming. They are 39 million strong, including some 8 million illegal immigrants—bilingual, bicultural, mostly younger Hispanics who will drive growth in the U.S. population and workforce as far out as statisticians can project (charts). Coming from across Latin America, but predominantly Mexico, and with high birth rates, these immigrants are creating what experts are calling a "tamale in the snake," a huge cohort of kindergarten to thirtysomething Hispanics created by the sheer velocity of their population growth—3% a year, vs. 0.8% for everyone else.

It's not just that Latinos, as many prefer to be called, officially passed African Americans last year to become the nation's largest

minority. Their numbers are so great that, like the postwar baby boomers before them, the Latino Generation is becoming a driving force in the economy, politics, and culture.

CULTURAL CLOUT

It amounts to no less than a shift in the nation's center of gravity. Hispanics made up half of all new workers in the past decade, a trend that will lift them from roughly 12% of the workforce today to nearly 25% two generations from now. Despite low family incomes, which at $33,000 a year lag the national average of $42,000, Hispanics' soaring buying power increasingly influences the food Americans eat, the clothes they buy, and the cars they drive. Companies are scrambling to revamp products and marketing to reach the fastest-growing consumer group. Latino flavors are seeping into mainstream culture, too. With Hispanic youth a majority of the under-18 set, or close to it, in cities such as Los Angeles, Miami, and San Antonio, what's hip there is spreading into suburbia, much the way rap exploded out of black neighborhoods in the late 1980s.

Hispanic political clout is growing, too. In a Presidential race that's likely to be as tight as the last one, they could be a must-win swing bloc. Indeed, the increase in voting-age Hispanics since 2000 now outstrips the margin of victory in seven states for either President George W. Bush or former Vice-President Albert Gore, according to a new study by HispanTelligence, a Santa Barbara (Calif.) research group. Bush opened the election year with a guest-worker proposal for immigrants that pundits took as a play for the Latino vote. He will follow up by rekindling his relationship with Mexican President Vicente Fox, who's due to visit Bush at his

Which Scenario For Hispanics?
Experts see three broad possibilities for Hispanics' role in American life:

Melting in - Hispanics follow the path of all other immigrant groups and gradually meld into American life, giving up Spanish and marrying non-Hispanics

Acculturation - Most Latinos speak both languages and retain much of their own culture and ties to their home countries, even as they adapt to U.S. lifestyles

Mexifornia - Many remain in Spanish-speaking enclaves and set the cultural and political agenda in soon-to-be-majority-Hispanic states like California and Texas

Data: BusinessWeek

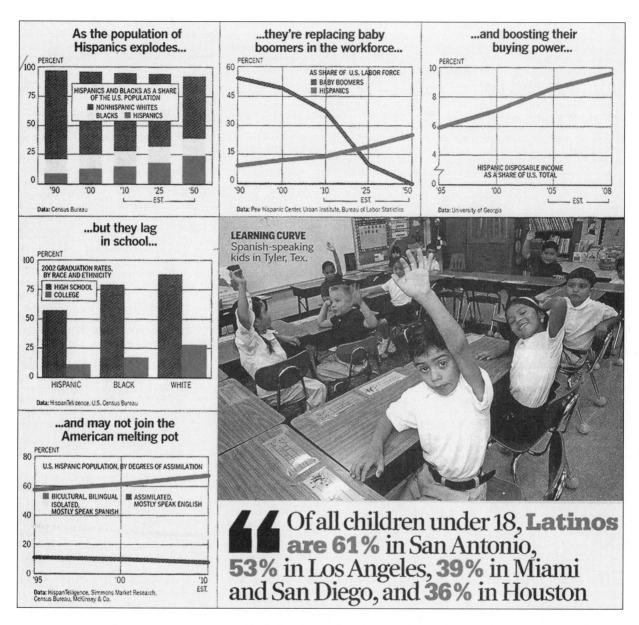

As the population of Hispanics explodes...

PERCENT

HISPANICS AND BLACKS AS A SHARE OF THE U.S. POPULATION
■ NONHISPANIC WHITES
■ BLACKS ■ HISPANICS

'90 '00 '10 '25 '50
EST.

Data: Census Bureau

...they're replacing baby boomers in the workforce...

PERCENT

AS SHARE OF U.S. LABOR FORCE
■ BABY BOOMERS
■ HISPANICS

'90 '00 '10 '25 '50
EST.

Data: Pew Hispanic Center, Urban Institute, Bureau of Labor Statistics

...and boosting their buying power...

PERCENT

HISPANIC DISPOSABLE INCOME AS A SHARE OF U.S. TOTAL

'95 '00 '05 '08
EST.

Data: University of Georgia

...but they lag in school...

PERCENT

2002 GRADUATION RATES, BY RACE AND ETHNICITY
■ HIGH SCHOOL
■ COLLEGE

HISPANIC BLACK WHITE

Data: HispanTelligence, U.S. Census Bureau

LEARNING CURVE
Spanish-speaking kids in Tyler, Tex.

...and may not join the American melting pot

PERCENT

U.S. HISPANIC POPULATION, BY DEGREES OF ASSIMILATION

■ BICULTURAL, BILINGUAL ISOLATED, MOSTLY SPEAK SPANISH   ■ ASSIMILATED, MOSTLY SPEAK ENGLISH

'95 '00 '10 EST.

Data: HispanTelligence, Simmons Market Research, Census Bureau, McKinsey & Co.

Of all children under 18, Latinos are 61% in San Antonio, 53% in Los Angeles, 39% in Miami and San Diego, and 36% in Houston

Crawford, Texas, ranch on Mar. 5. Democrats, traditionally the dominant party among Hispanics, are stepping up their outreach, too. New Mexico Governor Bill Richardson, a Mexican-American and potential Vice-Presidential candidate, delivered a first-ever Spanish-language version of the Democrat's rebuttal to the State of the Union address.

The U.S. has never faced demographic change quite like this before. Certainly, the Latino boom brings a welcome charge to the economy at a time when others' population growth has slowed to a crawl. Without a

steady supply of new workers and consumers, a graying U.S. might see a long-term slowdown along the lines of aging Japan, says former Housing and Urban Development chief Henry Cisneros, who now builds homes in Hispanic-rich markets such as San Antonio. "Here we have this younger, hard-working Latino population whose best working years are still ahead," he says.

Already, Latinos are a key catalyst of economic growth. Their disposable income has jumped 29% since 2001, to $652 billion last year, double the pace of the rest of

the population, according to the Selig Center for Economic Growth at the University of Georgia. Similarly, the ranks of Latino entrepreneurs has jumped by 30% since 1998, calculates the Internal Revenue Service. "The impact of Hispanics is huge, especially since they're the fastest-growing demographic," says Merrill Lynch & Co. Vice-President Carlos Vaquero, himself a Mexican immigrant based in Houston. Vaquero oversees part of the company's 350-person Hispanic unit, which is hiring 100 mostly bilingual financial advisers this year and which generated $1 billion worth of new business nationwide last year, double its goal.

Yet the rise of a minority group this distinct requires major adjustments, as well. Already, Hispanics are spurring U.S. institutions to accommodate a second linguistic group. The Labor Dept. and Social Security Administration are hiring more Spanish-language administrators to cope with the surge in Spanish speakers in the workforce. Politicians, too, increasingly reach out to Hispanics in their own language.

What's not yet clear is whether Hispanic social cohesion will be so strong as to actually challenge the idea of the American melting pot. At the extreme, ardent assimilationists worry that the spread of Spanish eventually could prompt Congress to recognize it as an official second language, much as French is in Canada today. Some even predict a Quebec-style Latino dominance in states such as Texas and California that will encourage separatism, a view expressed in a recent book called *Mexifornia: A State of Becoming* by Victor Davis Hanson, a history professor at California State University at Fresno. These views have recently been echoed by Harvard University political scientist Samuel P. Huntington in a forthcoming book, *Who Are We.*

These critics argue that legions of poorly educated non-English speakers undermine the U.S. economy. Although the steady influx of low-skilled workers helps keep America's gardens tended and floors cleaned, those workers also exert downward pressure on wages across the lower end of the pay structure. Already, this is causing friction with African Americans, who see their jobs and pay being hit. "How are we going to compete in a global market when 50% of our fastest-growing group doesn't graduate from high school?" demands former Colorado Governor Richard D. Lamm, who now co-directs a public policy center at the University of Denver.

Still, many experts think it's more likely that the U.S. will find a new model, more salad bowl than melting pot, that accommodates a Latino subgroup without major upheaval. "America has to learn to live with diversity—the change in population, in [Spanish-language] media, in immigration," says Andrew Erlich, the founder of Erlich Transcultural Consultants Inc. in North Hollywood, Calif. Hispanics aren't so much assimilating as acculturating—acquiring a new culture while retaining their original one— says Felipe Korzenny, a professor of Hispanic marketing at Florida State University.

It boils down to this: How much will Hispanics change America, and how much will America change them? Throughout the country's history, successive waves of immigrants eventually surrendered their native languages and cultures and melted into the middle class. It didn't always happen right

away. During the great European migrations of the 1800s, Germans settled in an area stretching from Pennsylvania to Minnesota. They had their own schools, newspapers, and businesses, and spoke German, says Demetrios G. Papademetriou, co-founder of the Migration Policy Institute in Washington. But in a few generations, their kids spoke only English and embraced American aspirations and habits.

Hispanics may be different, and not just because many are nonwhites. True, Maria Velazquez worries that her boys may lose their Spanish and urges them to speak it more. Even so, Hispanics today may have more choice than other immigrant groups to remain within their culture. With national TV networks such as Univision Communications Inc. and hundreds of mostly Spanish-speaking enclaves like Cicero, Hispanics may find it practical to remain bilingual. Today, 78% of U.S. Latinos speak Spanish, even if they also know English, according to the Census Bureau.

One out of 10 small businesses will be Hispanic-owned by '07, jumping to 2 million from 1.2 million today

---

BACK AND FORTH

The 21 million Mexicans among them also have something else no other immigrant group has had: They're a car ride away from their home country. Many routinely journey back and forth, allowing them to maintain ties that Europeans never could. The dual identities are reinforced by the constant influx of new Latino immigrants—roughly 400,000 a year, the highest flow in U.S. history. The steady stream of newcomers will likely keep the foreign-born, who typically speak mostly or only Spanish, at one-third of the U.S. Hispanic population for several decades. Their presence means that "Spanish is constantly refreshed, which is one of the key contrasts with what people think of as the melting pot," says Roberto Suro, director of the Pew Hispanic Center, a Latino research group in Washington.

A slow pace of assimilation is likely to hurt Hispanics themselves the most, especially poor immigrants who show up with no English and few skills. Latinos have long lagged in U.S. schools, in part because many families remain cloistered in Spanish-speaking neighborhoods. Their strong work ethic can compound the problem by propel-

ling many young Latinos into the workforce before they finish high school. So while the Hispanic high-school-graduation rate has climbed 12 percentage points since 1980, to 57%, that's still woefully short of the 88% for non-Hispanic whites and 80% for African Americans.

MELD INTO THE MAINSTREAM

The failure to develop skills leaves many Hispanics trapped in low-wage service jobs that offer few avenues for advancement. Incomes may not catch up anytime soon, either, certainly not for the millions of undocumented Hispanics. Most of these, from Mexican street-corner day laborers in Los Angeles to Guatemalan poultry-plant workers in North Carolina, toil in the underbelly of the U.S. economy. Many low-wage Hispanics would fare better economically if they moved out of the barrios and assimilated into U.S. society. Most probably face less racism than African Americans, since Latinos are a diverse ethnic and linguistic group comprising every nationality from Argentinians, who have a strong European heritage, to Dominicans, with their large black population. Even so, the pull of a common language may keep many in a country apart.

Certainly immigrants often head for a place where they can get support from fellow citizens, or even former neighbors. Some 90% of immigrants from Tonatico, a small town 100 miles south of Mexico City, head for Waukegan, Ill., joining 5,000 Tonaticans already there. In Miami, of course, Cubans dominate. "Miami has Hispanic banks, Hispanic law firms, Hispanic hospitals, so you can more or less conduct your entire life in Spanish here," says Leopoldo E. Guzman, 57. He came to the U.S. from Cuba at 15 and turned a Columbia University degree into a job at Lazard Freres & Co. before founding investment bank Guzman & Co.

Or take the Velazquezes' home of Cicero, a gritty factory town that once claimed fame as Al Capone's headquarters. Originally populated mostly by Czechs, Poles, and Slovaks, the Chicago suburb started decaying in the 1970s as factories closed and residents fled in search of jobs. Then a wave of young Mexican immigrants drove the population to its current Hispanic dominance, up from 1% in 1970. Today, the town president, equivalent to a mayor, is a Mexican immigrant, Ramiro Gonzalez, and Hispanics have replaced whites in the surviving factories and local schools. It's still possible that Cicero's Latino children will follow the path of so many other immigrants and move out into non-Hispanic neighborhoods. If they do, they, or at least their children, will likely all but abandon Spanish, gradually marry non-Hispanics, and meld into the mainstream.

But many researchers and academics say that's not likely for many Hispanics. In fact, a study of assimilation and other factors shows

(Cont.)

that while the number of Hispanics who prefer to speak mostly Spanish has dipped in recent years as the children of immigrants grow up with English, there has been no increase in those who prefer only English. Instead, the HispanTelligence study found that the group speaking both languages has climbed six percentage points since 1995, to 63%, and is likely to jump to 67% by 2010.

The trend to acculturate rather than assimilate is even more stark among Latino youth. Today, 97% of Mexican kids whose parents are immigrants and 76% of other Hispanic immigrant children know Spanish, even as nearly 90% also speak English very well, according to a decade-long study by University of California at Irvine sociologist Ruben G. Rumbaut. More striking, those Latino kids keep their native language at four times the rate of Filipino, Vietnamese, or Chinese children of immigrants. "Before, immigrants tried to become Americans as soon as possible," says Sergio Bendixen, founder of Bendixen & Associates, a polling firm in Coral Gables, Fla., that specializes in Hispanics. "Now, it's the opposite."

SELLING IN SPANISH

In its eagerness to tap the exploding Hispanic market, Corporate America itself is helping to reinforce Hispanics' bicultural preferences. Last year, Procter & Gamble Co. spent $90 million on advertising directed at Latinos for 12 products such as Crest and Tide—10% of its ad budget for those brands and a 28% hike in just a year. Sure, P&G has been marketing to Hispanics for decades, but spending took off after 2000, when the company set up a 65-person bilingual team to target Hispanics. Now, P&G tailors everything from detergent to toothpaste to Latino tastes. Last year, it added a third scent to Gain detergent called "white-water fresh" after finding that 57% of Hispanics like to smell their purchases. Now, Gain's sales growth is double-digit in the Hispanic market, outpacing general U.S. sales. "Hispanics are a cornerstone of our growth in North America," says Graciela Eleta, vice-president of P&G's multicultural team in Puerto Rico.

Spanish-language TV is likely to see the largest revenue gains this year, climbing 16%, vs. 8% for the industry as a whole

Other companies are making similar assumptions. In 2002, Cypress (Calif.)-based PacifiCare Health Systems Inc. hired Russell A. Bennett, a longtime Mexico City resident, to help target Hispanics. He soon found that they were already 20% of PacifiCare's 3 million policyholders. So Bennett's new unit, Latino Health Solutions, began marketing health insurance in Spanish, directing Hispanics to Spanish-speaking doctors, and translating documents into Spanish for Hispanic workers. "We knew we had to remake the entire company, linguistically and culturally, to deal with this market," says Bennett.

A few companies are even going all-Spanish. After local Hispanic merchants stole much of its business in a Houston neighborhood that became 85% Latino, Kroger Co., the nation's No.1 grocery chain, spent $1.8 million last year to convert the 59,000-sq.-ft. store into an all-Hispanic *supermercado*. Now, Spanish-language signs welcome customers, and catfish and banana leaves line the aisles. Across the country, Kroger has expanded its private-label Buena Comida line from the standard rice and beans to 105 different items.

As the ranks of Spanish speakers swell, Spanish-language media are transforming from a niche market into a stand-alone industry. Ad revenues on Spanish-language TV should climb by 16% this year, more than other media segments, according to TNS Media Intelligence/CMR. The audience of Univision, the No.1 Spanish-language media conglomerate in the U.S., has soared by 44% since 2001, and by 146% in the 18- to 34-year-old group. Many viewers have come

from English-language networks, whose audiences have declined in that period.

In fact, Univision tried to reach out to assimilated Hispanics a few years ago by putting English-language programs on its cable channel Galavision. They bombed, says Univision President Ray Rodriguez, so he switched back to Spanish-only in 2002—and 18- to 34-year-old viewership shot up by 95% that year. "We do what the networks don't, and that's devote a lot of our show to what interests the Latino community," says Univision news anchor Jorge Ramos.

The Hispanicizing of America raises a number of political flash points. Over the years, periodic backlashes have erupted in areas with fast-growing Latino populations, notably former California Governor Pete Wilson's 1994 effort, known as Proposition 187, to ban social services to undocumented immigrants. English-only laws, which limit or prohibit schools and government agencies from using Spanish, have passed in some 18 states. Most of these efforts have been ineffective, but they're likely to continue as the Latino presence increases.

For more than 200 years, the nation has succeeded in weaving the foreign-born into the fabric of U.S. society, incorporating strands of new cultures along the way. With their huge numbers, Hispanics are adding all kinds of new influences. Cinco de Mayo has joined St. Patrick's Day as a public celebration in some neighborhoods, and burritos are everyday fare. More and more, Americans hablan Espanol. Will Hispanics be absorbed just as other waves of immigrants were? It's possible, but more likely they will continue to straddle two worlds, figuring out ways to remain Hispanic even as they become Americans.

By Brian Grow with Ronald Grover, Arlene Weintraub, and Christopher Palmeri in Los Angeles, Mara Der Hovanesian in New York, Michael Eidam in Atlanta, and bureau reports

Buying Behavior

25

NOT YOUR FATHER'S... WHATEVER

What does Gen Y want in a car?
To auto makers' surprise, it's price and value

When it comes to young car-buyers, the '70s and '80s haunt Detroit like a ghost. During the oil shock, the Big Three were late making the move toward small, fuel-efficient cars, and handed a new generation of penny-pinchers to Toyota and Honda. Later, U.S. auto brands compounded their error, offering horrible styling and quality to newly affluent baby boomers. Many fled to Mercedes-Benz and BMW. The resulting love affair fueled import growth for almost 30 years. The Big Three bled market share and eventually had to kill struggling brands like Oldsmobile and Plymouth.

That epic shift in loyalties explains why U.S. and foreign auto makers devote so much attention to Generation Y, today's 16- to 24-year-olds. The group already buys 850,000 cars a year, about 6% of U.S. vehicle sales. According to Toyota, about 63 million kids will be driving by 2010. "This generation is bigger than the boomers," says James Press, COO of Toyota Motor Sales USA Inc. "We need to build the same relationship with them that we have with their parents."

Imports still have an edge with kids. Because Toyota, Honda, Nissan, and Hyundai refresh their small-car lineups more frequently than Detroit, many of their models boast younger average buyers. But no brand—import or domestic—has truly locked up the loyalty of the youth market, despite millions spent on wild designs and brash marketing. The most aggressive looks, from cars like the Pontiac Aztek, Chrysler PT Cruiser, and Toyota Echo compact, all struck out with kids. Honda Motor Co.'s boxy Element hit the market with a splash last year, but it has lured more fortysomethings than hipsters. "A big mistake car companies make is they assume that because kids have three piercings that they want to drive something obnoxious," says Wesley R. Brown, an analyst at Iceology, a trend research firm.

LONG WARRANTIES

In truth, carmakers are discovering yet again that the primary selling points for kids are the same as 30 years ago: price and value. The average sticker price for a new car sold to buyers under age 24 (most of them buy used cars) is $15,000, says CNW Marketing Research Inc. Says Eric Noble, president of The Car Lab, which has studied the market for auto makers: "A youth car is just a cheap car."

Little surprise that two South Korean cars—Hyundai Motor Co.'s $10,000 Accent and $13,000 Elantra—have the youngest average buyers of any on the market, at age 24. It helps a lot that Hyundai has seriously improved the styling of its cars in recent years. But the company's biggest advantage comes from playing up its long warranties. Hyundai guarantees its cars for five years and 60,000 miles—at least a year longer than a standard warranty. Engines and transmissions carry a 10-year, 100,000-mile warranty. Says Hyundai Motor America marketing director Paul Sellers: "That removes one element of risk." It also keeps ownership costs low for years.

Hyundai's long-term strategy is much like that of Toyota 25 years ago: Get younger buyers to graduate from its econo-cars to bigger and more expensive vehicles. In fact, the average age of Hyundai's buyers has been rising as it sells more SUVs, midsize

Youth Will Be Served
After several failed attempts to design cars for kids, manufacturers found that value is the best draw

	HONDA ELEMENT	⌃ CHRYSLER PT CRUISER	VOLKSWAGEN JETTA	TOYOTA SCION XB	⌃ HYUNDAI ACCENT
	Edgy design caught some young eyes, but its price and roominess mostly appealed to middle-aged drivers	Old-school styling gave the car a retro appeal for Mom and Dad, who were around for the original roadsters	Young people love Volkswagen, but this sticker price is too high for most young consumers	Funky looks and underground marketing efforts have just about concealed the car from older buyers	Dirt cheap, and the long warranty makes it the "What, me worry?" car
	$16,100-$21,350	$18,000-$30,000	$18,000-$24,000	$13,680-$14,480	$9,999-$11,399
AVERAGE AGE OF BUYER	44	41	34	29	24

Data: CNW Marketing Research, Inc., *BusinessWeek*

(Cont.)

cars, and its XG350 "near-luxury" sedan. Meanwhile, Hyundai hopes to secure its hold on young drivers by launching a low-priced compact SUV, the Tucson, this fall.

Toyota's Scion family of cars may be the industry's most radical step toward offering young buyers great value in an unconventional package. But even it has had just modest success. The jarring, slab-sided Scion xB compact sport-ute comes standard with automatic windows and locks, remote keyless entry, and a premium sound system that can read MP3 sound files, for just under $15,000—about $3,000 less than Honda's Element. Toyota sold 11,000 Scions in just five months, even though it was available only in California. And the cars attract younger buyers than Toyota's current 40-plus average. Still, the xB can hardly be seen as a teen magnet: Its average buyer is 29, and the more plain xA compact's average buyer is 32, according to CNW. That will rise even higher for the bigger, more expensive Scion tC sports coupe, which arrives in July.

And that's with Toyota practically hiding the cars from older buyers. Scion buys little network TV airtime; most ads run in select shows on Comedy Central and MTV. "We choose our programming very carefully," says Scion sales and promotions manager Brian Boulain. Scion also uses lots of "buzz" marketing, holding test drives at restaurants and popular music and clothing stores.

LONG IN THE TOOTH

Scion offers so much for such a low price that Toyota probably won't make money on

---

Some cars aimed at hipsters end up snagging parents instead

---

the brand this year. And it'll have to hit sales targets of 100,000 vehicles just to make a slim profit by '05. Toyota has the strongest balance sheet and biggest cash hoard in the industry, so it can afford to sell loaded cars at little or no profit. "We take a long view," says Press. "We're lucky that we can operate this without having to worry about how much money each car is going to make."

U.S. auto makers, however, don't have that luxury. With their higher cost base and emphasis on big-margin trucks in recent years, GM, Ford, and Chrysler devoted little attention to the small-car market. All the domestic carmakers offer deep discounts on compact cars, but most of those models have grown long in the tooth. General Motors Corp. will try to change that this fall, when it finally replaces its decade-old Chevy Cavalier with the Cobalt, a fresh-looking compact with interior craftsmanship that makes it competitive with Japanese models. GM has had some success targeting younger buyers with the $17,000 Pontiac Vibe—the average age of Vibe buyers is 38, vs. 46 for all Pontiacs. Ford Motor Co. has no discernible youth strategy but sells its Focus compact and a

stripped-down Mustang for below $17,000. The all-new Mustang coming next year will cost a bit more.

Detroit has tried to make up the lost ground in other ways, with little success. GM is importing the Chevy Aveo from its Korean operations—a move that faltered when the car was temporarily pulled from the market for safety checks. GM also tried to leverage the huge inventory of used cars by styling some sporty body accessories and performance parts for second-hand Chevy Cavaliers and Pontiac Sunfires. But the effort flagged when GM didn't back it up with marketing dollars. Meanwhile, Detroit has yet to fully tap its big advantage: GM, Ford, and Chrysler could use their strong reputations for trucks by coming out with cheap SUVs. CNW's survey says 70% of young buyers want a truck of some kind.

Even if aging brands like Toyota and those from the Big Three figure out a way to reach kids, it's tough to keep them. GM grabbed young buyers when Saturn was launched in 1991, but the fledgling division couldn't keep them. Toyota could have the same problem once its thirtysomething Scion buyers move on. Surveys show that young buyers most admire BMW, Mercedes, Lexus, and Volkswagen. That is, they like the brands that consistently come up with great cars. In that way, they're just like their parents.

By David Welch in Detroit

COKE: WOOING THE TIVO GENERATION

The cola giant's quest for brand loyalty is leading it away from 30-second TV spots

When the marketers at Coca-Cola Co. recently wanted to reach out to teens like Lauren Salapatek, a 17-year-old high school junior in suburban Chicago, they didn't do it through TV ads during the Grammys or Super Bowl. Instead, the soda giant lured her to the Coke Red Lounge, a gathering area for mall rats that it built in a shopping center in the northern 'burbs. The lounge, which offers exclusive music, movies, and videos piped in via sound domes and a plasma-screen media wall, has quickly become a regular afternoon and evening gathering spot for Salapatek and her friends. "It's cool, it's comfortable, it's in the middle of the mall," she nods approvingly as Linkin Park's *Faint* blares from the hooded speakers.

Coke's lounges, created with the help of the trendy Rockwell Group design shop, symbolize the sea change in marketing that's under way at the once-fabled marketing icon. For decades, Coke was the master of the 30-second TV spot: *Advertising Age* ranked Coke's classic "Hilltop" and "Mean Joe Greene" ads as two of the best ever. But thanks to media fragmentation and the growing use of devices like TiVo that let viewers skip ads altogether, megamarketers can now hit no better than 15% of the population with an ad in prime time—far less than the 40% reached as recently as the mid-1980s. Coke signaled the shift early last year when President Steven J. Heyer rattled Madison Avenue with a speech warning that "the days of mass, homogenous marketing are behind us."

BONDING EXERCISES

In the past year, Coke has accelerated its shift beyond passive TV ads toward a so-called experiential approach that uses events and activities to build a closer bond with consumers. So far it's hard to see a payoff in terms of more Coke sales. But the decision of such a hugely influential marketer to shift big dollars away from traditional ads is making ripples far from Coke's Atlanta headquarters.

The idea is that instead of bombarding consumers with hard-sell ads that they're going to tune out anyway, the brand will do better if it subtly infiltrates their daily routines. While management won't discuss how it allocates its marketing dollars, ad tracker TNS Media Intelligence/CMR estimates that last year through October Coke spent just $188.7 million on TV advertising in the U.S., a sharp drop from $268.1 million in 2001.

Coke has diverted money into new initiatives that allow it to embed itself into the favorite activities of its target audience, everything from sports to music to the Internet. In Spain, Coke launched a Web site where the large share of twentysomethings who still live at home can design their own "virtual apartment," *Sim-City*-style. In Britain, the soda giant created a Web site, myCoke-Music.com, that lets surfers mix their own tracks—and then submit them for a "thumbs up" or "thumbs down" review by peers.

Coke has a lot riding on Heyer's grand experiment because its marketing has seriously stumbled in recent years. Former CEO M. Douglas Ivester made no secret of his distrust of Madison Avenue, pumping money into merchandising and trade promotion. While sales volume soared, Ivester's heavy reliance on promotions led to deep discounting that depressed North American profits for a considerable stretch.

When Douglas N. Daft took over as CEO in 2000, he vowed to return Coke to its marketing greatness. But at a time when admakers' "big ideas" have a harder time resonating with a splintered audience, the company has been criticized for its erratic efforts—one oddball ad featured a wheelchair-ridden grandmother going ballistic after being told there was no Coke at a party. "Brand allegiances have changed so drastically. You are no longer a Chevy family or a Coke family," says Tom Pirko, president of New York consultants BevMark LLC. "They're an old company trying to be a new company—that's going to take some time."

Some believe Heyer is a leading candidate to succeed Daft—provided his strategy works. Heyer notes that "purchase intent"—the likelihood that consumers will buy a product—has risen 21% for the flagship Coke Classic brand under the new approach. However, sales volume in North America, which generates a quarter of Coke's sales and profits, remained flat in 2003, thanks to oversaturation and stiff competition.

Under Heyer, even the nature of Coke's TV spending has changed. Now, the company increasingly wants to be part of the show. It paid $20 million-plus to get red Coke cups on the desks of the judges of Fox Network's *American Idol* and to have the traditional "green room" guest waiting area renamed—and repainted—the Coke Red Room.

To be sure, this new approach isn't without risks of its own. Paying for product placement or program sponsorships can backfire if the show gets canceled. But with consumers increasingly tuning out TV ads, the Atlanta soda giant may have no choice but to find ways of marketing a New Coke to consumers.

By Dean Foust in Atlanta, with Brian Grow in Chicago

New Beverage From Snapple Seeks to Avoid Stigma of Dieting

By SHERRI DAY

Trying to take some of the public embarrassment out of dieting, Snapple yesterday announced a new meal-replacement product that it hopes looks less like a weight-loss aid and more like, well, a Snapple.

Snapple-a-Day, a fortified juice smoothie that will be on store shelves next month, is the beverage company's entry into the $1-billion-a-year meal-replacement business, which is dominated by Slim-Fast from **Unilever** and includes products like Ensure and protein-laden powder drinks associated with the Atkins diet. Snapple-a-Day has 210 calories—10 fewer than Slim-Fast—as well as vitamins and minerals including calcium, zinc, potassium and folic acid.

Snapple's drink may also represent the first wave of new products from soda companies that are aimed at consumers, particularly women ages 22 to 44, who worry as much about their waistlines as about flavor. The **Coca-Cola** Company is working on a whey-based drink called BeginIt and **PepsiCo** is exploring the category as well, according to company spokesmen. Snapple is a unit of **Cadbury Schweppes.**

Snapple's edge, according to Jack Belsito, the company's chief executive, is that the product will not be marketed as a diet aid. By packaging Snapple-a-Day in 11.5 ounce plastic bottles swathed in bright red, yellow and peach labeling and promising a brighter, more Snapple-like taste, the company hopes to remove the stigma associated with drinking frothy meal-replacement drinks from stubby metal cans.

"Very rarely do you actually see people drinking this product," Mr. Belsito said, referring to Slim-Fast. "It's usually consumed in some type of shroud of mystery. I don't want to be asked questions about am I on a diet? Or how many pounds did I lose? It's not a conversation that I want to have at work."

Like many of its beverage counterparts, Snapple's juice business has registered steady returns but extremely slow growth, analysts said. To stem declining market share for carbonated soft drinks and other core brands, beverage companies have been looking for new products.

"To continue growing, they have to extend their product offerings," said John D. Sicher, the editor and publisher of Beverage Digest. "We've certainly seen that in the last few years with bottled water. Five or six years ago, neither Coke nor Pepsi sold bottled water in the U.S. Now they have the leading bottled water brands. That model will be duplicated in other beverage categories in the years to come."

But Snapple did not want to duplicate the chalky taste of some diet products. That challenge fell to the company's research scientists in the Flavor Lab, a suite of four laboratories deep in the bowels of the company's headquarters in White Plains.

The lab, which smells like a combination of apple, strawberry and citrus, is run by Smita Patel, the vice president for research and development and Snapple's most trusted palate. Ms. Patel, who has worked as a food scientist for 20 years on products like French's Dijon mustard and Cadbury Schweppes' cranberry ginger ale, took nearly a year to create Snapple-a-Day.

To avoid the appearance of simply copying Slim-Fast, Ms. Patel decided early against using a chocolate or vanilla base for its new drink. Snapple's food scientists tried using whey, but abandoned it soon after they discovered that it had a pungent odor that was difficult to mask. They also decided against soy milk because it tasted like soy beans, and ruled out skim milk powder, which when mixed with flavors smelled acrid and overcooked. After two months, Ms. Patel chose soy protein for its ability to maintain a relatively neutral taste. The company also decided to add some carbohydrates and soluble fiber that would help to make consumers feel full.

But with so many minerals then packed into the drink, the biggest difficulty, according to Ms. Patel, was finding the right flavors to counteract the "liquid vitamins" taste of the early prototypes. The peach-flavored drink and its tropical-blend counterparts proved fairly easy to formulate but the strawberry-banana version was particularly challenging. Ms. Patel said her team mixed at least 180 combinations to create just the right mix so that the product both smelled and tasted like strawberries mixed with bananas.

"We have to identify the right levels; it's 0.02 percent or 0.01 percent in each bottle," said Ms. Patel, who is credited with some of Snapple's best-selling products, including peach iced tea, apple juice and WhipperSnapple. "If you overdo it, it's perfumey and can cause a burn. If you don't have enough flavor, then you wonder what's in the product."

On Monday, even as mass quantities were already being produced in factories, the scientists were still mixing new concoctions.

"It's just constant monitoring, week to week, day to day, especially if it's a new product," Ms. Patel said. "We kind of baby it to check to make sure nothing is going off."

Once the base and flavors were settled upon, Ms. Patel's team conducted stability tests to see how the product would hold up in a variety of storage conditions. To simulate a beverage warehouse on a hot summer day in Georgia, the scientists put their new beverages into an oven. They also checked Snapple-a-Day's performance over six-month periods at room temperatures and in refrigerators. The final test, however, occurred when Ms. Patel poured herself a glass of Snapple-a-Day on ice.

Snapple-a-Day will sell for $1.59 a serving, more expensive than Slim-Fast, but unlike a lot of diet products it will be available in single servings in corner stores. Mr. Belsito said the company expected to have 10 percent of the sales in the category within the next two years. Slim-Fast has about 38 percent of the market and recorded $396 million in beverage sales last year, according to Information Resources.

"For them to be a home run they don't have to be as big as Slim-Fast," said Michael Bellas, the chief executive of Beverage Marketing. "They will be able to leverage the Snapple direct store distribution to put that in venues where you don't see Slim-Fast. They're in single-serve. They're in the immediate-consumption channel. It's a perfect place. It fits with the convenience-on-the-go lifestyle that we have today."

But some nutritionists warn that consumers looking to lose weight or eat healthier foods should be wary of any meal substitute.

"This is a vitamin-supplemented soft drink," said Marion Nestle, the chairwoman of the department of food studies at New York University and the author of "Food Politics: How the Food Industry Influences Nutrition and Health" (University of California Press, 2002). "It's the equivalent of a candy bar. It's got an ounce of sugars in it. You bet it's not for dieters. It's got 200 calories of which most of them come from sugars. If I were going to advise someone to diet, the first thing I would do would be to tell them to cut out stuff like this."

Will Soft Touches Mean Softer Sales for the Mighty F-150?

By DANNY HAKIM

DEARBORN, Mich. — THE 2004 F-150 pickup truck from the **Ford Motor** Company will not even go on sale until this summer, but the debate over its design, which Ford has unsuccessfully tried to keep a secret, has been raging for months. At Web sites like F150online.com and Ford-trucks.com, message board postings burst with spy photographs and taut emotion: love, devotion, outrage.

"The F-150 is a truck," wrote a man who identified himself as Matthew from Stillwater, Okla., "not a freaking glorified car."

Matthew was particularly dismayed by the presence of what will surely be the new truck's most controversial feature. For the first time on an American full-size truck, some of the high-end F-150's will have an automatic gearshift positioned between the seats instead of on the steering column.

Like a car's.

This is welcome news to some people. "If the new F-150's are gonna look like that,"
wrote Arturo from Miami, "I'm just gonna go ahead and put my name on the waiting list now!"

But it is heresy to others. "It might go over O.K. with women," said Shawn Crowe, 24, a Ford enthusiast from Lawrenceburg, Ky., in an interview about the gearshift, "but most men will throw an absolute fit."

The redesigned F-150 is the American auto industry's most important vehicle introduction in years. It will be unveiled to the news media tomorrow at the North American International Auto Show in Detroit; some models are shown for the first time in the official photographs accompanying this article.

Ford's F-Series trucks, dominated by the F-150, have been the most popular vehicle line in America for two decades. To Ford, they are at least as important as sport utility vehicles like the Explorer, the best-selling S.U.V. and the third-best-selling vehicle of any kind after the F-Series and the Chevrolet Silverado pickups.

But competition is mounting on all sides, and Ford has little margin for error. Not only will the new F-150 have to contend with other full-size trucks from Chevrolet, GMC, Dodge and Toyota, but for the first time this year Nissan will try to steal some of Ford's market share with its own full-size pickup.

Of even more concern to many analysts are the production costs of the truck, which was lavishly developed during the bull market. In a penny-pinching industry, the new F-150 will actually cost more to make than the current one, a problem that Ford executives have pledged to fix after production begins.

"Can they get the cost down to leave sufficient profit?" said David E. Cole, the president of the Center for Automotive Research, an industry consulting and research firm. "It's a tough hurdle. Everything I've seen and heard about it says it's a well-executed truck. The real question is: Can it be as profitable as it has been historically? And the answer is probably no because of the added competition and the added cost."

Both Ford and **Nissan Motor** will give official first looks at their new big pickups at the auto show, which opens to the public on Saturday.

As the migration of the shift lever indicates, Ford is trying to fend off competitors by making the F-150 a truck for every taste and driver, from the Marlboro man to the soccer mom. In all, there will be more than a dozen major configurations of the pickup, compared with the current eight, which range in price from $18,500 to $37,000.

The top-end versions of the new trucks, which Ford has not yet priced, even accomplish the modest feat of looking better inside than most American-made luxury cars.

Can one truck line be all things to all people? Can it appeal to desk jockeys and, at the same time, to construction workers who want pickups they can wash out with a hose? A true reading of public reaction is not possible from the spy photographs, which generally show snippets from only one of many versions of the truck. The formal debut at the auto show will offer a better indication of customer sentiment.

What is clear is that Ford, which turns 100 in June, can ill afford to lose ground with the F-150. The company has rarely been more beleaguered. After a staggering $5.5 billion loss in 2001, it

Jeffrey Sauger for The New York Times

Julie Kurcz, a vehicle engineering manager at Ford, with a model of a new F-150 FX4. She said she tried to bring her personal perspective, as a 5-foot-2 woman, to the design.

rebounded with a slim profit last year. But overall sales fell 8.8 percent in 2002, Ford reported on Friday. That will only add to Wall Street's skepticism about the pace of Ford's year-old corporate turnaround plan.

Ford's bonds are hovering near junk status, and its stock fell 40.8 percent in 2002. Its market share has been plunging as foreign automakers open plants in the United States and continue to flood the market with cars and trucks. Even **General Motors,** long moribund, has had small gains in market share for two years in a row.

"We take every launch seriously, but the F-150 is our flagship," said James J. Padilla, Ford's chief of North American operations. The truck, he added, "means a lot to our bottom line, and it means a lot to our dealers."

"Nearly a quarter of our North American sales comes from F-Series alone," he added.

In fact, the F-Series probably put Ford into the black last year, all by itself. Gary R. Lapidus, an auto analyst at Goldman, Sachs, estimated that the F-Series generated $2.6 billion in pretax income for Ford in 2002, $1 billion more than his projection for the entire company.

Ford executives have said they expect the F-Series to remain as profitable as it is now. Most analysts, though, say that will be difficult to achieve because of the cost of upgrading the trucks and because the F-150 will have a new competitor in Nissan.

Ronald A. Tadross, an analyst at Banc of America Securities, called the truck's high costs a holdover of the Jacques Nasser era. Mr. Nasser was Ford's chief executive until William Clay Ford Jr., the Ford family scion and chairman, forced him out in October 2001 and took over as chief executive himself.

Mr. Nasser was heavily criticized for not paying attention to the basics of the industry—what Ford spends to build each vehicle, for example. Last summer, Mr. Ford installed David W. Thursfield, who also heads international operations, as the head of purchasing. Mr. Thursfield is a veteran cost cutter, but analysts say major changes can take years to show results.

Reducing costs is "really hard to do in an existing model," Mr. Tadross said.

"Where you have your best opportunities is when you're developing new models," he added, and cost savings can be designed and engineered from the ground up. Going back, he said, is considerably more complicated.

The F-150 "was designed on the old regime's watch, which means it has a lot of new content, a little higher cost structure than the old one and probably a little more complexity," he said.

Mr. Lapidus said he doubted that "the next-generation F-Series in aggregate will be as profitable as the last generation."

"No matter what they do," he added, "it will be very difficult to hit that objective."

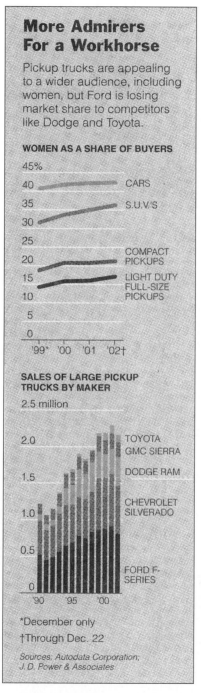

More Admirers For a Workhorse

Pickup trucks are appealing to a wider audience, including women, but Ford is losing market share to competitors like Dodge and Toyota.

WOMEN AS A SHARE OF BUYERS

45%
40 —— CARS
35 —— S.U.V'S
30
25
20 —— COMPACT PICKUPS
15 —— LIGHT DUTY FULL-SIZE
10 PICKUPS
5
0
'99* '00 '01 '02†

SALES OF LARGE PICKUP TRUCKS BY MAKER

2.5 million

2.0 —— TOYOTA GMC SIERRA
—— DODGE RAM
1.5
—— CHEVROLET SILVERADO
1.0
0.5
—— FORD F-SERIES
0
'90 '95 '00

*December only
†Through Dec. 22

Sources: Autodata Corporation; J. D. Power & Associates

Already, the F-Series' share of the full-size pickup market has slid. It was 38 percent last year, compared with nearly 43 percent in 1998, according to the Autodata Corporation, a research firm. The top competitor is

General Motors, which has about 30 percent of the market with its Chevrolet Silverado, the second-best-selling vehicle in the country, and an additional 9 percent with the GMC Sierra. But **Toyota Motor** has perhaps the most to do with the F-Series' recent share slide.

Toyota's first full-size pickup, the T100, fizzled in the mid-1990's, but the company has gained traction with a new full-size pickup, the Tundra, since it was introduced in 1999. In 2001, at the peak of full-size pickup sales, Toyota sold more than 100,000 Tundras, versus sales of more than 900,000 F-Series trucks by Ford and 700,000 Silverados.

For years, the pantheon of the American pickup truck was an uncomplicated place. Mostly men drove trucks, slogans were blunt ("like a rock" or "built Ford tough") and the music in commercials was left to the likes of Bob Seger, Chevy's former pickup pitchman known for his blue-collar anthems.

Lately, though, confusion has set in. Light trucks in general—a government classification that includes pickups, S.U.V.'s and minivans—now outsell passenger cars. Luxury car makers are increasingly making their money from trucks—BMW, Toyota's Lexus brand and Mercedes have all introduced S.U.V.'s—because many customers are willing to pay more for bigger vehicles.

In recent years, pickups have also become more luxurious. This trend reached an apotheosis in 2001, when Cadillac, of all unlikely brands, started selling a pickup. At a time when passenger-car sales are limping, manufacturers say pickups can offer much the same appeal that S.U.V.'s do: an aura of toughness with the trappings of comfort.

The growing popularity of light trucks has caused the fuel economy of the average American automobile to plummet to a 20-year low, despite many advances in technology. And light trucks pose dangers both to their own drivers, because of their increased risk of rollovers, and to car occupants because of the greater damage they inflict.

The new F-150 will have five major classes—varying mostly in interior glitziness—compared with just three now. In order, from no frills to fancy, are the XL, STX, XLT, FX4 and Lariat. Customers can order three different cab sizes: a regular cab has two seats, while the SuperCab and the jumbo SuperCrew have two rows of seats. The pickup bed is available in different lengths, and the sides of the truck can be ordered curvy ("flareside") or straight ("styleside"). Ford is also likely to continue offering limited-edition F-150's, like the upscale King Ranch and a model produced with **Harley-Davidson.**

Like many other American trucks and S.U.V.'s, the F-150 is getting bigger, with several inches added to its basic pickup bed and to the passenger compartment. The biggest version will cross the four-ton threshold

(Cont.)

for the first time. The grille is more imposing, and the oval Ford emblem at the back will almost double to nine inches in width.

The basic truck, the XL, is geared to the working man and has rubber floors in the passenger compartment that allow for hosing it out. At the top of the line, the Lariat is "geared toward buyers who view their trucks as a reward for achievement," according to the press kit.

The Lariat's interior comes in colors including "medium pebble" and has plenty of chrome, brushed steel and wood grains. It is not intended to be hosed out, nor is the FX4, which with its black leather seats looks more suited to a goateed bachelor—or, to the dismay of some male pickup enthusiasts, a woman.

Women now buy 18 percent of all pickups, up from 15 percent in 1999, according to J. D. Power & Associates, which monitors sales data from more than 5,900 dealer franchises nationwide. Even the basic F-150 has features tailored to nonconstruction workers, like a tailgate that is half as heavy to lift as the current version.

"I wanted it to be comfortable and smooth, a quiet and smooth ride free of shakes and head tossing," said Julie Kurcz, the highest-ranking female engineer on the F-150 project.

"I like to think that that's something I can bring to the part, my perspective; I'm 5-2

without high heels," said Ms. Kurcz, a baby boomer who declined to give her age. She and her husband are rebuilding a home with the help of her 2002 F-150.

Among the pickup's other options are heated seats and a selection of modular overhead storage areas that accommodate things like DVD players and Palm Pilots. (The F-150 already offers adjustable foot pedals for smaller people.) And, of course, there is the shift lever.

Mr. Padilla said he thought such features would help Ford attract a wider range of customers for the F-150. "I'll bet some of them are soccer moms," he said.

One of the F-150's most potent competitors last year was the Dodge Ram, whose surging sales were bolstered by the seven-year, 100,000-mile powertrain warranty offered by its parent company, **DaimlerChrysler.** (Ford offers a three-year, 36-month bumper-to-bumper warranty.) Dodge's advertising cranks up the machismo. The guy who drives the Ram in the company's television commercials looks as if he were chiseled from granite, and the Ram's grille has become cartoonishly muscle-bound. But this has an appeal.

"I see the Ram as the strongest competition from my standpoint, personally," said Roger Lemere, an F-150 driver in Sacra-

mento, Calif., who sells aftermarket parts for Fords. "I describe it as bold and a man's-looking truck," he said. "I do like it."

But for many people, including Mr. Lemere, buying anything but Ford is unthinkable. He worships his black 1997 F-150, which he outfitted with a custom tweed interior; the truck "doesn't see rain and it's a big money pit," he said.

Mr. Lapidus of Goldman, Sachs, who has seen the new F-150's in the flesh, said their exteriors would hold up well and were "manly, like a truck should be."

He also said the transformation of pickups into luxury vehicles meant a fundamental change in how they are marketed and designed.

"I don't think they're ever going to replace the S-Class," he said, referring to the fancy Mercedes sedan, "but this is consistent with what we see all over the light-truck category."

"They're turning them into fashion-oriented private-use vehicles, and they do require more of the accouterments. The trouble is, they are more of a fashion item and will require more frequent upgrades and replacements. You're going to have to be constantly reinventing them to keep them fresh."

Advertising

China's Cultural Fabric Is a Challenge to Marketers

*Toyota's **Prado** campaign hit a nerve with some Chinese consumers. Critics say the lions resemble those at the site of the opening battle during Japan's 1937 invasion of China.*

BY GEOFFREY A. FOWLER

STRIKING A PATRIOTIC chord might not help you win customers in China, but offending national pride is a surefire way to lose them.

It is a lesson that **Toyota Motor** of Japan learned the hard way. In December, the auto maker had to pull and formally apologize for 30 magazine and newspaper advertisements depicting stone lions—a traditional sign of Chinese power—saluting and bowing to a Prado Land Cruiser sport-utility vehicle.

"These ads were intended to reflect Prado's imposing presence when driving in the city," says Julie Du, account manager with **Publicis Groupe's** Saatchi & Saatchi, which made the ads.

"You cannot but respect the Prado," the ad says.

But Chinese words often hold multiple meanings. Prado translates into Chinese as *badao,* which also means "rule by force" or "overbearing."

Consumer critics who called Toyota and posted scathing—occasionally profane—messages in Internet discussion groups said the lions resembled those flanking the Marco Polo Bridge, the site near Beijing of the opening battle in Japan's 1937 invasion of China.

The Toyota fiasco highlights the tricky cultural and historical pitfalls that afflict marketing for even the savviest China-based foreign companies. On one hand, the ad industry increasingly agrees that despite rampant nationalism, patriotism doesn't build brands. But Toyota and others recently have discovered that they can't ignore how strongly politics shapes Chinese consumer sentiment.

As China's economy grows at breakneck pace and it prepares for the 2008 Olympics in Beijing, Chinese people may be growing more nationalistic. An October 2003 survey by **WPP Group's** Ogilvy & Mather advertising firm found that 34% of young people in prosperous southern China found patriotism to be "extremely important"—a 10 on a scale of one to 10.

"Young people are indoctrinated from very early on in school to be patriotic," says Joseph Wang, Ogilvy's group managing director for Hong Kong and southern China.

Some Chinese brands such as **Coca-Cola** competitors **Jianlibao** and **Fei Chang Kele** try to tap that patriotism in ads. "The Chinese people's own Cola!" exhorts ads for Fei Chang Kele.

But an increasing number of ad agencies are finding that a patriotic appeal doesn't lure Chinese shoppers to sportswear brands such as homegrown favorite **Li-Ning Sports Goods** over **Nike** just because it originates in China.

Indeed, the Ogilvy survey found that the strongest patriots were just as likely to buy foreign brands as shoppers who claimed to be indifferent. Ninety-four percent of the "more patriotic" drank Coke, compared with 100% of the "moderately patriotic." Only 19% considered country of origin a factor in brand choice.

"Brand-buying today is a personal activity. Patriotism is [a] collective activity," Ogilvy's Mr. Wang explains.

As a result, agencies are dumping patriotic pitches in favor of pragmatism. "It's the same as in politics: A political party can go only so far on a patriotic platform. Ultimately, if they don't deliver the goods, voters give them the boot," says Mickey Chak, planning director of DDB Worldwide Communications Group Inc. China.

Foreign sportswear makers who sponsor local Chinese teams often receive a lukewarm response. As a result, brands increasingly are highlighting their global significance instead. "Many sports fans in China aren't just interested in a sport because there are Chinese players in it," Mr. Chak says. "Long before Yao Ming, basketball enjoyed popu-

larity, and Chinese consumers bought into the NBA."

But even though they are dumping patriotism, advertisers such as Toyota have bungled by going too far and ignoring it.

Despite longstanding wartime antagonisms, the Chinese have become major consumers of Japanese products—which carry a high-quality cachet—even as they complain about accidents involving Japanese products, or Japanese service manuals that make political gaffes by identifying Taiwan as separate from China.

Bayerische Motoren Werke of Germany faced weeks of negative publicity in state-run newspapers during October after a woman in the northeastern Chinese city of Harbin crashed into a crowd with her BMW X53.0 Diesel Sport. Marketed to China's elite upper-class, the BMW brand became a target of populist resentment from millions of laid-off former state workers left behind by China's economic boom.

Many agencies have implemented "disaster checks" before their campaigns go live to make sure that they haven't been blinded to a political sore spot.

Toyota will establish a "supervisory system" for its marketing, a public-relations officer in charge of its Chinese office says.

Saatchi & Saatchi, which declined to discuss the role of patriotism in advertising, is working on new Toyota Prado ads but doesn't yet have a release date for them.

Top Online Chemical Exchange Is Unlikely Success Story

By Julia Angwin

IN 1999, John F. Beasley bragged that his Web start-up **ChemConnect** Inc. was likely to become the "largest business-to-business exchange on the Internet, period." Now, his assessment is a bit different: "It's better to own a smaller piece of a watermelon than an entire grape," he says.

Times have changed since the heady days when online business-to-business exchanges like ChemConnect thought they could revolutionize the world. Most of the entrepreneurs who built online trading platforms for industries ranging from steel to auto parts failed. The Old Economy companies that were supposed to be crushed by the upstarts have generally prevailed with their own online exchanges.

ChemConnect, however, is an unlikely success story. It is now the biggest online exchange for chemical trading, with volume of $8.8 billion in 2002, the latest figure available. Customers like Tom Garner, president of **Vanguard Petroleum** Corp. in Houston, have come to rely on ChemConnect for their business.

Mr. Garner says about 15% of his spot purchases and sales of natural-gas liquids are conducted on ChemConnect's commodities trading site. "Before, I would have had to beat the phones to death," he says. Now, "I'll post it online and 150 people are seeing it. It would take me all day to canvass that many people."

One key to ChemConnect's survival was speed. It was first to market, launching an Internet bulletin board in 1995. It was also the fastest and best fund-raiser among its dozens of competitors—bringing in $105 million by the time the stock-market bubble burst in 2000, compared with $50 million for its chief competitor, **CheMatch.com.** Mr. Beasley also realized that the only way to persuade traditional chemical companies to trade online was to allow the industry to

profit from ChemConnect—so he sold about one-third of the company to more than 40 chemical companies.

ChemConnect still isn't profitable, although it expects to break even this year. And while it is used by about 44% of the industry, many sellers wish there were more buyers online, according to a survey of 250 chemical buyers and sellers by AMR Research. "The key now is to basically be as patient as you can, but to continue to push the adoption curve," Mr. Beasley says.

When he founded ChemConnect in 1995, Mr. Beasley was 31 years old and a vice president of mergers and acquisitions at First Physician Care, an Atlanta physician-management practice. Bored with that, he decided to become an entrepreneur. He had no computer and knew nothing about the chemical business. But when he went to the library to search for ideas, he was intrigued by books about a giant network of computers called the Internet. So he asked his friend Jay Hall, who had some computer experience, to meet him for pizza.

Over beer and thin-crust pies, Mr. Beasley proposed some ideas he thought might work on the Internet, such as selling motorcycles or jeans overseas. But Mr. Hall had other ideas. Although he was an electrical engineer by training, he had been drafted to help sell his father's chemical business. "I said, 'The chemical industry is the most backward industry in the world,'" Mr. Hall recalls. (He says his view has changed since then.) Messrs. Beasley and Hall decided to set up a way for chemical companies to find suppliers online.

Together, they invested $10,000 in computer equipment and set up shop in Mr. Hall's spare bedroom—a loft that was "blistering hot and very cramped," Mr. Hall recalls. After work and on weekends, the two taught themselves Web programming and typed in lists of chemical suppliers to create an online directory. Within a month and a half, they had built an Internet bulletin board and were accepting classified advertising from chemical companies. Each listing cost $100.

In the spring of 1996, the partners hired Patrick van der Valk, a Dutch chemist, to build a Web site that would allow buyers and sellers to electronically post their listings, and eventually they made him a partner in the business. Their first customers were Indian and Chinese companies aiming to sell chemicals in the U.S. By 1998, they had 10,000 customers.

Competitors also were popping up. "We knew if we didn't raise money we'd be dead," Mr. Beasley recalls. So the team made the rounds of investors in Silicon Valley, eventually raising $4 million from Institutional Venture Partners and relocating to the San Francisco Bay area.

The pressure to get big fast was intense. More than a dozen chemical exchanges had emerged by 2000, led by CheMatch.com, which had lined up support from **DuPont** Co., while ChemConnect had backing from **Dow Chemical** Co.

Mr. Beasley launched himself into a frenzy of fund-raising, flying around the world to meet with chemical companies. In the spring of 2000, he raised $72 million from 38 of them. To keep the exchange neutral, he limited each company to, at most, a 5% stake. His success scared his rivals. "His ability to raise money was constantly sticking in my side," recalls Dave Tabors of Battery Ventures, who was an investor in CheMatch.

Mr. Beasley had his own moment of panic when CheMatch filed for an initial public offering before ChemConnect did.

"It was a pretty scary moment," Mr. Beasley recalls. "Had they been successful, they would have had a very significant amount of capital." Ultimately, neither firm went public because each failed to launch an IPO before the dot-com bubble burst.

With its hefty cash hoard, ChemConnect took the opportunity to buy competitors, including CheMatch.com and an industry-owned exchange. Mr. Beasley also recruited a seasoned chemical executive, John Robinson, to run the company as chief executive, while Mr. Beasley remained chairman.

The company has since moved from its flashy San Francisco offices to more modest quarters in Houston. Its staff has shrunk to 60 from about 190 during the boom era. And Mr. Beasley, who still lives in San Francisco, has more time for his hobby of motorcycle racing.

On a clear San Francisco day, he takes a visitor for a ride on his limited-edition Italian motorcycle. The sign overlooking the Golden Gate Bridge says "15 MPH," but he takes the hairpin turn at about 50 miles per hour. "The faster you go, the more intensely you have to focus," he says.

Wal-Mart's Low-Price Obsession Puts Suppliers Through Wringer

Duct tape manufacturer welcomes efficiencies that Wal-Mart requires.

. . . .

By Marilyn Much
Investor's Business Daily

Remember the rush on duct tape after the Homeland Security Department raised the terror alert to orange last February?

If you don't, Bill Kahl, executive vice president of marketing at Henkel Adhesives, can clue you in. As the maker of Duck brand duct tape, Henkel saw a spike in demand following the announcement.

During that time, Kahl and his team worked hard to keep a steady flow of the product in stores. Key customer Wal-Mart helped ease the burden. Using Wal-Mart's online Retail Link system, which gives its suppliers daily point-of-sale data, Kahl's team tracked inventory levels in the discount chain's regional warehouses.

When Wal-Mart centers in peak selling areas ran low, Henkel was able to fill the void by diverting shipments from other regions. The result? Henkel kept Wal-Mart stores fully stocked with duct tape even in the face of huge demand.

Wal-Mart's relentless pursuit of lower prices reaches well beyond creating efficiencies for its suppliers. The chain has helped drive down prices of goods, which benefits consumers. And through improvements in technology, it's bolstered the nation's productivity rate, economists say.

It's no secret that in its quest to create cost efficiencies throughout the retail supply chain, Wal-Mart helps its suppliers become leaner and more efficient.

"Working with Wal-Mart has made us a better company," Kahl said.

But Wal-Mart's pricing power is a double-edged sword. Smaller discount chains such as Caldor and Ames couldn't compete, and have gone out of business. And Wal-Mart's size and efficiency were key factors in Kmart's filing for bankruptcy in 2002.

Wal-Mart is the world's biggest retailer. It has close to 3,500 stores in the U.S. and 4,844 worldwide. In fiscal 2004, it boasted an estimated $253.5 billion in sales. Wal-Mart accounts for about 10% of total U.S. retail sales, excluding autos. It holds between a 25% and 30% share of sales of most consumer staples—everything from detergent and batteries to toothpaste.

It's also the nation's No. 1 retailer of groceries, toys, DVDs, CDs and entertainment software, apparel and home textiles.

Pricing Pressure

Pricing is the most obvious effect Wal-Mart has on retailing and the economy, says Frank Badillo, senior economist at consulting firm Retail Forward Inc.

"Its (impact) is like a ripple in a pond," Badillo said.

With its huge negotiating power and economies of scale, Wal-Mart boasts retail's lowest cost structure. It passes those savings on to consumers. Though Wal-Mart has an impact on all retail prices, it's been exerting the most pressure in segments where it competes directly—discount chains and department stores, Badillo says. In 2003, prices in these segments fell at more than a 3% annual rate, on top of a more than 2% drop the year before.

> "By going back to a supplier and saying, 'Lower your costs by say 5%,' Wal-Mart is shifting (pricing pressure) downstream."

The effect of Wal-Mart's pricing power has rippled throughout the economy.

When Wal-Mart enters a new geographic market, general merchandise, food and apparel prices fall in that area by 2% to 10% in the course of a year, says Carl Steidtmann, chief economist at Deloitte Research.

Mapping Out Costs

Similarly, when Wal-Mart lowers prices in a product category, other stores typically follow suit. For instance, since Levi Strauss debuted its Signature brand of clothes for the mass merchandise channel in Wal-Mart stores last July, the entire basic denim category has experienced a big price reduction, says analyst Jeffrey Klinefelter of Piper Jaffray & Co. Overall, U.S. consumer goods prices fell by 2.5% in 2003 from 2002. Analysts say Wal-Mart played a roll in that decline.

As Wal-Mart has grown, it's had a direct impact on the total retail supply chain, says Michael Niemira, chief economist for the International Council of Shopping Centers.

Wal-Mart executives wouldn't comment for this story. But here's how Wal-Mart might work with a vendor, says James Allen, a Bain & Co. consultant: During negotiations, a Wal-Mart rep maps out how much the store intends to lower prices for consumers. If the supplier wants to do business with Wal-Mart, it has to bring its yearly costs down the same amount, says Allen.

"By going back to a supplier and saying, 'Lower your costs by say 5%,' Wal-Mart is shifting (pricing pressure) downstream," Niemira said.

For suppliers, working with Wal-Mart is a mixed bag. On the plus side, Wal-Mart will agree to large-scale, long-term contracts in return for lowered costs. That can motivate firms to seek ways to cut costs and improve their productivity.

But there are minuses. Wal-Mart's relentless cost pressure can lead vendors to cut corners, Allen says. For instance, in an effort to pare labor costs, a maker might end up sourcing through countries that have low safety and environmental standards and poor labor conditions.

U.S. firms have been outsourcing production to lower-cost nations for years. But the growth of Wal-Mart has accelerated that trend.

"With its scale and competencies, Wal-Mart has made the need greater for brand

(Cont.)

owners to (lower) costs because the prize is distribution at its stores," Allen said.

In its quest to pare costs, Wal-Mart has been one of the leaders in sourcing goods directly from China.

"This creates a chain reaction and forces other companies to follow.... We're seeing the pattern more and more," said Badillo of Retail Forward.

He notes that No. 2 discounter Target set up a sourcing center in Shenzhen, China, in September. Chris Huber, Target's director of sourcing services, told China Daily that the retailer expects to double procurement from China this year over last. Badillo also cites the fact that early this month, Levi Strauss closed its last two U.S. sewing plants, and this spring it will shut its three plants in Canada, completing a shift to production in China and other countries with cheaper labor.

Then there's the effect Wal-Mart has on other retailers. Not only is the store making it tough for discounters to compete, but as the nation's No. 1 grocer it's also creating headaches for supermarkets.

A lot has to do with Wal-Mart's low-cost structure. It's more efficient than traditional supermarkets in terms of logistics and distribution. It's also a nonunion shop that pays lower wages and offers fewer costly benefits than supermarkets, which are unionized.

When you combine all its efficiencies, Wal-Mart has a 20% to 30% cost advantage over supermarkets, says Sandy Skrovan, a vice president at Retail Forward.

Wal-Mart charges 15% to 20% less on core items like beverages and paper towels. In so doing, Wal-Mart has increased its share of total consumer spending on consumable goods to 8% of the total in 2002 from 5% in 1997, Skrovan says.

As Wal-Mart has expanded its share of the grocery market and made the field more competitive, it's helped drive 13,000 mom and pop stores out of business in the last decade, Skrovan figures. She expects another 2,000 stores to close in the next five years, due largely to Wal-Mart's competitive stance.

"Wal-Mart's Low-Price Obsession Puts Suppliers Through Wringer," *Investor's Business Daily,* January 30, 2004. Reprinted by permission.

32

BlackBerry Maker Finds Friend In Uncle Sam

Targeting Public Sector.

. . . .

By PATRICK SEITZ
Investor's Business Daily

For Research In Motion Ltd., the daily scene on Capitol Hill is a dream come true. Practically everywhere, congressmen, staffers and lobbyists are using RIM's BlackBerry handheld e-mail devices.

A few years ago, RIM focused its sales efforts on New York City and the financial community. But the world changed after 9-11, and so did RIM's business.

Government customers, such as Congress and the Defense Department, have become in aggregate the largest category of BlackBerry users, says Don Morrison, chief operating officer of RIM. Government officials are using "tens of thousands" of the palm-sized devices with their distinctive thumb keyboards.

"Since 9-11, because of BlackBerry's performance under crisis situations, the government market has eclipsed the finance market in terms of actual number of users," Morrison said.

He estimates government users account for 10% of the more than 1 million subscribers to BlackBerry's wireless data service.

One question facing RIM is whether the widespread use of BlackBerry devices in Washington, D.C., is a unique situation or something it can replicate elsewhere.

After 9-11, Congress spent $6 million to buy 3,000 BlackBerrys for members and their staffs and to set up secure wireless messaging.

The move was criticized because RIM is a Canadian firm and Congress rushed ahead with the purchase. U.S.-based rivals such as Palm Inc. didn't get a chance to bid.

As chairman of the House Administration Committee, Rep. Robert Ney, R-Ohio, made the decision to buy BlackBerrys for all 435 members of the House and their staffs and link them to the emergency communications network. Ney was sold on BlackBerrys because they worked on Sept. 11, 2001, when cell phone networks were overloaded, says Ney's spokesman, Brian Walsh.

At the time, the BlackBerry was the only device available that met Congress' data encryption and communications needs, Walsh says. The House network now supports 3,700 BlackBerrys, Walsh says. BlackBerrys aren't as widespread or coordinated on the Senate side, he says.

On Feb. 2, after the discovery of the poison ricin in the Dirksen Senate Office Building, House members and their staffs were alerted on their BlackBerrys, while many Senate staffers were left in the dark because they don't have a comparable messaging system.

For House members, that was an improvement over the poor showing for the emergency communications system last Halloween. That's when two staffers' costumes and a plastic gun prompted an office lockdown while SWAT teams searched House offices. A message didn't go out over the BlackBerry network until almost an hour after the incident became known,

according to The Hill newspaper. Staffers had to get updates by watching TV news. The BlackBerry messaging system was improved soon afterward.

Congress' purchase of BlackBerry devices worked like an endorsement for the firm. Soon, federal agencies and branches of the armed services signed on too, Morrison says. The Canadian government became a big user around the same time as Congress, he says. Plus, state and local governments have become converts to BlackBerry.

Government use of BlackBerry devices has helped RIM sell to commercial customers, Morrison says. Corporate buyers have a higher comfort level knowing that government users are satisfied when it comes to security, he says.

"The inside-the-Beltway customers are very high-profile customers," he said.

RIM has doubled its subscriber count in the past year. In early March 2003, it had 534,000 subscribers. It reached 1 million subscribers on Feb. 3. "It's really taking off," Morrison said.

By year-end, RIM could have 2.2 million subscribers, says Tom Sepenzis, an analyst with ThinkEquity Partners. "They really do have a wonderful platform for delivering e-mail," he said.

The Waterloo, Ontario-based company is getting a boost from new BlackBerry phones that merge a cell phone with a RIM e-mail device, he says. And RIM is gaining subscribers in Europe and Asia, he says.

Coming soon are devices from other hardware makers, such as Nokia, that will use RIM technology. RIM doesn't have much competition today, but small, privately held Good Technology Inc. could give it a run for its money, says Todd Kort, an analyst with Gartner Inc. Sunnyvale, Calif.-based Good has signed up hardware makers Dell and PalmOne to use its technology.

RIM wants to move beyond e-mail, giving customers wireless access to information stored behind firewalls in server computers. For example, salespeople can use their BlackBerrys to update customer

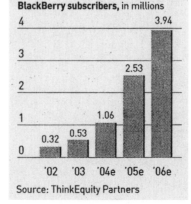

Picking BlackBerrys

The government market makes up roughly 10% of RIM's subscribers

BlackBerry subscribers, in millions

'02: 0.32
'03: 0.53
'04e: 1.06
'05e: 2.53
'06e: 3.94

Source: ThinkEquity Partners

(Cont.)

records, check on the status of an order or get information before a sales call. "Principally today it's a communications medium," Morrison said. "Increasingly it also will be an information medium."

RIM can see Congress and other government customers finding similar uses for BlackBerry devices.

House members and their staffs originally got BlackBerrys for emergencies, but now mostly use them for routine communications.

"A lot of members have become dependent on them," Walsh said. Some admit being addicted to the devices, calling them "crack berries."

In the nation's capital, you'll see congressmen and their support people using them in restaurants, theaters and at committee hearings.

Washington has a love-hate relationship with BlackBerrys, says Abraham Genauer, a staff writer for The Hill. "Members love it because they can bother their staffs any time, no matter where they are, whether they're in the district or on the road. And the staffs don't like being bothered all the time," he said. "It used to be if the congressman was away, you may not hear from him for a day or two. Now there's no getting away from them."

"Blackberry Maker Finds Friend in Uncle Sam," *Investor's Business Daily,* February 20, 2004. Reprinted by permission.

Getting Information for Marketing Decisions

THIS VOLVO IS NOT A GUY THING
The company turns to women to learn how to make the ideal car—for everyone

Burning rubber. Roaring engines. Grease and gas. Cars are a guy thing, right? The industry sure seems to thinks so. Auto ads tend to emphasize big, fast models, usually driven by a man—with a woman at his side, if at all—over user-friendly touches such as ergonomic seats. It's no surprise the crowd that designs, develops, builds, and sells autos remains a boys' club.

Yet on the other side of the sales desk, women sway a disproportionate share of car sales. According to industry studies, women purchase about two-thirds of vehicles and in-fluence 80% of all sales. It's this gender gap that Volvo is trying to bridge with a concept car unveiled at the Geneva Auto Show on Mar. 2. Shaped by all-female focus groups drawn from Volvo's workforce, the two-door hatchback was created by an all-woman management team. Dubbed Your Concept Car, or YCC, the resulting show car cost some $3 million to design and build and is packed with thoughtful design twists that attracted a big, spirited crowd in Geneva. "We found that by meeting women's expectations, we exceeded those of most men," said Hans-Olov Olsson, president and CEO of Volvo Cars, a unit of Ford Motor Co.

There's no guarantee the YCC will ever make it to a showroom. The auto industry uses concept cars as test beds for designs and technical innovations, and to gauge the public's reactions. Packed as it is with the latest gizmos, the YCC would be expensive: Volvo estimates a road version would cost about $65,000 and compete with luxury coupes built by the likes of Audi and Mercedes.

More James Bond than Soccer Mom, the YCC may just create enough buzz to hit the roads. Its gull-wing doors—which resemble the line of a bird's extended wings—are there as much for convenience and accessibility as for design chic. A button on the key fob stirs the YCC to life, raising the whole chassis a few inches to meet the driver, just as the upper door lifts hydraulically and the sill—the lower part of the door—slides under the car. The oversize opening makes stepping in and out a breeze, says Maria Widell Christiansen, the YCC's design manager. And because they're motor-driven, "the driver doesn't even need to touch the car to get in," she adds.

This hands-off approach is deliberate and consistent. Rather than a dirty, tough-to-unscrew gas cap, the YCC borrows a technology from race cars: When the gas button is pressed in the cockpit, a ball valve on the outside of the car rotates, exposing an opening for the fuel pump. Ditto for wind-shield-wiper fluid. Body panels are low-maintenance, too. Clad in a nonstick paint, they repel dirt.

SMART PARKING

Much of the advanced technology in the YCC is hidden from view. Women in Volvo's focus group weren't willing to give up power but wanted cleaner, more efficient perfor-mance. Hence the 215-horsepower, five-cylinder, near-zero-emissions gas engine, which shuts off when not in motion and then fires up instantly with the help of an electric motor. This delivers a 10% boost in mileage, says Olsson. There's also a nifty parallel-parking aid. When the car is aligned in front of an empty spot, sensors can confirm that, yes, it's big enough. Then, while the driver controls the gas and brake, the system self-steers the car into the spot.

EASY DOES IT
Press a button in the cockpit, get out, insert gas pump nozzle—you'll never unscrew a gas cap again

In the cockpit, the design team focused on ergonomics and styling. "Access for women, in particular, can be difficult," says Jennifer Stockburger, an automotive-test engineer at Consumer Reports, who has been testing vehicle ergonomics into her ninth month of pregnancy. For small women, especially, "reaching out to shut a heavy door, or adjusting pedals, can be tough."

To tailor the cockpit to drivers, the YCC team developed and applied for a patent on the Ergovision system. At a dealership, the driver's body is laser-scanned in a booth. Volvo then calculates optimal positions for the seat belt, pedals, headrest, steering wheel, and seat, all of which is saved in the key fob. Each driver is "automatically custom-fitted" when they get in the car, says Camilla Palm-ertz, YCC's project manager.

Whether or not the YCC is eventually built, some of its design innovations are likely to show up in future Volvo models, says Olsson. The concept car will make its U.S. debut on Apr. 7 at the New York International Auto Show. And no doubt plenty of gearhead guys will be there to admire its feminine wiles.

By Adam Aston in New York with Gail Edmondson in Geneva

By **Women**, For All

Designed by a five-woman team, Volvo's YCC show car is packed with features any driver can love.

NO-TOUCH DOORS Press a key fob, and the gull-wing doors lift automatically.

EASY ENTRY As the gull wings rise, the door sill retracts, the car lifts up 3 in., the steering wheel pulls in, and the seat slides back, making a wide path in.

GOOD-BYE, GAS CAP Adapted from race-car technology, a ball valve rotates to expose a hole for a gas pump nozzle.

EASY CARE Clad in no-stick paint, the body panels repel dirt. Seat covers can be removed, washed, and customized.

SAFER SIGNALS When braking hard, extra panels of LEDs fire up, boosting the brake lights' intensity.

HAIR-FRIENDLY HEADRESTS An open area leaves room for a ponytail, and improves whiplash protection.

Labatt Gets Boost from Under-30 Set

20somethings at McCann help speed new brew

By: Lisa Sanders

When the low-carbohydrate craze spread among consumers nationwide, Labatt USA's Jon Genese took note and shifted his marketing plans for a low-carb beer launch into a high gear one year ago with some aid from an unknown group called the MU-30s.

Rival Anheuser-Busch Cos., first to market with its low-carb brew Michelob Ultra in September 2002, had a hit with beer drinkers, and numerous competitors had launches in the works. Mr. Genese, director-marketing, domestic specialty brands, wanted Labatt USA's low-carb beer Green Light on store shelves and in consumers' hearts and minds before the brands of his competitors.

Proper product positioning was crucial to the launch's success. But months-long research studies were impractical. "Speed was our mission," Mr. Genese said.

An unusual resource offered by his Interpublic Group of Cos.' advertising agency, the TAG unit of McCann Erickson Worldwide, delivered the market research necessary to get Green Light on a fast-track to market. TAG chief Lori Senecal tapped an often-overlooked resource within the New York office: employees aged 30 years old or younger, and rallied a dozen of them to conduct on-the-street investigations last July in several key Labatt USA markets.

The MU-30s (short for McCann Under 30) interviewed bar patrons, bartenders and folks in the beer trade for insight into the low-carb phenomenon and brand-positioning opportunity. "We used the street-team findings as a filter," Mr. Genese said. "They were a first step in deciding which positioning ideas to test."

The findings of the MU-30 team, which were that Green Light should live more in the world of beer than athleticism, led to a positioning of "great beer, great fun, low carbs." That sets the new offering in contrast to Michelob Ultra's fitness positioning.

"There's a feeling from people in bars that they didn't relate to Michelob Ultra. What they want in a beer is fun and great taste, and if you get the low carbs too, that's great," Ms. Senecal said. The findings help lead to the tagline, "You've got the Green Light." The beer rolled out nationally Oct. 1.

LARGE SUPPLY

Today the MU-30s opinions, investigations and input are increasingly being used in numerous ways for various TAG clients, which include Cadbury Schweppes' Dentyne and Microsoft's Xbox. Throughout the fall, McCann expanded the group beyond an informal team working in the agency's New York headquarters, and just last month the agency initiated a global recruitment drive to encourage participation from any of its 300 offices in 132 countries. Additionally, every new McCann Erickson under-30 employee receives an invitation to join. A Web site connects all MU-30 participants, offering a bulletin board for interacting.

"This is an opportunity to engage our large supply of young people," Ms. Senecal said. "It gives them a change to participate right at the outset of their careers." To understand the role music plays in the lives of young adults, the MU-30s kept a log recording how, when and why music intersected their lives; for another client, MU-30s discussed their favorite leisure activities.

Labatt USA's Mr. Genese appreciates the speed, efficiency and potential savings of the in-house tool. "It is very costly to do research, and this can help to get through to positioning ideas that make sense," he said. The MU-30s contribute in numerous ways, Ms. Senecal said.

Insight into the young-adult population is valuable, said David Morrison, president, consulting firm Twentysomething, "because they are the early adopters and the influencers. Those in their 20s and early 30s are young of heart and mind, but have a bit more money than the college set."

The New Science of Focus Groups

by Alison Stein Wellner

Last fall, 15 million students headed off to college, many moving into that mysterious world known as the dorm. These first-time dorm denizens, along with their other college peers, spent an estimated $210 billion in 2002 on everything from microwave ovens to shower loofahs, representing a tantalizing marketing opportunity.

Yet how can retail-product designers, well beyond their college years, know what their young customers do not: what life in a dorm is like today? How can they help young adults away from home for the first time figure out how to navigate communal bathrooms as well as the intricacies of the clothes washer and dryer?

These are questions that intrigued *Target,* the Minneapolis-based discount retailer, primed to launch a product line aimed at the college segment. In search of qualitative research that would elicit deep insights, emotions and motivations from college students, Target hired San Mateo, Calif.-based research firm *Jump Associates.* What Jump delivered was a different spin on the traditional focus group, exemplifying the type of creative, eclectic approach to qualitative research that's becoming increasingly popular. The research enabled Target to hear firsthand from college-bound students about their concerns when shopping for their dorm rooms and to get a sense from college students of what life in a dorm is like.

"We were fascinated with the underlying social dynamic of going to college," says Dev Patnaik, managing associate at Jump. So the firm sponsored a series of "game nights" at high school grads' homes, inviting incoming college freshman as well as students with a year of dorm living under their belts. [Each was paid an incentive, similar to a focus group participant.] To get teens talking about dorm life, Jump devised a board game that involved issues associated with going to college. The game naturally led to informal conversations—and questions—about college life. Jump researchers were on the sidelines to observe, while a video camera recorded the proceedings.

The research paid off. Last year, Target launched the Todd Oldham Dorm Room product line designed for college freshman. Among the new offerings: Kitchen in a Box, which provides basic accoutrements for a budding college cook; Bath in a Box, which includes an extra-large

bath towel to preserve modesty on the trek to and from the shower; and a laundry bag with instructions on how to actually do the laundry printed on the bag. Thanks in part to the Dorm Room line, Target held its own during the back-to-school season. In the third quarter of 2002, when most of the year's back-to-school shopping for college students was done, revenues at Target stores increased 12 percent over the third quarter of 2001, to $8.4 billion, while comparable store sales increased by only 1 percent.

Patnaik calls the game night "the antidote to the traditional focus group," a process he views as "a customer terrarium, with people behind glass," much the same way plants and lizards are taken out of their natural surroundings and observed for scientific purposes. In Patnaik's view, traditional focus groups often make it impossible for market researchers to learn the truth about what customers are feeling. Still, many companies rely on focus groups, in which 8-to-12 people are gathered in a room that has a two-way mirror, to make their marketing decisions. But according to Patnaik, "Focus groups are the crack cocaine of market research. You get hooked on them, and you're afraid to make a move without them."

Whether or not focus groups are addictive, marketers are certainly heavy users. In 2001, companies spent $1.1 billion on qualitative research, most of this for focus groups, says Larry Gold, editor and publisher of *Inside Research,* a monthly publication based in Barrington, Ill., that tracks the market research industry. But in an era of rising expectations, qualitative research, especially focus groups, is increasingly under the gun. In fact, despite the proliferation of focus groups that are held prior to product launches, an astonishing 80 percent of all new products or services fail within six months or fall significantly short of projections, points out Harvard marketing professor Gerald Zaltman, in his new book, *How Customers Think: Essential Insights into the Mind of the Market* [Harvard Business School Press, 2003].

Of course, it's not reasonable to place the blame for these product failures squarely on the shoulders of traditional focus groups—but even those who conduct them admit that the method has room for improvement. Today, the field of qualitative research is changing, not only in

(Cont.)

response to its critics, but also to benefit from advancing technology and research methodology. Some are turning to cutting-edge segmentation science to ensure that they're studying the right group of respondents. Still others are taking a page from ethnographic research, creating focus group experiences that are less clinical and a lot more like real life. And as research from the 1990s, dubbed the decade of the brain, wends its way into the business world, cutting-edge qualitative researchers are opting for one-on-one interviews and borrowing cognitive science techniques, such as response latency and neuroimaging, to access emotions and feelings that consumers don't even know they're having. Qualitative researchers predict that such creative and effective approaches may ultimately leave the traditional construct of focus groups far behind.

THE SCIENCE OF RECRUITING

The heart of qualitative research is still the interview: A market researcher talking to consumers in a group of 12, in smaller groups of two or three, or even one-on-one. Of course, the people recruited to participate are critical to the success of the focus group. "The way you screen for the respondents separates a successful group from a nonsuccessful group," says Marie Joan Cohen, president of Marketing Insights, a Summit, N.J.-based qualitative research firm, whose clients include AT&T and Crayola. While researchers using traditional focus group often divide consumers into groups according to standard demographic breaks and with product usage history as a guideline [i.e., women ages 35 to 44 who have used toothpaste in the past year], a growing number of researchers recruit groups based on psychographics also. "We're looking beyond simple demographic differences," explains Trenton Haack, director of qualitative services at the research firm Burke, Inc., in Cincinnati.

In looking beyond demographics and product usage history, some qualitative researchers are tapping into the expertise gained over the past few decades by segmentation scientists, who divide consumer markets according to demographic and psychographic characteristics. For example, over the past 30 years the research powerhouse RoperASW in New York City has studied a consumer segment it calls "The Influentials"—the one American in every 10 who has significant word-of-mouth clout. Drawing on a database of more than 10,000 questions, and interviews with more than 50,000 Influentials and 500,000 other Americans, RoperASW uses its knowledge of this segment to help its clients recruit candidates for qualitative research, says RoperASW CEO Ed Keller.

"Influentials are two to five years ahead of the curve in their involvement with new trends and new products and lifestyle choices. They have this bellwether nature to them," he explains. Recruiting Influentials is particularly useful when a marketer is trying to determine how to launch a new product or how a product's use is changing over time, he says. "We'd never say that this is a panacea for every eventuality, but to the extent that you're looking

---

Whither *online* Focus Groups?

Back in the heady dotcom days, it seemed as though online polling was poised to make a clean sweep of market research—revolutionizing the way companies conducted quantitative and qualitative research. But although the Internet is firmly ingrained on the quantitative side, the qualitative side has not faired as well. From 2000 to 2001 alone, spending on online survey research increased by 53 percent to $400 million, according to Larry Gold of Inside Research, while spending on online qualitative remains negligible.

The problem seems to be tied to the dotcom bust. In gauging respondents' emotional reaction to a product or an advertising campaign—one of the key goals of qualitative research—focus groups that were assembled online were never as effective as those that met in person. However, online groups were particularly well suited to examining Web-based business. Two years ago, for example, when Ruth Stevens was senior vice president of marketing at NatWest Bank's now-defunct CyBuy division [she's currently president of eMarketing Strategy in New York City], she found great value in online focus groups. "We were a launch business, so we literally only had a handful of people using our service. But we really wanted to understand what their experience was like. The fact that we could get them to log in from their homes and offices, all over the country, made it possible for us to fill up the virtual room," Stevens says. Now that the bumper crop of dotcom companies has shriveled, the market for online qualitative research is smaller.

Still, the ability to pull consumers together from all over the country to get quick, gut-level reactions is not without its fans. Companies are finding that online bulletin boards, where a moderator posts a question and consumers respond when they want—and thus are able to give their responses more thought—are useful, says Gerry Katz, executive vice president of Applied Marketing Science, in Waltham, Mass. Although spending on this type of online research is still negligible today, over time, these bulletin boards are likely to become more popular.

(Cont.)

for people knowledgeable, informed and open-minded, and ahead of the curve, Influentials are very appropriate to study in qualitative research," adds Keller.

Naturally, there seems to be an infinite number of ways to segment the U.S. population, and qualitative researchers are also taking advantage of advances in geodemographics to improve their recruiting pool. As it happens, segmentation science is advancing to the point where psychographic and demographic characteristics, as well as media usage and purchasing behavior, can be overlaid, down to the neighborhood level—and now down to the household level. "Knowing exactly who you're going to get in a focus group is a way of eliminating respondent bias. It gives you a more accurate and more efficient method of identifying intended targets for focus groups, and of learning more about their lifestyle and media preferences even before they come in the door," says Josh Herman, product manager for segmentation at research firm Acxiom, in Little Rock, Ark.

Last Spring, Acxiom began to offer a database called Personicx, a system which assigns to each U.S. household a specific segment based on life stage, purchasing behavior and attitudes. While databases like this have long been available at the neighborhood level, the ability to target households within a neighborhood is a more specific form of segmentation that should be particularly useful to focus group researchers, says Herman. [The database is updated monthly.]

A case in point: Though the United States Department of Agriculture [USDA] isn't necessarily the first entity you'd think of as being on the cutting-edge of marketing, it relied on Personicx last year. The agency wanted to get a food-safety message out to households who were most at risk of improperly cooking burgers or mishandling salmon. The system enabled the USDA to recruit focus groups from households it believed fit a target demographic and psychographic profile, and it was also able to use its knowledge of the segments to help analyze the results.

DIGGING DEEPER

Once the respondents are recruited, focus group researchers plan their strategy for getting at what consumers really think and feel. It's a task that has always been a challenge for qualitative researchers—one that has depended on the skill of the moderator, says Kirk Ward, formerly director of new-product development at Hershey and now president of Innovation Focus Research in Lancaster, Pa. Phil Johnston, senior vice president at

Cleveland-based ad agency Marcus Thomas, LLC, whose clients include the Cleveland Indians and Alcoa, agrees, saying that as Americans are sampled more frequently, they become more research-savvy.

"As people are exposed to more research, they begin to understand what's expected of them," he says. Frequently, consumers will simply parrot back marketing or advertising messages, which offers little to companies seeking consumer insights.

To help consumers relax and thereby elicit more authentic responses, qualitative researchers have been turning to approaches proven effective in ethnographic research. For one thing, they might downplay the marketing agenda of the research experience. "What will increasingly happen is moderators will acknowledge the importance of environment," says Insights' Cohen. "I've always been a big believer in using environments that are much more comfortable and that are more adaptive to the product," she says. She finds it more effective, for example, to speak to women about female health products in a living room setting rather than at a conference table, and to speak to children in a room arranged like a play area. Some companies are starting to offer researchers this flexibility, she says. INGather Research in Denver, Colo., offers facilities where focus groups can be held that look just like a living room, a kitchen, a playroom, a bar and even a courtroom—and all are equipped with large two-way mirrors along one wall.

Some qualitative researchers are turning away from focus groups entirely, believing that one-on-one interviews are more valuable then group interviews in obtaining fresh insights.

Other qualitative researchers are breaking through people's defenses by resorting to subtle trickery. Rather than simply holding up print advertisements in a focus group and asking for reactions—which is not the way that consumers would encounter the ads in the real world—the Marcus Thomas firm inserted the print ads for a campaign it was testing into magazine mock-ups. "We then had the moderator, before leaving the room, tell the respondents that in addition to the task at hand, we were evaluating certain publications, and to take a few minutes to flip through the magazines," says Johnston, senior vice president at Marcus Thomas. As a result, the firm was

(Cont.)

able to observe the focus group recruits interacting with the advertising in a more authentic manner.

JUST YOU AND I

Some qualitative researchers are turning away from groups entirely. Gerry Katz, executive vice president of Applied Marketing Science, in Waltham, Mass., says that for new-product development, one-on-one interviews are more valuable than group interviews in obtaining fresh insights. Katz says that when a company conducts "voice of the customer" research for new product development, searching for wants and needs not yet met in the marketplace, the goal is to hear something new—and group dynamics can often make that difficult. [He points to a 1993 study by Abbie Griffin and John Hauser, published in the journal *Marketing Science,* that compared focus groups to one-on-one interviews. Griffin and Hauser found that, hour for hour, individual interviews elicited more useful comments.]

Zaltman, at Harvard, is also a fan of the one-on-one interview. He believes that one-on-one interviews are better poised to take advantage of the cutting edge of cognitive science. He's highly skeptical about consumers' ability to report on their decision-making process accurately—or on the true state of their emotions. Zaltman argues that consumers rarely are rational when making decisions, that they rely far more on emotions than on rational thinking when they decide what to buy. Further, he maintains that consumers can't really describe their decision-making process because they "have far less access to their mental activities than marketers give them credit for—95 percent of thinking takes place in the unconscious mind." [For more on Zaltman's approach, see "The Power of Images" in *American Demographics,* Nov. 2001.] In his view, self-reported descriptions of a decision-making process may provide next to no insight into what actually motivated that person to behave in a certain way.

Zaltman believes that smart companies will start to exploit the advances made in the 1990s in physiological and psychological research. Market researchers can now study the movements of subjects' pupils, for example, to gain a window into unconscious emotions, and can measure the lag time in responses to questions, known as "latency response," to gain useful insights. On the frontier is the use of neuroimaging in market research. By hooking people up to a magnetic resonance imaging machine [MRI] and showing them advertisements, researchers could visually track bloodflow to the parts of the brain associated with positive or negative emotions, or the parts of the brain associated with memory, and get a more accurate read on how the participants are feeling and whether they will remember an advertisement.

This doesn't mean that scientific advances and whizbang technology will put focus groups out of business. Even Zaltman concedes that "there are circumstances where I think focus groups are warranted." For example, he says that if you want to learn the vocabulary a group of consumers uses to describe an experience or if you want to know about how word-of-mouth operates, focus groups are appropriate. "But you shouldn't use focus group to get in-depth insights," he says. Since focus groups typically run two hours and involve 10 people, he argues that each person gets only 12 minutes of time. "You can't get very far—you can't get very much depth—in 12 minutes with any one individual," Zaltman says. And since depth is the goal, the group approach that has been a fixture in marketing research for the past six decades may go the way of the dinosaur.

36

Mystery Shoppers Going High-Tech

They 'Spy' On Retailers
. . . .

Small digital cameras
and laptop computers
now tools of the trade
. . . .

By Stephanie Wilkinson
Investor's Business Daily

The man sits in his car in a Krispy Kreme parking lot, but he's not eating doughnuts.

He's tapping into his laptop computer. He stops and opens the box of doughnuts on the seat next to him. He cuts open a jelly-filled morsel, looks at it and places it on the box top. He reaches into his briefcase and takes out a small, pen-shaped camera. Then he snaps digital photos of the cut-open doughnut.

He clicks the camera into a cradle attached to his laptop to transfer the photos to the computer. He uses a cable to link his cell phone to his laptop, log onto the Internet and then e-mail the photos to headquarters.

Doughnut fanatic? No, this man is one of the new breed of high-tech mystery shoppers.

In the old days, individuals armed with nothing more than a paper questionnaire would make unscheduled visits to stores to check up on product quality and customer service. Their paper reports took days to process, creating a crucial lag between the time of the visit and the time when corporate decision-makers got the full report.

In some cases, companies found, certain mystery shoppers weren't bothering to go to the target stores at all. They made up answers. Mystery shopping got a few black eyes.

Today, thanks to such things as digital photography, camera miniaturization and the Internet, mystery shopping has been rejuvenated. One company bringing technology to the mystery-shopper/quality-control field is Pacific Research Group Inc. of Costa Mesa, Calif.

Steve Anderson, customer experience manager at Krispy Kreme Doughnuts

Corp., based in Winston-Salem, N.C., says his company switched to PRG 18 months ago to conduct its ongoing mystery shopper program. Its previous mystery shopping company relied on paper, film-based photography and other low-tech methods.

"We made the shift because of PRG's use of newer technologies," he said. "We used to have to wait five weeks to see a report. Now we see them within 48 hours (of a mystery shopper's visit). If a store is inspected on Saturday and you get the report on Monday, you're much more likely to see problems get fixed."

PRG contracts with thousands of freelance shoppers around the country to perform surprise visits to fast-food outlets, gas stations, airlines and a host of other kinds of businesses.

PRG Likes PenCam

In total, PRG shoppers average 12,000 store visits a month, he says.

To qualify as a mystery shopper, candidates are required to have a Windows-based laptop and a minidigital camera. PRG has a link at its Web site to that of the PenCam, a tiny $59 digital camera made by Aiptek Inc. of Irvine, Calif. But mystery shoppers can use any such camera that works. For laptops, the PRG Web site includes links to the Dell Computer Corp. and Compaq Computer Corp. Web sites.

Before shoppers are given an assignment, they must take an online tutorial tailored to the specific client company and pass a test. "With digital photography, we can include photos in the tutorials to let the trainees know exactly what they should be looking for," said Darren Magot, vice president of sales at PRG. "We can show them exactly what constitutes a clean bathroom, or what a perfectly filled doughnut looks like."

"We use to have to wait five weeks to see a report. Now we see them within 48 hours."

Steve Anderson, *Krispy Kreme Doughnuts*
. . . .

The retail client company works with PRG to create an electronic questionnaire. Typically a mystery shopper looks at such things as trash in the parking lot, friendliness of the store's staff and the serving temperature of the food.

Armed with minidigital camera and laptop, the shopper visits the store, makes a purchase and discreetly takes photographs.

Usually, shoppers retreat to their cars to fill out the questionnaire on the computer. Then they choose which photos to include. The reports are e-mailed to PRG editors, and then go to the customer's headquarters or store managers. The photos provide a lot of detail and remove much subjectivity, says Magot. "There's less opinion and more fact," he said. "It's hard to argue with photos."

The reports, though, serve many purposes, say Magot and Anderson. "They're not just used as a whipping stick," said Magot. "Many positive incentives are tied to the results of these stores."

Krispy Kreme franchisees, for instance, can earn trips to national conferences by doing well in these random spot checks. Each of the company's 215 stores is visited by a mystery shopper once a month.

New Camera Focus

Key to the evolution of the mystery shopper is the advent of cheap, small digital cameras. As the prices of digital cameras continue to fall and their resolution improves, other business uses of these small cameras will surface, says Michelle Slaughter, an analyst at InfoTrends Research Group Inc. in Boston.

That will be good news for the makers of these products. The market for sub-$100 digital cameras has actually declined, Slaughter says, from $136 million in revenue in 2000 to $46 million in 2001.

Several factors contributed to the big decline. For one, market leader Polaroid Corp. filed for bankruptcy reorganization. It's discontinuing its line of digital cameras. Slaughter says other makers also closed down or stopped making the cameras.

"Until recently, small cameras have been perceived as mere novelties, with manufacturers coming and going in the market rapidly," she said.

(Cont.)

Companies made the mistake of targeting these small cameras to kids, who turned out not so interested in digital photography, she says.

"But as performance of sub-$100 cameras gets better and the learning curve eases, corporate consumers ought to help the market bounce back," Slaughter said. "Many industries such as real estate, insurance and construction already are taking advantage of digital photography."

Reprinted from *Investor's Business Daily,* May 3, 2002. Used with permission.

37

Data Mining: Welcome to Harrah's

You give us your money. We learn everything about you. And then you thank us and beg for more. How's that for a business model?

By: Joe Ashbrook Nickell, **April 2002 Issue**

If you ever want to witness, close up, the unheralded magic of the modern gaming business, just wander down any aisle full of chirping, chiming slot machines and watch the folks clutching the plastic buckets and pulling the levers. One afternoon last May at the Rio Resort in Las Vegas, I did just that—and plopped down in front of a 25-cent video poker machine to experience it all first-hand. For 10 minutes or so, I dolefully fed quarters into my Bally's "Deuces Wild" until I'd dropped $20. Then I moved on to a handful of other machines—a "Monopoly" slot game, video blackjack, and several more varieties of video poker. After nearly two hours on the floor, I'd notched just one decent jackpot ($40), I was out $350, and I wanted to leave.

Not exactly a magical experience for me. But for Harrah's Entertainment (HET), the parent company of the Rio and two dozen other casinos around the country, even brief slot binges like mine are worth far more today than their weight in quarters. As I moved from machine to machine, a tangle of computers in a Harrah's office in Memphis, Tenn., was collecting the biggest prize of all—an astonishingly detailed account of each second I spent at the Rio. Harrah's took note of how many different machines I had played on (nine), how many separate wagers I placed (637), my average bet (25 cents), and, of course, the total amount of money—called "coin-in"—I'd deposited in the machines. By the time I left the Rio, Harrah's had compiled enough information about me to build a detailed profile of my gambling habits, a plan for luring me back to the casino, even an individual profit-and-loss projection by which the company would gauge its future marketing investment in me. If traditional slot machines are one-armed bandits, these things are one-armed diabolical geniuses in the Dr. No/Goldfinger class.

And for all that information, Harrah's has an innocuous little piece of plastic to thank: a colorful card with a magnetic stripe that Harrah's slot players insert into machines while they play. Twenty-five million Harrah's customers, in fact, use these personalized frequent-gambler cards, called Total Rewards, to earn free trips, meals, hotel rooms, and other freebies while they test the decidedly long odds of slot playing. Harrah's, in turn, uses that data to refine its customer database, which now includes 90 targeted demographic segments, each of which receives custom-tailored direct-mail incentives to visit any of Harrah's 25 properties around the United States.

There's a reason, of course, that Harrah's works so hard to glean all the data it can from the slot crowds. Slots and other electronic gaming machines account for the majority of Harrah's $3.7 billion in revenue, and more than 80 percent of the company's operating profit. Largely on the strength of its new tracking and data-mining system for slot players, Harrah's—once an also-ran chain of casinos—has emerged in recent years as the second-largest operator in the United States (behind MGM Entertainment) with the highest three-year investment return in the industry.

> **HARRAH'S NATIONWIDE SLOT-TRACKING SYSTEM DOES WHAT EVEN ITS BEST CUSTOMERS CAN'T: MAKE GOOD BETS.**

If you believe the man who built that system for Harrah's—former Harvard business professor Gary Loveman, now the company's chief operating officer—the company's recent prosperity has little or nothing to do with cultivating his customers' impulses to gamble. It has everything to do, he says, with simply getting to know them so well through data profiling that he can give them the perfect reasons—a steak here, a free hotel room there—not to spend money at other casinos, where the odds, after all, aren't any better. "This is a whole new world that we couldn't get our hands around before," Loveman says. "All we used to know was how much money we made on each machine, but we couldn't connect what kind of customer used them. Now," he says, "I can get on

Who Gets the Free Steak?

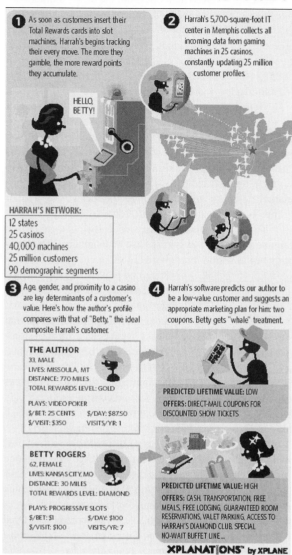

① As soon as customers insert their Total Rewards cards into slot machines, Harrah's begins tracking their every move. The more they gamble, the more reward points they accumulate.

HELLO, BETTY!

② Harrah's 5,700-square-foot IT center in Memphis collects all incoming data from gaming machines in 25 casinos, constantly updating 25 million customer profiles.

HARRAH'S NETWORK:
12 states
25 casinos
40,000 machines
25 million customers
90 demographic segments

③ Age, gender, and proximity to a casino are key determinants of a customer's value. Here's how the author's profile compares with that of "Betty," the ideal composite Harrah's customer.

④ Harrah's software predicts our author to be a low-value customer and suggests an appropriate marketing plan for him: two coupons. Betty gets "whale" treatment.

THE AUTHOR
33, MALE
LIVES: MISSOULA, MT
DISTANCE: 770 MILES
TOTAL REWARDS LEVEL: GOLD

PLAYS: VIDEO POKER
$/BET: 25 CENTS $/DAY: $87.50
$/VISIT: $350   VISITS/YR: 1

PREDICTED LIFETIME VALUE: LOW
OFFERS: DIRECT-MAIL COUPONS FOR DISCOUNTED SHOW TICKETS

BETTY ROGERS
62, FEMALE
LIVES: KANSAS CITY, MO
DISTANCE: 30 MILES
TOTAL REWARDS LEVEL: DIAMOND

PLAYS: PROGRESSIVE SLOTS
$/BET: $1 $/DAY: $100
$/VISIT: $100   VISITS/YR: 7

PREDICTED LIFETIME VALUE: HIGH
OFFERS: CASH, TRANSPORTATION, FREE MEALS, FREE LODGING, GUARANTEED ROOM RESERVATIONS, VALET PARKING, ACCESS TO HARRAH'S DIAMOND CLUB, SPECIAL NO-WAIT BUFFET LINE...

XPLANATIONS™ by XPLANE

Archaic as they might seem now, the clubs proliferated and triggered an important shift in the industry: By the end of the 1980s, machines surpassed table games as the major casinos' biggest source of income.

Customer service, however, remained stuck in the 1970s. Casino managers who had long recognized the importance of building relationships with their most profitable clientele reserved star treatment for so-called whales, the big spenders that Las Vegas traditionally coveted, but only an occasional free drink for the folks toting plastic buckets.

All of that began to change in the early 1990s, when casinos began installing computerized systems that kept records on individual players. Using the magnetic strips on plastic cards, they allowed casinos to build records for an unlimited number of customers, and offer "comps" and other incentives based on the amount of money inserted into machines, not the amount won. At about the same time, state and federal laws changed to legalize gambling on riverboats and Indian reservations, and operators raced to open their doors in new markets. Between 1990 and 1997, Harrah's alone tripled the number of casinos it operated.

But as new markets grew more competitive, the business reached the point of diminishing return: Harrah's often found its early arrival usurped by grander, more extravagant casinos that opened next door. Making matters worse, each Harrah's casino operated and marketed itself separately from the others—"a system of feudal fiefdoms," says John Boushy, Harrah's chief information officer. "While management at each of our properties had been thinking, 'This is my customer,' customers had been wondering why they didn't get the same treatment at different Harrah's properties," Boushy says.

By 1997, Boushy and CEO Phil Satre understood that devising the means to keep their 25 million slot players loyal to Harrah's was the key not only to capturing the biggest share of their wallets, but also to staying a step ahead of competing chains. They began to consider the idea of electronically linking all of Harrah's players clubs—so that when Harrah's riverboat gamblers in Mississippi flew to Vegas, they could redeem their reward points for free Harrah's meals, rooms, or shows.

Enter Loveman, then a 37-year-old associate professor of business administration at Harvard who had never, he says, set foot in a casino. But occasionally he taught special classes on the service industry to Harrah's executives. The classes, as well as Loveman's research, focused on the profitability-through-customer-loyalty equation that intrigued Satre.

the system and say, 'Where are all the 60-or-older females from North Carolina playing?' Boom, I'll know. This is the replacement of intuition and hunch with science."

How Loveman's system led to a turnaround of sorts for Harrah's underlines how painfully slow one of America's biggest service industries has been in getting to know its customers. In the first slot-machine "players clubs" introduced in the 1980s, the best slot customers were given punch cards, which attendants notched whenever customers hit jackpots; once the cards had enough notches, customers redeemed them for meals or other incentives.

(Cont.)

As he got to know the company and the gaming business, Loveman saw an opportunity to stress-test his theories. After trading notes with Satre, he outlined his idea to turn card data from each casino over to a central marketing brain for the company. Loveman soon found himself in Vegas, sitting in on executive strategy meetings and building support for his plan. In 1998, Satre gave Loveman the post of chief operating officer and a mandate to launch the system.

Today, Harrah's network links more than 40,000 gaming machines in 12 states, and operates on the belief that customers will, given the right inducements, become "brand-loyal" to Harrah's. In just the first two years of the Total Rewards program, the company saw a $100 million increase in revenue from customers who gambled at more than one Harrah's casino. "We were getting 36 cents of every dollar that our customers spent in casinos," Loveman says. "We realized that if we could just get to 40 cents, that would be monstrous." Harrah's current "wallet share" now stands at 42 percent. "If you increase that number ever so slightly," he adds, "the benefit to income statement and shareholder value is astronomical." He has a point: Since 1998, each percentage-point increase in Harrah's share of its customers' overall gambling budgets has coincided with an additional $125 million in shareholder value.

The central feature (and perhaps the greatest irony) of Loveman's system is its ability to do what its 25 million customers cannot—that is, consistently make good bets. Before I even sat down for my round of video poker at the Rio, for example, Harrah's had a pretty good hunch that I wouldn't be financing its next round of employee bonuses. It suspected that from the moment I signed up for my Total Rewards card in the casino lobby and filled in my name, address, date of birth, and driver's license number. Since I was a 32-year-old man from the distant state of Montana, Harrah's predicted that my long-term potential was already low. I was at the Rio three nights, yet I spent a total of just four hours and 40 minutes gambling. As Loveman explains, "It's important to know when to pull away from an investment in a customer [who] is not going to return." He attributes $20 million in annual cost reductions to the Total Rewards program.

Starting with four key pieces of information—your gender, your age, where you live, and what you play—Harrah's software predicts which customers are most likely

> I KNEW I WASN'T COMING BACK AS SOON AS I FINISHED MY FIRST ROLL OF QUARTERS. SOMEHOW, HARRAH'S KNEW THAT TOO.

to become big spenders. Then it designs appropriate marketing strategies—direct-mail offers are the most common—to lure those customers back. "Most companies look at it on a product-by-product basis: 'I want to generate this much revenue on a particular product,'" says Rich Mirman, a veteran of consulting firm Booz Allen Hamilton, whom Loveman hired as Harrah's marketing chief. "We flip that around: We want to maximize every relationship."

To make his point, Mirman sketches out the example of a Las Vegas vacationer who spends a week at the Mirage, blowing $1,000 a day in the casino. If that person wanders into the Rio, she may spend only $300 in its casino—yet she is exactly the kind of customer the Rio wants to draw. If the Rio doesn't match or beat the direct-marketing offers from the Mirage, "it doesn't take a lot of brains to realize she's not coming back," he says.

That's why Harrah's decided early on to approach each new customer as a long-term acquaintance. The company began sifting through gigabytes of customer data collected by player-tracking systems at the various Harrah's properties during the previous five years. Loveman and Mirman found that the 30 percent of their customers who spent between $100 and $500 per visit to a Harrah's casino accounted for 80 percent of company revenues—and almost 100 percent of profits. That's because those gamblers were typically locals who—unlike me—visited regional Harrah's properties frequently.

Loveman eventually began to reverse-engineer profiles of the ideal Harrah's customer. "Age and distance from the casino are critical predictors of frequency, coupled with the kind of game you play and how many coins you play per game," Loveman explains. He paints a picture of the perfect player: a 62-year-old woman who lives within 30 minutes of Kansas City, Mo., and plays dollar video poker. Such customers typically have substantial disposable cash, plenty of time on their hands, and easy access to a Harrah's riverboat casino (in this case, on the Missouri River in North Kansas City). "If we only observe her once in a quarter, it's likely that's because she's playing three or four times a quarter at our competitors," Loveman says. "So we're going to make an educated guess and market to her as if she were a more frequent visitor, and we'll let her confirm or disconfirm that. Then we'll update the profile based on what she does."

Once the Harrah's system identifies high-value customers, it places them into corresponding demographic seg-

(Cont.)

ments. (Harrah's maintains 90 such segments.) Customers who live far away from Harrah's properties typically receive direct-mail discounts or comps on hotel rooms or transportation, while drive-in customers get food, entertainment, or cash incentives. Most offers are time-sensitive, with tight expiration dates, in order to encourage visitors to either return sooner or switch a visit from a competitor to a Harrah's property. For each direct-marketing pitch, the company tracks response rates and return on investment, and adjusts its future campaigns according to the results—all of which is recorded at the company's central database in Memphis. "When I meet with our marketers," Loveman says, "anything we've done new, I ask, did we test it first? And if I find out that we just whole-hogged, went after something without testing it, I'll kill 'em. No matter how clever they think it is, we test it."

As bulletproof as Harrah's system appears to be, it's utterly invisible to customers who, while they might under-stand the long odds of slot playing, know little or nothing about the betting Harrah's does behind the scenes on every scrap of information they provide. Mirman brushes off sug-gestions that the program is deceptive. "If they don't want their play tracked, they don't have to use the card," he says. He acknowledges that certain practices—such as using face-recognition cameras to identify customers—would likely backfire. But, Mirman says, customers needn't worry about the most common privacy affront: Harrah's, he says, will never sell its customer lists to anyone.

Nor would Harrah's—God forbid—ever dream of getting people to actually increase their overall gam-bling. When asked about this, Loveman parries deftly with rhetoric worthy of a tobacco lobbyist. "It's all about customers bringing their existing gaming business to us," he says. "It's rarely about more gambling. It's a lady who lives in Philadelphia, comes to Atlantic City 10 times a year, visits Harrah's three times, but now she's got a reason to come to Harrah's six times." But it doesn't take a cynic to realize that, by offering credits toward comps based on the amount of "coin-in" (the ratio is approxi-mately one reward credit per $10 gambled), and by pro-moting tiered programs such as Total Platinum, Harrah's and other casinos are giving customers more reason than ever to justify more gambling.

Ethical nuances aside, the cold logic behind Love-man's tracking methods has proved to be good medicine for Harrah's. The company's record earnings of $3.7 billion in 2001 were up 11 percent from 2000. And more than half of the revenue at Harrah's three Las Vegas casi-nos now comes from players the company already knows from its casinos outside Nevada.

As for me, well, I already knew I wasn't coming back to Harrah's as soon as I'd finished off that first roll of quar-ters. Somehow, Harrah's knew that too, despite my having generously dropped $350 in one of its casinos in just a few hours. But as Mirman explained before I left, "You live in Montana, you're relatively young, you're playing in Las Vegas, and I would guess that your bankroll is not sufficient to push you into the high-value group." He was right: Since my visit, I've received a single piece of mail from Harrah's: a foldout flier offering discount admission to shows at the Rio, which I promptly tossed. "We would probably predict you'd be unresponsive to the kinds of offers you would qualify for," Mirman said, "so you prob-ably won't hear much from us. But don't worry," he added. "It's just a segmentation, not a personal evaluation."

Like, What's a Spin Cycle?

Trying to Get GenY Psyched About Appliances, Whirlpool Tests Sleek, Portable Wares

By Elliot Spagat

When **Whirlpool Corp.** started studying how it could sell appliances to the 18-to-24-year-old crowd, it dared to watch how young people do their laundry.

The Benton Harbor, Mich., company put cameras in dorm rooms and apartments. It interviewed young adults. And a few things came out in the wash.

Sometimes, doing the laundry meant rinsing jeans in the sink and leaving them to drip. Sometimes, it meant spraying a shirt with deodorant. Unlike those over 30, who often own houses and have families, 20-somethings couldn't care less about spin cycles and water temperatures, said Charles Jones, Whirlpool's vice president of global consumer design. Their ideal machine would have just a single push button.

"If you talk to a Gen-Y'er about laundry and washing and drying clothes, their eyes glaze over and you immediately lose them," he said.

With its traditional market saturated and sales slowing, Whirlpool is looking for ways to reach a relatively untapped group who has

been ignored for good reasons: young adults, who rarely have much money, floor space or interest in appliances. The nation's largest appliance maker is hoping to appeal to young buyers with well-designed products.

The company is testing a sleek and small silver refrigerator, as well as a microwave oven and an air purifier with orange-colored accents, in Best Buy stores in Dallas, Chicago and Los Angeles. It has other items on the drawing board, including a microwave dryer just big enough for a pair or two of jeans. Whirlpool declines to comment on sales; Best Buy, the only retailer where the appliances are being tested, says it is angling to get young customers interested in appliances. Meantime, a **General Electric** Co. spokesman says GE also is developing appliances targeting Gen Y, but wouldn't elaborate.

The efforts come as the Association of Home Appliance Manufacturers estimates that shipments of stoves and ovens will slide 4.3% this year, the first decline since 1995, and shipments of refrigerators will slip 2.6%, only the third drop in 12 years. Shipments of microwave ovens are expected to fall 5.2%.

People under 30 were the least likely to own laundry equipment and full-size refrigerators among any age group tracked last year by the Washington, D.C., industry association.

"These are people who don't have a set lifestyle," says Marise Kumar, Whirlpool's vice president of developing categories. "They move from place to place. They'd like to put all their appliances and household goods in the back of a truck and move to the next location."

Whirlpool studied the group by watching students last year at the University of Illinois at Chicago and the University of Notre Dame in Indiana. In other cities, it doled out disposable cameras to people under 30 and asked them to photograph likes and dislikes.

In addition to discovering that washing clothes is rare, it learned that leftover pizza is a real problem to store.

So an orange refrigerator in the works for the "Pla" (as in "play") line features special internal handles to hold a large pizza box and wheels to make the fridge more portable. The prototype dryer, also orange and shaped like bowling pin tipped on its side, is small enough to sit on a dresser, hold a couple of pairs of jeans, and do the job in 12 minutes. In choosing orange, the company borrowed a page from Apple Computer Inc., which is known for its sleek and coloful designs. The color "makes a statement," says Ms. Kumar.

Whirlpool's efforts began in 2000 when it exhibited funky microwave ovens and cookware, dubbed "Macrowave," at European museums and trade shows. A lightweight, battery-operated oven featured a pop-up top resembling a portable compact disc player and a strap to carry it over your shoulder, just like a purse or knapsack. Another oven had clear panels, so you could watch your frozen dinner turn to a boil. Macrowave ovens were experimental designs and never intended for store shelves.

It followed up with an unusual line of prototype washers and dryers—named "Project F," as in fabric—which made its debut at a Berlin trade show in February. A silver floor-to-ceiling "personal cleaning" box combined separate compartments for a shower, sink, washer and dryer. An environmentally correct washing machine had six small tubs separated by water hyacinth plants that absorb phosphorous from detergent.

Apartment-dwellers say Whirlpool faces a tough sell with its new commercial line. In many parts of the country, apartments come equipped with basic appliances. Lauren Bloxom, a 24-year-old saleswoman for Guess jeans in Dallas, said the sleek wares would have worked in her dorm room but the three-bedroom pad she shares with two roommates includes a full-size refrigerator, microwave oven, washer and dryer.

In high-rent areas, by contrast, apartments may be too small for even the smallest appliances. Gabe Banner, 24, wouldn't mind a few, but the two-bedroom rental he shares with a roommate in Manhattan's East Village is too small even for that, he says. Shelves are stacked high on his walls, and he stashes out-of-season clothes under his bed. To make room for an appliance, he might have to get rid of stereo equipment, an unthinkable trade-off.

And Whirlpool isn't promising any savings. Prices are similar to traditional models, with the minirefrigerator going for $220, the air purifier for $190 and the microwave for $100. Adam Mitchell, a 25-year-old retirement home worker who rents a one-bedroom in Dallas, said he would rather spend spare cash on a TV, a stereo, beer, or on throwing a party.

Making Home Appliances Hip

Whirlpool products in trial stages that are targeted to young adults:

APPLIANCE	DESCRIPTION	PRICE
Compact Refrigerator	4.3 cubic ft., silver panels	$220
Microwave Oven	1.1 cubic ft., orange buttons, orange-tinted window, silver panels	$100
Air Purifier	Purifies 250-square foot-room, white with orange handle	$190
Compact Refrigerator	Orange door with clock, wheels	On exhibit only
Microwave Dryer (shown right)	No vent, small loads only, fits on dresser top	On exhibit only

Unmarked Paid Search Results, Good Or Bad?

Issue Presents Conflicts

. . . .

Web portal Yahoo starts offering such online ads, but top rival Google isn't

. . . .

By Pete Barlas
Investor's Business Daily

All companies can have a tough time pleasing both customers and investors, but the conflict is causing a little more soul-searching for Internet search service providers.

And the two leaders, Google Inc. and Yahoo Inc., are making opposite moves in this delicate dance, just at a time when their search rivalry is heating up.

Web portal Yahoo this week began selling ads in places that had been off-limits to advertisers.

The ads—basically links to an advertiser's Web site—will appear in a user's search results. Apparently, they won't be marked as "sponsored" links or as paid ads. Google, which is mulling what many analysts say will be the biggest Internet IPO since the dot-boom, says it won't sell such ads.

Yahoo could reap millions of dollars in new revenue from selling these ads—and Google could be leaving those dollars on the table. But Yahoo's move could backfire, and Google's could succeed, if users believe the new ads compromise Yahoo's ability to deliver good, objective search results.

The financial rewards from these ads could be huge for Yahoo, says Steve Schepke, a vice president at Internet ad firm Meandaur Inc.

"It's a big deal because it's a new revenue opportunity," he said. "The numbers I have heard are upward of $100 million a year potentially if this product is successful, which I think it's going to be."

Generates Traffic

This new type of ad is called paid inclusion. Advertisers pay just to be guaranteed a place in the search results of a given search keyword or term.

This differs from so-called pay per performance listings. Those guarantee that an advertiser's link will appear at or near the top of the rankings of a given search result.

These ads, though, are marked as sponsored links and often are shaded or in some other way indicate to users that the company paid.

Getting a spot in Yahoo's search results could attract many users to a Web page. In December, Yahoo ranked as the No. 1 U.S. Web property with 11 million unique visitors, says market tracker comScore Networks Inc.

Google also ranked high, at No. 5.

The issue for Yahoo is that consumers might not appreciate it including unmarked, paid links in an area of search results that have been ad free, says Greg Sterling, an analyst the Kelsey Group, a research firm.

"Yahoo has to strike a delicate balance," he said. "They want to maximize revenue, but preserving a good user experience has got to be the paramount concern."

Yahoo began rolling out its paid inclusion program late Tuesday night. The company plans to roll out the program over all of its international sites over the next few weeks.

Yahoo says consumers need not be wary of paid inclusion. Advertisers in the paid inclusion plan get their Web sites updated faster than those not in the program.

The service helps bring more sites with more relevant information to a consumers' attention, says Jeff Weiner, senior vice president of Yahoo search and marketplace.

"It works well for our content providers and it works well for our users because we are improving relevancy," he said, "and it works well for Yahoo."

Yahoo also is looking to find new sources of revenue. And its search results offer a lot of space that can be leveraged into big bucks, says Danny Sullivan, editor of Search EngineWatch, an online news service on this market. "The vast majority of the Web pages on Yahoo don't generate any money for Yahoo," he said. "So if you go to paid inclusion, you are maximizing the real estate."

Yahoo will use search software from Inktomi to introduce the paid listings to its search results. Yahoo bought the search software unit of Inktomi last year for about $235 million.

Yahoo will sell the paid search results to an advertiser at a fixed price. Analysts estimate that 20 cents per click is a likely amount. Advertisers will pay only when a consumer clicks on their site as a result of a Yahoo search.

Yahoo and other search companies, such as Ask Jeeves Inc. and FindWhat.com Inc., have cashed in on pay per performance ad revenue. It helped Yahoo report a fourth-quarter per-share profit of 11 cents, up from 8 cents in the year-ago period. Revenue jumped 132% to $663.9 million.

With pay per performance, advertisers bid for a high placement for a given search keyword or phrase.

Search Is On

Paid search revenue on sites such as Yahoo and Google is expected to grow faster than online ad or classified revenue in the U.S.

Source: Jupiter Research

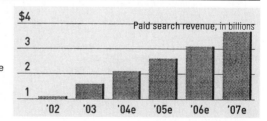

Paid search revenue, in billions

(Cont.)

The more they pay, the higher they rank among search results when a consumer does a Web keyword query. Here, too, advertisers don't pay a cent until a consumer clicks on their ad from a search results page.

The Federal Trade Commission requires that search companies label their pay per performance ads as "sponsored links."

But no such labeling is required for paid inclusion listings.

Other sites already include such listings. Microsoft Corp.'s MSN Internet service mixes paid inclusion listings from Inktomi with normal, unpaid listings.

Could Be Backlash

Yahoo hasn't said whether it will provide any label for its paid inclusion listings. But it's unlikely to do so unless the FTC requires it, says Matthew Berk, an independent analyst in New York.

"If they don't have to, then why should they?" he said.

The FTC is less concerned about paid inclusion than pay per performance ads, since the former doesn't guarantee a ranking in a search. "With paid inclusion, there's no guarantee that (a company link) shows up first," Berk said.

Advertisers can, of course, simply trust that their Web site will appear in a search result. But by paying, they guarantee it will happen. And they pay far less to Yahoo and other search engines for paid inclusion than they would for the high ranking of pay per performance.

But if consumers can't tell between paid and other listings, and they want to, that could be a problem for Yahoo, says Sullivan.

"There could be a backlash from consumers," he said.

Yahoo must make sure it balances paid and unpaid listings in its search, says Kelsey Group's Sterling.

"If Yahoo integrates too much paid content into search results, the company risks compromising that user experience," he said.

Yahoo has become one of the largest Internet companies in part by providing a reliable search service.

The company says it plans to use a staff of human editors to make sure that only the most relevant paid inclusion ads appear in any search query. Analysts say adding another layer of human editors sometimes helps provide more relevant search results than using just software.

The additional cash, though, is a big lure to start paid inclusion, says Schepke.

"The $100 million sitting out there is the real reason they are going to push that stuff out," he said.

Google, though, has stayed away from paid inclusion listings, and it says it will continue to do so. Paid listings violate the trust of delivering unbiased search results, says Jonathan Rosenberg, vice president of product management for Google.

"A paid inclusion result is not in the best interests of the consumer," he said.

But if Google's investors see Yahoo getting big bucks from paid inclusion, they could nudge Google executives to give it a try.

Said Berk, "How can you say to investors, 'We're not going to do this because we think it's philosophically bad,' but then Yahoo says it's ringing up the cash register?"

Reprinted from *Investor's Business Daily*, February 19, 2004. Used by permission.

40

Never Heard Of Acxiom?
Chances Are It's Heard Of You.

How a little-known Little Rock company—the world's largest processor of consumer data—found itself at the center of a very big national security debate.
■ *by Richard Behar*

Last summer a sheriff in Cincinnati stumbled onto what may have been the biggest security breach of consumer data ever. Searching the home of Daniel Baas, a 24-year-old computer-systems administrator at a data-marketing firm, detectives found dozens of compact discs containing the personal data of millions of Americans. The information, it turned out, had been hacked by Baas over a period of two years from a giant server in Arkansas belonging to a company called Acxiom.

Never heard of Acxiom? The publicly traded, politically connected Little Rock company is the world's largest processor of consumer data, collecting and massaging more than a billion records a day. Its customers include nine of the country's top ten credit-card issuers, as well as nearly all the major retail banks, insurers, and automakers. It's a business that generates $1 billion in sales annually and, after a few bumpy years, is expected to produce $60 million in profits. Analysts project earnings to grow 15% annually over the next five years.

For most of its life, Acxiom (the "c" is silent) has kept a low profile—its corporate customers like it that way. But lately it has found itself at the center of a white-hot swirl of anti-terrorism, national security, and consumer-privacy issues. Remember the flap about JetBlue giving passenger records to a government contractor? And the one about John Poindexter's terrorism futures exchange? They all touched Acxiom.

And in the middle of all that, it now turns out, Acxiom itself was getting hacked. While there's no evidence that Baas—who pleaded guilty in December to federal cybercrime charges—used the stolen data for any commercial purpose, the case raises serious questions about the vulnerability of databases at companies like Acxiom, which should be the most secure.

Indeed, another electronic break-in was discovered during a self-audit by Acxiom following a tip-off from authorities about another intrusion. Acxiom reported the second incident to government investigators.

The group of hackers in Boca Raton, Fla. who had penetrated the same Acxiom server for three months last year also accessed data on millions of Americans. Once again, it doesn't appear that consumers were defrauded, but indictments aren't expected before March. "We dodged a howitzer with that one," admits Charles Morgan, Acxiom's longtime chairman and CEO. "It was a whole company—a bunch of crooks. If it had been the Russian mafia, we would have been in a hell of a mess."

Such embarrassments come at a bad time, not just for Acxiom but for America. Since 9/11, the company has been campaigning for crucial federal contracts in homeland security.

> "We dodged a howitzer," says Morgan. "If it had been the Russian mafia, we would have been in a hell of a mess."

Retired general and presidential candidate Wesley Clark and the Clintons have helped. But until recently, Acxiom officials were unaware that their own homeland had been breached. Baas easily cracked Acxiom's passwords, helping himself to unencrypted data belonging to 10% of Acxiom's customer base—upwards of 200 large companies. "This is a wake-up call for us and our industry," says Morgan.

As Morgan knows, the stakes go way beyond the privacy of consumers. Since 2001,

Acxiom has engaged in research with the Pentagon and other agencies to find ways to consolidate, link, and share data. The federal Transportation Security Administration recently announced that this summer it will roll out its controversial second-generation Computer Assisted Passenger Prescreening System, or CAPPS II—a scheme that color-codes airline passengers in terms of their likelihood to be terrorists. The project will rely heavily on Acxiom's data and its identity-matching logarithms. Privacy advocates worry that systems such as CAPPS will hurt the innocent by producing streams of false positives. But the opposite may be the case. In late December several flights from Paris to the U.S. were grounded because intelligence intercepts misidentified a half-dozen people as possible threats, including a 5-year-old child mistaken for an al Qaeda pilot. Had Acxiom's identity-resolution system been in place, that probably wouldn't have happened.

Many say the use of private-sector data is critical in the fight against terrorism. "Government must have access to that information," concludes a recent report by the Markle Foundation, which focuses on technology policy and whose 36-member security task force includes Clark. "The travel, hotel, financial, immigration, health, or educational records of a person suspected by our government of planning terrorism may hold information that is vital."

By most accounts, nobody does a better job of identity verification than Acxiom, which is rapidly expanding its reach in Europe and Asia. "The Acxioms of the world—these are citizen patriots in this new war," says David Aufhauser, the Treasury Department's recently departed general counsel. "It's as if it's 1776 all over again. A great deal of the intelligence that we receive in the shadow war on terror is suspect—the product of capture, interrogation, bribery, deceit, false feints, or, abroad, torture. Information in financial or personal databases provides a measured counterpoint."

But as much as the country may need Acxiom, the hacking incidents could be rocket fuel for those who oppose CAPPS and similar programs. Clark, for one, appears to be distancing himself from his lobbying for the data giant. "Had I still been on that [Acxiom] board when all this was going through," Clark said in a presidential candidates' debate last month, "I would have insisted that ACLU and others be brought in to preapprove CAPPS II." (In fact, Clark was on the board through most of the process.)

Acxiom itself has been downplaying the hacking breaches—it hasn't said anything publicly about the Florida attack—as it tries to maintain the confidence of both its corporate clients and its federal benefactors. Even so, an Acxiom team is beefing up the company's computer security in ways that may also become a model for Washington. That need is pressing: A recent government report concludes that many federal agencies, including the Department of Homeland Security, are failing in computer security.

To grasp what is at risk, one need only take a walk through Acxiom's five-acre data center in Conway, Ark. Thousands of servers and storage units—a city of blinking six-foot boxes —quietly process the billions of data bits that flow into the company each second. As silent as Mars, Planet Acxiom has few signs of life beyond a handful of geeky traffic controllers monitoring the liftoffs and landings of data in cyberspace on NASA-sized screens. "Think of it as an automated factory, where the product we make is data," says a manager. In a separate, locked glass room known as the shark tank, black plastic fins jut from the tops of some of the 70 servers and storage units. "Some clients don't work well in the same sandbox," explains Jeff Kauble, who co-manages the complex. Citigroup? Allstate? Homeland Security? He won't say. Another client insists its data be stored miles away, in the sealed underground vault of a former government building.

Once upon a time in America a savvy store clerk knew that you had, say, three kids, an old Ford, a pool, and a passion for golf and yellow sweaters. Today Acxiom is that store clerk. It manages 20 billion customer records, has enough storage space to house all the information in the Library of Congress 50 times over, and maintains a database on 96% of U.S. households that gives marketers a so-called real-time, 360-degree view of their customers.

How? Acxiom provides a 13-digit code for every person, "so we can identify you wherever you go," says the company's demographics guru, Bruce Carroll. Each person is placed into one of 70 lifestyle clusters, ranging from "Rolling Stones" and "Single City Struggles" to "Timeless Elders." Nearly one-third of Americans change their clusters annually as a result of a "lifestyle trigger event," Carroll says. Acxiom's catalog also offers hundreds of lists, including a "pre-movers file," updated daily, of people preparing to change residences, as well as lists of people sorted by the frequency with which they use credit cards, the square footage of their homes, and their interest in the "strange and unusual." Says Carroll: "We're pushing a new paradigm."

The man behind the paradigm is Morgan, who joined the company in 1972 and built the industry's first large-scale, multisourced database in 1978. Although he just turned 61, the IBM-trained engineer still drives a Harley to work, pilots the company plane, and until last year drove in NASCAR races. "Charles is the guy you want to have flying the airplane if something goes wrong," says Acxiom's general counsel, Jerry Jones. "He can take in lots of information and make decisions. He tweaks algorithms in his spare time and loves to drill down into the data."

A decade ago Morgan got rid of most titles

> "This is very powerful data," Clark said— "absolutely what the government needs to be aware of."

at Acxiom and sardined top executives, himself included, into ten-by ten-foot offices. The moves have paid off: For five of the past seven years, Acxiom was among FORTUNE's 100 best places to work in America. Morgan is two years ahead of the marketplace in using grid-based processing—replacing expensive servers with cheap, interconnected PCs to dramatically drive down costs and improve processing speeds. He's also critical of the government's anti-terror infrastructure. While the two-year-old Patriot Act sanctions the sharing of data between the government and private parties, Congress only recently approved the FBI's expanded power to demand records from securities and car dealers, travel agencies, and currency exchanges. But operators of ships, trains, and planes still don't have the ability or authority to verify a simple driver's license. "Homeland Security has done a poor job of doing just about anything," Morgan says.

When America was attacked on 9/11, Acxiom was in a unique position to help. Shortly after the FBI released the names of the 19 hijackers on Sept. 14, Acxiom located 11 of them in its databases. "Call the FBI," suggested company director Mack McLarty, former chief of staff in Bill Clinton's White House. By day's end, subpoena in hand, a team of FBI agents had moved into Acxiom's headquarters. "Isn't there something you guys can be doing to help?" former President Clinton, a friend of Acxiom counsel Jones's, asked in a call to the company a few days later. "We are," said Jones.

Clinton visited the company's Little Rock offices on Oct. 5, 2001, and phoned Attorney General John Ashcroft to encourage him to use Acxiom for passenger ID verification. Clark, too, was impressed when he was given a demonstration. "This is very powerful data—absolutely what the government needs to be aware of," Clark said at the time. Clark, who had declined to join Acxiom's board a year earlier, started working as a consultant and lobbyist. He joined the board in December 2001 and, according to Acxiom, was paid $460,000 in fees by the company. (Clark refused to talk to FORTUNE about his activities on behalf of Acxiom.)

Morgan was dumbfounded, he recalls, when the FBI arrived at Acxiom. "Their technology was unbelievably bad," he recalls, "and the international terror experts were computer illiterate." For one thing, the agents were toting laptops with Intel 286 processors—slow, low-memory computers that went out with the 1980s. "I thought, 'This has to be a joke,'" he says.

The FBI-Acxiom collaboration lasted for months. Morgan won't provide details, but he says current and former addresses helped identify housemates of the hijackers, as well as suspects with whom they may have been in contact. "We were always paranoid about people looking at the data in that way—as an investigative tool," says Morgan, who wrote much of the software code for the FBI. "It was a slow-going, laborious discovery process, with some amazing moments."

Acxiom's work led to "deportations and indictments," says an executive, as well as thank-you calls from Ashcroft and FBI boss Robert Mueller. In one case, Morgan says, Acxiom was enlisted after the capture in Texas of two Muslim immigrants with expired visas who had boarded planes on 9/11 with box cutters. The two were never linked to the hijackings, but Acxiom's data helped convict them of involvement in the sale of fraudulent credit cards, which led to their deportation.

Meanwhile, Clark began opening doors in Washington, looking to convert the good will toward Acxiom into business opportunities. He arranged and attended meetings at the CIA, Treasury, the State Department, and the Pentagon. By all accounts, officials from Paul O'Neill to John Poindexter were impressed, as was Health and Human Services Secretary Tommy Thompson, who met with Clark in October 2002 and agreed to initiate a test using Acxiom data to help reduce fraud. Beyond tracking terrorists, connecting the government's disparate and archaic databases can help drive down identity theft, the nation's fastest-growing crime. In one test, Acxiom found more than 100 people using the same Social Security number.

Morgan recalls joining Clark for a meeting at the Pentagon, where they made their way to the front of a long security line. As soon as guards spotted the retired general, they whisked the two inside under armed escort. "A lot of the headway we have made lies in the access that General Clark has provided," states a memo from Morgan in 2002. "Here's the approach he takes to helping position Acxiom: 'IT has a role to play because we'll never be safe enough if we try to build walls and conduct searches and screenings. We have to really know who our neighbors are and what their interests are.'"

The highest-ranking official Clark and Morgan visited was Vice President Dick Cheney. Clark led the July 2002 presentation, which laid out the firm's capabilities in a 40-page white paper that cited the example of American Airlines hijacker Waleed Alsheri—Acxiom consumer No. 254-04907-10006. Cheney was "very positive," recalls former Arkansas Senator Tim Hutchinson, who arranged the meeting. "He said he would 'ring the bell'—as he put it—and try and let people know about it."

One of Acxiom's biggest cheerleaders was Hillary Clinton. According to Morgan, Clinton expressed support for a system that would gather detailed data on every passenger during the ticketing process. After a visit with Clinton in November 2001, Morgan reported to his staff: "It was very gratifying when the president of one of Lockheed Martin's companies approached Jerry [Jones] and me after one meeting and said she had heard from Senator Clinton that Acxiom was a company she really needed to get to know." Clark also played a significant role with Lockheed, and in February 2003, when the TSA named the company as its prime contractor on CAPPS II, Acxiom got a key subcontract.

Just when things were looking up for Acxiom's government business— which accounts for less than 1% of the company's annual revenue— the wheels came off. Hutchinson says the company got "bogged down" in federal bureaucracy. Others at Acxiom wonder if politics might have been at play. Certainly Clark's harsh attacks on the Bush administration throughout 2003 didn't help. Nor have Clark's post-Acxiom diatribes against the two-year-old Patriot Act, which sanctions the sharing of data between government and the private sector.

And the timing of the computer hacks couldn't have been worse, occurring just as Acxiom's key government projects were coming under fire. In September the Senate wiped out funding for the Terrorism Information Awareness project (TIA), a global surveillance database launched in January 2002 by DARPA, the Pentagon's advanced research agency. Clark had gotten Acxiom in the door. But before it could land a contract, the project was shut down—and its director, John Poindexter, forced out—when a TIA subcontractor posted information on its website about a proposed futures market in terrorism and assassination.

Jones, Acxiom's lawyer, says killing TIA was an overreaction. For one thing, it was purely a research project using artificial data, not a mandate to build and implement a product. "You can't create a system on the fly to make it useful," Jones says. "You must at least build the infrastructure and have things running in the background." A public debate in advance would have been better, he adds: "Starting the debate afterward, the outcome is certain."

Acxiom was also caught in the blowback over CAPPS II. Last February, Torch Concepts, a Pentagon subcontractor, included the real Social Security number of a passenger in a PowerPoint presentation to a trade group. The information came from Acxiom, which had been asked by one of its customers, JetBlue, to provide detailed information on two million passengers to Torch for an Army study. A privacy activist eventually found out about the breach and posted the Social Security number on the Internet. In September, Congress blocked funding for implementing CAPPS II until the GAO issues a report on privacy concerns, which is expected this month.

Today the situation is as complicated as the hunt for terrorists. The Federal Trade Commission is examining Acxiom's role, JetBlue is fending off class-action lawsuits, and one of Clark's former campaign rivals, Senator Joseph Lieberman, has requested that the Secretary of Defense investigate whether the Army violated the Privacy Act by not informing JetBlue's passengers. "There wouldn't be politics in that, now would there?" asks Morgan about the Lieberman effort. Adds Jennifer Barrett, Acxiom's chief privacy officer: "We're not having a thoughtful and deliberative debate. Shut down the funding and you don't fix the problem."

That Acxiom was caught snoozing by hackers is ironic. Despite its Big Brother capabilities, the company gets praised—even by critics—for being a pioneer on privacy issues. Every employee undergoes regular and rigorous training about privacy. Morgan often butts heads with his trade group, the Direct Marketing Association, on everything from e-mail spam to the federal do-not-call list. He understands that agitated consumers are bad for business. "The first time I brought up privacy policy at the DMA was 1992, when I joined the board," he recalls. "Everyone looked at me like I was an idiot. It wasn't on the agenda." Acxiom was among the first in any industry to appoint a chief privacy officer with power to nix unethical projects like selling data linked to Social Security numbers to marketers. Yet it was only in the wake of the hacker intrusions that Acxiom created the post of chief security officer, with full-time responsibility for preventing cybercrime and mandating encryption.

The lack of encryption was a colossal oversight. "So often the thing you don't think about comes and bites you," says Morgan. "Most of our customers didn't want to go through the trouble of encryption." Yet that seems reckless at a time when the credit card industry is under siege by hackers and identity thieves. "The losses [to business] are in the billions," Morgan says. Acxiom maintains that its two breaches were the only ones in its history. How can the company be sure? Baas was nailed almost by accident, after investigators examined the computer of another hacker they were probing. And he had taken up residence inside their server for two years.

If Acxiom expects to hold itself up as the gold standard for technology linking and processing, Morgan has to seal his own leaky roof. Investigators say Baas offered Acxiom's data to other hackers if they would help him organize the information into his own database. Luckily he found no takers. "Large

> It was a colossal oversight. "So often the thing you don't think about comes and bites you," says Morgan.

(Cont.)

> "Large corporations need to realize they are the trustees of the personal information of millions of Americans."

corporations need to realize that they are the trustees of the personal information of millions of Americans," says Robert Behlen, a federal prosecutor in the Baas case. "Had the defendant chosen to post the stolen information on the Internet or used it to open credit card accounts, the amount of damage would have been significantly higher."

Last June, in an appearance before the FTC, Morgan said that Acxiom conducted "risk assessments and regular audits on all internal and external information systems to ensure the integrity of client data and Acxiom data." And Morgan's clients have for years performed their own security audits of Acxiom's network, testing it for penetration weaknesses. But the file transfer protocol (FTP) server penetrated in both computer hacks had miserable protection.

Think of an FTP server as an electronic mailbox sitting outside the firewall—a landing spot used by customers and vendors to send and receive files. Baas used a password issued to his employer, an Acxiom vendor, to access the server. From there he managed to crack hundreds of passwords, including one that acted like a master key to the internal systems, letting him scoop up unencrypted data on millions of consumers. "Once you're in the family, so to speak, we're probably more trusting and not as careful as we probably should be," explains Morgan. "We must change that."

In October, Acxiom told securities analysts that new projects and contracts were largely on hold as the firm scrambled to improve its security. It put a SWAT team in place, hired two independent auditing firms, and bought third-party tools to detect intrusions. The company also changed its access and password procedures, and is rapidly moving toward full and automated encryption. Jones held a conference call with 100 general counsels of the affected companies, while other firms flew to Arkansas to see for themselves what had happened. But publicly Acxiom has tried to play down the breaches. "I think this was a much bigger deal than the company let on to investors," says analyst Brad Eichler, who follows Acxiom for Stephens, the Little Rock investment bank that took Acxiom public. "They spent a lot of time that quarter patching things up with customers who were really ticked off."

Acxiom executives say the breaches haven't resulted in any customer defections. Nor have they affected the company's stock price, which recently hit a 52-week high of $19.32.

The larger question is whether the hacking incidents and the concerns about privacy will derail efforts to create a linked infrastructure of databases to help in the war on terrorism. In the debate between privacy and national security, Congress should not lose sight of its own joint congressional inquiry into 9/11, which concluded that law enforcement was unable to connect the dots before the attacks because technology "has not been fully and most effectively applied" in terror prevention. The hijackers followed patterns that could have been detected: purchasing tickets with cash, sharing residences and post office boxes, even using the same frequent-flier number. One terrorist had an expired visa. Another went to a travel agent to buy his ticket, only to discover that his debit card had insufficient funds. He paid in cash and offered a fake Virginia driver's license for ID. Asked for a telephone number, he gave one that was disconnected and had never been his. Acxiom's database could have provided real-time data to connect those dots.

Product

Now Low-Carb: Unilever's Skippy, Wishbone, Ragu

By Sarah Ellison and Deborah Ball

IN A SIGN that low-carb dieting may be more than just a passing fad, Anglo-Dutch marketing giant Unilever is launching a line of 18 new low-carbohydrate products hitched to some of its most venerable brand names. Dubbed "Carb Options," the new line includes carbohydrate-conscious relatives of Skippy peanut butter, Ragu spaghetti sauce and Wishbone salad dressing, along with other condiments, spreads, snacks and shakes.

Costly and risky, Unilever's move is a measure of how far into the mainstream the hot low-carb diet trend has moved. An estimated 30 million to 50 million people are carb-conscious, according to Unilever, which figures the low-carb category could generate as much as $1 billion in sales in 2005.

Separately, snack-food giant Frito-Lay, a unit of **PepsiCo** Inc., is expected to announce today the launch of low-carb Doritos and Tostitos tortilla chips, containing 60% fewer carbs than the regular chips.

But betting so much on a diet craze is risky, particularly for Unilever, which has struggled over the past year to meet quarterly sales growth targets. Unilever is well aware of the dangers of chasing diet fads. One of its biggest brands, Slim-Fast shakes and snacks, has lost luster as dieters have turned away from meal-replacement products in favor of low-carb dieting. By linking some of its oldest trademarks to the latest trend in weight-loss, Unilever risks diluting their brand image.

The Carb Options line is meant both for people following strict low-carb diets and for people who are just "watching their carbs," says John Rice, chief executive of the Unilever Bestfoods North America unit. But Unilever, like most other big marketers, is unwilling to make an explicit "low carb" claim on its labels. The Food and Drug Administration hasn't issued labeling guidelines for the term "low carb," as it has for "low fat." The FDA is expected to issue carb guidelines as early as this year, following talks with major food companies and nutrition experts.

Each serving of the Carb Options products has six grams or less of "net carbs"—a term that also isn't approved by the FDA but is increasingly used on food labels to describe those carbs with a measurable effect on blood sugar. Net carbs are sometimes known as "bad carbs," such as those found in sugar, bread and potatoes, and excluding those from fiber or sugar alcohols.

Unilever reformulated some of its most popular products for its low-carb line. For example, while regular Ragu Chunky Gardenstyle sauce contains 20 grams of carbohydrates per serving, the Carb Options version has only five grams of net carbs. Unilever also is using Carb Options as a stand-alone moniker for low-carb shakes and snack bars.

The low-carb craze began back in the 1970s with the late Robert Atkins's diet book; in recent years, the resurgent popularity of "Dr. Atkins' New Diet Revolution" has inspired a slew of similar regimes, including the South Beach diet, and low-carb products. Until now, niche marketers dominated the category of low-carb packaged food. Foremost among them has been **Atkins Nutritionals** Inc., the corporate designation for the Atkins empire. Analysts estimate it generated some $200 million in revenue last year; in October, Goldman, Sachs & Co. and Parthenon Capital, a Boston private equity firm, bought a majority stake in the company for an estimated $600 million to $800 million.

Unilever is pricing its Carb Options products at a premium of 20% to 25% above the existing brands. But the company notes they will be far less expensive than rival products from the niche marketers. A jar of Skippy Carb Options peanut spread, for example, has a suggested retail price of $2.89, while a comparable jar of regular Skippy costs $2.49. But both are a steal compared to Carb Not Beanit Butter, a soy-based spread costing $6.99.

Anheuser-Busch Cos. has led brewers with a plunge into low-carb beer. And fast-food restaurants have become carb-conscious, too. At some locations, **McDonald's** Corp. and **Burger King Holdings** Inc. have posters making suggestions on how to choose low-carb, low-calorie and low-fat meals. For example, McDonald's will serve a burger wrapped in a lettuce leaf, not a bun.

But most big packaged-food marketers have watched the carb-counting trend from the sidelines. When **H.J. Heinz** Co. introduced a ketchup with only one gram of carbohydrates per serving last year, the product was the exception rather than the rule.

Unilever is returning for more of the diet-fad game after watching one of its biggest brands, Slim-Fast, triumph and tumble.

Founded in 1977, Slim-Fast took off in the 1980s, riding consumers' passion for quick-loss dieting based on meal replacements. Following Oprah Winfrey's weight loss, Slim-Fast used celebrity endorsements to stoke growth and by 1990 was a mainstream brand with $600 million in annual sales.

But over the next five years, Slim-Fast's sales plummeted as consumers tired of celebrity endorsements and the taste of its shakes, turning instead to other diet fads based on grapefruit and cabbage soup. By 1996, Slim-Fast's global sales had shriveled to about $200 million.

New marketing and new products helped turn Slim-Fast around, and in 2000 Unilever bought the brand. The global marketer expanded distribution and put some marketing muscle behind it, turning it into a $1 billion dollar brand by 2002. But then the cycle repeated itself last year, and Slim-Fast fell victim to the Atkins craze. Sales began falling in early 2003, but Unilever's management was unfazed, calling Atkins a short-term trend that wouldn't slow Slim-Fast's growth. Unilever doesn't break out sales for Slim-Fast, but revenue in its Health & Wellness category, of which Slim-Fast is the biggest part, declined 15% in the first half of 2003 and 23% in the third quarter, according to the company. Sales of Slim-Fast fell 32% in the fourth quarter of 2003, according to estimates by Sanford C. Bernstein.

Slim-Fast's roller-coaster ride mirrors that of SnackWell's, a fat-free cookie brand launched by Nabisco (now part of **Kraft Foods** Inc.). In the early 1990s, SnackWell's rode the low-fat craze and reached a sales peak of $600 million, then quickly fell off. The brand has since reintroduced some fat into the products, but it remains a small player.

Unilever, in addition to launching the Carb Options products, also will make a labeling change. To its venerable Hellmann's mayonnaise, Unilever will add the phrase, "As always, zero grams of carbs per serving."

Unilever plans to spend more than $10 million marketing its new low-carb products this year, reassuring customers that the food tastes good, and referring to the durability of the accompanying brand names. The slogan for the print campaign: "Taste you can count on."

Care, Feeding and Building of a Billion-Dollar Brand

Pringles manager Niccol mounts Stax defense

By: Jack Neff

It's Friday morning at Procter & Gamble Co., and while you'd never know it by his demeanor, Brian Niccol is under attack.

Not personally. But Mr. Niccol is North American brand manager for Pringles at a time when his potato-crisp brand faces its biggest-ever direct challenge in the form of Lay's Stax from PepsiCo's Frito-Lay. Stax launched in the U.S. in September and crossed the border in January to open a second front in Canada.

In a company known for its stiffness, particularly under fire, Mr. Niccol isn't showing it. He's relaxed and quick with a wisecrack, belying a P&G stereotype of unpersonable managers. At one point, he mentions his plans to host a "Survivor" party on a Sunday night when most of America will be at Super Bowl parties. The reason: His athletic-themed spoof ad for Fiery Hot Pringles lost out in P&G's internal Super Bowl derby to Charmin, but its runner-up status won time on the premiere of "Survivor 8" following the Super Bowl.

Mr. Niccol is a rare under-30 brand manager at P&G. Even before he took the Pringles job in December 2002, he had spent two years as brand manager launching Therma-care heat wraps. That stint is commemorated by a ballcap and other brand memorabilia that liven his cubicle—one of many cube farms throughout the very cubic P&G "central building" in Cincinnati.

WUNDERKIND

Already managing one of P&G's billion-dollar brands at 29, Mr. Niccol has the markings of a wunderkind. He also has the added bonus, according to one former P&G executive, of working on a snack business considered "non-core," and thus relatively free of senior management meddling.

But his day is quite typical of the grindstone sharpening that noses get around here. Mr. Niccol gets in around 7:45 this morning, typical for him and many other P&G brand managers who trickle in before 8, despite snow-snarled traffic. The time before 9 will be one of the few quiet, meeting-free segments he'll spend alone in his cubicle as he catches up with e-mail, voicemail and reading. The rest of his day, which ends around 7 p.m., is filled mainly with meetings, both scheduled and impromptu.

Besides his 55-hour-plus workweek, Mr. Niccol takes his work home on the weekend. From Chairman-CEO A.G. Lafley and Global Marketing Officer James Stengel comes the drive to spend more time with consumers. For Mr. Niccol, that usually means taking his wife on a Saturday shopping trip that spans four stores, representing the gamut of classes of trade, so he can check displays and chat up consumers.

He's been married three years. And while he didn't meet wife Jennifer at work, like many office-bound P&Gers do, he was introduced to her by a colleague. "I was complaining that I hadn't had any dates," Mr. Niccol recalls. "And at P&G, a culture of action, they took care of it for me."

His Friday morning starts with *The Wall Street Journal*. An article makes him wonder whether Pepsi's "It's the Cola" campaign reflects a broader shift by PepsiCo, including Frito-Lay, to focus on products and advertising ideas rather than celebrities.

Mr. Niccol's mind is on the competition a lot these days. His first meeting, around 9 a.m., is with Jason Thacker, assistant brand manager in charge of "Stax defense" and new-product initiatives. It's a natural combination in Mr. Niccol's mind: "Obviously, I'm cognizant of what my competitors are doing," he says later. "But I strongly believe the best defense is a good offense."

With Mr. Thacker, he's reviewing the weekly sales and share data from ACNielsen Corp. Stax recently has lowered its retail price under $1 at a major store account, and now P&G is tracking a wide array of other retailers starting to follow.

Pringles' cheddar-flavor version—comparable to a cheddar version of Stax—is 7% below forecast, but Mr. Thacker chalks it up to lingering effects of a tornado that shut down Pringles' Tennessee factory for several weeks last summer and made it miss out on back-to-school promotions.

CONFERENCE CALL

Mr. Thacker also passes on what he learned at a bar over the weekend from an acquaintance—that another package-goods company has been working up plans for a co-branded flavor to pitch to Pringles. But the same marketer already has a deal with a regional competitor, Mr. Niccol notes.

Mr. Thacker is one of five ABMs who report to Mr.

(Cont.)

Niccol, along with a marketing specialist in retail design and a clerical support staffer. Mr. Niccol tries to meet with each daily, and his next stop is a conference room at 9:45, where he pulls ABM Nate Lawton to go over the comprehensive business review he'll present in the next few weeks to Jamie Egasti, VP-North American snacks.

Around 10, Mr. Niccol starts a conference call with two executives from his ad agency, Grey Global Group's Grey Advertising, New York. He goes over a laundry list of issues big and small—how music royalties are keeping them from getting extra mileage for the "Athlete" ad on CBS.com; an ABM's maiden voyage to a commercial shoot planned for Los Angeles the next day; plans to "on-board," in P&G-speak, African-American shop Carol H. Williams Advertising, Oakland, Calif., on marketing plans.

Mr. Niccol notes a corporate goal of spending 10% to 15% of media dollars on African-American ads for the top 10 to 15 brands, including Pringles. "It's got to be qualified copy [in other words, hit minimum copy test scores] to release the funds," he says.

Then he gets to the bigger picture. "In the mid-'90s, we had better advertising," he tells Grey's Lynn Janovsky, VP-group management supervisor, and Liz Mason, account supervisor. That was a period when now-defunct Wells, Rich, Greene handled the business. But, he adds: "I think we have a lot of momentum now coming out of the 'Athlete' spot" set to break on "Survivor."

'GET ON BOARD'

Talk shifts to work being done by Grey's Canadian agency team. "They need to get on board with the pace we want to go in," he says. "The pace is only going to go faster."

By 10:45, Mr. Niccol's focus has shifted to the store and a different conference room, as he meets with two sales managers and a finance manager to go over promotion plans. Item one: a promotion with a nontraditional retailer that has spun out of control, with prices so low they're upsetting other retailers.

"Does Jamie know about this yet?" Mr. Niccol asks, referring to Mr. Egasti. A sales executive shakes his head, somewhat sheepishly. They talk over ways to structure a new trade deal to help combat the more aggressive pricing on Stax in a way that treats all the classes of trade fairly, but they need more data to reach a conclusion.

Lunch arrives, to the same room, about 10 minutes ahead of the "Stax defense" meeting, which Mr. Niccol and crew will eat their way through.

From meeting to meeting, Mr. Niccol is spending as much time influencing decisions as making them. By the end of the day, he'll have had input on almost every aspect of the brand.

"The brand manager job is becoming a place where it's about influencing your cross-functional counterparts," Mr. Niccol says later. "I feel accountable to raise the red flag when we're saying we want to achieve X but we haven't resourced correctly to do it. . . . I view it as carrying the torch of the brand equity."

He continues to carry that torch in two new-product initiative meetings, and regroups at the end of the day with his ABMs.

Then it's off to the weekend and that party themed to "Survivor," where the reality show's own torch-carrying tribe members are constantly reminded that "Fire is life."

With Names Like These . . .

By Laura Shanahan

"WHAT'S IN A name?" pondered Shakespeare, famously noting that a rose by any other appellation would smell as sweet. Good thing William could spin sonnets and speeches, because marketing clearly wouldn't have been his calling. Sure, a rose or a hose would be the same by any other name; but the $64,000 question is: Would it sell? Sorry, Will, but the pay, not the play, is the thing here.

Increasingly, it seems names are noteworthy, for better or worse, for products as diverse as four-wheelers and films.

"Nearly as unwatchable as it is unpronounceable," the *Los Angeles Times* critic clearly enunciated about the motion picture Gigli, in which the titular character had to repeatedly advise "Jee-lee," while audiences got restlessly jiggly and inappropriately giggly. Would a less-annoying name have saved this turkey? Probably not, but it unnecessarily added yet another target for critics' and talk-show hosts' tossed tomatoes.

Volkswagen recently rolled out the well-received luxury SUV Touareg, which is so patently pronouncement-challenging that various reporters added something rarely seen in reviews: a phonetic spelling, so consumers wouldn't feel like total nimrods in front of car dealers. One particularly diligent reviewer noted that while "toor-egg" seems to be the way to go, he's also heard "ter-egg," "twor-regg," "twahr-reg," "too-reg" and even "twah-ray," concluding "suit yourself."

Ah, but the problem is, consumers don't like to risk looking like unschooled fools in front of sales and service staff. That's why we point to what we want on French menus. Sometimes on English ones, too. Or we order something else. Or nothing else. As the saying goes, better to stay silent and seem stupid, than to open one's mouth and confirm it.

Then there are the names we can pronounce all too well; we're just not comfortable saying 'em. At least not to folks we don't know very well.

"I'd like to get 'extra close,'" is at least one variant of what I'd have to say to philosophy's sales associate, in order to indicate a desire to purchase a shaving kit. (And yes, the company's name and products are lowercased, making the statement even more ambiguous in print.)

Alternately, I could say, "I need 'extra help,'" if I wanted to purchase a men's zit-zapping kit. Dunno about you, but I'm always fearful that if I feed people a straight line like that they'll turn into Triumph the Insult Comic Dog: "Lay-dee, tell me sahmtheeng I don't know—before I poop on you!"

Then there's the cosmetic cream by Fresh (now, that's a *great* name for a toiletries company; short, vividly descriptive, modern and, um, fresh!). Alas, in nearly stark contrast is the product's name: Crème Ancienne; shades of the French menu, with a *soupçon* of unfortunate association. No, the cream won't make you ancienne, but your wallet might look the worse for wear, having $250 extracted.

Speaking of unfortunate associations, I recently bought a sweater in a shade I'd call pale lime. "Frozen Frog," ribbit'd the hangtag, which I read *apres*-purchase. Now every time I wear it, I have visions of being trapped in a frigid school lab. I also liked a Coach pistachio-green suede bag, until I read the catalog description of "pear." Prickly. As sounds Cactus Club orange juice—yeah, that's what you want for liquid refreshment; associations of aridity and sharp needles.

> *Prickly. As if Cactus Club orange juice is what you'd want for liquid refreshment.*

Of course, much association is idiosyncratic; Smucker's, a fine brand, famously acknowledges the potential pitfall of a less-than-elegant moniker: "With a name like Smucker's, it has to be good." But my friend Jon loves the name. "It actually has the word 'muck' in it," I point out, but all Jon hears is a sound that smacks of smacking one's lips, which he does when he eats the make's jams.

What can we conclude? Other than that Jon is an idiot? Avoid names that evoke moribund animals, or are hard or embarrassing to say—and opt for the pithy and the positive.

Unless you're pitching to rebel youth, of course. Or selling hot sauce. I hear Screaming Sphincter is doing real well.

Don't Devour The Company's Sales

Branding—Roll out new items without cannibalizing existing product lines
. . . .

By Kirk Shinkle
Investor's Business Daily

In November, Sharper Image Corp. unveiled an entertainment system that has pretty much everything.

The Personal Entertainment Center is a portable DVD/CD/radio/TV system, replete with 20 or so "soothing sound" environments (from church bells to rain). The device, which sells for about $600, also has an alarm clock and temperature readout.

But the gadget retailer already sells dozens of versions of all of those electronics.

Wouldn't its other product lines suffer with the introduction of the combo unit?

"The personal entertainment center was a great product for the holidays," said Aimee Cooper, the firm's head of public relations and human resources. "We didn't see a lot of cannibalization."

Cannibalization is an ugly word, but it's a problem companies regularly face. Keeping new offerings from cutting into existing sales is an inexact science.

Unfortunately, firms can't always innovate fast enough when competition comes knocking at the door. From DVD players to breakfast cereal, firms have to keep their brands fresh or risk getting trounced.

They also must face the fact their latest idea is probably going to steal some thunder from products they already have on the shelves.

But companies have ways of making sure innovative products steal market share from rivals, not from their own bottom line.

Cooper says Sharper Image customers were asking for a product with all the features found in the Personal Entertainment Center.

The retailer held focus groups to zero in on what features customers most wanted.

Defensive Pricing

Sharper Image stays cautious when it introduces a product that competes with existing wares. It manufactures about 20% of its products, so initial orders can be small—5,000 to 15,000 units to start. Those sales are a gauge of how well the new product will sell overall.

Cannibalization can also be a problem when a firm rolls out a new version of an existing product. For instance, each year Sharper Image introduces an update of its signature Ionic Breeze air purifier.

> It's a good anti-cannibalization strategy: Introduce brands at different price points, and also get more shelf space."
>
> **John Lister,** *brand consultant*

For the 2003 holiday season, it put out a desktop version of its filter. The new unit carried a cheaper price and extra features.

"There was zero cannibalization. These are people who wanted to buy it for the office," Cooper said, noting that earlier sales patterns showed Ionic Breeze customers were likely to be repeat buyers.

Pricing is another key defense against cannibalization.

The $600 tag on the do-everything DVD player is higher than most of the firm's other electronics. Most of its other combination audio-products go for between $100 and $300. Sharper Image also sells a 20-inch Toshiba TV/DVD/VCR that sells for $400.

Other firms combat cannibalization using a host of tactics, depending on the nature of their products.

John Lister, a branding expert with New York-based Lister Butler, says while many companies try to figure out how much cannibalism will occur, most go out of their way to avoid it.

"The strategy many people are taking is to minimize cannibalization as opposed to quantifying it," he said.

One way to do that: Created a separate brand image. That's what big consumer product companies continue to do.

"Consumer goods companies like Kraft have a smart strategy," Lister said. "They have their own barbecue sauce, but then they have the Bull's-Eye line at a different price point. It's a good anti-cannibalization strategy: Introduce brands at different price points, and also get more shelf space."

Another example: "How does Kellogg's justify having 18 breakfast cereals next to each other? I guess they don't really care as long as you pick one of them," Lister said. "And why are there six versions of Ritz crackers? Well, somebody's buying them all."

Some companies avoid cannibalizing their own products by offering just one product at a time.

Harman International Inc. is known for high-end speakers like Harman Kardon and JBL. Joe Milano, director of strategic accounts at the firm's multimedia unit, likes to keep it simple.

He introduced in January the JBL Creature II, a small, three-piece computer speaker system. The first version was unveiled in 2002. Harman cut the price by $30 on the new version and added new features, and Milano opted to discontinue the old line.

"We don't plan to have both on the market at the same time," he said. "We try not to have products that compete with each other on performance."

No Stuffing Allowed

Milano likes to keep products priced at least $50 apart, and keep technical

> The firm unveils a version of Ionic Breeze each year, but positions is so as not to steal sales from earlier models.

(Cont.)

specifications decidedly disparate. Other offerings—the JBL Duet and the JBL Invader—go for about $60 and $180, respectively. That strategy has kept cannibalization to a minimum, he says.

Brand consultant Lister notes that Procter & Gamble employs a similar strategy by keeping just one or two market-leading products in each of its segments, rather than stuffing a category full of competing products.

He says different approaches at different companies are just part of everyday business, and says there's still a fair bit of guesswork when it comes to fighting cannibalization.

"I'm not sure you're always going to get numerical data or even clear-cut strategies. A lot of stuff might boil down to common sense marketing," Lister said.

Reprinted from *Investor's Business Daily,* February 17, 2004. Used by permission.

45

Salad in Sealed Bags Isn't So Simple, It Seems

By AMANDA HESSER

YUMA, Ariz. — For millions of Americans, preparing a mixed green salad is as easy as opening a sealed plastic bag. But here in the land of lettuce, complexity is a given, and time is the enemy.

There is a reason bagged lettuce costs more than twice as much as a head of iceberg. It is not easy getting those perfectly formed leaves, washed and still fresh, from the soil to the table. The process requires speed, technology, secrecy about that technology and plain-old farmers' ingenuity.

Bagged salad sales in the United States have soared in the past decade, exceeding $2 billion last year, according to ACNielsen, the market research company. And while iceberg may still be king, accounting for 73 percent of all lettuce grown in this country, that is a decline from 84 percent in 1992. Consumption of romaine and leaf lettuces like green leaf and red oak has more than doubled since the early 1990's.

"We have a department working on lettuce breeding," said Peggy Miars, a spokeswoman for Earthbound Farm, a grower here whose annual sales have grown an average of 55 percent since 1995. "You don't want a bagful of lettuces that are all flat. That is the main reason we have the frisee in there—for texture. They are also breeding for better colors. Deeper reds are desirable."

Whatever the color, speed is of the essence. The moment the plants are shaved from the ground, the clock starts ticking. Six days is allowed for washing and bagging the lettuce and transporting it around the country, and about a week more to sell it. After that, the leaves turn slimy.

And slimy lettuce can be disastrous. As Bill Zinke, vice president for marketing at Ready Pac Produce of Irwindale, Calif., which processes bagged salads, said, "It's constantly a business of staying up to and ahead of what fields you will be harvesting, not just today and this week but weeks and months in advance."

Earthbound said it was the first company to package lettuce in bags, starting in 1986. And by packaging whole baby leaves instead of mature heads cut into bite-size pieces, it can move lettuce to market without giving it the "nitrogen flush" that bags of cut-up romaine or iceberg lettuce need to keep the cut edges from browning.

But baby greens have to be harvested in just a few days, before they grow too big. Each bag of what the company calls its "mixed baby greens" has at least eight varieties of specialty lettuce, nearly all of which have to be ready for harvest the same day.

For Earthbound Farm, the country's largest producer of organic salads, it all begins in fields here. More than 90 percent of all lettuce in the United States is grown in Arizona and in California, mostly from two regions—Yuma in the winter, and the Salinas Valley in the summer.

The places where the greens are sorted look like a Rube Goldberg drawing. Bins of freshly cut leaves are rushed from nearby farms to the packing plant in refrigerated trucks. Then the bins are lifted into a vacuum tube the diameter of a subway tunnel.

In 20 minutes, the vacuum brings the temperature of the lettuce down to 36 degrees, and it goes into cold storage. Maintaining that temperature until it reaches the grocery will keep it fresh for about 15 days.

Inside, the packing plant is cold and wet, and loud as a jackhammer, as enormous production lines ferry the tiny greens from bin to bag. First, they are upended onto conveyors, passing a row of inspectors and sweeping down a flume into the world's largest salad spinners. Then up conveyors they go, to giant scales and bagging machines. More than 14,000 pounds of lettuce can be processed every hour.

This is where the secrets are kept. The way the flume swishes the lettuce and how harshly the spinners treat it affect how much it is damaged and how nearly perfect and dry the leaves are in the bag. A photographer sent to capture the process was not permitted to take close-ups of the newest machines. Pen and paper were heavily discouraged.

"It is a very competitive environment," Drew Goodman, the president of Earthbound Farm, said. "At most, you get six months" before new ideas are picked up by rivals.

"With the different service providers and maintenance people," he added, "most any new development is going to be—*available*, let's say, to others."

Mr. Zinke would not discuss Ready Pac's salad washing or drying process. "It's a very slim-margin business," he said. "So you hang closely on your points of difference that give you a competitive edge."

Almost none of the technology now used in the industry existed 15 years ago. Mr. Goodman and his wife, Myra Goodman, the founders of Earthbound Farm, started growing lettuce in their backyard in the 1980's. Last year the business, which specializes in baby organic lettuce, had sales of more than $200 million.

The Goodmans developed much of their machinery out of necessity—a salad spinner, for example, that dries smaller batches of lettuce at lower speeds, causing less damage to the leaves. Machines like it are now widely used in the industry.

In Earthbound's new 115,000-square-foot plant in Yuma, the water flumes have swirling jets to keep the delicate leaves from clumping. The temperature throughout the plant is controlled by a master computer. Charles Sweat, the chief operating officer, travels by company jet between here and the summer plant in San Juan Bautista, Calif., and he can adjust the temperatures by remote control on his laptop.

Once the lettuce is bagged, it is sent off in refrigerated semitrailers to stores around the country. Company officials can only hope that the cooling units on the trucks work well and that the markets store the salad in a cool place.

Fresh Express, which deals mostly in head lettuce that is cut and put into bags, has processing plants around the country, so its workers can cut the heads into bite-size pieces closer to their destination, increasing shelf life. Other companies, including Ready Pac, simply have to hurry to get lettuce on the road.

One of the most important advances in keeping baby and cut lettuce crisp from the time it is packed on the West Coast until it arrives on the East Coast was the development of a new bag to pack it in.

"We had a breakthrough in 1989 that allowed us to take it national," said Robin Sprague, a spokeswoman for Fresh Express, one of the companies that began using the process. The packaging, a plastic film that her company calls "modified atmosphere packaging," gives the cut lettuce a longer shelf life by slowing the rate of decay.

At nearly the same time, Ready Pac came up with two more innovations: a system for washing the lettuce three times and a "pillow pack," a bag that is inflated with extra

(Cont.)

nitrogen to protect the leaves from bruising during shipping.

Organic lettuce is still just about 4 percent, of a giant industry whose change and growth is rippling through other businesses. "What we're talking about," said Ken Hodge, the communications director for the International Fresh-cut Produce Association, "is a phenomenon that has cut across the whole produce industry." Freshly cut fruits are expected to be the next big thing.

Still, salad makers are fighting to take their industry to a new level. They are busy reducing the amount of salad that clumps in the machine. They are improving the tatsoi's texture, and the time it takes lettuce to go from the Arizona field to a dinner table in Bangor, Me.

"This business is really about performing every day," said Mr. Goodman of Earthbound Farm. "So that means having the best quality every day and innovating every day. So hopefully, we're on to our next innovation while our competition is figuring out our last one."

46

Let There Be L.E.D.'s

Tiny, Glowing and Efficient, Chips Take On the Light Bulb

BY IAN AUSTEN

It started innocently enough. Marcel Jean Vos, an interior and commercial designer in London, bought some light-emitting diodes to create a small lighting system in the kitchen of his apartment. Now, four years later, Mr. Vos has transformed a neighboring one-bedroom apartment into a space lighted entirely with L.E.D.'s, the solid-state technology more commonly associated with the tiny lights on electronic gadgets.

The apartment has 360 L.E.D. arrays, and about 20 yards of plastic ribbons embedded with the glowing semiconductors. The lighting effects include a kitchen counter that changes color, an illuminated shower stall, a candle that has chips instead of a wick, and a light sculpture.

"Everyone is looking for an excuse to ditch the incandescent light bulb," said Mr. Vos, the chief executive of Vos Solutions, his design consultancy. "And it is about time. We are using extra energy for nothing."

But his project demonstrates both the advantages and the drawbacks of replacing incandescent light, a technology that has not changed substantially since Thomas Edison developed his first successful bulb in 1879.

Despite its enormous number of light fixtures, Mr. Vos's apartment uses no more electricity than four 100-watt incandescent bulbs would, he said. ("And what kind of fun can you have with just four light bulbs?" he asked.)

But offsetting the frugality is the staggering cost of the installation. Mr. Voss estimated that he spent $50,000 to create the apartment's lighting system.

"Right now it's something that's only for the rich and famous," said Mr. Vos.

While Mr. Vos's apartment is unusual—he makes the unverifiable claim that it is the world's first residence entirely lighted by chips—he is not alone in his thinking that L.E.D.'s may help end the reign of the conventional light bulb. Major manufacturers like G.E. Lighting and Philips Lighting, along with some much smaller newcomers, want to find a place in every home for L.E.D. illumination.

What began with Christmas tree lights and under-the-cabinet lights may eventually lead to inexpensive, solid-state lighting systems. Researchers are promising lights that will be more like wallpaper than bulbs.

The research into solid-state lighting is motivated by light bulb makers who want to create new and profitable products. But

saving energy is a consideration, too. About 20 percent of all electricity in the United States is used for lighting. A shift from bulbs to L.E.D.'s and other more efficient kinds of lighting could cut that percentage in half, easing the strain on power systems and reducing the chances of a blackout like the one that affected the northeastern United States and Canada last August.

"What we're looking at here is really changing the way people think about their environments," said Mark Roush, a former lighting designer who is now a senior marketing executive at Philips Lighting. "And there's nothing that drives awareness of lighting more than not having it."

In the incandescent bulb, it would seem that Mr. Roush and his counterparts at other companies have an easy target. "The standard by which we judge all light sources is the incandescent," he said. "But the incandescent has very poor color rendering."

The incandescent bulb, which works by heating a thin metal filament so that it emits light, is also inefficient. About 90 to

95 percent of the electricity that goes into most incandescent bulbs is converted to heat rather than light.

"It's absolutely the least efficient light bulb you can buy," said Anil R. Duggal, the manager of G.E.'s light energy conservation program. And you don't have to be an engineer to know how little it takes to shatter an incandescent bulb or how frequently the filament burns out.

But one factor sweeps all those considerations aside when most household users go shopping: incandescent bulbs are very inexpensive. Standard bulbs commonly sell for as little as 50 cents each, and even brighter and longer-lasting halogen incandescent bulbs can be had for a few dollars. That makes more efficient alternatives like compact fluorescents, at $10 or more, seem extravagant, and leaves little or no room in the market for the even more expensive lights that use L.E.D.'s.

L.E.D.'s are tiny devices, made of semiconductor material, that allow an electric current to travel in only one direction and produce light as a byproduct of current flow. Like fluorescent lights, L.E.D.'s do not have filaments, so they run cooler and last longer. Their higher prices might be offset by longevity and lower operating costs, but few consumers do those calculations while pushing a shopping cart. "I know that when I go into a store, I mostly look at what's in my wallet," said Gert Bruning, a lighting researcher at Philips Research.

Plug It In

Something New Under the Counter

Aside from some Christmas lights, L.E.D. lamps designed for consumers are scarce. The first consumer offering from GELcore, an L.E.D. lighting company partly owned by General Electric, has more than a little commercial lighting in its genetic makeup.

The GELcore Flexible L.E.D. Accent Lighting System is an 18-inch cord dotted with five light-emitting diodes, each about a half-inch high.

Scott Hearn, the president and chief executive of GELcore, said the flexible lighting was descended from a system that the company sells as a replacement for neon tubes. Retail stores using the product, known as Tetra lighting, noted that its flexibility and low heat level would make some variation of it ideal for use inside display counters, he said.

The consumer version—which costs about $25 and is available at several retail stores, including Wal-Mart—was introduced in the fall.

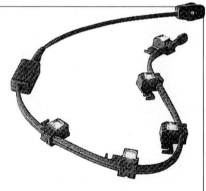

Mr. Hearn said it had been particularly popular with hobbyists who light display cabinets filled with their handiwork.

For installations with little room to spare, the compactness of the lamps may be offset by the electrical power converter attached to its plug. Also, phosphors applied to the L.E.D.'s are designed to create a bluish light similar to a florescent fixture. While ideal for department store cabinets, that cold light may seem out of place in the home. *Ian Austen*

(Cont.)

For now, that has made L.E.D. lighting mostly of interest to the commercial world, where energy use and maintenance costs are carefully watched. The vast video screens and animated signs that cover buildings in Times Square are the most dramatic commercial use of the technology. But the most common applications tend to be prosaic. Many traffic signals, Walk/Don't Walk signs and indicator lights on trucks and buses use L.E.D.'s.

GELcore, an L.E.D. lighting maker owned by G.E. and Emcore, a semiconductor company, recently unveiled an L.E.D. technology for illuminated street signs. Similarly, what appear to be neon tubes on new buildings are often plastic ribbons embedded with L.E.D.'s.

The major barrier to creating inexpensive L.E.D. lights for homes is not the semiconductors themselves. The real obstacle is the cost of overcoming several basic limitations of the chips.

The first is the nature of their light. Incandescent or fluorescent bulbs diffuse their glow over a wide area. L.E.D.'s, in contrast, are very bright only at a single point. That's handy for showing that a cellphone is charged or for making up one subpixel in a huge video billboard, but a drawback for filling rooms with light. "L.E.D.'s are very good at lighting effects," Mr. Roush said. "Now they are coming across the threshold to effective lighting—delivering the light where you want it."

Most of the bulbs in Mr. Vos's apartment, which are the kind used for signs, achieve that result by combining several L.E.D.'s under a plastic lens.

Light color is also a problem. Currently no L.E.D. produces light of a color that is suitable for everyday household use. The best produce a white light that has a pronounced and very unflattering blue tinge.

At the moment there are two ways around the color problem. Many L.E.D. bulbs create white light by blending the output of separate red, green and blue diodes.

Scott Hearn, the president and chief executive of GELcore, said his researchers were developing an alternative in which the L.E.D.'s generate invisible ultraviolet light. That light in turn causes phosphors on the chip to glow. As with fluorescent lights, producing a specific color becomes a matter of adjusting the phosphors' chemical recipe.

GELcore began selling a $25 under-cabinet accent light this fall that uses a variation of the concept. The light has a series of blue L.E.D.'s that have been coated with yellow phosphors to improve their light color.

Most people in the L.E.D. lighting industry have already conceded the business of replacing standard incandescent bulbs to efficient compact fluorescent lamps. They're hoping to use the technology to introduce entirely new kinds of household fixtures.

Replacing incandescent lights with chips can save electricity, but the cost of installation is steep.

"Having these flat things is a totally different way of looking at lighting," Mr. Roush said. "All of a sudden I have dynamic color, color that can change. Inside spaces can be illuminated to match the whiteness of daylight outside, while buildings can change their colors outside."

The most successful L.E.D. lighting product for consumers so far emerged from a desire to overcome a common seasonal annoyance. Frustrated by the need to climb a ladder to replace burned-out Christmas lights on his house in Yardley, Pa., David Allen began looking into alternatives.

At first Mr. Allen looked at developing fiber-optic systems. But along the way he discovered that, contrary to industry assump-

tions, it was possible to assemble strings of L.E.D.'s that could be plugged into wall outlets without a power converter. The lights are rated for up to 200,000 hours of use.

This holiday season was the second that his Forever Bright lights were widely distributed in North America. While Mr. Allen declined to give sales figures, he said that sales of the lights increased by 500 percent over 2002, partly because of promotions by some electrical utility companies.

But even if more houses start to resemble Mr. Vos's futuristic apartment, the glory days for L.E.D.'s may be cut short by their younger sibling, organic light-emitting diodes, or O.L.E.D.'s. Because they are based on plastics, O.L.E.D.'s do not have to be manufactured in semiconductor factories. Nor are they limited to relatively small sizes.

"Organic L.E.D.'s can potentially be made with a low-cost printing line, much like you print a newspaper," said Dr. Duggal of GE.

More important, they could be created on flexible materials, leading to new forms of lighting. Rolls of O.L.E.D.'s could be produced as a kind of luminous wallpaper. Table lamps could exchange their bulbs for shades that provide both light and decoration. But O.L.E.D.'s are in their infancy and so far have few applications. Phillips uses them in an electric razor, and they are found in some small displays in car dashboards. They are not very energy efficient, and the light output tends to decrease over time.

Dr. Duggal said that much work remained to be done to improve the technology. "How this gets adopted is going to be interesting," he said. "But making all this work is still a big challenge. It's not a done deal."

47

Makers Of Child-Tracking Technology Find Big Potential Market

Trackers Evolving, Shrinking

....

Kidnapping fears also are driving sales of cell phones, which parents give to kids.

....

By Patrick Seitz
Investor's Business Daily

Recent high-profile kidnapping cases have raised interest in technology for tracking and locating children.

Privately held Wherify Wireless Inc. soon will begin selling a pendant-sized device that combines a global-positioning-system receiver and cell phone, which kids can wear or put in their pocket.

The company says it's a big advance over its first-generation product—a bulky wristwatch.

Cell phone companies in general are benefiting from child safety concerns as parents buy mobile phones for their children at younger ages than a year or two ago, analysts say.

Steve Wozniak, co-founder of Apple Computer Inc., also has designs on the kid-tracking market with his venture called Wheels of Zeus Inc.

"It's likely to become a crowded space," said Keith Waryas, an analyst with market research firm International Data Corp.

Wherify sold thousands of its first product, but hopes to sell millions of the new product after it becomes available this summer, says Timothy Neher, chief executive of the Redwood Shores, Calif., company.

The new device is about the size of an Oreo cookie. It includes a cell phone with a two-way speaker. It comes with a panic button for calling 911 and a programmable button for calling home. It has "aided GPS" capabilities for locating people in-side buildings. Normal GPS devices can't penetrate buildings.

"We've gone light years ahead of where we were," Neher said.

The original Wherify wristwatch bracelets were similar to the first cell phones in that they were brick-sized and expensive, he says.

That first Wherify product can't be used for voice communications, but works as a GPS locator, pager and watch. The company is both a service provider and product maker. That first product now sells for $199, with service plans starting at $20 a month.

"It was more of a technology statement than anything else," Neher said. "Any first-generation product is going to be limited. We sold thousands of them, but not hundreds of thousands. We think with this next generation we can get to millions of units."

Wherify expects the pendant device, called the GPS Locator Phone, to sell for less than $149, with service plans starting at $10 a month. The basic service would include three "locates"—times when people can go online and locate their child—and 15 minutes of talk time. More expensive plans would offer more locates and talk time.

Wherify also plans to sell a new version of its watch starting in the fourth quarter or the first quarter next year, Neher says. It will be 80% smaller than the current

---

Locating Your Kids

Wherify's first wristwatch bracelet for tracking children was fairly large and expensive. Its new locator product, which also can be used for voice communications, fits in the palm of a hand.

---

version, Neher says. The first wristwatch locator weighs 3.9 ounces and has been sold since fall 2002.

The new model, he says, will come with "Dick Tracy stuff" like two-way voice communications and downloadable games. The expected price is $149.

"It targets a market that has a huge amount of potential," said David Hilliard Williams, an analyst with E911-LBS Consulting in Wilton, Conn.

But many parents aren't waiting for special tracking and communications devices for children. They're buying regular cell phones for their kids, analysts say.

A few years ago, the generally accepted minimum age for cell phone usage was 16. Today it has fallen to 12 or even younger, IDC's Waryas says. The Columbine school shootings and frequent Amber alerts have raised awareness about the need to track kids and communicate with them in emergencies, he says.

"It's not just limited to tracking. It's the ability to get in touch with your kids in this increasingly connected society," Waryas said.

Surveys show that people want family tracking capabilities with their cell phone service, Waryas says. At 11 p.m. or midnight, when a kid has missed curfew, parents want to be able to go to their PC, push a button and find out where their child is, he says.

But that sort of service raises legal and privacy concerns, Waryas says. It raises questions such as: Who has rights to access the data, and how long will the data be stored? Can law enforcement agencies get the data, especially given the scope of the Patriot Act?

The child-tracking services raise liability concerns, such as what happens when the device fails to locate a missing child, Williams says.

All cell phones soon will come with a location-tracking ability to meet the Federal Communications Commission's wireless Enhanced 911 requirements. About 60% of cell phones sold today have E911, which can be used to locate a caller in an emergency, Waryas says.

Giving children cell phones is a tough call. He says it can be expensive, especially if they lose or break their phones. Plus, parents want to place limits on usage.

(Cont.)

Wozniak says one benefit of his WozNet system is it will be low cost. He envisions his system being used to track small devices on kids, pets and Alzheimer's patients, and also used to track assets like cars and briefcases.

But Wozniak is counting on homeowners and communities to put in place a new local wireless infrastructure for his system to work. That's a drawback. "That's reinventing the wheel," Wherify's Neher said. "There's going to be a lot of dead spots with that concept."

An early use for WozNet will be home security, Wozniak says. The system can notify users remotely when something happens, such as a break-in at the house, he says.

WozNet is still in development, but the firm has signed up Motorola Inc.'s broadband communications unit as a partner.

Reprinted from *Investor's Business Daily*, March 1, 2004. Used by permission.

48

Wi-Fi Changes Virtually Everything

Users say they'll never go back

ByMichelle Kessler
USA TODAY

Watching football on TV doesn't cut it anymore for John Furrier and his son, Alec, 8.

Broadcasters can't spew enough statistics to satisfy the two. So the Furriers rely on a laptop with wireless Internet, called Wi-Fi, to get the latest data from the living room couch while watching the game.

Wi-Fi sends Web pages and other information through the air via radio waves. The Furriers' Wi-Fi laptop receives up-to-the-minute scores and trivia from ESPN.com, though it's not plugged into a phone line. That allows father and son to swap stats without missing a minute of the game.

Hankering for some nachos? They can take the laptop with them to the kitchen and not miss a play. John Furrier, 38, even admits to surfing the Web from the bathroom.

Wi-Fi is catching on fast—and changing the way people use the Internet. Fans say it leads them to do more things online: They pay bills from the living room, search recipes from the kitchen and check e-mail on the go. Tech analysts say that's just the beginning of what Wi-Fi can do. In the future, it will connect all kinds of devices—lamps, stereos, computers—and, for the first time, truly integrate the Internet into daily life.

"It's going to connect all kinds of things that need to be connected together," says Matt Peterson, co-founder of a San Francisco-area Wi-Fi users group. "It could really make your life easier."

Wi-Fi has been in the mainstream only about four years, but it's already causing a rise in laptop computer sales. Laptops made up 22% of PCs sold in the USA in late 2002. By the end of 2003, they made up 30%, says researcher Gartner.

Now, Wi-Fi is starting to appear in consumer electronics. Gateway, Microsoft, Samsung and others are building TVs, DVD players, stereos and other gadgets that can talk to one another—and to nearby PCs. That makes it possible to download a movie or song from the Internet and send it wirelessly to your home entertainment system.

That's just the beginning. Researchers are working on a tiny version of Wi-Fi that can be used to send very simple commands to household appliances. You could use it, say, if you wanted to turn on your lights remotely, via the Internet. Or adjust your thermostat. Or check whether you left the iron on. There are thousands of possibilities, Peterson says.

That means big opportunities for enterprising companies, says Nielsen/NetRatings analyst Charles Buchwalter. Six million people buy something online each day, and millions more use the Web for research and reservations, according to the Pew Research Center's Internet & American Life Project. As Wi-Fi makes the Web more convenient, those numbers will rise, he says. Companies that sell online goods and services—and adapt quickly to Wi-Fi—could have a huge, new customer base, he says.

Wi-Fi will prompt companies "to take the Internet much more seriously," Buchwalter says. "It's revolutionary."

FROM COUCH TO KITCHEN

Wi-Fi is taking off fast. More than 64 million Wi-Fi systems are expected to be sold this year, up from 24 million in 2002, says researcher IDC.

Already, Internet companies such as ESPN.com are tailoring features to customers with Wi-Fi. In September, ESPN.com launched a host of features. Among them: live chats with sports experts, more video clips of big plays and tools to help fantasy football fans track their teams.

It's a big change from ESPN.com's initial design, based on targeted users who watched the game in the living room and dashed to an office PC to check scores or stats. ESPN launched the redesign after focus groups said they were using Wi-Fi to take the site into the living room.

The new interactive features "give a little bit of a sports bar feel, even though you're sitting alone on your sofa watching the game," says General Manager John Kosner. ESPN.com is considering additional interactive features, such as instant messaging during games, he says.

Cooking Web site Allrecipes.com underwent a similar overhaul. The site's original users were people who browsed recipes at a desk and printed them to

(Cont.)

What you need for Wi-Fi

► Wi-Fi antenna. Found in most electronics stores for $50 to $150. Often called an "access point."
► Broadband Internet connection. The most common types are a digital subscriber line (DSL) or cable modem.
► Laptop equipped for Wi-Fi. Most new ones are. Wi-Fi attachments are available for most older laptops for about $80.

take to the kitchen. Now, anecdotal evidence suggests, users are sorting recipes in the kitchen on a laptop with Wi-Fi, says marketing director Esmee Williams.

In November, Allrecipes redesigned its site, in part to make it easier for Wi-Fi users. They've simplified navigation and made it easier to view a whole recipe on one screen, without a flood of ads.

Epicurious, another cooking site, boosted its offerings of how-to videos that users can watch while cooking. It also enhanced its online "recipe box" feature, which stores favorites for users, and is continually adding recipes to the site.

Entertainment portal Yahoo TV caters to Wi-Fi users, too. Customers are starting to use a Wi-Fi-equipped laptop while watching TV for interactive viewing, says Director Doug Hirsch. When a big show is on, traffic on the Yahoo site jumps, he says.

To capitalize on the trend, Yahoo TV recently signed a partnership with Television Without Pity, a TV gossip site that features real-time chats about shows as they air. "This is convergence. You're talking about your show while you're watching," Hirsch says.

And customers keep coming up with ways to use Wi-Fi. Rajesh Vasireddy, a graduate student at the University of Illinois at Urbana-Champaign, hates using his remote to navigate program listings that come with cable TV. So he uses a Wi-Fi laptop to breeze through the listings online. Anna-Marie Claassen, who works for a Wi-Fi company, likes to do crossword puzzles online from her couch. Tim Pozar, another co-founder of the San Francisco Wi-Fi group, uses it to check his e-mail from a personal digital assistant while following his 4-year-old son around the house. "It's handy," he says.

WI-FI IN THE WAREHOUSE

Wi-Fi is also transforming the way businesses use the Internet. The technology first was used by business travelers, who needed an easy way to go online while on the road. Some businesses use Wi-Fi to replace costly wires or provide connectivity in hard-to-reach places, such as warehouses. By making it easier for employees to work wherever, whenever, Wi-Fi often boosts productivity and provides a return on investment of 200% or more, says Bill Clark, a wireless analyst with researcher Gartner.

Myrtis Smith, who runs a career-coaching service from her Cincinnati home, worried that a new baby would make working tough. She installed a Wi-Fi network just before her son was born. Now, Smith, 30, can check e-mail while watching her 8-month-old son play. "I'm free from my desk," she says.

Unique ways to use Wi-Fi are expected to flourish as it gets cheaper and easier to use. Two years ago, a home Wi-Fi antenna, sometimes called an access point, cost $300. Now it's less than $100, says IDC technology analyst Abner Germanow.

Wi-Fi fans say they'll never go back. "I'm addicted to it," John Furrier says. "I can't imagine life without it."

49

Twilight Of the CD? Not if It Can Be Reinvented

BY LAURA M. HOLSON

Tonight in Manhattan, rock stars, divas and rappers will descend en masse on Madison Square Garden, arriving at the Grammy ceremonies in a parade of glamour and attitude. But the excitement they create will only mask the growing anxiety in the recording industry about the future of its fundamental product, the CD, which is threatened with the same obsolescence that it long ago foisted on the LP and then the tape cassette.

Introduced in the United States 20 years ago, the CD is losing its allure. From 2001 to 2002, some 62.5 million fewer of them were sold—a decline of 9 percent to 649.5 million, according to Nielsen SoundScan. Online swapping of songs is growing at a crippling rate, forcing almost every corner of the music industry to try to divine exactly what role, if any, the CD will play in a future dominated by Internet delivery and competition from popular new technologies like the DVD.

Most analysts and industry executives agree that selling music online is the future. But they say it will take at least two years for companies to devise a business plan for it that makes financial sense. In the meantime, the CD will remain the biggest source of revenue for both music retailers and recording companies, who will try to squeeze as much profit as they can out of each and every sale.

As a result, the CD is being rethought, repackaged and, in some cases, repriced. Experiments to resuscitate this ailing product are growing. In January, Bon Jovi created a compact disc, with eight previously unreleased songs, exclusively for **Target** stores. Priced at $6.99, it was intended to help bolster sales of other Bon Jovi albums, including the newest, "Bounce."

Best Buy, the No. 1 electronics chain in the country, is selling prepaid cards good for 10 downloads that allow consumers to create compilations to play either on discs or on computers. And last year, the Interscope recording label gave a DVD to the first million buyers of "The Eminem Show" as an incentive to buy the CD.

All this is happening as the economic underpinnings of the CD continue to deteriorate, endangering the music business altogether. With the rising popularity of online music, much of it available free, technology-wise teenagers, the industry's most voracious buyers, can easily use CD-burning technology to make bootleg copies and sell them at school for as little as $1.

Companies are showing signs of cracking. Two industry veterans have recently lost their jobs: Thomas D. Mottola, the head of **Sony Music Entertainment,** which lost more than $132 million last year; and Jay Boberg, president of **MCA Records.** The music retailer **Wherehouse Entertainment** announced in January that it was filing for bankruptcy protection, partly because of lackluster sales. And the **EMI Group,** based in London, the only major music company that is not a part of a media conglomerate, is struggling with debt and is believed by analysts to be considering merger prospects.

"Large companies tend to wait until they feel pain to act," said Dan Hart, chief executive of Echo, a recently formed consortium of retailers that hope to sell music online. "Now they feel pain."

Doug Morris, chief executive of the Universal Music Group, said: "We are definitely in the middle of a transition. It was always a packaged-goods business, but that is changing. We are slowly moving forward."

Compact disc sales have slipped for several reasons, not all of them related to piracy or online music swapping. Critics complain that there is a dearth of blockbuster acts these days and that those with hits, like Britney Spears, often have short-lived careers. And with the average price of a compact disc at $14.21, they contend that music is simply too expensive for frequent purchases.

But Hilary B. Rosen, chief executive of the Recording Industry Association of America, countered that a recent study by the association found that only 3 percent of the consumers polled said they were buying less music because prices were too high.

Still, there is no question that other activities are taking up listeners' time, thanks to the growth of electronic games and multichannel cable and satellite television. Perhaps most threatening is the popularity of the DVD, which emerged in the mid-1990's. By 1999, DVD players had gained mass-market appeal, and they now cost as little as $50, about the same price as a portable boom box. In some retail stores, DVD sales have surpassed those of CD's.

"The DVD is moving into the bedrooms of the next generation of young kids," said Gary L. Arnold, senior vice president for entertainment at Best Buy, which announced in January that it was closing 107 stores. The next generation of young people has no af-

Has the Music Stopped?

After climbing in the 1990's, compact disc album sales dropped 9 percent last year.

finity for the compact disc. For them, he said, "it's about gaming and PlayStation."

To thwart online swapping, several music companies, including Sony and Universal, have experimented with copy-protected compact discs, much to the ire of paying consumers, who complain that they cannot listen to some of those discs on their computers. The industry does not use a standard copy-protected format, so consumers do not know what kind of disc they are buying. Fearing a consumer backlash, the industry has slowed down those copy-protection efforts.

Software makers are trying to come up with alternatives that address the needs of both consumers and recording companies. At a recent music conference in Cannes, France, **Microsoft** said it had developed technology to allow music companies to record two sets of identical songs on a compact disc, one that could be played on a home or car stereo and the other, called second session, that could be copied to a personal computer. The second-session songs would have limitations, perhaps barring consumers from sharing files or copying songs onto another disc.

Recording companies probably placed too much hope on super audio CD's, which are said to have superior sound compared with regular CD's. The technology, introduced two years ago, has not taken off because super audio CD's cost nearly four times as much to buy as regular CD's—and they require a special machine to experience the full impact.

And super audios, championed by Sony and **Philips,** are not alone in offering sound quality that surpasses that of the typical CD: a dueling new technology in DVD audio, supported by **Panasonic** and **Pioneer,** is setting up a battle reminiscent of the VHS-Betamax wars.

Until all these new technologies are sorted out, recording companies and retailers are betting on promotions and marketing deals to increase sales. Bruce Kirkland, a member of Bon Jovi's management team, said the album that Bon Jovi put together for Target had also increased sales of the "Bounce" album in its stores. In the first week of the promotion, Target's share of the market for "Bounce" for all retail stores jumped to 26.1 percent from 15.9 percent, he said.

"I think the onus is on the retailers to take care of this because the recording companies always shoot themselves in the foot," Mr. Kirkland said.

Mr. Arnold of Best Buy said he believed that DVD's could well replace the CD in the future because they play not only music but also video images. In the last 12 months, sales of DVD's have surpassed those of compact discs at Best Buy, he said.

But before they can become a new industry standard, he added, they will have to more adeptly meld music and video.

Music distributors and retailers, battered by the slump in compact disc sales, are embarking on their own efforts to give consumers more and easily accessible music. Last month, six music retailers, including

> # The compact disk could join the LP in the dustbin of technology.

major outlets like Best Buy, Wherehouse and **Tower Records,** said they would form the Echo consortium to sell music on the Internet through their retail Web sites. As recently as a year ago, that would have been unthinkable, as retailers and music companies were at odds about how best to tackle online distribution.

In another joint effort, **Anderson Merchandisers,** one of the largest magazine and music distributors in the United States, bought technology from **Liquid Audio,** an online music pioneer that distributes 350,000 songs through retailers, in the hope of exploiting the growth in digital music.

"It has not been the norm that retailers should be the ones helping us rethink our business," said John Esposito, president of United States distribution for the Warner Music Group. "But retailers are telling us the current model does not work."

Best Buy has been one of the most active retailers in this regard. It recently began testing a program in 30 stores that allowed consumers

to buy a card with a preset value that could be used to buy downloads to a computer or disc. Scott Young, vice president for digital distribution at Best Buy, said the experiment had had limited success and was under review.

Mr. Hart of Echo said retailers would primarily seek to sell downloads over their Web sites that consumers could call up from their homes. But as well as selling digital downloads, partners of Echo are likely to explore several options, including the use of store kiosks where consumers can make personalized compact discs.

Such a venture, like any in the digital music world, is fraught with risk. In 1999, Sony Music Entertainment tried a similar strategy but consumers did not respond, analysts said.

There are, of course, other problems facing distributors and retailers, most notably acquiring the rights to distribute whole catalogs of music online. The music companies faced that issue early on, when starting their own Web sites. Competing companies declined to offer all their music on both PressPlay, a joint venture of Sony Music and Universal Music, and MusicNet, which was formed by Warner Music, EMI and **BMG.** It took months for them to begin sharing music, leaving consumers disillusioned and frustrated.

For all of these ventures, companies will still have to grapple with why consumers would pay for music they can easily get free. One major retailer, according to a music executive, has suggested to several recording companies that it might put a cap on the price of any compact disc it sold in its stores. Only a store like **Wal-Mart** would have the strength to pull that off, he added.

"I think the biggest problem is, the industry doesn't know how to get started and take steps where you get an incremental gain," said Phil Leigh, a digital media analyst at Raymond James & Associates in Tampa, Fla. "If compact disc sales continue to drop and there is no increase in online sales, then artists will be mad and your bosses are mad, too. There is an old expression that pioneers are the ones with arrows in their backs. The one thing executives don't get paid for is rocking the boat."

50

Savvy Safety Systems Are Developed for Cars

Devices Are Available On Some Luxury Cars, Could Become Widespread

By Al Karr

Debra Bezzina was driving on Interstate 96 in Michigan last month when she reached for a pack of gum in her pocket.

Suddenly, an urgent voice said, "Not, Not, Not," alerting her that the car was drifting to the right, starting to cross the solid white line by the side of the road.

It wasn't a back-seat driver. Ms. Bezzina, a field-test program manager for auto-parts maker **Visteon** Corp., has been driving an experimental Nissan Altima equipped with a warning system that alerts drivers to road departure and lane shifting.

"Who knows? I might have drifted all the way out of the lane without realizing it," except for that warning signal, she says.

The test system signals other potentially dangerous situations as well. On another day, as Ms. Bezzina circled the Nissan off the Southfield Freeway onto I-96, at a speed judged by the system to be too high for the cloverleaf curve, an icon flashed on the dashboard, and the seat vibrated in front, behind her knees.

These warnings are part of a growing number of savvy systems being developed by auto makers and researchers at universities and transportation authorities. The federal Department of Transportation has supported such efforts under its Intelligent Vehicle Initiative, with the aim of helping—or even forcing—motorists to make better on-the-road decisions and thereby avoid crashes.

Some crash-avoidance systems are already available on certain luxury cars. The Cadillac DeVille, for instance, has military-style night-vision aids. Certain models of Lexus, Mercedes-Benz, Infiniti and Jaguar have "adaptive cruise control" that controls acceleration and braking to maintain, say, a two-second gap between your vehicle and the one ahead of you.

But beyond that, a wide range of "smart" systems are being developed. Motorists may see some of them in the next two to four years, and many will be in widespread use

Smart Wheels

Car makers and transportation researchers are developing a range of "intelligent" vehicle systems to help avoid crashes and improve driving safety. Motorists may see some of them in the next two to four years, and many are predicted to be widespread before 2010.

❶ **Rear-end collision avoidance**
'Adaptive Cruise Control' uses forward-looking radar to adjust vehicle speed to maintain safe distance. More advanced systems would be able to cut down on acceleration or apply brakes if driver didn't heed warnings. Some versions already available.

❻ **Intersection collision avoidance**
Technologies would sense the position and motion of other vehicles at intersections and determine whether they are close enough to pose a risk for someone entering intersection or turning. Late stage development.

❷ **Lane change and merge collision avoidance**
Combining 'Adaptive Cruise Control' with sensors that alert drivers to nearby moving traffic. In early research stage.

❸ **Lane or road departure warnings**
Systems and sensors would warn the driver when his vehicle is likely to deviate from the lane of traffic or go off the road. Late stage development.

before 2010, predicts the Intelligent Transportation Society of America, an association of industry and academics.

Products under development include systems that, in theory at least, would prompt motorists to slow down sooner or stop before entering dangerous intersections, while others would provide warnings for inadvertent lane change or road departure. Still others would alert a driver that his or her vehicle is closing the gap with the car ahead too fast, and then, if the driver doesn't respond, move to reduce the accelerator pressure and apply the brakes in time to avoid a crash.

"In the next few years, you will see a lot more technologies coming into vehicles which are geared toward preventing crashes," says Joseph Kanianthra, associate administrator for vehicle safety research for the National Highway Traffic Safety Administration.

The IVI program, which received $28 million in funding for fiscal 2003, is directed at the most common types of crashes: rear-end, intersection, road-departure, lane-change and merger collisions that are responsible for the majority of highway fatalities. In 2002, there were more than six million car crashes in the U.S., resulting in 42,815 deaths, 2.9 million injuries, and $230 billion in costs, according to NHTSA.

It is uncertain how effective these new systems will be because considerable development and field testing remains to be done. There is also the question of how motorists will react: Will they welcome the new assistance, be distracted by it, resent the "interference," or cede too much control? Researchers also want to know how drivers will respond to each specific warning device, and where to draw the line on the driver's authority versus the car's.

General Motors Corp. heads a group that has conducted a 10-month field test that involved 80 drivers and 10 Buick Le Sabres,

combining two technologies for avoiding rear-end crashes: "adaptive cruise control" and forward-collision warnings and control. The system uses audio and heads-up displays on the windshield, to warn drivers who are bearing down on a slowed or stopped vehicle ahead, advising them to brake or swerve. If the driver doesn't respond, the system itself would cut down on acceleration and apply the brakes.

Massachusetts Institute of Technology's Age-Lab focuses on technology to aid older drivers, but the systems under development also could improve safety for drivers of any age. One would display warnings on the windshield, showing the vehicle's speed, how much it is above what would be considered safe, and a suggestion to start braking. But, in a further step toward science fiction, dashboard monitors might also record the driver's heart rate, blood pressure or other stress factors, which could affect safe driving.

Researchers ask where to draw the line on the driver's authority versus the car's.

Of course, there is a danger of overloading the driver with too much information, which could itself cause an accident, says Joseph Coughlin, the Age-Lab director. "We tend to be so optimistic about the technology and know so little about the human element," Mr. Coughlin says. So far, "we're getting lots and lots of data to the driver, but not a drop of knowledge about what to do with it," he adds.

Many "intelligent transportation" experts believe that such problems can be overcome,

(Cont.)

contributing to a safer driving environment. Cautious drivers probably won't notice the systems, because they won't function if drivers are acting prudently, adds NHTSA's Dr. Kanianthra, though he says that more aggressive drivers might see the systems as a "nuisance."

Some crash-avoidance efforts focus on systems outside the car.

The University of Minnesota's Intelligent Transportation Systems Institute is aiming to reduce crashes at rural intersections that don't have any traffic signals, those junctions where low-speed traffic on rural "collector" roads enters a highway carrying high-speed, high-volume traffic.

This spring, the Minnesota DOT plans to demonstrate a crash warning system at such an intersection along a four-lane divided expressway in the southern part of the state. The system will use radar detectors along the highway to measure gaps in traffic and then flash roadside warning signs to drivers on the collector road, indicating whether it is safe to get onto the highway. If funds are available, some such systems could begin in 2005, says Max Donath, the ITS Institute's director.

The Virginia Tech Transportation Institute is working on two similar systems. One uses roadway technology to flash a stop signal when a vehicle's speed and distance show that it will soon run a red light or stop sign. The other would signal a device in the vehicle to produce a noise and flash a stop-sign icon on the dashboard to warn the driver of the imminent hazard.

When put into operation, all these systems are going to produce "a sea change in the way we drive," says Neil Shuster, president of the ITSA.

From *The Wall Street Journal,* March 2, 2004. Reprinted by permission of Dow Jones & Co., Inc. via The Copyright Clearance Center.

51

Nokia's Hit Factory

The cell-phone giant's unorthodox research-and-development machine has cranked out innovation after innovation, thanks to an eccentric leader known as Mr. Advice.

By Paul Kaihla

Yrjö Neuvo's name is tricky to pronounce, even for fellow Finns, so let's just call him Mr. Advice. That's a literal translation of his surname, and slyly fitting for a former university professor. On a recent Sunday at a remote farmhouse on Finland's south coast, Mr. Advice's face is flushed and sweaty. Clad in Kevlar overalls, he has just chainsawed down an ash tree the size of a telephone pole. His wife is feeding branches into a bonfire. Mr. Advice begins enthusing about his hobby of collecting farm tractors. He proudly shows off a 13-horsepower Chinese job. Without explanation, he fires up a second model, a green beast with a hinged body that looks like a giant insect. He talks a reluctant visitor into taking the controls. "Turn here!" he commands with a wave.

The term "nutty professor" may be coming to mind about now. But there is a lot more going on at this little house on the tundra than at first meets the eye. Neuvo is always trying to figure out how to get people to try something new, anything new. It could be getting a stranger to ride a tractor. Or it could be getting greenhorn engineers to ponder wild avenues of thought that lead to revolutionary cell-phone innovations—which, as it happens, Mr. Advice has done, repeatedly. Neuvo is the humble, if eccentric, technologist who heads research and development at Nokia (NOK), arguably the best product-driven R&D organization in the world.

Nokia's R&D apparatus is unlike anything in multinational corporate history. Most large-scale R&D operations are centralized, hierarchical, no-nonsense—science as brute force. Nokia's 18,000 engineers, designers, and sociologists are scattered across the globe and form a kind of federation of rule-breaking, risk-taking hackers. Most of them answer not to countless layers of managers but to Neuvo, who considers it his missionary duty to break

down his people's mental inhibitions, freeing their minds to roam toward the next big breakthrough. "We operate the way a great jazz band plays," Neuvo says. "There is a leader, and each member is playing the same piece, but they can improvise on the theme."

That approach has made some beautiful music for Nokia. Since Neuvo took over Nokia R&D, its engineers have churned out an unmatched string of technical firsts: the first mass-market cell phone with the antenna on the inside, the first one-chip phone, the first compact battery with long-lasting power. Breakthrough features mean hot phones, and no competitor has come close to equaling Nokia's record of monster product hits—it has had half a dozen models that sold as much as 50 times the company's own internal projections. That run has enabled Nokia to amass a 38 percent share of the cell-phone market, roughly equal to that of its four biggest competitors combined. A decade ago, Nokia was close to bankruptcy; now it's closing in on $30 billion in annual sales. It makes the vast majority of the profits generated by the entire mobile-phone industry.

Of course, that's not as big a deal as it once was. The cell-phone business has been hammered; Nokia's stock has fallen 70 percent during the past two years. And the company's freewheeling R&D approach has produced some duds. Still, Mr. Advice seems to have pulled off one of the trickiest balancing acts an R&D chief can achieve: unleashing the combined creative energy of thousands of engineers without being swamped by anarchy.

* * * * * * *

Nokia, headquartered just outside Finland's capital of Helsinki, has a storied history. The company was founded in 1865 as a forest products concern and went

The Big Winners

Phone model	Year released	Unit sales (in millions)
101	1992	12
2100	1994	20
5100	1998	100+
3200	1999	45*
8200	1999	35
3300	2000	70+

*Europe only. SOURCE: Industry estimates

(Cont.)

through many reinventions on its way to becoming a consumer electronics conglomerate. The most radical came in 1992,when Nokia decided to shed everything except a business that at the time represented only 10 percent of the company: mobile communications.

When Neuvo came to Nokia in 1993 from the electrical engineering faculty at Finland's University of Tampere, Motorola (MOT) and Ericsson (ERICY) were the engineering heavyweights of the wireless world. Ericsson was outspending Nokia on R&D by a 5-to-1 ratio. Nokia was seen as an upstart that got by on thinly engineered fad phones. Neuvo seemed an unlikely choice to blast Nokia forward: He's a lanky, soft-spoken man, described even by friends as unprepossessing and vaguely odd. He still carries the same kind of briefcase he lugged around campus, a leather satchel that resembles a doctor's bag. It's crammed with gadgets like cell-phone speakers, as well as a tool kit he uses "to fix certain things if they are broken—somebody's eyeglasses or computer parts." A multimillionaire, he rides his bike to work every day, even in the fierce Finnish winter.

Nokia had already begun to disperse its R&D operations before Neuvo arrived. In the traditional corporate model, R&D is centralized and manufacturing is distributed. Siemens, for instance, directs most of its research out of a single huge complex in Munich. Nokia, by contrast, lets teams at 69 sites—from Boston to Bangalore, India—run their own projects. Nokia has far less R&D hierarchy than its competitors do, says Lauri Rosendahl, Deutsche Bank's Nokia analyst. "That's why freaky ideas from junior engineers can end up in a product rather quickly," he says.

The bare bones of Nokia's distributed R&D system may have existed when Neuvo arrived, but he put the

meat on them. One of his first steps was to drastically accelerate the expansion of R&D sites, while keeping the teams within them small. His reasoning is simple: The smothering influence of the home office can lead to tunnel vision. "If you just have R&D campuses around headquarters, you might become what we call 'home blind,'" Neuvo says. "You need to have your finger in the wind in many places" to fuel the imagination. Colleagues say he used his international academic connections like an intelligence network to cherry-pick acquisitions ranging from hot startups to R&D sites that other companies had put on the block, as well as to identify rising young talent. In three to four years, Neuvo's division had tripled in size; today it's eight times bigger than when he started.

But Neuvo's crucial achievement was to infuse his burgeoning operation with a hacker spirit, to make his staff, as he puts it, "challenge and not shrink from making mistakes." Building that kind of a culture isn't easy. It helped that, in Finland, Neuvo is an engineering legend, an inspirational figure whose research in digital signal processing brought him international renown. He kept himself close to his engineers and waged daily warfare against hierarchy (in Nokia as a whole, there are only three layers of decision-making between the most junior engineer and the president of the company). Neuvo constantly prowls the far-flung R&D labs, prodding engineers to be audacious in pursuit of their scientific muse, and makes it clear that no idea is too harebrained to receive a hearing. Neuvo "is a techno-freak who is always crossing the line," says Erkki Kuisma, a veteran Nokia engineer. "He encourages people to do crazy things if they believe their crazy idea is right."

Kuisma knows this firsthand. In 1996 he came up

FIVE WAYS TO UNLEASH INNOVATION

1 DON'T LOCATE ALL YOUR R&D IN A SINGLE PLACE, ESPECIALLY IF IT'S NEAR THE SMOTHERING INFLUENCE OF HEADQUARTERS. DISPERSE IT AROUND THE GLOBE.

....

2 KEEP TEAMS SMALL—NO LARGER THAN 50 IF POSSIBLE—AND GIVE INDIVIDUAL ENGINEERS AND THEIR MANAGERS A LOT OF POWER AND AUTONOMY.

....

3 FLATTEN HIERARCHY AND STAY AS CLOSE AS POSSIBLE TO YOUR ENGINEERS. HIERARCHY DISSIPATES ENERGY.

....

4 ENCOURAGE ENGINEERS TO GENERATE CRAZY NEW IDEAS OUTSIDE THEIR OFFICIAL WORK ASSIGNMENTS BY CELEBRATING SECRET TINKERING AND SIDE PROJECTS—AND GET INNOVATIONS INTO PRODUCTION WITH ROCKET SPEED.

....

5 WELCOME MISTAKES. IF YOU'RE NOT MAKING THEM, YOU'RE NOT PUSHING THE ENVELOPE HARD ENOUGH.

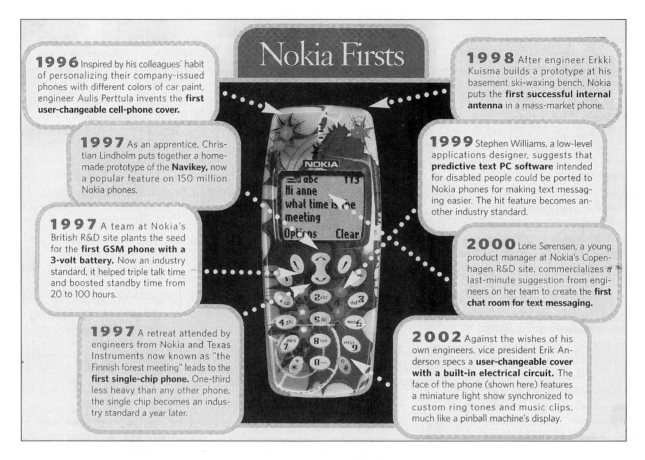

Nokia Firsts

1996 Inspired by his colleagues' habit of personalizing their company-issued phones with different colors of car paint, engineer Aulis Perttula invents the **first user-changeable cell-phone cover.**

1997 As an apprentice, Christian Lindholm puts together a home-made prototype of the **Navikey,** now a popular feature on 150 million Nokia phones.

1997 A team at Nokia's British R&D site plants the seed for the **first GSM phone with a 3-volt battery.** Now an industry standard, it helped triple talk time and boosted standby time from 20 to 100 hours.

1997 A retreat attended by engineers from Nokia and Texas Instruments now known as "the Finnish forest meeting" leads to the **first single-chip phone.** One-third less heavy than any other phone, the single chip becomes an industry standard a year later.

1998 After engineer Erkki Kuisma builds a prototype at his basement ski-waxing bench, Nokia puts the **first successful internal antenna** in a mass-market phone.

1999 Stephen Williams, a low-level applications designer, suggests that **predictive text PC software** intended for disabled people could be ported to Nokia phones for making text messaging easier. The hit feature becomes another industry standard.

2000 Lone Sørensen, a young product manager at Nokia's Copenhagen R&D site, commercializes a last-minute suggestion from engineers on her team to create the **first chat room for text messaging.**

2002 Against the wishes of his own engineers, vice president Erik Anderson specs a **user-changeable cover with a built-in electrical circuit.** The face of the phone (shown here) features a miniature light show synchronized to custom ring tones and music clips, much like a pinball machine's display.

with what at first seemed like a truly crazy idea: removing the antenna from the cell phone and hiding it inside the device. Kuisma, whose official assignment at the time was to conduct radio frequency research, had kicked around internal antenna specs with a couple of colleagues. He brought it up with Neuvo at the Helsinki airport while the two were on a business trip; Neuvo's eyes lit up. In no time, Kuisma was in his basement at home, cutting the aerial off an existing 1611 GSM phone and patching the hole by remolding the plastic casing after melting it with a blow-dryer he uses for waxing cross-country skis. Kuisma fashioned an antenna from a square piece of copper tape and inserted it beneath the phone's back plate.

The idea immediately hit resistance. Some Nokia executives were afraid customers would assume that a phone without a visible antenna wouldn't be powerful enough. But Neuvo began showing Kuisma's prototype to top Nokia executives, pinning them in lobbies and meetings, putting his personal credibility on the line. That's what Neuvo does when he believes his engineers

are on to something, and he has one advantage from his days as a professor. More than 100 of his former students work at Nokia—including the president of the mobile-phone division (Neuvo was his master's thesis adviser). If he finds an executive who needs more convincing, Neuvo lets the engineers do the talking. "What counts for a lot in this company is how committed the engineers themselves are," explains Erik Anderson, a close Neuvo colleague and head of two of Nokia's largest R&D sites. "We tell the engineer, 'Go sell this guy.' We pick the key people, and we aim the engineer like a missile."

In Kuisma's case, Neuvo put him through an exhaustive coaching session about how to make the pitch to doubters, like a thesis adviser would with a student doing an oral defense. Thus prepped, Kuisma won the day, and his internal antenna debuted in 1998 in Nokia's 8800 series "luxury phone," the model that was famously launched on haute couture runways rather than at wireless industry trade shows. It became one of the most profitable products in Nokia history, with gross margins of 70

(Cont.)

to 80 percent. The internal antenna was quickly imitated by competitors—a point of great pride for Neuvo, and validation that Nokia had closed the engineering gap.

* * * * * * *

Many of the other pioneering features in Nokia phones similarly bubbled up from the culture of uninhibited dabbling Neuvo has fostered. Nokia's signature Navikey, the user interface that radically reduced the number of buttons above a phone's keypad by combining three of them into a single fat bar, is regarded as one of the great design innovations in cell-phone history. It was sketched out by a 28-year-old Nokia apprentice during his first few weeks on the job.

In 1995, Christian Lindholm, who was still finishing his master's degree in economics and had never worked in telecom before, was assigned to a group studying user interfaces. He started tinkering on his own. "I was just talking to myself—'Let's get rid of some keys, and make the keypad more universally intuitive,'" he recalls. Lindholm and another young newcomer created 10 prototypes. One of them found its way to Neuvo; he wasn't particularly focused on user interfaces at the time, but he seized on Lindholm's idea. "It was a radical technical innovation," Neuvo says with relish.

Lindholm hadn't been at the company long enough to even meet Neuvo, but Mr. Advice immediately began working the corridors and company cafeteria, excitedly showing senior colleagues what Lindholm's interface could do, and improvising new ways to use it. Within a year, the Navikey was on the market, wowing consumers with its ease of use. Navikey-equipped models like the low-end 5100 and 6100 became huge blockbusters, making the Navikey one of the company's most important subbrands.

Nokia takes flat hierarchy and free-range engineering culture so seriously that some innovations have gotten into phones without even being approved by senior managers. For new features that involve modest risk and resources, product managers have authority to simply build them into a phone. One of Nokia's current rising stars is Lone Sørensen, who at the age of 24 was put in charge of Nokia's 3310, a phone that has sold more than 70 million units since its release two years ago. She slapped a program into a phone that allows users to send text messages to each other in a chat room—another mobile industry first. She cooked up the feature as a secret side project, and added it to the phone at the last minute without consulting her nominal boss, Anderson. "It just shows up," Anderson says with a shrug. "If you try to pay an organization to work full-time coming up with ideas like this, you won't get it. You need some jackass down in R&D who just says, 'Hey, let's do this.'"

* * * * * * *

Sometimes, though, a jackass is just a jackass. Neuvo's long leash means there's tremendous potential for some lightly supervised project to go off the rails. It seems to have happened with Nokia's 5510 MP3 phone, introduced last fall amid much trumpeting. The phone, which allows users to listen to FM radio and play MP3s, has proved too bulky and too expensive, and Nokia is quietly pulling it off the market. (Nokia officials concede that the phone is a disappointment but won't elaborate.)

Such screwups, most observers agree, have been relatively rare. But can that last? R&D hot streaks are like hot streaks in other fields: They often spring from a mysterious confluence of good timing, good talent, and good luck, and they can end suddenly. Sometimes the music just stops. At Nokia, keeping the hits coming is complicated by the swirling technological changes the company faces; phones that have dominated the market will soon be rendered obsolete by devices that will allow users to access the Internet at high speeds. There's no guarantee that Nokia—and not, say, Sony, Samsung, or even Microsoft—will come up with the R&D breakthroughs that define the new generation of phones.

Back at his seaside farmhouse, sipping sausage soup, Neuvo is calm about the future and Nokia's place in it. He notes that Nokia now spends roughly $3 billion a year on R&D. While rivals have been cutting R&D spending during the tech slump, Nokia increased R&D outlays 16 percent last year. Neuvo talks about an upcoming phone that will allow users to take a picture and send video clips. It's an advertisement for his distributed approach: The phone's software was written by Nokia engineers in Copenhagen, Dallas, Tokyo, and Finland. Colleagues in Britain designed crucial wireless protocols. The Hong Kong R&D unit came up with the cradles.

But always, Neuvo returns to his deep belief in innovation as art and his faith that if his engineers chase their muse, the breakthroughs will come. "When an artist is really excited and does a sculpture day and night, then he is energized by it, because it's in his hands and he owns it," Neuvo says. "This is how you get art. Our artists aren't just closing their eyes and waiting until the innovation comes. We are innovating all the time."

Place

52

Losing Focus

As Kodak Eyes Digital Future, A Big Partner Starts to Fade

Amid Difficult Transition, Film Maker Sees Relations With Walgreen Suffer

The Trouble With Minilabs

BY JAMES BANDLER

To understand the massive challenge facing Eastman Kodak Co., step into a Walgreens drugstore.

Just a few years ago, Kodak was the exclusive provider of photo-developing services to Walgreen Co., America's largest drug chain. These days, about 1,500 of the company's stores rely on one-hour developing equipment made by Fuji Photo Film Co., Kodak's archrival. Walgreen has also installed more than 4,000 computer kiosks from Fuji that let customers get prints in minutes from their filmless digital cameras. Fuji, in short, is becoming the future of photo developing for Walgreen, a retailer with 4,290 outlets that sells more than two billion photo prints a year—second only to Wal-Mart Stores Inc.

The story of how Kodak's relationship with Walgreen deteriorated so rapidly illustrates the perils it faces as it tries to manage a difficult transition away from its signature product: film. Digital cameras threaten to make traditional film irrelevant, and Kodak, hungry for new sources of income, plans to dramatically reduce its reliance on film sales in favor of new digital technologies, including inkjet printers. As part of this radical restructuring, Kodak, based in Rochester, N.Y., said yesterday that it plans to shed as many as 15,000 jobs, or more than 20% of its work force, by the end of 2006. It also will take charges of $1.3 billion to $1.7 billion.

But as Kodak embarks on its new path, the company has struggled to maintain relationships with retailers such as Walgreen, which remain vital partners in the company's older businesses of selling and developing

film. That's a big concern, because there's still lots of money to be made in those businesses, and Kodak needs the income to fund its leap into the digital future.

One big problem is that it isn't clear what role retail outlets will play in the photo business once digital cameras become more common. Although most consumers still visit stores to get prints of their photos and buy film, digital technology now allows consumers to take pictures, store them on the Internet or a personal computer and print them at home without ever visiting a store.

So to hedge its bets, Kodak is juggling several strategies at once. It has offered retailers including Walgreen kiosks that let digital shutterbugs print out photos for a fee. It has also gone around the retailers with its Ofoto Web site, to which consumers can upload their digital pictures and order paper prints of them without ever stepping into a store. Kodak is also investing heavily in printers that consumers can use to print their digital photos at home.

Some of those strategies created confusion and alienated Walgreen executives, who feared Kodak was cutting them out of the business. As a result, according to a Walgreen official and an internal Walgreen document, Kodak should receive less than $400 million in revenue from Walgreen this year. That compares with about $500 million in 2000. The figures include rebates and allowances that Kodak pays back to Walgreen. The drop is a big blow for Kodak, which has suffered a $600 million decline in annual revenue since 2000. Kodak disputed the $500 million figure for 2000, saying the amount was considerably lower.

Some of the drop stems from the decline in travel that followed the 2001 terrorist attacks and the overall trend toward more filmless digital photography. But much of the lost Walgreen revenue, according to a person familiar with the numbers, is related to Walgreen's decisions to shift more business to Fuji.

"There's a saying at Walgreen: 'You have to earn your way in, but you also have to earn your way out,'" says Gordon Addington, the former head of photo developing at Walgreen until he retired in 2001. "Kodak did its best to earn its way out."

Gerald Quindlen, general manager of world-wide consumer sales for Kodak, has acknowledged that Walgreen and Kodak have had differences without going into specifics. But he said in an interview that the drug chain remains an important customer. "We continue to work through a lot of issues with them," he said.

Kodak still sells Walgreen lots of film and retains a diminishing film-developing franchise there. It also has strong relations with other key photo retailers, including CVS Corp. and Target Co. But Kodak has had other stumbles in the retail world. In 2001, it

signed a multimillion-dollar exclusive photo-developing deal with Kmart Corp., only to see the discount retailer file for bankruptcy and shut down hundreds of stores. Just a few years earlier, Kodak watched as Fuji signed a 10-year deal with Wal-Mart that gave Fuji exclusive rights to critical elements of Wal-Mart's photo-developing business.

Photo developing, which includes processing fees and paper and chemical sales, generated about 20% of Kodak's $13 billion in revenue in 2002, according to an analyst at Buckman, Buckman & Reid, a brokerage firm. The business is also important because its helps Kodak build brand identity, fueling more sales of its traditional film, which accounted for roughly 28% of revenue in 2002, according to the brokerage firm.

Kodak's relationship with Walgreen began, as Walgreen history recounts, after Kodak founder George Eastman enjoyed a lunch at Charles Walgreen's original store on the South Side of Chicago. A 1909 photo of the second Walgreens store shows a Kodak sign in the window.

The relationship continued to flourish into the 1990s, when consumers began demanding more one-hour photo developing. Previously, consumers tended to drop off rolls of film at retail stores, with the rolls then shipped to labs run by Kodak and others. Kodak helped Walgreen set up a national one-hour-photo business. It provided machines called minilabs that could handle the developing on-site—collecting fees to lease the equipment—and trained Walgreen employees to operate them. It even gave Walgreen a $31.6 million interest-free loan, since repaid, to help Walgreen implement the systems, according to a Kodak letter to Walgreen officials.

But problems eventually surfaced. Mr. Addington, the former head of photo developing at Walgreen, said the equipment leased from Kodak broke down as often as 11 times a month, often because of paper jams and software glitches. Film would get overexposed when jammed machines had to be opened up and fixed. Getting the machines serviced could take two to three days, a person familiar with Walgreen's photo business says.

When Daniel Carp, then Kodak's president, visited Walgreen's Deerfield, Ill., headquarters in 1999, Walgreen's top brass asked Mr. Carp what Kodak planned to do about the photo-developing machines. As recalled by a person at the meeting, his reply was: "We're not in the one-hour photo business." Long after the meeting, Walgreen's then-chairman, L. Daniel Jorndt, would frequently repeat Mr. Carp's words inside the company: "Not in the one-hour photo business!"—often adding, "Is that guy for real?"

Mr. Carp, now Kodak's chief executive, says through a spokesman that he didn't say Kodak wasn't in the one-hour developing business. He said his actual remark was simply,

(Cont.)

"We don't make the minilabs," referring to the fact that Kodak bought the machines from a Swiss manufacturer. In an earlier interview, Mr. Carp added that when the supplier filed for bankruptcy in 2002, Kodak went to great lengths to help its customers by buying up spare parts to continue servicing the minilabs. "We stood by all our customers at a very critical time," Mr. Carp said.

Walgreen stuck with Kodak and its minilabs, partly because it was locked into long-term leases on the equipment.

But soon, relations frayed over another matter—plans to give Walgreen a photo-developing outlet on the Internet. Web sites such as Snapfish and Shutterfly had begun offering digital-camera users the ability to upload photos onto the Web, store them, and order prints to be mailed to them. Kodak, too, had invested in a system it then called PhotoNet. It allowed customers who dropped off film at retail outlets to elect an option for a fee that would convert their pictures to a digital format and send them to a Kodak Web site, where they could be e-mailed or printed out—sometimes for another fee, paid directly to Kodak.

Walgreen, concerned that digital photography would cut into its developing business, badly wanted its own presence on the Web, and began talking to Kodak about setting up a joint Web site. Planning and negotiations moved ahead during 2000. Among other services, the site would allow customers to upload photos from digital cameras and have them printed and mailed to them.

But Walgreen officials grew uncomfortable with the fine print of the Kodak deal. Although customers arriving at the site would see a Walgreen page on entry, getting any kind of photo services would require them to click onto a Kodak site, reducing the visibility of Walgreen's brand name. Also, while Walgreen would get a cut from any fees for the photo developing performed by Kodak, Kodak would keep the pictures on its site, thereby gaining more control over future business with the customers.

Despite the concerns, Walgreen's Mr. Addington still preferred Kodak to other photo companies, mainly because of its strong brand and marketing prowess, and he was ready to sign a Web pact. But when Mr. Addington and his boss retired in early 2001, Kodak lost two of its strongest Walgreen allies. Walgreen killed the deal and began developing its own Web photo service with Fuji, which was comfortable taking a less visible role. The service, linked to the main Walgreen site, was launched late in 2003, and relies on Fuji photo developing.

Mr. Addington's successor as Walgreen's head of photo developing was Michael Navarro, who had come to the drug chain from rival Rite Aid Corp. Looking over old contracts Walgreen signed to lease Kodak's one-hour minilabs, he was startled to discover Walgreen was paying Kodak about 10 cents per print, which was substantially higher than what Rite Aid had been paying for similar services.

Walgreen began pressing Kodak for answers. Kodak eventually responded by lowering the fees. But Walgreen still wasn't happy because the old machines kept breaking down.

Walgreen officials had other problems with Kodak's one-hour minilabs. While Kodak's machines were designed only to handle traditional film, comparable Fuji machines used by Wal-Mart could make prints from digital cameras, too. Kodak began selling kits to allow the minilabs to make prints from digital-camera memory devices. But Walgreen officials also thought the Kodak prints were noticeably worse than those from Fuji's minilabs.

In late 2001, Walgreen quietly began installing Fuji one-hour developing machines in Southern California stores. To date, Walgreen has installed Fuji minilabs in about 1,500 stores, with plans to buy another 800 or so this year, displacing more Kodak-leased machines.

Because Kodak hasn't been willing to let Walgreen out of its leases on its old minilabs,

Walgreen is bearing both lease costs and the expense of buying the Fuji machines, which normally sell for about $115,000 apiece.

Walgreen still has about 3,200 of the old Kodak-leased minilabs in its stores—about 500 of them sitting idle in storage—with a total lease liability to Kodak of about $200 million stretching out over the next several years.

The shift to Fuji equipment could cause even more problems for Kodak by undercutting one of its key forays into digital technology, a walk-up kiosk called Picture Maker. The kiosks, which are already in place in thousands of stores, can make prints from digital cameras. But Walgreen didn't like the fact that the Kodak kiosks can't be connected to its new Fuji developing minilabs, so it decided to install competing Fuji kiosks in each of its stores. Walgreen now uses the Kodak Picture Makers primarily as a means for customers to make copies of old photos.

Kodak says it has tried to address Walgreen's concerns, and Kodak has replaced numerous senior-level executives in charge of retail operations. Some other retailers, including Eckerd, say they've noticed a change in the photo giant's attitude over the last year. Mona Furlott, the vice president in charge of Eckerd's photo-finishing business, said in a recent letter to Kodak that the "Eckerd/Kodak relationship has been improved beyond my expectations" in recent months, adding that the company has gotten better at listening to concerns.

But there aren't many signs that the new team has helped much yet at Walgreen. Kodak recently came back to Walgreen with an offer to provide new, better minilabs made by another manufacturer. Walgreen didn't reject the deal outright. But it hasn't committed so far, because it doesn't want to be locked in to another long-term Kodak deal, a Walgreen official says.

From *The Wall Street Journal,* January 23, 2004. Reprinted by permission of Dow Jones & Co., Inc. via The Copyright Clearance Center.

53

Blockbuster Set to Offer Movies by Mail

Rental Giant's Shift in Approach Is Expected to Keep Prices Low; A Netflix Binge for $19.95

By Martin Peers
And Nick Wingfield

Coming soon to your nearest mailbox: a Blockbuster movie.

Blockbuster Inc. is planning to launch a service that allows customers to order DVDs online for delivery through the mail. If the service sounds familiar, that's because it is. **Netflix,** the Los Gatos, Calif., company, has built a devoted following offering consumers an array of videos through the mail.

While successful, Netflix has only 1.49 million subscribers, compared with the Blockbuster's 48 million member accounts. The move by the rental giant is expected to give the movies-by-mail concept a major boost and spark an intense contest to give consumers a good deal. **Wal-Mart Stores** Inc., which uses cheap DVDs to attract customers, has started a similar program.

The new services are the latest attempt to keep the video rental business relevant to consumers, who can now choose from an increasing variety of ways to watch movies at home. Not only can you now buy a new DVD for under $20 at mass merchants such as Wal-Mart, but cable-TV operators and even the movie studios have started services that allow consumers to order a movie over the TV or computer to watch immediately for $3 or $4. These offerings have all the convenience of a video: the movies can be paused, rewound or fast-forwarded for as long as 24 hours after the initial rental. The big attraction? No late fees.

Not surprisingly, the video-rental market is shrinking. **Viacom** Inc., parent of Blockbuster, said yesterday it would divest its stake in the video company.

The big appeal of the new plans is the promise of multiple movies, for a single monthly price. With Netflix's most popular plan, subscribers can rent an unlimited number of movies for $19.95 a month, keeping as many as three DVDs at a time. Once they send the movies back, by popping them into a postage-paid envelope and dropping them in a mailbox, they can immediately get more. The services don't limit the number of DVDs that can be ordered in any one month, making them a good deal for couch potatoes who love movies.

Blockbuster hasn't unveiled details of its online service but it will be competitive with Netflix's, says a person familiar with Blockbuster's plans. That means Blockbuster will likely have a $20 a month subscription fee for three or four titles. Blockbuster plans to launch the service in the fourth quarter.

Blockbuster has one big advantage over Netflix—its ability to integrate the mail-order service with the convenience of its more than 5,500 stores. Blockbuster has already launched a subscription service that, for $24.99 a month, lets people borrow as many DVDs as they want through the month, with a limit of three at any one time, by going to the store. Blockbuster will extend this service to all its stores by the middle of this year.

Next year, Blockbuster says, it will integrate the mail-order and store services, allowing people to order a movie online or from the store, returning either at the store or through the mail. This hybrid service overcomes one of the big disadvantages of Netflix, the inability to get a movie instantly if you suddenly decide Saturday night you want to rent something.

Netflix's CEO, Reed Hastings, says he doesn't think the combination of Blockbuster's store and online service will be especially appealing to consumers, adding that similar efforts by Web retailers to offer in-store pickup of merchandise haven't taken off. He believes Blockbuster will have a hard time overcoming certain associations some consumers have with it. "To consumers, Blockbuster represents late fees," he says.

A few years ago, Blockbuster argued that mail-order was a niche business, although it acquired a small company offering a mail-order DVD service, Film Caddy, to WATCH the market. Film Caddy charges $19.95 for four titles at a time.

Blockbuster has said most people decide to rent movies on impulse and wouldn't want to have to order several days ahead of time. But since the end of 2002, Netflix has almost doubled its subscribers, a growth rate that surprised Blockbuster. Along the way it became a Wall Street favorite, its stock increas-

Movies by Mail

A comparison of some key movie rental services.

SERVICE	PRICE	COMMENT
Blockbuster	Not announced but to be competitive with Netflix, possibly $19.95 a month for three or four titles	The video-rental giant will eventually allow its customers to pick up a movie in the store and return it through the mail
Netflix Netflix.com	$13.95 for up to 4 DVD rentals a month, with two titles at a time; $19.95 unlimited rentals, with three titles at a time; $39.95 with eight titles at a time	The pioneer of online DVD rentals with 1.5 million subscribers and speedy delivery throughout most of the country
Wal-Mart DVD Rentals Walmart.com	$15.54 for unlimited rentals with two titles at a time; $18.76 for three titles at a time; $21.94 for four titles at a time	Puts promotions for the service in shopping bags with DVD players purchased in Wal-Mart stores. State sales tax may erase the price advantage, depending on where subscribers live.
DVD Avenue Dvdavenue.com	$14.95 for unlimited rentals with two titles at a time; $19.95 for three titles at a time; up to $44.95 a month for eight titles at a time	In addition to movies, rents PlayStation video games
CleanFilms Cleanfilms.com	$19.95 for two titles at a time; $24.95 for three titles at a time; up to $39.95 for eight titles at a time	Sanitizes standard Hollywood movies, from "Jungle Book" to "Independence Day," removing nudity, bad language and graphic violence

Source: the companies

(Cont.)

ing more than sixfold since the beginning of last year, making it worth $1.8 billion. While Blockbuster still doesn't expect the market for online-only rental DVDs to ever get much bigger than 3 million people, Blockbuster Chairman John Antioco acknowledged yesterday that those people are "movie lovers who are obviously important to us."

Blockbuster's move poses a potentially serious threat to Netflix, whose stock dropped $3.76, or 5%, to $72.80 on news of Blockbuster's plans. Netflix is also facing competition from Wal-Mart, which says it has been pleased with the number of subscribers it has gotten for its own online DVD rental service. Later this year, Wal-Mart says it will expand the number of facilities it has around the country for delivering movies, a move that should speed up shipment of titles. "We're seeing superb growth in this business," says Cynthia Lin, a spokeswoman for Walmart.com.

Some consumers are moving beyond Netflix and Blockbuster. Josh Felser, an entrepreneur in Mill Valley, Calif., says he plans to cancel his Netflix subscription after getting a TiVo, on which he has recorded about 50 movies from his satellite television service. He doubts the Blockbuster rental service will appeal to him. "I haven't been to a Blockbuster in so many years I don't even know where they are," Mr. Felser says.

From *The Wall Street Journal,* February 11, 2004. Reprinted by permission of Dow Jones & Co., Inc. via The Copyright Clearance Center.

Online Sales Up 25%, But They're Small Piece Of Retail Pie

By Brian Deagon
Investor's Business Daily

U.S. consumers spent $17.2 billion buying goods online in the fourth quarter, up 25% from a year ago.

For the year, consumers spent $55 billion, up 26% from $43.5 billion in 2002, according to Commerce Department figures released Monday. The e-tail industry has continually posted double-digit growth rates since Commerce started tracking the sector in late 1999.

"It shows that 2003 is on the record as another fast-growth year for e-commerce," said Kate Delhagen, an analyst at Forrester Research Inc.

For now, e-tail sales are just a sliver of total retail sales. In the fourth quarter, U.S. retail sales totaled $918 billion. E-commerce represented just 1.9% of that amount, up from 1.5% in the third quarter, says the Commerce Department.

The Commerce survey is based on a random sampling of 11,000 retail firms whose sales are weighted and benchmarked to represent a universe of 2 million retail firms. The sampling takes into account online retailers, as well as online auctions and car sales. But it excludes online travel, brokerage and ticket sales because they are not classified as retail in government categories.

The Commerce report is the most recent of a string of online sales reports that have been released during the past few weeks. Researchers' tabulation methods differ somewhat, but the overriding trend is unmistakable. Online retail is a fast-growing business that is gaining in prominence.

"Sales and profits in online retailing are hitting a point where proponents of the technology are getting a seat in the corporate boardroom of big retailers," said Patti Freeman Evans, an analyst at Jupiter Re-

search. Moreover, she said, retailers are getting savvier at mining data from their Web sites and using it to adjust how and what they sell at their physical store locations.

"When you're cruising down an aisle, the store can't tell what you are browsing, or what you put in your shopping cart then take out, or that buying one item led to buying another," said Evans.

But you can collect that information from people who shop online. "How a consumer searches for something on your Web site says something about the attitudes they have toward those products," she said.

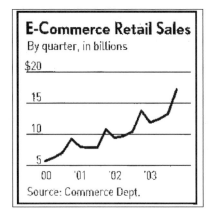

E-Commerce Retail Sales
By quarter, in billions

Source: Commerce Dept.

Jupiter Research predicts online retail sales will reach $65 billion in 2004, up 24% from last year. They will continue to grow at a compound annual rate of 17% through 2008, to top $117 billion, or 5% of U.S. retail sales.

But Forrester Research, which includes travel sales and ticket reservations in its data, predicts online retail will account for 10% of retail sales by 2008, or nearly $230 billion.

In 2003, travel and ticket sales accounted for $30.5 billion in commerce, according to Forrester, and will grow to $61 billion in 2008.

Among the trends fueling the growth in online sales is the increase in high-speed Internet connections. The easier it is to browse, the thinking goes, the more willing consumers are to shop online. About 71 million households have an Internet connection. Thirty percent of those have a broadband connection, Forrester reports. That's up from 10% in 2000. By 2008, says Forrester, 74% of Internet users will have a broadband connection.

A second trend fueling growth is just simple math: More people go online each year. Another five million will get an Internet connection in 2004, says Delhagen.

"More and more people are getting connected and they are shifting their buying behavior as a result," she said.

As to what sells online, the fastest growth categories in the fourth quarter included computers, music and movies. Also moving up in the rankings were furniture, appliances and jewelry, according to research firm comScore Networks.

"It shows that people are getting more comfortable buying high-ticket items online," said Gian Fulgoni, comScore chairman.

Goldman Sachs, in its most recent survey of the e-commerce market, said the mass market adoption of online shopping is a direct result of increased consumer satisfaction. That's especially true when it comes to ease of use, reliability and selection.

What is not factored into the e-tail sales figures are goods researched online but purchased at a store. According to Jupiter, nearly 30% of offline retail purchases will be influenced by research done online.

Reprinted from *Investor's Business Daily*, February 24, 2004. Used by permission.

Retailers Rely More on Fast Deliveries

BY ELIZABETH SOUDER
Dow Jones Newswires

NEW YORK—When **Nintendo** Co. shipped its new "Mario Kart: Double Dash" videogame to stores in November, most retailers agreed to pay a little extra to have the games sent directly to the stores within nine days.

For about 60% of the stores, the games went from a packaging plant near Seattle straight to the retail-store shelves, no stops at warehouses or distribution centers, which can increase the time a product gets to the shelf to as long as six weeks.

As it turned out, speed was crucial. The game, which features characters racing go-carts while throwing things at each other, was out of stock by the first week of December, after sales of almost 500,000 games. Nintendo was able to restock shelves in time for the critical pre-Christmas rush—thanks to Atlanta-based **United Parcel Service** Inc.—and Nintendo sold more than 900,000 games in the U.S. by the end of the year.

This past holiday season, retailers turned to shipping companies to help maintain supply lines. That demand has prompted transport companies such as UPS and Memphis, Tenn.-based **FedEx** Corp. to offer new services directed at retailers and to use their transport networks differently, bringing in new sources of revenue.

The trend toward just-in-time retail shipments has been growing over the past decade. Nintendo began shipping videogames that way 10 years ago. But in 2003, with the economy sputtering, retailers strove to keep inventories low. So when an item like "Mario Kart" sold well, some retailers were in a bind, and relied on faster shipping of merchandise to stores to accommodate customers.

"Really the biggest time of year for us is November and December," said George Harrison, senior vice president of marketing for Nintendo of America Inc., the U.S. unit of the Japanese company. "If it goes out of stock for a while, customers tend to lose interest in it."

Quantifying the trend is slippery, but experts across the industry agree the amount of direct-to-store shipping is growing, and will continue to grow until most retailers receive at least some of their merchandise that way.

"We're moving more to a continuous replenishment of inventory," said Adrian Gonzalez, a logistics expert with ARC Advisory Group.

The retail industry is moving away from the cycle of building up inventory and letting it decline when the economy hits a rough spot, he said. "The inventory build will not be as great as it was in the past" as the economy improves, Mr. Gonzalez said.

UPS and FedEx have beefed up their services for retail shipments, not only delivering packages to stores on a tight schedule, but also handling customs or packing the goods exactly as the retailer wants. UPS goes so far as to inspect goods for retailers and to put clothes on hangers.

UPS spokeswoman Lynnette McIntire said the company's supply-chain services unit makes up about 8% of UPS's total business. And the unit's revenue is set to increase by a double-digit percentage this year, she said.

Other transport companies are using their extensive delivery networks in new ways to handle direct-to-store shipments. Closely held truckload carrier **Schneider National** Inc., Green Bay, Wis., sees itself as a "rolling warehouse," delivering goods to retail stores as they are needed, said Tom Nightingale, vice president of marketing for the carrier.

Schneider uses the same equipment to load goods on trucks or on trains, which has turned out to be one of the company's strengths as a retail-goods carrier. A shipment in the Schneider network can change its destination without having to be reloaded on different equipment, he said.

Mr. Nightingale said most of the direct-to-store shipments Schneider handles are for one-time promotions or special sales, rather than as a constant method of replenishing shelves.

Gus Pagonis, head of logistics for **Sears, Roebuck** & Co., Hoffman Estates, Ill., said he sometimes sends full truckloads of goods directly to stores for special promotions. He said that is among the cheapest methods of direct-to-store delivery. But he doesn't like to inundate stores with so much inventory all the time.

"The backroom of a store is like a quagmire," said Mr. Pagonis, who as a lieutenant general in the U.S. Army ran logistics during the Gulf War.

For smaller loads, retailers often turn to less-than-truckload carriers to ship directly to stores. Bill Zollars, chief executive of **Yellow Roadway** Corp., said the Overland Park, Kan., less-than-truckload carrier has seen an increase in direct-to-store shipments in the past year, benefiting Yellow's expedited service.

"It's the same amount of goods, probably shipped a little more frequently," he said. Where Yellow captures more revenue is when a shipment must be expedited to meet a deadline, he said.

One deadline Yellow was asked to meet was the release of the latest Harry Potter book. Beth Ford, a senior vice president with New York-based **Scholastic** Corp., which published the book in the U.S., said 94% of the shipment went directly from the presses to book stores on trucks operated by Yellow and **J.B. Hunt Transport Services** Inc., of Lowell, Ariz.

Last June, Scholastic shipped 8.5 million copies of the book, the fifth of the bestseller series, within two days in order to meet the launch deadline. By planning the loads carefully, the shipping costs per book actually dropped below those of the fourth Harry Potter book, which hit stores in 2000, Ms. Ford said.

Direct-to-store deliveries don't always make sense for Scholastic, which also publishes textbooks that are stored in a warehouse and sent out a few at a time.

Ms. Ford said Scholastic has been focusing in the past few years on improving its logistics system to cut overall costs. She said it is also a priority for many of Scholastic's bookstore customers, who want to keep less inventory in the stores and are returning unsold books to Scholastic more quickly. "Logistics companies are becoming more sophisticated with their offerings, and we're looking at what we can use," Ms. Ford said. "I might pay more for the logistics side" if it means cutting costs elsewhere or keeping a commitment to customers.

Working closely with retail stores to reduce inventory requires implementing expensive technology to track where products are selling the best. Transport companies must have the technology to track shipments and get them to the retailer at a specified time, and manufacturers must install their own tracking systems to match that of the retailers.

Suppliers such as Scholastic and Nintendo tend to bear most of the costs of getting goods to the retailer, and in some cases that means paying to store inventory on behalf of the retailers.

Mike Peters, a vice president for warehouse operator ProLogis, said he has seen a shift in the company's customer base toward more manufacturers than retailers, as retailers demand that manufacturers handle more inventory.

Retailers have been "very cautious about investing in inventory" of late, said Mr. Peters, who runs the consulting business of the Aurora, Colo., company. "Some of that inventory will be pushed upstream and held by manufacturers."

The question for retailers: "Are they willing to share in that risk, or are they just pushing the goods upstream?" he said.

As for Nintendo, a 10-year veteran of direct-to-store deliveries, the game maker has managed to pass along some of the shipping costs to retail customers.

Marketing head Mr. Harrison said retailers that participate in the direct-to-store shipping program must pay extra, amounting to about 2% of total sales, allowing Nintendo and retailers to share the costs.

"We try to show them the benefits" of cutting down on their own inventory and cycling fresh products on the shelves more quickly, he said.

66,207,896 BOTTLES OF BEER ON THE WALL

Every time a six-pack moves off the shelf, Anheuser-Busch's top-secret nationwide data network knows. Here's how BudNet gives the company its edge.

By Kevin Kelleher

When Dereck Gurden pulls up at one of his customers' stores—7-Eleven, Buy N Save, or one of dozens of liquor marts and restaurants in the 800-square-mile territory he covers in California's Central Valley—managers usually stop what they're doing and grab a notepad. Toting his constant companion, a brick-size handheld PC, the 41-year-old father of three starts his routine.

"First I'll scroll through and check the accounts receivable, make sure everything's current," he says. "Then it'll show me an inventory screen with a four-week history. I can get past sales, package placements—facts and numbers on how much of the sales they did when they had a display in a certain location." After chatting up his customer, Gurden "walks the store, inputting what I see." What he sees, that is, about his *competitors'* product displays, which goes into the handheld too. "It's no extra work to get the competitive info," he says. "You always want to walk the store."

All done, Gurden jacks the handheld into his cell phone and fires off new orders to the warehouse, along with the data he's gathered. "Honestly? I think I know more about these guys' businesses than they do," he says. "At least in the beer section."

What makes Gurden so smart? He's a sales rep for Sierra Beverage, one of about 700 U.S. distributors that work for Anheuser-Busch. Gurden and several thousand reps and drivers serve as the eyes and ears of a data network through which distributors report, in excruciating detail, on sales, shelf stocks, and displays at thousands of outlets.

Called BudNet, it the King of Beers's little-known crown jewel, and the primary reason that Anheuser's share (by volume) of the $74.4 billion U.S. beer market inched up to 50.1 percent from 48.9 percent during the past year—a huge gain at a time when a week economy, lousy weather, and the threat of higher state taxes and tighter drinking laws have kept sales of Coors, Miller,

and other brewers on ice. No wonder Anheuser-Busch is so tight-lipped about its data-mining operation. (Only one executive agreed to be interviewed for this story.)

According to dozens of analysts, beer-industry veterans, and distributor execs contacted for the article, Anheuser has made a deadly accurate science out of finding out what beer lovers are buying, as well as when, where, and why. The last time you bought a six-pack of Bud Light at the Piggly Wiggly, Anheuser servers most likely recorded what you paid, when that beer was brewed, whether you purchased it warm or chilled, and whether you could have gotten a better deal down the street.

Anheuser uses the data to constantly change marketing strategies, to design promotions to suit the ethnic makeup of its markets, and as early warning radar that detects where rivals might have an edge. "If Anheuser-Bush loses shelf space in a store in Clarksville, Tenn., they know it right away," says Joe Thompson, president of Independent Beverage Group, a research and consulting firm. "They're better at this game than anyone, even Coca-Cola."

As recently as six years ago, the beer industry was a technological laggard. Distributors and sales reps returned from their daily routes with stacks of invoices and sales orders, which they'd type into a PC and dial in to breweries. They, in turn, would compile them into monthly reports to see which brands were the hottest. But Anheuser changed the rules in 1997, when Chairman August Busch III vowed to make his company a leader in mining its customers' buying patterns.

While most brewers were experimenting with Internet-based record keeping, Anheuser began amending its contracts with wholesalers to demand that they start collecting data on how much shelf space their retailers devoted to all beer brands, which ones had the most visible displays, and the locations of those displays. At first, it was left up to the distributors to figure out just

(Cont.)

how to amass the data and deliver reports to Anheuser; many resorted to sending in Excel spreadsheets, a method that grew cumbersome as Anheuser demanded more data. A cottage industry quickly emerged for software developers who, working with Anheuser execs, simplified the process for distributors. It then fell to Joe Patti, Anheuser's vice president for retail planning and category management, to fine-tune the system into BudNet. "Wholesaler and store-level data has become the lifeblood of our organization," Patti writes in an e-mailed statement.

Understatement is more like it: Collecting the data in a nightly nationwide sweep of its distributors' servers, Anheuser can draw a picture each morning of what brands are selling in which packages using which medley of displays, discounts, and promotions. Anheuser then sends its distributors out with new marching orders. "Since Michelob Light (an Anheuser brand) serves as an official sponsor of the LPGA Tour," Patti explains, "if someone asks how the brand is distributed on golf courses, we can quickly calculate our distribution and develop plans to address the courses that don't carry Michelob Light."

That's an advantage Anheuser enjoys for two reasons. First, the company wields Wal-Mart-like clout with wholesalers and insists on exclusive deals with as many as possible, offering incentives for those that comply, IBG's Thompson says. Second, none of the other brewers approaches Anheuser's data-mining savvy. "It's not just collecting data," says Harry Schuhmacher, editor of *Beer Business Daily*. "It depends on brainpower. Anheuser-Busch is the smartest in figuring out how to use it."

The trick has served Anheuser beautifully since Busch III announced the company's tech blitz. Anheuser has posted double-digit profit gains for 20 straight quarters, while its nearest competitors, Coors and Miller, have flatlined. Today it's the only major brewer to rely heavily on data from Information Resources Inc.—which tracks every bar-coded product swiped at checkout and per-

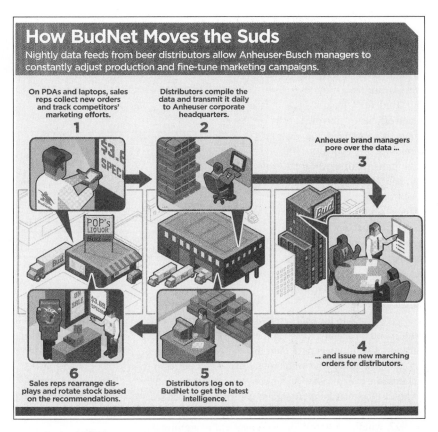

How BudNet Moves the Suds

Nightly data feeds from beer distributors allow Anheuser-Busch managers to constantly adjust production and fine-tune marketing campaigns.

1. On PDAs and laptops, sales reps collect new orders and track competitors' marketing efforts.

2. Distributors compile the data and transmit it daily to Anheuser corporate headquarters.

3. Anheuser brand managers pore over the data ...

4. ... and issue new marching orders for distributors.

5. Distributors log on to BudNet to get the latest intelligence.

6. Sales reps rearrange displays and rotate stock based on the recommendations.

forms Nielsen-style consumer surveys—and to conduct its own monthly surveys to see what beer drinkers buy and why. Parsing the aggregate data tells Anheuser what images or ideas to push in its ads, and what new products to unveil—such as low-carb Michelob Ultra, Anheuser's most successful launch since Bud Light.

This data, crossed with U.S. Census figures on the ethnic and economic makeup of neighborhoods, also helps Anheuser tailor marketing campaigns with a local precision only dreamed of a few years ago. The data reveals trends by city (Tequiza may be hot in San Antonio, but Bud Light plays better in Peoria), by neighborhood (gay models appear on posters in San Francisco's Castro district, but not on those in the Mission), by holiday (the Fourth of July is a big seller in Atlanta, but St. Patrick's Day isn't), and by class (cans for blue-collar stores, bottles for white-collar). "They're drilling down to the level of the individual store," Thompson says. "They can pinpoint if customers are gay, Latino, 30-year-old, college-educated conservatives." Anheuser's most sought-after demographics? Twenty-somethings and Latinos. Not only are both more likely to drink beer than the overall

(Cont.)

population, but these groups are also projected to grow by more than 3 percent a year through 2010, according to Census Bureau estimates.

BudNet hasn't just added efficiency into the beer chain, it's changed the dynamics of the industry. The data juggernaut has turned the beer wholesaling business from an unruly network of mom-and-pops into an industry in which only the most tech-savvy survive. (Three of the six biggest distributors in the country—Ben E. Keith Beers, Silver Eagle Distribution, and Henley & Co.—handle only Anheuser suds.)

According to the Independent Beverage Group, operating income for the average Anheuser wholesaler is $2.2 million—five times greater than the average for Miller or Coors distributors. And wholesalers that don't perform to Anheuser's ever stricter standards are unceremoniously dumped. One distributor, founded by former Yankees slugger Roger Maris after his 1968 retirement, sued Anheuser in 1997, winning $50 million in damages after arguing that the beer company unfairly cut it loose. "Anheuser-Busch keeps their distributors under its thumb," says Madison McClellan, an attorney for Maris Distributing.

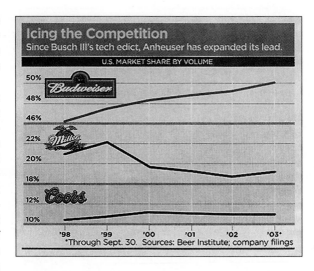

Icing the Competition

Since Busch III's tech edict, Anheuser has expanded its lead.

U.S. MARKET SHARE BY VOLUME

Budweiser

Miller

Coors

'98 '99 '00 '01 '02 '03*

*Through Sept. 30. Sources: Beer Institute; company filings

The case is under appeal, but Anheuser shows no signs of letting up. At a recent gathering of beer distributors, August Busch IV, president for domestic operations, promised his audience that "brewers and wholesalers with a clear data-driven focus will have a distinct competitive advantage." According to Bal Maraj, president of MIT Systems, which makes software for devices used by several Anheuser distributors, the company will soon require all of its drivers and sales reps to carry handheld computers for wireless data uploads, just as Gurden does.

Three years ago, still toting around clipboards and invoices, Gurden didn't even bother keeping track of the Coors and Miller displays in his customers' stores. Today those are among the most important data fields in his handheld. And Coors and Miller are paying dearly for what he knows.

E-Commerce Report

Some Web merchants fill a void, and make a profit, by selling coffins and other funeral supplies online.

BY BOB TEDESCHI

With so many consumer purchases proving popular online—whether books, concert tickets or prescription drugs—the question was eventually bound to arise. Why not coffins?

Funeral industry executives and analysts say that consumers are increasingly interested in being able to shop online for their funeral needs and that some Web merchants are stepping up to serve them.

"When you visit casket dealers online, you can look at something over and over again," said Jay Kravetz, editor of Death Care Business, a trade publication. "You're not pressured—you have time to look with relatives and friends. It's really easier online."

And it can be cheaper, given that some funeral directors mark up their coffins as much as 300 percent over wholesale, knowing that most consumers are reluctant to haggle or shop around.

On the Web, **Funeral Depot,** which sells funeral supplies both online and offline from its Hallandale Beach, Fla., store, is able to earn a profit of about 40 percent by charging double the wholesale price of its coffins—and still significantly beating funeral homes' prices. The average price of Funeral Depot coffins sold online is about $1,500.

"I'll offer the same coffin at a fraction of what a funeral home charges, deliver it overnight for free, and still make substantial profit and walk away the hero," said Dean Magliocca, president and owner of Funeral Depot.

Mr. Magliocca is among the more successful online merchants of funeral supplies, with projected revenue this year of $1.5 million—the bulk of it from his Web operation. It is a modest number, to be sure, but Mr. Magliocca is not complaining. "We're very pleased with our progress," he said. "It's taken us a little over three and a half years to get us where we're at, but we've finally perfected what we do, and we're starting to generate a lot of revenue with nice margins."

At the time he started the Web operation, Mr. Magliocca had been selling only monuments and grave markers from his storefront. "I started to hear from families that they didn't have enough money to spend on markers because the coffins were $5,000," he recalled. "I found out it wasn't necessarily because of the wholesale costs."

Mr. Magliocca, who started the online business "with about $400 worth of Web publishing software and a lot of elbow grease," offers nearly 300 different coffins, with prices ranging from $745 for an unsealed thin-metal box to $18,500 for a solid-bronze model that he says "looks like it belongs in space, not the ground."

FuneralDepot.com also sells "theme" coffins made by **White Light** Inc., which are painted in various motifs, including an auto racing theme. For the whimsical there is a coffin done up like a special-delivery package and stamped "Return to Sender."

Mr. Magliocca sells coffins from all leading manufacturers, like **Hillenbrand Industries'** Batesville Casket Company and **Matthews International's** York Group. But he has to buy them from third parties because he says that none of the major manufacturers will sell their coffins directly to him, or to any online coffin merchant, for that matter.

The problem, which has plagued manufacturers and online retailers in many industries, is referred to in business parlance as channel conflict. Manufacturers or their distributors either do not trust Net sellers to protect the image of their brands, or they do not want to upset their established resellers—in this case, funeral homes—by allowing online retailers to sell their wares at a discount.

To work around this problem, Mr. Magliocca has set up a nationwide network of about 45 independent funeral homes that are authorized to sell coffins from well-known manufacturers and have agreed to ship orders on Funeral Depot's behalf. These funeral homes earn a small percentage of each of these sales—business they would not have otherwise gotten—and many have received referrals from FuneralDepot.com customers who call or send e-mail messages to ask the company to suggest funeral homes in various cities.

Funeral Depot's arrangement with the independents has drawn legal fire from at least one manufacturer, Batesville, which says it has a lawsuit pending against Funeral Depot. While Batesville would not comment on the suit, a Funeral Depot lawyer said the case focused on whether the company could legally continue to use the Batesville name when offering Batesville coffins on FuneralDepot.com or link to images from the Batesville catalog that are shown on other Web sites.

Other online coffin sellers are coming up with their own work-arounds to secure brand-name merchandise. Kim Powers, president and founder of **Memorial Concepts Online,** which sells coffins and other funeral-related items on the Web, declined to say exactly where her company bought its coffins.

Ms. Powers, whose three-year-old company is based in Ponca City, Okla., said Memorial Concepts was now profitable, despite the fact that she could not sell in her home state. In Oklahoma, as in nearly a dozen other states, the law prohibits anyone without a funeral director's license from selling a coffin—critics say the policy is meant to protect the interests of funeral homes.

Last year, Ms. Powers sued the state, arguing that the law violates, among other things, her right to economic liberty under the United States Constitution's "Privileges or Immunities" clause.

In December, a Federal District Court in Oklahoma ruled against Ms. Powers, observing the longstanding practice of federal courts to defer to the judgment of state legislatures when the lawmakers regulate "nonfundamental rights," like those involving working conditions or the right to earn a living (as opposed to "fundamental rights," like the right to privacy). Ms. Powers and the organization that is representing her, the Institute for Justice, a libertarian advocacy group in Washington, are appealing the case to the United States Court of Appeals for the 10th Circuit in Denver.

A similar case brought by the Institute for Justice on behalf of a non-Internet coffin seller in Tennessee could help Ms. Powers's cause. In that case, in which the plaintiff is challenging a law that is nearly identical to Oklahoma's, a Federal District Court struck down the Tennessee regulation, saying it served "no legitimate governmental purpose." Tennessee's attorney general has yet to decide whether to appeal to the United States Supreme Court.

Even though the Oklahoma law prevents Ms. Powers from selling coffins in the state and has cost the company time and money, she said the publicity had been helpful. "Our business has always been very good in other areas, like markers and monuments," she said. "But since we brought this case, our coffin business has more than quadrupled."

While buying coffins online may be a way for consumers to save money, it may not necessarily be the best thing for the newly bereaved, according to Robert M. Fells, general counsel of the National Funeral Directors Association.

Mr. Fells, who said his group was "just fine" with allowing independent coffin sellers to operate online, said grief counseling experts advised people to visit funeral homes in person to help select coffins or urns as a way to ease the grieving process.

Yet, he said, "more and more, instead of going to the funeral home, people are saying, 'I don't need that—I'll e-mail you.'"

One Nation Under Wal-Mart

How retailing's superpower—and our biggest Most Admired company—is changing the rules for corporate America. ■ *by Jerry Useem*

Bentonville, Ark., does not come to the world. The world comes to Bentonville. Whether you're a media mogul or a toy tycoon or King Tut, you drive your rent-a-car north on Walton Boulevard, past Smokin' Joe's Ribhouse and the Lube N' Go, and into one of the parking spots marked SUPPLIER. Don't expect a welcoming party. You make your way into a packed waiting room that reminds you of the Department of Motor Vehicles and have a seat. Thirsty from your trip? Coke machine in the back. Coffee? Ten cents in the box, please. Change machine over there if you need it.

The young buyer who emerges to greet you has a paycheck that's far smaller than yours, a name that's far less celebrated, and a budget of about $1 billion. He ushers you into a seven-by-ten-foot blue roomlet—one fluorescent light, one table, one photo of Mr. Sam. So, says the buyer in his unfailingly polite manner, how can Disney help Wal-Mart?

If you are an executive from Walt Disney, you've been here before. Your company sells movies, Pooh merchandise, and many other items to Wal-Mart. But when the buyer wonders whether Disney could make a short video involving Wal-Mart and a Disney character— you know, something to get the store associates fired up or perhaps to play on Wal-Mart's in-store TV network—you have to say no: Disney characters aren't allowed to be so crassly commercial. Well, that's okay. Jeffrey Katzenberg was down here, and his team at DreamWorks made the nicest video of Shrek doing the Wal-Mart cheer ...

Not only was the *Shrek* video a huge hit, but Katzenberg has spent more time around Bentonville than anyone might suspect. "I've been there three times in the last 45 days," he confirmed recently. "I cannot tell you how much I respect and love the bare-essentials efficiency... I'm flattered by the opportunity they've offered." If this strikes you as unconvincing, you haven't seen Katzenberg do the Wal-Mart cheer.

That an important studio boss like Katzenberg would answer calls of "Give me a W." with fist raised might generate snickers among his peers. But nobody was laughing

in 2001 when Wal-Mart—its stores bristling with displays of the green ogre—helped turn *Shrek* into the year's bestselling DVD. "Jeffrey figured out something his competitors didn't," says Warren Lieberfarb, the former Warner Home Video chief, who is known as the father of DVD. "Wal-Mart is the largest single revenue generator for Hollywood in the world."

And so, you see, there are two types of executives these days: those who have learned to play by Wal-Mart's rules, and those who still haven't learned the right answer to the cheer's closing question: "Who's No. 1?"

"The customer! Always! Whoomp!!!"

For most of Wal-Mart's 41 years, Corporate America refused to acknowledge the retailer as one of its own. Wal-Mart was Podunk, U.S.A., Jed Clampett, Uncle Jesse's pickup—and worse yet, a *discount store*. This year its transfiguration is complete. Wal-Mart is FORTUNE's most admired company, marking the first time the world's biggest corporation—yes, it replaced Exxon Mobil atop the FORTUNE 500 last year—is also its most respected. You might say that Wal-Mart finally belongs in corporate America. More accurately, you could say corporate America belongs to Wal-Mart.

To understand this astonishing development, you need to grasp the difference between a big company—what Wal-Mart was at the time of Sam Walton's death in 1992, when it was about one-fifth its present size— and a company that has created a whole new definition of bigness. If conventional metrics, like Wal-Mart's $240 billion-plus in sales or its 1.3 million "associates," don't do the trick, these may help:

► Wal-Mart's sales on one day last fall— $1.42 billion—were larger than the GDPs of 36 countries.

► It is the biggest employer in 21 states, with more people in uniform than the US. Army.

► It plans to grow this year by the equivalent of—take your pick—one Dow Chemical, one PepsiCo, one Microsoft, or one Lockheed Martin.

► If the estimated $2 billion it loses

through theft each year were incorporated as a business, it would rank No. 694 on the FORTUNE 1,000.

What this means for Wal-Mart's lowprofile CEO, Lee Scott, is that he runs what is arguably the world's most powerful company. What it means for corporate America is a bit more bracing. It means, for one, that Wal-Mart is not just Disney's biggest customer but also Procter & Gamble's and Kraft's and Revlon's and Gillette's and Campbell Soup's and RJR's and on down the list of America's famous branded manufacturers. It means, further, that the nation's biggest seller of DVDs

It employs the most
Wal-Mart is the largest employer in 21 states (in red).

It buys the most

COMPANY	% OF ITS TOTAL SALES TO WAL-MART
Tandy Brands Accessories	39%
Clorox	23%
Revlon	20%
RJR Tobacco	20%
Procter & Gamble	17%

It sells the most

PRODUCT	WAL-MART'S U.S. MARKET SHARE*
Dog food	36%
Disposable diapers	32%
Photographic film	30%
Toothpaste	26%
Pain remedies	21%

*Percent of all sales through food, drug, and mass-merchandisers.

FORTUNE CHART/SOURCES: ECONOMY.COM; SEC FILINGS; A.C. NIELSEN is also its biggest seller of groceries, toys, guns, diamonds, CDs, apparel, dog food, detergent, jewelry, sporting goods, videogames, socks, bedding, and toothpaste—not to mention its biggest film developer, optician, private truck-fleet operator, energy consumer, and real estate developer. It means, finally, that the real market clout in many industries no longer resides in Hollywood or Cincinnati or New York City, but in the hills of northwestern Arkansas.

If this sounds fanciful, then you haven't visited Newell Rubbermaid's new Bentonville office, just a 60-second drive from Wal-Mart headquarters. One of 200 corporate embassies here that form a ring known as "Vendorville," it's home to the 50 members of Newell's Wal-Mart Division. "Everything in here is like Wal-Mart," says one manager, and he means it literally. The carpets mirror those in Wal-Mart headquarters. Same with the cheap cubicles. The first floor has an "exact replica of a Wal-Mart store" showing the placement of Newell glassware, Sharpie pens, trash cans, Levelor blinds, and so forth. Upstairs, Sam Walton's image and aphorisms hang on the walls, while even the Gregorian calendar has given way to "Wal-Mart time": Week 9 is understood to mean nine weeks into the company's fiscal year, starting Feb. 1. "You need to *be* your customer," explains my host.

Newell's reasoning comes down to one number: 15, the percentage of its merchandise that passes through Wal-Mart cash registers. That number helps explain why Newell CEO Joe Galli spends four weeks a year touring Wal-Mart stores, and why Newell seldom designs or launches a new product without Wal-Mart's involvement, and why division president Steven Scheyer gives every new employee a copy of Sam Walton's autobiography. (It also helps explain why there are no direct flights from New York City to Little Rock, but you can catch one of American Airlines' two daily nonstops from LaGuardia to Bentonville.) "We live and breathe with these guys," says Scheyer. "People are focusing on 'What's the right Sharpie for Wal-Mart, what's the right closet product for Wal-Mart, what's the right stroller?'" Little wonder that Stockholm Syndrome—the phenomenon in which hostages come to identify with their captors—has been a problem for some companies. "At first there's resistance, then they break down, then they go to the other side," says Steve Cleere, a consultant at TradeMarketing. "They're thinking like Wal-Mart people instead of brand people, and they need to be rotated out."

How Wal-Mart thinks has never been a big mystery: Buy stuff at the lowest cost possible, pass the gains on to the consumer through superlow prices, watch stuff fly off the shelves at insane velocity. (Critics who say Wal-Mart is obsessed with its bottom line have one thing wrong: Wal-Mart is obsessed with its top line, which it grows by focusing on the consumer's bottom line.) Suppliers are expected to offer their best price, period. "It's not even negotiated anymore," says Paul Kelly of Silvermine, a consulting company that helps manufacturers sell to big retailers. "No one would dare come in with a half-ass price." As for a supplier *raising* prices, good luck: In some cases Wal-Mart has been known simply to keep sending payment for the old amount. "The days of the price increase," Joe Galli has told his troops, "are over."

By systematically wresting "pricing power" from the manufacturer and handing it to the consumer, Wal-Mart has begun to generate an economy-wide Wal-Mart Effect. Economists now credit the company's Everyday Low Prices with contributing to Everyday Low Inflation, meaning that all Americans—even members of WhirlMart, a "ritual resistance" group that silently pushes empty carts through superstores—unknowingly benefit from the retailer's clout. A 2002 McKinsey study, moreover, found that more than one-eighth of U.S. productivity growth between 1995 and 1999 could be explained "by only two syllables: Wal-Mart." "You add it all up," says Warren Buffett, "and they have contributed to the financial well-being of the American public more than any institution I can think of." His own back-of-the-envelope calculation: $10 billion a year.

That, mind you, is Wal-Mart today. "As Wal-Mart grows," writes consultant Ira Kalish of Retail Forward, "it will transform its competitors, its suppliers, and the industries it dominates." In apparel, for instance, Wal-Mart is moving from staples into cheap-chic fashion, exemplified by its new George line, which offers career basics like skirts and blazers priced between $8.87 and $28.96. That in turn is pressuring everyone from Bloomingdale's to Banana Republic to compete on price as well as image. "Wal-Mart has caused the fashion industry to go topsy-turvy," says Marshal Cohen, co-president of NPDfashionworld.

In Hollywood, Wal-Mart's push for cheap DVDs (as low as $5.88) has exacerbated a schism between studios like Universal, which don't want to cannibalize the lucrative rental business, and those like Warner, which are pushing a high-volume, low-margin approach. Caught perilously in the middle is Viacom's Blockbuster. "We don't plan to participate in the below-cost DVD madness," says CEO John Antioco.

Convenience stores, meanwhile, are threatened by the 700 gas stations now in Wal-Mart parking lots, causing petroleum sellers to lobby vigorously for protective legislation. "We are seeing margins on fuel that we haven't seen this low in a decade or more," says Jeff Lenard, a spokesman for the National Association of Convenience Stores.

The battle of the brands, too, is increasingly played out on Wal-Mart turf. In batteries, perennial third-place Rayovac has used a low-cost "Wal-Mart *über Alles*" strategy to challenge Energizer and Gillette's Duracell. Tattered Levi Strauss, once too cool for discount stores, has bet its future on sub-$30 jeans to hit Wal-Mart racks this summer. And toy companies anxiously watch the fate—and try actively to boost the fortunes—of Toys 'R' Us, fearing a unipolar world. "If Toys 'R' Us goes under, and then Kmart too, are you selling 60% of your toys to Wal-Mart?" asks Alex Lintner, a retail expert at Boston Consulting Group.

Wal-Mart in 2003 is, in short, a lot like America in 2003: a sole superpower with a down-home twang. As with Uncle Sam, everyone's position in the world will largely be defined in relation to Mr. Sam. Is your company a "strategic competitor" like China or a "partner" like Britain? Is it a client state like Israel or a supplier to the opposition like Yemen? Is it France, benefiting from the superpower's reach while complaining the whole time? Or is it ... well, a Target? You can admire the superpower or resent it or—most likely—both. But you can't ignore it.

I t is an odd fact that the public face of Wal-Mart continues, after all these years, to be the folksy visage of Sam Walton. Spend enough time inside the company—where nothing backs up a point better than a quotation from Walton scripture—and it's easy to get the impression that the founder is orchestrating his creation from beyond. The explosive growth of the past decade has, of course, actually occurred under the earthly apostleship of David Glass and, since 2000, 53-year-old Lee Scott.

Yet the best way to understand Wal-Mart is to talk to people like Shelly Chandler. Daughter of a Marine colonel, she started out sorting invoices for $4.65 an hour. As a $50,000-a-year apparel buyer in the mid-1990s, she controlled a budget of $1 billion. "Tough as I am—thank you, Sam—I got good deals," recalls Chandler, who still speaks of the company as "we" despite having left in 1996, when her child fell ill. "Sam taught us to be tough but fair. That's what makes Wal-Mart go round and round and round." Pressed on how it felt to control a thousand million dollars, Chandler paused. "I had the biggest pencil in the United States of America," she said, "and if someone didn't do what fit with our program, I could break my pencil, throw it on the table, and never come back."

Early power retailers like Sears and A&P started out with the upper hand. A 1930 FORTUNE article noted that "A&P's terms become, practically, Economic Law." (The magazine also marveled that "if every person in New York City were a hen laying regularly, there would not be enough eggs to fill the A&P demand.") It was the coming of television, plus laws that prevented stores from selling products below their listed price, that shifted the advantage to mass-marketers like P&G, Coke, and Revlon (which not only sponsored but owned the top-rated '50s TV show *The $64,000 Question*). "What Wal-Mart has done," says Harvard's Tedlow, "is turn that on its head again. The store has a helluva lot of power."

How Wal-Mart chooses to wield this power is today's $244 Billion Question. Many assume that the company uses it crudely, cracking suppliers' heads and stealing their lunch money. But if that were the case, you'd expect to see manufacturers' margins shrinking. And? According to Value Line, operating margins of household product makers actually grew 48% between 1992 and 2001; food processors' went up 30%; soft drink makers' rose 14%. Though horror stories do circulate (some entrepreneurs have accused Wal-Mart of knocking off their product proposals), Wal-Mart also towered as the "best retailer with which to do business" in a Cannondale Associates survey of 122 manufacturers. "I think most would say that Wal-Mart is their most profitable account," says Silvermine's Paul Kelly.

How can that be? It begins to make sense if you consider the byzantine demands that most retailers impose on suppliers. Slotting fees. Display fees. Damage allowances. Handling charges. Late penalties. Special sales and rebates. Super Bowl tickets. Each is a small inefficiency that benefits the retailer at the supplier's expense and, ultimately—since the supplier builds those costs into its prices—the consumer's. Wal-Mart, by contrast, is famous for boiling everything down to a one-number negotiation. "It's very pure," says Newell Rubbermaid's Scheyer. "All the funny money—1% for this, 2% for that, 'I need a rebate ... I need a special fund for our annual golf event'—it isn't there. They'll negotiate hard to get the extra penny, but they'll pass it along to the customer."

While this part of the negotiation is strictly arm's-length (figuratively anyway, given the cubby-like dimensions of the blue rooms), Wal-Mart also operates in "partnering" mode, in which both sides swap information to streamline the flow of goods from raw materials to checkout counter. "They would rather extract fat from the process than ex-

tract their suppliers' profits," explains Ananth Raman, a Harvard Business School professor who studies supply chains. So while Newell Rubbermaid's "We ♥ Wal-Mart" strategy can seem the ultimate in corporate vassalage, consider what Newell gets out of the deal: not only huge volume but, thanks to Everyday Low Prices, *predictable* volume, which lets it keep its factories running full and steady. There are no advertising costs, no "funny money." And Wal-Mart will even back up its trucks to Newell's factories. Many suppliers, including P&G, like the model so much that they've pushed it on their other customers.

There's more. Newell gets product ideas from Wal-Mart. Hundreds of them. A store associate in Arizona mentions that Hispanic customers are looking for a kind of cookware called a *caldero*. Done. The hardware department sees an opportunity for "light industrial" cleaning products. Time to market: 90

The company of giants

Wal-Mart's share of the economy isn't the biggest ever, but it will be in four years if its recent growth rate continues.

YEAR	COMPANY	% OF GNP
1917	US Steel	2.8%
1932	A&P	1.5%
1955	GM	3.0%
1983	Sears	1.0%
1990	IBM	1.2%
2002	Wal-Mart	2.3%*

*Estimate.

days. Shoppers, in effect, get direct control of the nation's manufacturing facilities—reason to see Wal-Mart as the world's most finely articulated tool for turning customer wants into reality. A win-win-win.

Playing this game, however, requires constant hustle. Besides continually cutting your costs, you need to handle all that data pouring off RetailLink—the system that lets suppliers track their wares through Wal-Mart World—since you wouldn't want to annoy Wal-Mart with excess inventory or, worse yet, not enough. An electronic "vendor scorecard" will let you know how you're doing.

In the meantime, you should also be peppering Wal-Mart with "retail-tainment" ideas about how to make its stores more fun. If you're the maker of Power Rangers, that means creating the world's largest inflatable structure—a 5,000-square-foot moon—for a tour of Wal-Mart parking lots. If you're

Coke, it means routing your L.A.-to-Atlanta Olympic Torch Run past every Wal-Mart possible. You may be "encouraged" to buy time on the instore TV network. And should you enjoy the privileged position of "category manager," you'll be expected to educate Wal-Mart on everything happening in the jelly or lingerie or Hulk Hands markets. Above all, you'd better start thinking like a retailer. "If you're focused on your shipments, you're screwed," says Dennis Bruce, a vice president with Newell Rubbermaid's Bentonville team. "You gotta be worried about what's moving through the registers."

"Vendor offenders," as some Wal-Marters jokingly call them, don't last long. "People think they're wired in at the top of the company, but the relationship is nothing if you don't perform," says Newell's Scheyer, whose father sold to Sam Walton in the 1960s.

Then, too, Bentonville isn't above dropping the occasional bomb. Procter & Gamble's storied partnership with Wal-Mart began on a 1987 canoe trip when Walton and a P&G boss agreed to start sharing information instead of hoarding it. Yet there was little warning when, in 2001, Wal-Mart unveiled its Sam's American Choice detergent at roughly half the price of P&G's family jewel, Tide. (The move "in no way strains our relationship," a P&G spokeswoman said at the time. Uh-huh. And we have no problem with a McDonald's brand FORTUNE.) Now there are rumors—which Wal-Mart does not confirm—that the retailer is planning to introduce a second, even cheaper detergent under its Great Value label. "I'm not sure [P&G] didn't pay way too high a price to achieve that partnership," says TradeMarketing's Cleere. "They taught Wal-Mart about the laundry business."

Tide still commands about four times the shelf space of Sam's Choice, and Tom Coughlin, chief of Wal-Mart's US. stores, says manufacturers' brands will remain the company's cornerstone. But Wal-Mart's private-label assault has turned even its most trusted suppliers into its competitors. With little fanfare and no advertising, Wal-Mart's Ol' Roy dog food (named for Sam Walton's English Setter: 1970-81) has charged past Nestle's Purina as the world's top-selling brand. Great Value bleach outsells Clorox in some stores.

That raises a tricky question: What, exactly, is the brand here? As Wal-Mart flexes its muscle as a marketer and not just a merchandiser, it could accelerate the demise of weaker brands. Even P&G has refocused on just 12 powerhouses, like Crest and Pampers. Now manufacturers worry about losing their direct connection to the consumer. Two decades ago

65% of their ad budgets went to television and other mass media, while today 60% go to retailers for in-store promotions and the like. The worry, as a Forrester report predicts, is that "Wal-Mart will become the next Procter & Gamble." The nightmare: Wal-Mart becomes your company's new VP of marketing.

If the trip on Gulliver's coattails is no joyride, it sure beats being a Lilliputian underfoot. Over the years Wal-Mart has thundered its way up the retail food chain, first flattening mom-and-pop stores, then stepping on discounters like Ames, Bradlees, and Kmart, and finally sitting on specialty retailers like Toys "R" Us—threatening, in effect, to kill the category killer. Now no category seems safe.

Just ask your grocer. The quintessentially low-margin business had benefited from a decade of consolidation and cost cutting by giants like Kroger and Albertsons. Yet most of the gains dropped to the companies' bottom lines, not the consumers'. Now, feasting on fat margins in the presence of Wal-Mart is a bit like tucking into a juicy sirloin in the presence of a grizzly: Your dinner won't be there for long, and unless you start running, neither will you. Only ten years after launching its food business amid much guffawing, Wal-Mart is the world's biggest grocer, driving down prices an average of 13% in the markets it enters, according to a UBS Warburg study. The effect has been seismic: Kroger has gone on a cost-cutting drive to narrow the price gap, Albertsons has abandoned some markets entirely, and an army of consultants now advise grocers on how to grapple with the 800-pound gorilla. When Wal-Mart moves, it adheres to the Powell doctrine of overwhelming force.

Now imagine you're a Wal-Mart strategic planner on the prowl for other high-value targets. Where else are middlemen taking fat profits and stiffing consumers? Did someone say used cars? Of course! The last castle of medieval retailing. Visit the parking lots of several Houston Supercenters, and you'll find a dealer quietly testing a no-haggle approach under the name Price 1.

What else? Well, what about Microsoft? Its margins are—can this be right?—44%, and it's sitting on $38 billion in cash. Mr. Sam would not approve. Log on to walmart.com and you'll find $199 computers powered by a fledgling Windows competitor, Lindows.

Financial services! Regulators have twice thwarted Wal-Mart's attempts to buy a bank, but hey, you don't need a bank to offer wire transfers and money orders. And get this: Western Union charges $50 to wire $1,000 from Texas to Mexico. How about a flat $12.95 instead, and 46-cent money orders

instead of the 90 cents charged by the U.S. Postal Service? Available at a store near you.

Wal-Mart vacations. Internet access. Flower delivery. Online DVD rentals à la Netflix. All happening.

Wal-Mart stresses that many of these experiments are just that: experiments. But the company has long excelled at using itself as a testing lab, tweaking and refining a concept until—boom!—it's everywhere. That's why even the looniest speculation—Wal-Mart partners with a Korean auto company to make a private-label car, Wal-Mart acquires a drug chain, Wal-Mart becomes a wholesaler to other merchants—can't be dismissed. Just because you're paranoid doesn't mean Bentonville isn't out to get you.

Wal-Mart's zero-to-60 engine is driven by three powerful cylinders: scale, scope, and speed. The scale part is obvious. The scope part allows Wal-Mart to "flex" its toy section before the holidays and collapse it afterward, while Toys "R" Us is stuck selling toys year-round. (Scope also lets Wal-Mart use entire categories—gas, soft drinks, whatever—as loss leaders to pull people into the stores.) The speed part may be the most intimidating. Wal-Mart's turnover is so rapid that 70% of its merchandise is rung up at the register before the company has paid for it. Speed is why it routes ships from China through the Suez Canal and across the Atlantic, so that exactly 50% of imports end up on each coast—more expensive in the short run, but faster in the long. And while the interior of a Wal-Mart distribution center evokes the final scene of *Raiders of the Lost Ark*—42-foot-high corridors of toilet paper stretching toward a vanishing point—many items never hit the warehouse floor, moving directly from truck to truck along 24 miles of conveyor belts.

That leaves competitors with two options (surrender not one of them; Bentonville doesn't do acquisitions). Option No. 1 is to play Wal-Mart's game. Very risky. In the mid-1990s, Kmart proved it to be ritual suicide. On the other hand, companies already steeped in discounting—Costco, Family Dollar, grocery chain Publix—have more than held their own against Goliath. Option No. 1 should thus carry the warning found atop black-diamond ski runs: EXPERTS ONLY.

Option No. 2: Don't play Wal-Mart's game. Typically a better choice. Grocery folks regularly tromp through H-E-B, a Texas grocery chain that's held Wal-Mart at bay with such "destination products" as ice cream made from Poteet strawberries, a local favorite that H-E-B freezes in vast quantities. Not surprisingly, Wal-Mart is already thinking along similar lines, mining its mountains of data to tailor individual stores to local tastes.

The question on everyone's mind, of course, is, How much more dominant can Wal-Mart get? More than 70 million people already roam its aisles each week. Its truckers are trained to avoid deluded motorists who dream of a collision and a Wal-Mart-sized settlement. The U.S. Mint chose Wal-Mart, not banks, to introduce its Sacagawea gold dollar in 2000. Target had difficulty finding American flags on Sept. 12, 2001, because guess who had begun buying every flag it could the previous day. Hegemony, it would seem, doesn't get any more complete.

Yet a bit of fifth-grade math produces a startling result: If Wal-Mart maintains its annual growth rate of 15%, it will be twice as big in five years. "Could we be two times larger?" asks CEO Lee Scott. "Sure. Could we be three times larger? I think so."

Crazy talk? Maybe not. Roughly half of Wal-Mart's Supercenters (groceries plus general merchandise) are in the 11 states of the Old South, leaving plenty of room for expansion in California and the Northeast. And Bentonville is getting creative about overcoming the political and real estate hurdles there. In January it opened its first inner-city Supercenter in the Baldwin Hills neighborhood of Los Angeles, a three-story affair with special escalators for shopping carts. All told, Wal-Mart will open roughly a store a day this year.

As it expands outward, it's also filling in the gaps. "We've found that a smaller population than what we originally had thought can support a Supercenter," says Scott. "So you can put two Supercenters—Rogers (Ark.) and Fayetteville—roughly four miles apart. Same thing is true in Dallas, Houston, Atlanta." Within those four miles Wal-Mart is building new Neighborhood Markets, or "SmallMarts": smartly designed food/drug combos with conveniences like self-checkout, honor-system coffee and pastries, drive-through pharmacies, and halfhour film processing (this last based on a finding that 50% of women shoppers have an undeveloped roll of film in their purse). In Arkansas, Wal-Mart's even dabbling with stand-alone pharmacies. Throw in Sam's Club, with 46 million paid memberships, and walmart.com, with its mission of "easy access to more Wal-Mart," and you start to wonder: Is there any format Bentonville won't consider on its march to "saturation"? Well, yes, says Scott. "You're not going to see Wal-Mart casinos."

Which brings us to a final issue: Is someone going to decide that Wal-Mart has too much power? Doesn't the government break up companies that get this big? The short answer in this case is "not likely."

(Cont.)

Antitrust law is aimed at protecting consumers, not competitors. (In the US. anyway: A German judge last year ordered Wal-Mart to raise its prices.) Monopolists jack up prices. Wal-Mart lowers them—making it, in some instances, a more effective trustbuster than the trustbusters themselves.

Yet the company has grown self-conscious about its size. While Sears and Woolworth once announced their power by erecting the world's tallest skyscrapers, Wal-Mart strives to be everywhere and nowhere, hidden in plain sight—just your friendly hometown superpower. The reasons for that may be less calculated than cultural. Sam Walton used the language of service and democracy—customers, he said, "voted with their feet"—to build a republic of fervent consumer advocates. Today the company still sees itself that way—and seems confounded when the rest of the world does not. For lest we forget, America's most admired company has also been one of its most maligned, recently attracting headlines about class-action lawsuits alleging that associates were forced to work unpaid overtime. "In the past we were judged by our aspirations," says Scott. "Now we're going to be judged by our exceptions."

It's more than a little reminiscent of another fledgling republic that became a superpower and discovered to its shock that much of the world saw it as an imperial.

59

It's Not Only the Giants With Franchises Abroad

Leaping Cultural Divides to Add Markets

BY EVE TAHMINCIOGLU

Cynthia McKay was in business for more than a decade before her food basket company received a dreaded Better Business Bureau complaint in 2003. She assigned the blame, in part, to her sometimes overzealous plan to go global.

Le Gourmet Gift Basket Inc., which has 510 franchises, including 25 outside the United States, expanded into Hong Kong in 2002. The initial experience was no picnic for Ms. McKay, the chief executive. Last year, a customer ordered a basket to be sent to an American worker who had been transferred to China. So, Ms. McKay had her Hong Kong franchise make up a basket and send it to the homesick expatriate—but she underestimated the cultural divide. The client had ordered an American-themed basket but the basket delivered contained pickled octopus and rice cakes instead of smoked salmon and potato chips.

"The client came back to me, threatened a lawsuit and went to the Better Business Bureau," said Ms. McKay, whose company is based in Castle Rock, Colo. "Even though my contract with the franchisee says they are responsible for their own behavior, good will was involved." Ms. McKay mailed another basket overnight at a cost of $160 and sent a letter of apology to the customer. The complaint, the company's only one so far, was subsequently resolved.

For all the cultural misunderstandings and challenges ranging from currency fluctuations to language barriers that she has encountered since expanding abroad, Ms. McKay says she has no regrets. After moving first into New Zealand in 1999 and then into Australia, Canada and Hong Kong, her company is projecting $90,000 in international revenue this year. Her company has its sights on South Africa, the Philippines, Thailand and eventually Saudi Arabia, as well as Europe.

Big franchise players like McDonald's and Dunkin' Donuts have long seen the world as a business opportunity, but an increasing number of smaller franchise companies are now sharing this vision. Last year, 56 percent of franchise operators were in markets outside the United States, up from 46 percent in 2000, according to a survey of its 810 members by the International Franchise Association. "Much of that growth is attributed to the small and mid-sized firms," said Marcel Portman, the group's vice president for global development.

Experts say the main factors driving the trend are the Internet, the improved technology that allows a company to do satellite conferencing and produce low-cost training videos for foreign franchisees, a saturated domestic franchise market, growing international acceptance of franchising and a surge in international franchise shows.

"Two years ago we asked, 'Where is our future?' and we realized it was international," said Bill Powers, vice president and chief operating officer of Realty Executives International, a residential real estate franchise company based in Phoenix. It has franchises in Thailand, South Africa, Australia, Israel, Canada and Mexico. The company, he said, is close to running out of regions at home.

Smaller franchise companies should tread warily, however. Mr. Portman recites a catalog of pitfalls involving cultural hurdles, economic uncertainty (including the core question of whether local consumers will pay for the product), foreign-exchange instability, the difficulty of checking the financial backgrounds of potential franchisees and obstacles to securing intellectual property rights in countries with weak trademark laws. "Or maybe someone already trademarked your name or concept and is waiting for you to come down and pay for it," he said. "This is known as trademark piracy."

But large or small, American companies can find it tough to sell their franchise concepts abroad, especially in countries where English is not spoken and in those with unfamiliar laws and customs. In such places, recruiting competent local franchisees is crucial. "I tell my clients, especially those that have never gone overseas, to make more than one visit if you want to develop a market," said William Le Sante, the managing director of franchising consultancy for Le Sante International, a consulting firm in Miami. "You might get off a plane and say, 'Oh my gosh, this is not our market.'"

Mr. Le Sante offered an example of a fast-food company based in the United States that ran into trouble in Latin America by giving its international partner a free hand in the selection of locations, products and a distributor for its outlets. The partner signed leases the operation could not afford, resulting in a big financial loss to the company and damage to its image in its new market.

Gary Salomon, chief executive of Fastsigns International Inc., a company based in Carrollton, Tex., that makes signs and graphics for businesses, says he made the mistake more than once of expanding abroad without sending in an advance team to investigate conditions. In Colombia, for example, the company "had problems with security, political stability and a motivated working class that was reasonably well educated." The company left Colombia in 1996.

And while he has remained in other Latin American countries, both Mexico and Argentina have been plagued by currency devaluations and economic turmoil, he said. And Brazil, though it has a large middle class and a strong work ethic, is saddled with "tremendous inflationary problems and currency stability issues," he said.

Even Europe can throw a curveball at entrepreneurs in the United States. Initially, Fastsigns had difficulty with some British franchisees who balked at making aggressive sales pitches, Mr. Salomon said. "It's not the personality of a Brit," he said. But the company sent an operations team and continues

---

Getting It Right

Seven questions to ask before you franchise overseas.

1. Will local consumers buy your product?
2. How tough is the local competition?
3. Does the government respect trademark and franchiser rights?
4. Can your profits be easily repatriated?
5. Can you buy all the supplies you need locally?
6. Is commercial space available and are rents affordable?
7. Are your local partners financially sound and do they understand the basics of franchising?

Source: William Le Sante, managing director of franchising consultancy for Le Sante International, Miami

(Cont.)

to hold training sessions in Britain to make sure the local owners stay on track.

Fastsigns has 65 international franchises and aims to have 120 within three years, with most of the growth coming in Britain, Australia and Canada.

For all the perils of venturing into unknown territory, there can be pleasant surprises. When Partyland Inc. of Plymouth Meeting, Pa., went into Saudi Arabia in 1998, the company worried that consumers in that conservative Islamic society would not be receptive to its Barbie-theme party goods, said Kevin Pike, the company's assistant vice president franchise services. But the Barbie products sold well, as did whoopee cushions. Balloons are a staple; a Saudi prince recently ordered 4,000 of them at a Partyland store for his daughter's birthday. The company now has two stores in Saudi Arabia and two in Kuwait.

Partyland, which has 350 units in 20 countries, has had to tweak its format to take account of local circumstances. To beat the exorbitant rents in Singapore, the company created boutique-style shops rather than use the usual warehouse design. In tropical St. Lucia, the company permitted tile floors as well as the standard carpeting.

Many companies, including Fastsigns and Partyland, use what they call master developers or master franchisers when they enter a country. These entities, which act as middlemen between the company and the franchisees, are invaluable for their understanding of the local customs, but they do not come cheap.

Ms. McKay, a former lawyer, decided to do it all on her own, figuring any mistakes she made early on would cost her less than a master developer's fees. And she has learned from those mistakes. A prospective franchisee in the Philippines wanted to include a local meat pastry called siopao in the company's gift baskets. With the memory of the pickled-octopus fiasco in Hong Kong fresh in her mind, Ms. McKay knew the last thing she needed was a newspaper story about food poisoning linked to her company.

"I was trying to explain to them that we don't transport meat or anything perishable," she said. "I could just see it: 'We killed three people with tainted meat.'"

Promotion

60

CAN MAD AVE. MAKE ZAP-PROOF ADS?
It's blurring the lines between promotion and programming as DVRs gain ground

ndre Farris used to be a network executive's favorite viewer. Young, single, and with disposable income to burn, the 34-year-old San Francisco real estate broker was the kind of upscale bigspender whom TV advertisers crave. But since last year, when he ordered a digital video recorder from satellite operator DirecTV, Farris has been mostly zapping through Madison Avenue's lures. Says Farris: "The commercials got on my nerves."

POWERFUL THREAT
With millions more viewers like Farris poised to sign up for DVR services, network executives have plenty to worry about these days. Already scrambling as younger viewers drift off to play video games and watch DVDs, they face a potentially even more powerful threat: Over the next several years, DVRs, which record TV shows on hard drives instead of on videotapes, are set to hit the mainstream as cable and satellite operators start to offer them at huge discounts.

As a result, the number of DVRs in front of couch potatoes could nearly double, to 5.8 million by the end of 2004, according to tech consulting company the Yankee Group. That number could jump to 24.7 million—or more than one in every five TV households—by 2007. By then, SG Cowen Securities Corp. analyst James Marsh projects, TV users will be zapping through more than 60% of the commercials, ignoring an estimated $6.6 billion worth of ads. "The DVR has the potential to blow apart the entire network business model," says media consultant Blair Westlake, a former chairman of Universal TV.

Network executives, of course, have heard such doomsday predictions before. This time, however, the threat is real: DVRs make recording shows and skipping commercials a snap. And the equipment is cheap and easy to get. Already, satellite operator EchoStar Communications Corp. gives DVRs free to new subscribers who agree to pay $4.98 monthly for DVR service. And Rupert Murdoch, eager to take as many as 1 million subscribers a year from cable, says his newly acquired DirecTV will likely match EchoStar's offer.

Those moves have cable fighting back: On Dec. 3, giant Comcast Corp. said it would begin offering DVRs to its 21 million customers by the end of 2004. And Time Warner Cable Inc. is rolling out DVR service in 30 of its 31 markets, including New York and Los Angeles.

AUDIENCE EROSION
How will broadcasters and ad agencies retaliate? No clear strategy has yet emerged. Many top network execs insist the arrival of mass market DVRs doesn't present an immediate problem. With a nearly $50 billion ad market, TV executives are hardly shaking in their Guccis. "Worrying about it doesn't take up too much of my day," says NBC Entertainment President Jeffrey A. Zucker. "I know its coming—and it will be important—but it's not coming this fall."

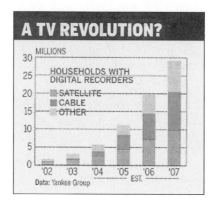

A TV REVOLUTION?

MILLIONS

HOUSEHOLDS WITH DIGITAL RECORDERS
- SATELLITE
- CABLE
- OTHER

'02 '03 '04 '05 '06 '07
EST.
Data: Yankee Group

Maybe not. But network execs do face the immediate problem of DVR owners zapping through promos that alert viewers to their new shows, which could further speed audience erosion. To fight back, many networks have been promoting their shows by running the names and times of their upcoming programs along the bottom of the screen. NBC, a 6% owner in DVR pioneer TiVo Inc., has gone a step further: For its recent promo of the Jan. 26 Golden Globe Awards show, it

gave TiVo owners the option of clicking on a "thumbs up" icon that lets them set their machines to record the show when it airs.

More important, as the use of DVRs catches on, TV executives could face a nasty revolt from advertisers. The rumblings are already beginning. The future "is away from broadcast TV as the anchor medium," warned Coca-Cola Co. President Steven J. Heyer last year. The company, which spends more than $300 million a year in TV ads, is veering away from 30-second spots with more money flowing into such areas as ad placements in DVDs and video games.

REAMS OF DATA
Still, broadcasters will have plenty of other opportunities to nab ad dollars. Coke, for instance, spent an estimated $20 million to put cups with its logo in the judges' hands during Fox's superpopular *American Idol TV* show. Coke isn't the only one: Product placements are booming elsewhere in TVland, says Devery Holmes, president of product placement firm Norm Marshall & Assoc. Her firm has seen its TV placements triple for its 60 clients, including placing a General Motors Corp. truck on cable channel Bravo's *Queer Eye for the Straight Guy* and *USA Today* on NBC's *West Wing*.

Moreover, the arrival of DVRs isn't all bad news for TV and ad executives. Ad-zapping may eventually force Madison Avenue to get more creative and up the amps on their TV spots. To get viewers' attention, they'll have to turn out must-see Super Bowl quality ads like the 90-second Britney Spears spot in last year's big game, says Ted Sann, chief creative officer of ad agency BBDO North America.

What's more, the devices can collect reams of demographic data that networks and agencies can use to tightly target or "telegraph" ads to desired audiences. Coke marketers in October began airing monthly 25-minute music programs for TiVo's Showcase service, a menu-style page that allows viewers to record 30-minute music shows sponsored by Coke for later viewing. And, using TiVo's demographic information, adbuying firm Starcom Worldwide plans to

(Cont.)

create tailored commercials for shows that TiVo watchers view most. Last year, it put Best Buy Co. ads featuring singer Sheryl Crow in the middle of MTV and VH-1 shows. DVR viewers could stop the ad and watch a longer performance by Crow that was sponsored by Best Buy.

As the DVR revolution catches on, that's just the sort of blurring of the line between programming and sponsorship that viewers could see more of. But if TV networks and advertising agencies aren't careful, it could also be just the kind of programming that viewers will increasingly zip right through.

By Ronald Grover in Los Angeles with Tom Lowry and Gerry Khermouch in New York, Cliff Edwards in San Mateo, Calif., and Dean Foust in Atlanta

61

As Consumers Revolt, a Rush to Block Pop-Up Online Ads

BY SAUL HANSEL

The boom in Internet pop-up advertisement may be about to, well, pop.

The big ads that flash in separate windows above or below Web pages are among the most intrusive, and to many people, the most obnoxious features on the Internet. Not coincidentally, the pop-up format is also among the most effective for advertisers and the most profitable for Web site publishers.

But the potential reach of these ads is starting to be sharply curtailed as major companies, like **Time Warner's** AOL unit, **Yahoo** and **Google,** distribute software that blocks pop-up ads from opening. This summer, **Microsoft** will put a pop-up blocking feature in the next release of Internet Explorer, the dominant Web browser.

"There is a consumer revolt as forms of advertising get more intrusive," said Rob Kaiser, vice president for narrowband marketing at **EarthLink,** the first big Internet service provider to distribute pop-up blocking software. The reaction to pop-ups, he said, is similar to the rush to join the government's do-not-call list to block telemarketing calls and the increase in the use of video recorders to block TV commercials.

Advertising executives, in television and the Internet market, note that consumers who block the ads are undercutting the economic model that provides them with free entertainment and information.

"I haven't spoken to any people who say I love pop-ups, send me more of them," said David J. Moore, the chief executive of 24/7 Real Media, an online advertising firm. "But they are part of a quid pro quo. If you want to enjoy the content of a Web site that is free, the pop-ups come with it."

But even companies like Yahoo and Microsoft, which receive significant revenue from advertising, have decided to bow to complaints from Web users.

"We are adding a pop-up blocker based on feedback from customers," said Matthew Pilla, a senior product manger for Windows at Microsoft.

Long a feature of AOL, pop-ups became widespread on the Internet about three years ago, as Web sites sought ways to replace the torrent of ad money that dried up after the dot-com boom. And a few advertisers, like X10, selling wireless cameras, and Orbitz, the online travel company, jumped onto the format early.

In December 2001, 1.4 percent of the Web ads measured by Nielsen/NetRatings were pop-ups or "pop-under" ads, which appear behind the main browser window. That rose to 8.7 percent in July 2003. But it has declined since, to 6.2 percent in December.

AdvertisementBanners.com, which places pop-under ads on Web sites, has found that 20 percent to 25 percent of Web users have pop-up blocking enabled on their computers, double the rate of a year ago, said Chris Vanderhook, the company's chief operating officer. Some advertising companies say that a smaller percentage of people are using blockers, but there is agreement that use of pop-up blocking is increasing.

In the year and half since EarthLink offered blocking software, one million of its five million customers have installed it. AOL added pop-up blocking to its software in 2002. Google added a blocker to its toolbar, a small program that adds some features to Internet Explorer. Yahoo, more recently, added a similar feature to its toolbar. And Microsoft's MSN just added a pop-up blocker to its most recent software.

The biggest potential impact will come this summer when Microsoft releases its Service Pack 2 for Windows XP, which will add a pop-up blocker and many other features to Internet Explorer. For now, Microsoft says Internet Explorer will not block pop-ups unless users enable the feature.

Still the prospect of nearly ubiquitous pop-up blocking unsettles some big advertisers.

"I don't want to see pop-ups blocked," said Matthew R. Coffin, the chief executive of LowerMyBills.com, a site that sells long distance and other services. Pop-up and pop-under ads, he said, attract more people than any other ad format. "People wouldn't click if they weren't interested."

The decline of pop-ups, he said, is all the more troublesome because it comes after the company had to slash use of e-mail advertising in response to the public backlash against spam. As a result, the company is moving to older forms of marketing.

"I'm very gung-ho on TV ads," he said.

Smaller Web publishers have fewer alternatives. Many independent Web sites are part of networks that pay them $3 to $5 for every thousand pop-ups they display.

"These pop-up blockers, as they become too widely used, will definitely cut into my income," said William Smith, who runs 40 Web sites from Winnipeg, Manitoba.

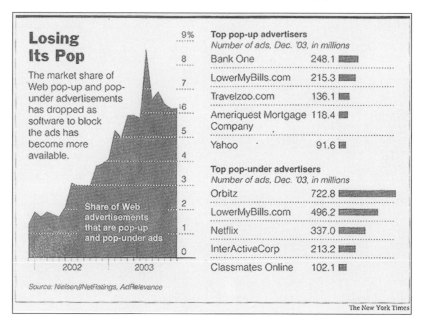

Losing Its Pop

The market share of Web pop-up and pop-under advertisements has dropped as software to block the ads has become more available.

Share of Web advertisements that are pop-up and pop-under ads

2002   2003

Source: Nielsen//NetRatings, AdRelevance

Top pop-up advertisers
Number of ads, Dec. '03, in millions

Bank One	248.1
LowerMyBills.com	215.3
Travelzoo.com	136.1
Ameriquest Mortgage Company	118.4
Yahoo	91.6

Top pop-under advertisers
Number of ads, Dec. '03, in millions

Orbitz	722.8
LowerMyBills.com	496.2
Netflix	337.0
InterActiveCorp	213.2
Classmates Online	102.1

The New York Times

(Cont.)

He says that 10 percent to 20 percent of his income comes from pop-up ads. Some of his sites, like thewinnipegpages.com focus on travel and others are pornographic.

Both types of sites take pop-up ads for products like Internet Eraser, software that eliminates records of what Web sites people visit. He said he tries not to have too many pop-ups interfere with users viewing his Web sites, but he does display pop-ups as they decide to leave.

"A guy has to make money," he said.

The larger Web publishers, by contrast, have reduced use of pop-up and pop-under ads. At Sportsline, pop-ups represented 5 to 10 percent of its ad revenue a few years ago, but now account for less than 1 percent. "We are totally ready for the day when you can't have any pop-ups," said Mark J. Mariani, Sportsline's president for advertising.

"Clients have started to shy away from pop-ups and pop-unders," he said. Sportsline now sets a quota of no more than one pop-up ad for each user in any 12-hour period. Instead, Sportsline, like many other publishers, is emphasizing larger advertisements woven into their main sites.

The Interactive Advertising Bureau, the major trade group representing both advertisers and Web publishers, has decided not to fight the pop-up blockers.

"If consumers tell us that pop-ups are a bad idea and they don't really like them, then it's time to stop doing them," said Greg Stuart, the group's chief executive.

Yet that is not a universal view even among major companies. DoubleClick, the big advertising software company, is developing technology that could let Web advertisers override the ad-blocking software in some cases. It is not planning to use that technology in instances where users have specifically chosen to activate the software.

"There are advertisers who want pop-up ads and publishers that want to serve them," said Douglas Knopper, general manager for online advertising at DoubleClick. "Our role is to help them do that."

Direct Response Getting Respect

As OxiClean moves to stores, Clorox and P&G try infomercials

By: Jack Neff

When OxiClean pitchman Billy Mays met Procter & Gamble Co. Chairman-CEO A.G. Lafley last summer at a wedding, the encounter may not have been as unlikely as it seemed.

Mr. Mays and his direct-response industry have married into conventional consumer-products marketing in more ways than one. Increasingly, they're selling their wares in stores while still taking toll-free orders from consumers. Mass retailers are shedding reluctance to carry such direct-response staples as Orange Glo International's OxiClean. Some, such as drug-chain heavyweight Walgreens, devote entire front-of-store sections to "As Seen on TV" goods.

OLD DOGS, NEW TRICKS

But wait, there's more. Noting success of these upstart rivals, package-goods stalwarts whose brands have been "seen on TV" for years in 30-second ads increasingly are dabbling in longer-form direct-response ads. P&G's Swiffer WetJet motorized floor-cleaning gadget made its U.S. debut on Comcast's QVC home-shopping network in 2001. More recently, a flight of WetJet infomercials helped propel the brand past Clorox Co.'s rival Clorox Ready-Mop in four-week data from Information Resources Inc. in November for the first time since ReadyMop launched last January, according to Alliance Capital Management's Sanford C. Bernstein.

P&G's Dryel home dry-cleaning kit, on the market since 1999, recently tried a bare-bones direct-response ad in addition to its ongoing 30-second ads, both from Red, Cincinnati. As with Swiffer, the pitch was for consumers to call in for coupons rather than the products.

"Both the brands are doing well," said a P&G spokeswoman. "They're seeing an increase in sales, shipments and awareness. . . . They attribute that to their overall communications mix, of which DRTV is a piece."

Clorox has been doing DRTV, too, including a two-minute ad to help launch ReadyMop last January. When Clorox launched OxiClean-rival Clorox Oxygen Action last summer, it turned to Encino, Calif. based direct-response shop Inter/Media Advertising to supplement conventional 30-second ads from Omnicom Group's DDB Worldwide, San Francisco.

Clorox is spending under 1% of its media budget on DRTV and is learning about the medium, a spokeswoman said, adding that the marketer is exploring how DRTV might help it develop alternative distribution channels for some products.

Joel Appel, president of Orange Glo, a Quaker Oats Co. marketing executive for Gatorade before leaving to join the business founded by his father, said, "We never could have put the kind of spending we've done behind our brands without direct response." Though industry insiders say brands can't turn a profit on DRTV ads once they have national retail distribution, direct sales still help pay the media freight.

Changing retail attitudes have opened the door for hybrid DRTV-to-retail rollouts, said A.J. Khubani, president of TeleBrands, marketer of such products as Amber Vision sunglasses and the Roll-A-Hose. "It used to take three to four years to get full retail distribution for DRTV products," he said. "Now, you see 'As Seen on TV' products in stores within a month of going on TV."

OTHER ADVANTAGES

The P&Gs of the world can afford big media budgets without those operators standing by. But direct-response offers other advantages. Brands such as Swiffer can develop a consumer database for direct-mail or e-mail offers aimed at building repeat sales of replacement supplies.

Mr. Khubani has no doubt OxiClean opened eyes of package-goods advertisers to direct-response. At a trade show last year, he said he met with P&G executives who quizzed him extensively about DRTV.

But the marriage isn't always a smooth blend. When Mr. Mays met Mr. Lafley, he says he needled him gently about informal complaints P&G had registered about Oxi-Clean ads. Mr. Lafley's "a really nice guy," said Mr. Mays, though he referred questions to company lawyers.

China Cracks Down on Commercials

Viewer Complaints Lead To Bans on Certain TV Ads; Prime Airtime Is Restricted

By Geoffrey A. Fowler

Beijing Resident Zhang Xiying recalls the awkward silence that fell over dinnertime conversation with her son and his friends when a TV commercial for a feminine-hygiene product appeared during the broadcast.

"What the ads bluntly said should only be talked about between women," says Ms. Zhang, 50 years old.

The Chinese government apparently agrees. In an attempt to bring decorum to China's often unruly broadcasting system, national regulators have banned ads for "offensive" products, such as feminine-hygiene pads, hemorrhoid medication and athlete's-foot ointment, during three daily meal times. Beer ads have been limited to two between 7 p.m. and 9 p.m. Regulators also sliced in half the amount of prime airtime available for ads on some stations—on some key channels, say media buyers, prime-time ads last year could run for up to 20 minutes straight.

The moves highlight the difficulties facing China, home to the world's biggest television audience, as it tries to apply cultural and broadcasting standards without driving away deep-pocketed advertisers.

Officials with the State Administration of Radio, Film and Television say they implemented the new rules Jan. 1 because viewers complained that commercials were too graphic—and too frequent—during dinner. They also instituted a special telephone hotline for viewers to report infractions, which already has resulted in 600 orders from the government to change ads. China's fast development is creating cultural rifts between sophisticated urbanites and millions of rural farmers, who don't always appreciate or understand the commercials beamed in on CCTV from Beijing.

Political content on the airwaves in China always has been strictly regulated. But because China has become an increasingly competitive and important market for consumer goods over the past few years, advertisers are eager to push the limit of what is considered socially acceptable in order to get their message across. And even though Chinese ads already pass through government censor boards, the process can sometimes be finicky. Censors sent one **McDonald's** ad back almost a half dozen times because they objected to a scene showing a man licking drippings from his juicy chicken burger off a magazine page, says Ruth Lee, creative director of **Publicis Groupe's** Leo Burnett Shanghai.

Ren Qian, the radio-film-TV administration's vice director of the department of broadcasting affairs supervision, says the new laws are an attempt to bring consistency to censor enforcement. "We want to level the playing field by regulating the national standard."

But advertisers and media buyers complain that the new rules are too broad and are out of step with the country's quickly changing mores. "Banning sanitary products is definitely the wrong move," says Ravi Morthy, the general manager of Publicis Groupe media buyer Starcom, which will now have to place ads for **Procter & Gamble's** Whisper feminine-hygiene products during lower-profile time slots.

China's $14.5 billion ad market, already the world's fifth largest, grew 30% in 2003 and is widely expected to become the world's second largest in under a decade, according to Nielsen Media Research. Prime-time TV is the main tool many marketers use to build brand reputations in China.

But the new restrictions could potentially crimp the growth of the country's ad market because they limit the total number of ads shown at prime time to nine minutes an hour from a previous average of 11. The U.S. average is 11 minutes and 16 seconds during prime time.

Some channels were so ad-heavy that the cutback in ad time has resulted in a drop of nearly 50% of prime-time ad revenue. Last year, ads took up 30% to 40% of the prime-time programming of provincial broadcaster Hebei TV. "Now we're facing a pretty big challenge to fulfill the growth target of ads revenue," says Huang Wenxia, head of Hebei's broadcasting department.

A Change in China

Average number of minutes used by advertising in 2003 prime-time TV programming

United States: 11 minutes, 16 seconds*
Singapore: 12 min.
Hong Kong: 10 min.
China: 11 min.

New in 2004:
China: 9 min.

* Includes only national commercial-minutes

Source: Universal McCann and CCTV Research

Don't worry, Whisper CD Ultra is here!

Ads by Leo Burnett China for **Procter & Gamble's** *Whisper brand of feminine-hygiene pads are among those now banned during meal times in China.*

Face-Off

An Unlikely Rival Challenges L'Oréal In Beauty Market

Procter & Gamble Draws On No-Nonsense Marketing To Battle Parisian Chic

Eureka in the Laundry Room

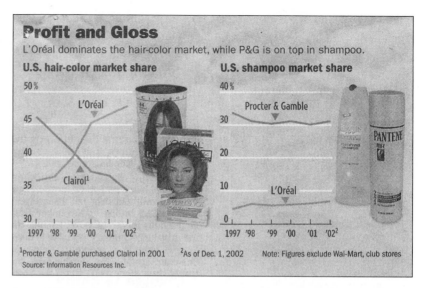

Profit and Gloss

L'Oréal dominates the hair-color market, while P&G is on top in shampoo.

U.S. hair-color market share

L'Oréal
Clairol[1]

50%
45
40
35
30

1997 '98 '99 '00 '01 '02[2]

U.S. shampoo market share

Procter & Gamble
L'Oréal

40%
30
20
10
0

1997 '98 '99 '00 '01 '02[2]

[1]Procter & Gamble purchased Clairol in 2001   [2]As of Dec. 1, 2002   Note: Figures exclude Wal-Mart, club stores
Source: Information Resources Inc.

What do women really want?

For two very different answers, step into the battle over the $90 billion beauty-products industry. For years one company, France's L'Oréal SA, has dominated the business by wooing women with Parisian chic, the promise of looking like its sexy spokeswomen, and the self-assured slogan, "Because I'm worth it."

What L'Oréal offers, says Chief Executive Lindsay Owen-Jones, is a "unique cultural heritage, which is Paris, which is beauty, which is fashion, which is an eye for things that are beautiful and that inspire consumers to spend more with the feeling of being special."

Now L'Oréal is feeling pressure from a rival with an entirely different approach to selling beauty. It's Procter & Gamble Co., wheeling out the no-nonsense comparative advertising that it's long used to sell soap and diapers, reciting statistics to show how its products are superior to "Brand X."

A current P&G promotion for Pantene conditioner offers a "10-day challenge," promising hair that is 60% healthier, 85% shinier, 80% less prone to breakage and 70% less frizzy. In another case, after using 60 different methods to measure the size of pores, length of wrinkles and the color and size of age spots, P&G researchers used results from one of the tests to proclaim in national ads that Olay Total Effects Night Firming Cream worked better than leading department-store brands. The ad featured a jar of Olay atop a stack of other products. The fine print listed the losers—among them, two products from L'Oréal's Lancôme.

P&G began the beauty wars in earnest in 2001, with its $5 billion takeover of Clairol—the biggest acquisition in the company's 165-year history. P&G thus leap-frogged L'Oréal's leading position in mass-market beauty, becoming the largest seller of cosmetics in supermarkets and club stores. P&G has the upper hand in skin cleansers, moisturizers and shampoos. L'Oréal, however, remains the world leader in beauty, and leads the U.S. market in color cosmetics and hair-color products.

Now the two are colliding more than ever. P&G is trying to penetrate the high-end market, where L'Oréal rules, while L'Oréal is trying to sell more shampoo and conquer Wal-Mart, P&G's biggest customer. And both P&G and L'Oréal have flirted with Beiersdorf AG, the German maker of Nivea skin cream, with P&G contemplating a $10 billion bid.

A.G. Lafley, P&G's chief executive, insists that his company can win by giving women an honest answer about how products stack up against competing brands. "Frankly, too much of beauty care has been promises unkept," he says.

Sitting in front of a row of L'Oréal products in his Paris office, Mr. Owen-Jones, a charismatic Briton who has run L'Oréal for the past 14 years, sniffs that L'Oréal ads don't "have the comparison of a T-shirt that's shrunk on one side and the one that hasn't on the other." In cosmetics, "you have to both inform, convince but also seduce consumers . . . and not just ram facts down their throats."

Mr. Owen-Jones adds, "You've got to decide whether something is beautiful, and by the way, even with the most sophisticated marketing methods, nobody is actually going to tell you whether this bottle is beautiful or not—you've got to shoot from the hip."

But today L'Oréal finds itself playing catch-up in some areas. After P&G launched Olay Total Effects anti-aging cream two years ago, L'Oréal quickly followed with a similar-sounding product called Visible Results, packaged in a bottle virtually identical to Total Effects'. "Imitation is the sincerest form of flattery," says Susan Arnold, P&G's president of personal beauty care, who started at P&G in 1980 as a brand assistant working on Dawn dish detergent. (L'Oréal says Visible Results is aimed at a different, younger demographic than P&G's product.) Total Effects, which has become the best-selling anti-aging cream in mass retailers in the U.S., retails for $19.99, one of P&G's most expensive products.

Keeping Up Appearance

P&G's interest in beauty is more than cosmetic. In the '90s the company's sales growth began to falter. Now many of its markets are mature, and profit margins for its core products, such as diapers and toilet paper, are under constant price pressure from generics and branded competitors. P&G has tried for years to relieve that pressure, and revive sales, by diversifying its product line.

Notably, Durk Jager, Mr. Lafley's predecessor as CEO, tried to move P&G heavily into the pharmaceuticals business—but his bid to purchase American Home Products Co. and Warner-Lambert Co., for more than $100 billion, fell through in January 2000. That March, P&G announced a steep earnings drop, sending its stock into a free-fall and capping a three-month stretch that saw the company lose nearly half its market value. Mr. Jager resigned that June.

When Mr. Lafley took over as CEO, he immediately set his sights on enhancing the beauty business. The company wasn't a complete stranger to the game: P&G made its first big foray into the field in 1985, when it picked up the Pantene and Olay brands with

(Cont.)

its acquisition of Richardson-Vicks. Until that point, the company's beauty revenue totaled just $1 billion, and its biggest beauty brand was Ivory soap, a product best known for its ability to float in bathwater.

Mr. Lafley, the company's first CEO from the beauty division, dramatically increased the size of the beauty business, snapping up Clairol and pouring money into P&G's other beauty brands, while slashing costs and improving operating efficiency. He also joked about his short, spiky white hair, saying he was one of the only people left who didn't use dye.

In the first half of 2002, ad spending on Olay, Cover Girl, Clairol and Pantene accounted for about one-fifth of the $900 million P&G spent on advertising in the U.S., according to Competitive Media Reporting. Moreover, P&G, like L'Oréal, pours hundreds of millions of dollars a year into beauty research and development.

This attention has lifted P&G's beauty business and helped the company reverse its slide. Roughly $8 billion of the company's $40 billion in revenue now comes from beauty products, and under Mr. Lafley, P&G's stock has risen 51.74%. It ranked as the second-best-performing stock in the Dow Jones Industrial Average last year.

L'Oréal, meanwhile, has been in the beauty business since the early 1900s, when a chemist named Eugene Schueller started the company by peddling hair dyes to French beauty salons. A century later, L'Oréal has become the world's largest cosmetics company, with $14 billion in annual sales and a long record of double-digit profit growth. Investors have rewarded the performance by making L'Oréal France's second-most valuable company, with a market capitalization of $50.4 billion.

That impressive growth has made Liliane Bettencourt, Mr. Schueller's only child, Europe's richest person. In an unusual three-decade-old arrangement that was meant to protect the company from a takeover, the 80-year-old Mrs. Bettencourt controls L'Oréal in a partnership with giant Swiss food group Nestle SA. Mrs. Bettencourt, who has never taken an active role in managing L'Oréal, owns 51% of Gesparal, a holding company that owns 53.7% of L'Oréal. Nestle owns the other 49% of Gesparal, a stake it bought in 1974.

Crossing the Channel

L'Oréal owes much of its recent success to Mr. Owen-Jones, who joined the company in 1969 at age 23 as a product salesman. Steadily climbing the corporate rungs, he rose to the top job in 1988, becoming the first and only foreigner to head a big French company. Mr. Owen-Jones, now 56, cuts an unusual profile in the clubby Gallic business establishment: Born and reared outside of Liverpool, he bypassed the elite French schools that groom the country's CEOs. In his spare time, he likes to race cars.

Mr. Owen-Jones diversified L'Oréal's French portfolio by adding some American brands to reach a broader audience. The new additions, ranging from Ralph Lauren perfume to the Matrix hair-salon line, now represent 20% of L'Oréal's overall sales. And L'Oréal today derives a third of its revenue from North America, compared with just 14% from France.

The most successful addition by far has been Maybelline. Since acquiring the lipstick maker in 1996, L'Oréal has increased its sales nearly fivefold to $1.4 billion. Part of the makeover involved jazzing up Maybelline's offerings with some flashy new colors, such as lemon yellow and peppermint green in the Miami Chill line. To give the brand more cachet, L'Oréal also moved its offices from Memphis, Tenn., to Manhattan, and quickly changed the brand to "Maybelline New York."

Under Mr. Owen-Jones, L'Oréal's polished image has edged ever more toward glamour. One of his coups was to hire the model and actress Isabella Rossellini to endorse Lancome when he was head of L'Oréal's U.S. subsidiary in the early 1980s. That move helped turn the company's premium brand into a household name in the U.S. and popularized the use of celebrities in cosmetics advertising.

These days, L'Oréal employs what Mr. Owen-Jones has dubbed "the Dream Team"—a stable of dozens of models and actresses to plug its wares in billboard ads and on TV. The team currently includes supermodel Claudia Schiffer, Destiny's Child singer Beyonce Knowles and actresses Andie MacDowell, Heather Locklear and Catherine Deneuve.

P&G acknowledges that it can't compete with L'Oréal in trendiness. For the most part, the women who speak for P&G's beauty products are unknowns.

Mr. Lafley brought Domenico De Sole, chief executive of Italian fashion house Gucci, onto his board and recently sent a group of P&G product designers to visit him. Lecturing the P&G executives on the essence of beauty and luxury, Mr. De Sole held up his Gucci watch to illustrate the point that products that weigh more give the impression of higher quality. He also described how Gucci uses special tissue paper in its stores. Impressed, P&G responded to the advice by printing "Olay" on the inside of its moisturizer packages, a move calculated to give the product a more upscale look.

At L'Oréal, P&G's ambitions draw snickers. "They're mainly laundry-detergent makers," says Bruno Bernard, a biology Ph.D. who heads L'Oréal's research into hair follicles at a Paris lab. "Their vision of hair is of something you can wash like you would a piece of clothing."

P&G researchers don't dispute that idea. In fact, P&G's strategy to revive Clairol's hair-color business started in the company's laundry room. P&G turned to researchers at the company's fabric-care division, home of Tide laundry detergent, for new insights on how tapwater affects fibers. The P&G scientists found that there are a lot of similarities between a strand of hair and a string of fabric. The result: a new technology to block trace amounts of copper in tapwater, which diminishes the ability of hair-color molecules to penetrate hair follicles. "You've got to lift the natural melanin out of the hair and at the same time deposit new color," explains Wilbur Strickland, a P&G researcher who worked for three years to help develop the new technology. "With fabric-care products there is the same dynamic of taking things out [such as dirt] and putting something back

Brand Battle

Mass-Market Brands

P&G	L'ORÉAL
Hair	
Clairol's Nice 'n Easy	L'Oréal Paris, Garnier
Clairol Herbal Essences	SoftSheen-Carson
Pantene	
Head & Shoulders	
Cosmetics	
Cover Girl, Max Factor	L'Oréal Paris
	Maybelline
Skin	
Olay	L'Oréal Paris
Noxzema	
Fragrance	
Old Spice	none

Prestige/Salon Brands

P&G	L'ORÉAL
Hair	
Miss Clairol	Mizani
Complements	Matrix Essentials
Textures & Tones	Redken, Kerastase
Cosmetics	
Max Factor Gold	She Uemura
(sold in Asia)	Helena Rubenstein
Skin	
SKII	Lancôme, Biotherm
Fragrance	
Hugo Boss	Ralph Lauren
Joy by Jean Patou	Giorgio Armani
Giorgio Beverly Hills	Lancôme

(Cont.)

in"—such as fragrance or fabric softeners.

The new ingredient will be added to Clairol's Nice 'n Easy hair color and is part of P&G's effort to stop a decades-long slide in Clairol's market position. Today, L'Oréal's two main brands, L'Oréal Paris and Garnier, control 47.9% of the U.S. hair-color market, according to Information Resources Inc. Clairol has 35%.

Now, both P&G and L'Oréal are looking to make big moves in each other's core markets. Mr. Lafley covets Beiersdorf, maker of Nivea cream, the biggest skin-care brand in the world—an acquisition that would provide P&G with a strong foothold in Europe. Mr. Lafley declines to comment on discussions with Beiersdorf, saying only, "If you're not in the habit of being a hostile acquirer, the seller always controls the timing." L'Oréal took a look at Beiersdorf over the summer but has since backed away, according to people familiar with the matter.

Meanwhile, L'Oréal's largest product launch of its 95-year history will land squarely in P&G's domain. L'Oréal's new shampoo and conditioner marketed under its Garnier brand, Fructis, is coming to the U.S. in February. Currently, L'Oréal ranks fourth among shampoo vendors in the U.S. and is No. 5 in conditioners—segments where P&G holds the top two slots with Pantene and Clairol Herbal Essences. P&G played a direct role in Fructis's creation. L'Oréal came up with the new shampoo in France after P&G blindsided it with a breakthrough product in the early 1990s: a silicon-based two-in-one shampoo and conditioner. Now selling in Spain, Germany, Mexico and Canada, the U.S. is Fructis's final hurdle.

Strolling through a Duane Reade drugstore on Manhattan's Fifth Avenue, Karen Fondu, one of L'Oréal's senior U.S. executives, peruses the aisles of lipsticks, eye shadows and hair colorants, pointing out the prime placement of L'Oréal's products. Pausing in the shampoo aisle, she lifts a perfectly manicured finger and points to the top shelf where she wants Fructis to be positioned. "We want to be right there," she says, indicating a spot between bottles of Pantene and Herbal Essences shampoos and conditioners.

L'Oréal executives are enjoying playing the underdog in the U.S. "We're a relative newcomer to this side of the Atlantic," says Joseph Campinell, president of L'Oréal's U.S. consumer-products division. Putting on a mock Southern twang, he says: "There are still a lot of people at Winn-Dixie who want to know what that 'Lowral' brand is."

Giving Buyers Better Information

What's In Store: Hired-gun reps spread the word about new products.

· · · · · · · · · · · · · ·

By Ken Spencer Brown
Investor's Business Daily

If you want something done right, the old saying goes, do it yourself.

That's why tech manufacturers, competing with a sea of rivals on retail shelves, often send their own representatives to stores to push their wares.

These on-site ambassadors answer customer questions, give demos and train the store staff on how to better sell the product. The aim is to persuade sales clerks to steer customers away from rival products and toward their own.

Fuji Photo Film USA Inc., better know as Fujifilm, wanted to do the same thing this winter to promote its new line of digital cameras for the holiday shopping season.

But Tony Sorice, who's in charge of the firm's hardware sales, knew he didn't have the budget to hire and train a brand new field sales team. So he put a new twist on the do-it-yourself approach: He outsourced it.

Sorice turned to sales and marketing company Campaigners Inc.

Campaigners saves clients money by quickly training a sales force to represent the manufacturer. Sometimes it trains retailers or pushes for better shelf placement. Other times, its workers stay in the stores during business hours, showing off the goods to customers directly.

"We were looking for an extension of our sales force as we became more involved in the digital imaging business," Sorice said. "There are tons of digital cameras out there, and it's important that we stay top of mind of the people on the (retail) sales force."

Such outsourced in-store marketing, long used by consumer products firms in grocery stores and at special events, is growing in popularity as a way of promoting tech products. Manufacturers can boost new product exposure in big chains such as Best Buy without having to hire a bigger sales staff year-round.

Hard To Explain

The effort doesn't replace the usual marketing work, which can include everything from ads to product reviews. But it does add a crucial step at that very point when customers make their final decision.

Redondo Beach, Calif.-based Campaigners isn't the only firm selling that type of marketing service. Its rivals include Acosta Sales and Marketing, Best Service Co. and Creative Channel Strategies Inc.

Samsung Electronics America uses Creative Channel for programs at Best Buy and other stores.

Erin Burns, Samsung's retail channel marketing manager, says it's not enough to just aim marketing at consumers. Keeping retailers abreast of current products is just as important.

For Fujifilm, the challenge was how to convey the benefits of its new digital camera. With just a product box sitting on a shelf, it wouldn't be easy to explain that the camera uses a new technology that doubles the resolution suggested by the 3.2 megapixel rating. With rivals offering higher megapixel models, Fuji knew it needed a way to stand out.

Campaigners tackled this by explaining the product better to retail clerks, who in turn did a better job explaining it to shoppers. That can be an improvement over a commercial or a Web site, since the message reaches the casual shopper at the very point of decision.

To do this, Campaigners needs to know the product nearly as well as the manufacturer. So the firm asks the clients lots of questions over a period of days to get familiar with the product and the company's style.

From there, the firm works with the client to craft a marketing message and approach.

One of the toughest parts is getting the right people. Campaigners culls a database of thousands of on-call workers to match skills, availability and other measures. Some work on a contract basis, and others are full-time employees.

Keeping up the pool of workers is key. To make sure Campaigners has enough workers ready for the next campaign, it often holds "casting calls" around the country to find people it can use.

The skills needed can vary from project to project.

"When you're on stage (representing) Microsoft, you need someone more technically competent than for Sierra Mist," said Campaigners CEO Melissa Orr.

Too Much Information?

Gathering attention on a college campus might be important in one setting. In others, it might be vital to keep loudmouth propeller heads in the crowd happy.

When auditioning, Campaigners puts wannabe reps through real-life scenarios to see how they react. After all, hecklers, product glitches and stolid crowds are routine in the field.

After selecting those who will work in the upcoming project, Campaigners brings them together for a two-to four-day training camp. Typically, the client directs the teaching, highlighting the intricacies of their goods.

"You would not believe how much there is to know about washing machines and dryers," Orr said, referring to client LG Electronics Co.

The final step of training is a day of rehearsed presentations. Campaigners puts workers through their paces, throwing all sorts of curves as they hone their performance.

Finally, the new reps are sent out into the field.

To retailers and shoppers, the Campaigners crew may as well be the manufacturer itself. Reps are decked out in outfits provided by the manufacturers and act as direct ambassadors.

One of their most valued functions is gathering field data: How familiar is the retail sales staff with the product? What do they think of rival products? For Fujifilm, the bottom line metric was sales. The company saw a noticeable spike in stores that got visits from the Campaigners staff. The work also keeps Fujifilm products on the minds of sales clerks.

If Sorice ever doubted that Campaigners was working closely enough with retailers, he got the proof he needed when one of his inhouse sales staff visited a store with a Campaigners rep. The store's staff recognized the Campaigners rep and greeted her by name. Familiarity won't guarantee the clerk promotes the product, but it's a crucial first step.

"The retailers know these people," he said. "And they pass that on to the end customer."

OUT OF CONTROL

Oracle's fabled sales culture has broken down. Customers are angry, and Larry Ellison knows it. Here's how he's trying to shape the future of the world's second-largest software maker.

By Ian Mount

Last August, North Dakota state senator Joel Heitkamp was on a commercial flight home from Texas when he struck up a conversation with a professionally dressed woman in the seat next to his. He had no idea what an earful he was about to receive.

The other passenger, it turned out, was Chris Brown, an Oracle Corp. (ORCL) saleswoman who was part of a team trying to sell software to several North Dakota state agencies. According to Heitkamp, she was livid at the prospect that Oracle might lose out in the bidding. She blasted the state's bidding process, which was being managed by Curtis Wolfe—the state's chief information officer and a man Heitkamp respected. And then, in an astonishing move, she said Oracle might sue the state if it lost the bid.

Brandishing lawsuits at customers isn't exactly high on the list of all-time winning sales tactics.

But when Wolfe heard about the conversation, he was not surprised. For months Wolfe had been steaming about other high-pressure moves by Oracle salespeople. In the end the state's $22 million contract went to Oracle archrival PeopleSoft (PSFT) because it had better software, Wolfe says. But the machinations of Oracle's sales team left a sour taste that's sure to linger. "You don't want them to be like used-car salesmen," he says.

Tales of hyperaggressive salespeople are nothing new to Oracle. The company is legendary for a sales culture that combines the fervor of tent revival preachers and the determination of combat Marines. Once the envy of the industry, it's a major reason Oracle became the world's second-largest software company, and its founder, Larry Ellison, one of the world's richest men.

The industry has changed, however, and so has Oracle's place in it. Competitors from IBM (IBM) to Microsoft (MSFT) are challenging the company's once-dominant position in the database software market. Oracle, in turn, is desperately trying to build a presence in applications that run other business processes. That thrusts Oracle's sales team into a much more crowded and nuanced market, face-to-face with seasoned competitors like Siebel Systems (SEBL) and SAP (SAP). The whole strategy has been rendered even more delicate by quality problems in its new business management application suite—called 11i—and by the steepest downturn in IT spending in recent memory.

Episodes like the North Dakota one suggest that Oracle's sales team either doesn't grasp the gravity of the company's situation or is simply unable to adapt its brute-force tactics to the new reality. State officials in places like South Dakota and Wisconsin have joined North Dakota in denouncing Oracle, complaining about everything from heavy-handed sales pitches to gouging on price. Many corporate clients have their own beefs; some say Oracle salespeople have lied about product capabilities. And in its most public debacle, Oracle has been dragged into a California political scandal in which the company is alleged to have stuck the state with as much as $41 million worth of software and services it will never use. There's no evidence yet that the company did anything wrong, and the scandal appears to be more about state politics than about Oracle; still, the headlines only reinforce the image of a sales force that routinely runs roughshod over customers.

Man with a Plan
Larry Ellison say's he's reforming Oracle's famously aggressive sales operation, but some wonder whether the hyper-competitive CEO is right for the job.

Oracle says it has done nothing improper in any of these situations. "It's almost counterintuitive to think that you can behave inappropriately for a long period and be successful," says Kevin Fitzgerald, who runs Oracle's government, education, and health-care sales. "It just doesn't happen that way." But the company admits that bad publicity has cost it business. Indeed, the catalog of complaints

(Cont.)

SELLING MEDICINE

Sick sales cultures can be cured. Here are some time-tested remedies.

Nothing taxes the health of a sales force like a recession. Sales dry up, commissions plunge, top performers walk. Yet tight times are the right times for diagnosing and curing sales force ills. Problems hidden—or caused—by easy growth are exposed, and change is easier because everybody expects it. "Salespeople know the shareholders are screaming, 'Fix something!'" says Andris Zoltners, managing director of sales force consultancy ZS Associates. Luckily, top-line torpor is usually caused by a few highly treatable conditions. And none need be terminal.—Andy Raskin

GREEDOPHILIA: Of all sales force motivators, greed is the worst. "Witness Enron," says Zoltners, who is also a marketing professor at the Kellogg School of Management. "When greed is the driver, salespeople overstate product advantage and do anything to get the sale—not good for long-term customer happiness."

TREATMENT: Go right to the top of the sales team, Zoltners says: "Get rid of the Ken Lay, and changes propagate down. You gotta cut out the heart, and put in a new one."

CALLPHOBIA: It's tough out there for salespeople who got used to the boom-era life of easy deals. And fear of today's more complex selling environment means less pavement-pounding. "Many companies give us a grandiose analysis of their problems, and it turns out their salespeople simply aren't talking to customers," says Sam Reese, CEO of Miller Heiman, a sales training firm. "They show up talking about widgets, and the buyer says, 'I already saw that on your website—I want to discuss financing, customer service, and logistics.'"

TREATMENT: Design a sales process with support from other departments, like finance and engineering. But, Reese warns, establish milestones that a salesperson must hit before resources become available. As Alec Baldwin admonished a poor-performing Jack Lemmon in *Glengarry Glen Ross,* "Coffee is for closers!"

INCENTIVITIS: Compensation plans that don't keep pace with industry changes fail to reward productive behavior. At Microchip Technology, a crucial selling step is getting manufacturing customers to design its microcontrollers into new products. But when Mitch Little became Microchip's VP for worldwide sales in 1999, he saw customers moving assembly overseas. "Our guy in, say, Boston was no longer motivated to get the design win," Little says, "because the customers were purchasing from a plant in Mexico—and the Mexico rep would get the commission."

TREATMENT: Little now compensates everyone on his 300-person team with a salary and an incentive based solely on corporate performance. He credits the move with helping Microchip hold its own in its beleaguered sector, though he admits that it drove some people out. "This takes a different kind of person," Little says. "We found that out real quick."

CHRONIC TEAM ROT: Companies that lowered hiring standards during the boom are paying the price. "A lot of pretenders wound up in sales when it was the land of milk and honey," Reese says. And it doesn't take many bad hires to ruin a quarter. "If you have a bad salesperson, you knock out a territory," Zoltners says. "If you have a bad sales manager, you knock out 10 or 12."

TREATMENT: List the skills your salespeople need—not only selling prowess but also things like industry experience and product knowledge. Then start hiring and firing. "Today is a great time to find out if you have the A team or the B team," Reese says, "and to start muscle-building if it's the latter."

percent for the fiscal year that ended in May and its share price off 90 percent to about $9 since June 2000, Oracle can't afford a sales force that's a liability. Whether Ellison and his team can civilize a program that has been addicted to aggressiveness for two decades—and whether the notoriously competitive Ellison is the person to lead the way—is a question Oracle must answer quickly. At stake are not only Oracle's customer relations, but also its push to become more than just a database vendor. And on that initiative rests the very future of the company.

A fire-breathing sales culture doesn't arise overnight. Oracle's started long ago, with the man Ellison called Genghis Khan.

His real name is Gary Kennedy. A Mormon bishop from a ranching town in the northeast corner of Utah, Kennedy came to Oracle in 1982 and soon built what is acclaimed to this day to be the toughest sales group ever seen in tech. Kennedy's team was heavy on working-class ex-athletes, people Kennedy believed were hungry to make an indelible mark on the world. "I loved to hire policemen's kids," says Kennedy, now semiretired and living outside Salt Lake City. They received the briefest gesture at training—a mere five days—and were unleashed on the world.

is serious enough to have engaged Oracle's sometimes remote founder and CEO. In an interview with *Business 2.0,* the usually defiant Ellison conceded that his sales operation has in some ways lost its bearings. "Culturally," he says, "Oracle is doing everything it can to operate differently." It has little choice. With its revenues down 11.8

Former Kennedy salespeople say he fostered a deeply Darwinian climate. "The motto was 'We Eat Our Young,'" recalls Marc Benioff, a former Oracle sales executive who's now CEO of Salesforce.com. One of Kennedy's blunter motivating tactics was a sales force ranking called "Hail to the Stars." Kennedy didn't just highlight the best salespeople in this regular e-mail—he listed them all, down to the absolute worst, and noted those who'd been canned or had otherwise departed. Each salesperson had a quota and a "commit," essentially a quasi-religious oath to bring in a certain amount of business. Written on Post-its stuck in Kennedy's desk, a salesperson's commit hung over him like a sword. "It was basically in blood," says Harry Gould, a former Oracle salesman who's now a top executive at SeeBeyond. "Gary boiled sales down to that one word."

The best salespeople got wealthy in very public ways. In a program he dubbed "Go for the Gold," Kennedy had Brink's truck drivers deliver gold coins to the desks of salespeople who beat quota. Details often got overlooked in the mad push for sales. Former executives say some salesmen who'd missed their quotas got gold by mistake, and Oracle later learned that it had paid out over $10 million more than it meant to because commissions had been miscalculated.

Kennedy's approach moved product: Oracle's sales rose from about $55 million in 1986 to nearly $1 billion in 1990. But that year, the relentless pressure to make quota that had been Kennedy's hallmark caught up with the company. Mired in a slump that made hitting sales targets that much tougher, some of Kennedy's salespeople tried to fill the gap by making under-the-table deals that boosted sales by allowing the customers to return software they didn't want. Oracle was forced to restate earnings, and Kennedy was ousted in a sacrifice to investors.

Today, Kennedy says he regrets some of what happened on his watch. He pushed hard, he says, but always emphasized playing by the rules. "What I didn't say, and wish I'd said, was 'Look, in a world of two bad choices—miss your quota or break the rules—it's much, much better to miss your quota,'" he says.

During the tech boom, rule-breaking was hardly necessary, but Oracle never totally lost its tough-as-nails sales culture. And as times have gotten leaner and the pressure to close deals has grown, some of the old aggression—and the damage it can do to customer relations—has resurfaced.

Wolfe, North Dakota's CIO, says the threatened lawsuit was just one of many instances where Oracle's sales tactics went over the line. For instance, North Dakota had set up a system under which all communication between the 25 or so members of the decision-making committee and the vendors was to be funneled through an independent consultant hired for that purpose. Sales-

people from PeopleSoft and the other bidders abided by that rule, Wolfe says. But Oracle's lead salespeople showed up unannounced and repeatedly lobbied committee members directly; in fact, he says, Oracle was so pushy that it learned that one company was going to be dropped from the bidding before the company itself even knew. "They try to go around you, try to go through you," he says. "That oversteps the bounds of propriety, as far as I'm concerned."

Oracle's Fitzgerald downplays the problems in North Dakota. He says Brown, the Oracle saleswoman, might have suggested a lawsuit out of frustration, but adds that Oracle "would never sue a state like North Dakota." Brown declined to comment.

For Infonet Services, a telecom based in El Segundo, Calif., the problem wasn't the pushiness of Oracle salespeople—it was their veracity. In June 2000, an Oracle sales VP started to lean on Infonet to buy its CRM software, says Jim deMin, a technical manager at Infonet. When deMin asked about reference sites, the salesman said the program was indeed up and running—then tried to wriggle free.

"Oracle's salespeople try to go around you, they try to go through you...." North Dakota CIO Curtis Wolfe says. "You don't want them to be like used-car salesmen."

"You guys actually have users of your CRM module, right?" deMin recalls asking him.

"Absolutely," he answered.

"Got a name?" deMin asked.

"Well, no," the salesman admitted.

DeMin says he then conducted his own hunt and finally found a company with the software. It was a rudimentary beta version that the company was testing only because its Oracle sales representative had promised a good deal on other software if it did. DeMin says he suggested that his Oracle rep "have Bob Ballard [the undersea explorer who found the wreckage of the Titanic] look for" an Oracle CRM user. Oracle was "trying to sell us CRM modules that really didn't exist," deMin asserts. In the end, deMin went with software from rival Siebel.

In other instances, distrust was sowed by Oracle's pricing policies. Earlier this year Wisconsin consolidated several of its Oracle databases on a smaller number of servers, to make them easier to manage. It was a minor thing and didn't involve buying more licenses, says Bill Langlois, a state acquisitions specialist, but the state needed recertification that it was in compliance with its Oracle contract. The problem was that Oracle had changed its pricing policy and the salespeople on the Wisconsin deal saw a way to cash in. Langlois recalls a group of three salespeople showing up for a meeting in his office and coming on strong. "They say, 'This is our new policy. This is the way it is,'" he says.

Eventually, Langlois talked down the price, but the negotiations ate up time (five meetings and 25 phone calls, he estimates) and the result wasn't cheap—the state coughed up more than $100,000 for what it says is no gain. "This is costing money for me to spend time dealing with these people to give them more money for which we're getting nothing," Langlois says. "There's no more usage, no more people using it, nothing has changed. Except we're paying more."

At least Wisconsin's software works. A recent lawsuit filed by rare-coin broker Wall Street Rarities alleges that Oracle salespeople hard-sold the company an e-commerce inventory program by claiming it had functions that didn't exist. The suit alleges that, on the last day of Oracle's first quarter of 2000, salesmen James Wiberly and Warren Gardner spent three hours trying to get the company's CEO, Bill Anton, to sign a deal, telling him that the discount they were offering was about to expire. Anton demurred, but in November, at the end of the next quarter, Wiberly again pressed Anton to sign up, promising a $300,000 cap on consulting fees. This time Anton agreed—to his chagrin. Wall Street Rarities alleges that the software never worked, causing consigned inventory to back up and driving away sellers. Moreover, the company alleges that it had to spend $500,000 in consulting fees—and still never got a working system. It seeks more than $10 million in damages.

Oracle has disputed Wall Street Rarities's account in court, but won't elaborate. In response to the complaints of Infonet's deMin and Wisconsin's Langlois, an Oracle spokesperson says only, "Oracle does not comment on hearsay or conjecture."

No customer has been publicly angrier than the state of California, causing a PR nightmare for the company. Late on the last day of Oracle's 2001 fiscal year, the state signed off on a $95 million contract for Oracle database software. There were no other bidders—odd for a deal that large—and the state auditor says a rushed decision may have left the state with far more software and services than it can use. (Oracle disputes that.) But

what really put the purchase under the microscope was a $25,000 campaign contribution to Gov. Gray Davis from an Oracle lobbyist and sales consultant days after the contract was signed. The check was delivered by Oracle's man to the state's e-government director, a proponent of Oracle getting the deal.

So far, the revelations from state legislative hearings have looked worse for the state's software buyers than for Oracle. Still, the controversy has hurt: Oracle chief financial officer Jeff Henley says the case prompted two potential government clients to put off multimillion-dollar purchases of software last quarter.

From Larry Ellison's perspective, the task of reforming Oracle's sales culture is in very good hands. His.

From Larry Ellison's perspective, the task of reforming Oracle's sales culture is in very good hands. His.

"This is the first time I've been this directly involved in the sales force," Ellison says. He explains that the sales team has always been the province of people like Kennedy and former chief operating officer Ray Lane, who left after a much-publicized run-in with Ellison over control in June 2000. "That sales aggression ... that was really their style," claims Ellison, a CEO famous for his own hypercompetitive tendencies.

But there were worse problems than simple aggression. For years, Oracle has organized its sales force in an "account manager" structure, where one salesperson would be responsible for selling all Oracle products to certain customers. In its infancy, Oracle sold one product—a database. But as it added applications for human resources, supply chains, CRM, and the like, the demands on salespeople for multifaceted expertise have soared. Often, the salespeople haven't been up to it, resulting in them either pushing the wrong software on customers or promising things the applications couldn't deliver. "We can't possibly have salespeople who are experts in everything from our database to our application server," Ellison says. "That's simply impossible."

But Oracle can do a better job by restructuring and changing the way its salespeople handle products. The company has reorganized most of its sales force in recent months. Fitzgerald, Oracle's government sales chief, says that as of June 1, each salesperson in his organization is assigned to specialize in a few particular products so he or she can concentrate on selling a customer the most appropriate software. George Roberts, Oracle's head of North American sales, converted 75 percent of his major-account sales force into specialists by the end of last year, and converted almost all of the rest as of June 1.

"Oracle does well when the products are good and poorly when they aren't. That's as simple as it gets." —Larry Ellison

---

Most important, Ellison says he's working to calm down Oracle's aggression in sales by doing the obvious— not rewarding it. He recently eliminated a long-established commission structure, called "accelerators," that rewarded salespeople for deals closed in a quarter's waning days. In some cases the commission was 12 percent if a deal was sealed on the day a quarter closed, compared with 2 percent if it got done the day after. That encouraged furious sales pushes, overpromising, and steep discounts. "You got more into how you were structuring the transaction financially rather than whether this product was right for this given customer," says Ken Martin, who was an Oracle sales manager in the late 1990s.

Now, Ellison says, the company is moving to a program that gives salespeople a flat commission of 4 to 6 percent. He calls the old incentives "perverse." "You can argue it's good for the company because the sales force is 'highly motivated' to get the deal into the quarter, but in fact I think it incents behavior that's not in the interest of the company, long-term, or in the interest of the customer," Ellison says. "You really can't reform the sales force until you clean up that problem."

Ellison insists that his new, soothing touch will modernize Oracle's sales culture and bring the company greater success than it has ever known. Oracle still has many strengths he can build on. Despite the bust, Oracle's database business remains a profit gusher; the company had operating margins of 44 percent last quarter, second only to Microsoft among major software firms. Oracle earned $656 million in the latest quarter. It has $5.8 billion in cash.

But even if Ellison is right about getting Oracle back on track, there remain questions about where the company will go next. Ellison's vision for the future includes more revenue from outsourcing, perfecting its applications, pushing its application server, selling database clusters, and building subscription revenue from existing customers. All are potentially good businesses, but none have the pop and growth potential of Ellison's original database idea or his as-yet-unfinished push into applications.

The more immediate issue is whether Ellison is really the man to permanently reform Oracle's sales culture. Contrary to Ellison's assertion that Oracle's aggressiveness was in part Ray Lane's "style," Lane was seen by many at the company as a calming influence—a kind of horse whisperer—for the sales force. "Larry is very aggressive and would drive an aggressive sales force," says Nimish Mehta, who spent 11 years at Oracle and is now CEO of Stratify. "Ray kind of buffered that."

Indeed, to many people who know the company, Oracle and Ellison are synonymous, and a change in one would require a change in the other. "Oracle had this culture when it had $25 million in sales. Oracle had this culture when it had $50 million in sales. And Oracle has it today with $10 billion in sales," says Benioff, who was at Oracle for 13 years. "Where did it come from? The guy who's still running the company today."

Ellison has little patience for such analysis. "Everybody talks about selling and the Oracle sales force and all of this other stuff," he says. "Oracle has done well when the products are good and poorly when the products aren't good. That's about as simple as it gets."

For Oracle's sake, he'd better be right.

Advertisers Adding Up Their New Options

As fewer folks watch TV, marketers study ways to pitch their messages.

. . . .

By Doug Tsuruoka
Investor's Business Daily

If you can't fight 'em, figure' em out.

That's what advertisers are being forced to do as young adults view less TV—especially TV commercials—in favor of more online content and use of digital video recorders such as TiVo.

Among the moves, advertisers are exploring ways to insert ads into increasingly popular online games. They're also doing more research on DVRs. The devices let people record TV shows, and it's easy to edit out commercials. So advertisers are looking to place their products right into shows or to otherwise find ways to get people to view their product pitches.

It won't be easy for advertisers, says Stuart Fischoff, a media psychologist at California State University, Los Angeles.

"The genie's out of the bottle," he said. "People are going to use technology to bypass ads. The old ideas of how you sell a product have to change."

Ford Motor Co. and, reportedly, PepsiCo Inc. and the National Football League are among the most active advertisers searching for ways to market their messages. There are many others, says Greg Stuart, president of the Interactive Advertising Bureau in New York City.

"I think advertisers are acting more out of desperation than experimentation," said Stuart. "People just aren't watching TV ads anymore."

Several studies back up this theory.

Nielsen Media Research's October/November figures showed that 7% fewer males in the advertiser-coveted 18-to-34 age group watched prime-time TV vs. the same period a year earlier. For women in that age group, viewership fell 2.9%. A study released in late November by the Pew Internet & American Life Project found that young adults were much more attached to the Internet than to the TV.

Pew and others say more younger people are multitasking. They're reading and writing e-mail, playing games, listening to music and watching movies, often at the same time.

That leaves less time for TV, and certainly less time for viewing TV commercials. If they do watch TV, many record TV shows on TiVo or similar devices and ax the commercials.

Analysts say advertisers must work harder to reach younger consumers. The result likely will be new types of ads.

Todd Smith, a 24-year-old junior executive with New York PR firm Starkman & Associates, is a multitasker who watches less TV. "I have a (Sony) PlayStation at home. You get into a video game and it becomes more important than TV," he said.

Viewer trackers such as Nielsen are paying more attention to people like Smith, even though DVRs are in only 2% of U.S. homes. Nielsen has been tracking TiVo use since August 2002, but it hasn't released any findings publicly and, says a spokesman, has no plans to. It has released findings to clients, which include many advertisers and TiVo Inc.

TiVo also tracks what its customers are recording and watching, and sells the data to clients.

People want the option of seeing or not seeing an ad, whether on a game, in a Web page or in the course of downloading a movie, says Charlene Li, an analyst with market tracker Forrester Research Inc.

Future ads will have options that let consumers control what they want to view, she says. Some will be fancier versions of today's interactive online ads. These ads often use eye-catching effects, such as a moving figure. People then can click on the figure if they want to learn more about the product.

"Younger consumers expect that level of control," Li said. "Most online ads have tended to be interruptive."

DVR users, says Li, will opt to view commercials that are interesting. "If advertisers make their ads more bizarre or entertaining, people will watch," Li said.

Advertisers also are looking at more low-key ways to get their message across. For example, they might have their products or services featured as part of an online game, Li says.

An online action game, for instance, could have characters driving Ford SUVs. Or game characters might wear clothes from, say, Abercrombie & Fitch. The practice resembles how some firms pay Hollywood filmmakers to feature their products prominently in movies.

Li also expects more use of marquee advertising online, in which one advertiser gets prominent placement and uses special effects. She says Ford did this last year with an ad on Web sites that seemed to make the screen shake when a Ford pickup drove across the screen.

IAB's Stuart also says product placement can be a bigger form of advertisement, and not just in movies and TV shows.

"Games," he said, "can be a huge ad market."

Reprinted from *Investor's Business Daily*, January 15, 2004. Used by permission.

In-Store Media Ring Cash Register

With media fragmentation stores find clever ways to catch, hold shoppers' eyes

By: Kate Fitzgerald

Add the supermarket to the list of culprits contributing to media fragmentation.

Retailers and marketers, armed with new technology, have transformed the store itself into a media channel, and they're jockeying for control within the store's walls.

The steady splintering of ad-supported print and TV media options has made it more important than ever for marketers to make their products shout at consumers from the store shelves. And retailers' new mantra is to brand the shopping experience itself so customers are constantly aware of where they're shopping. Just walk into a Target or Kroger near you to see the evidence.

It has gone so far that some supermarkets are trying to reduce the clutter of the marketing messages delivered inside their stores—which is potentially bad news for marketers. "All the gadgets thrown into the store to get consumers' attention have turned into a kind of marketing spam," says Kevin Kelley, a principal with Shook Kelley, Charlotte, N.C.

"Retailers want to turn down the noise while emphasizing their own names and private-label brands," says Mr. Kelley, whose retail store design consultancy works with supermarkets.

Despite this in-store tug of war between the retailer and the marketer, retailers never forget the widely cited fact that at least 70% of all buying decisions are made at the point of purchase, and brand marketers' in-store displays, promotions and contests play a big role in making cash registers ring, according to Dick Blatt, president-CEO of Point-of-Purchase Advertising International. POPAI represents makers of in-store marketing displays.

WORKING STRATEGICALLY

"Retailers are demanding more quality in their displays," Mr. Blatt says. "They want in-store devices to conform to their standards, and in the process, display makers are working more strategically with marketing agencies to get better results."

More than ever, trade dollars grease the shelves of all retailers, says Mickey Jardon, exec VP at DVC Co-Marketing, a Norwalk, Conn.-based division of DVC Worldwide. "The dollars keep going up, and although many retailers have put out a 'clean store' policy to limit in-store messaging, they know manufacturer-driven promotions push not just those specific brands but entire product categories," he says.

Budgets previously earmarked for traditional advertising are increasingly migrating into co-marketing funds

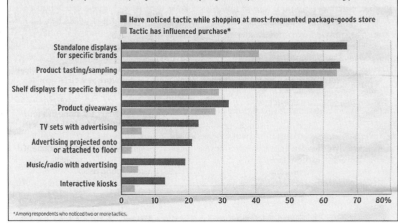

IN-STORE'S TARGET MARKET

According to a survey Knowledge Networks conducted for this report, spur-of-the-moment purchase decisions are made frequently or every time they shop by 30% of respondents.

QUESTION: How often do you purchase a particular product or brand on the spur of the moment?		TOTAL	MEN	WOMEN
	Every time I shop	6%	8%	6%
	Almost every shopping trip	24%	20%	26%
	Once in a while	63%	63%	63%
	Never	7%	9%	5%

Notes: The panelists KN surveyed do most or all of the grocery shopping for their households. Go to knowledgenetworks.com for more on this survey, including additional trends in package-goods purchases, and results broken down by race and household income.

WHAT BEGUILES IN THE AISLE

Among in-store tactics noted most by respondents to the Knowledge Networks survey were standalone displays and sampling. But it's sampling that tops the list for influencing purchase.

■ Have noticed tactic while shopping at most-frequented package-goods store
■ Tactic has influenced purchase*

- Standalone displays for specific brands
- Product tasting/sampling
- Shelf displays for specific brands
- Product giveaways
- TV sets with advertising
- Advertising projected onto or attached to floor
- Music/radio with advertising
- Interactive kiosks

0   10   20   30   40   50   60   70   80%

*Among respondents who noticed two or more tactics.

(Cont.)

for retailer-specific national promotions often backed by spot TV commercials. These efforts usually have a significant in-store marketing component, says Paul Kramer, president of the channel marketing group at Ryan Partnership, a Wilton, Conn.-based marketing agency.

Overall, mainstream supermarkets have given up on fighting discounter Wal-Mart Stores and club stores like Costco on price, and are reconfiguring their stores to focus on a more relaxed shopping experience, better customer service and products grouped around lifestyle needs such as entertainment or healthcare. High-profit categories such as dry grocery and general merchandise items are being showcased through new store fixtures that look less like aisles and more like islands, alcoves and attractive pantry layouts, say in-store experts.

"Supermarkets were traditionally set up like lumberyards, but now they're being designed more around the consumer's mind-set," Mr. Kelley says, "and in-store marketing displays must follow that logic rather than just blindly screaming for attention."

Other new trends include less reliance on kiosks and machines that spit out coupons when customers push but-

In-store's target market: According to a survey Knowledge Networks conducted for this report, spur-of-the-moment purchase decisions are made frequently or every time they shop by 30% of respondents.

MAKING THE CONNECTION ... OR NOT

Consumers often fail to make the connection between in-store ads and previous mass-media advertising they've seen for the same brands.

QUESTION: In the store where you buy most package goods, how many ads or displays are in some way familiar from advertising outside the store?	TOTAL	MEN	WOMEN
Most or all	10%	12%	10%
Many	29%	35%	27%
Some	39%	31%	41%
Very few	13%	12%	14%
None	9%	10%	8%

Notes: The panelists Knowledge Networks surveyed do most or all of the grocery shopping for their households. Go to knowledgenetworks.com for more on this survey, including trends in package-goods purchases, and results broken down by race and household income.

tons at the point of purchase, says Mr. Kramer.

During this past holiday season, Allied Domecq took the floor, literally, to tout Malibu coconut rum. The program using Floorgraphics' billboards followed similar efforts for Kahlua liqueur and Stolichnaya vodka.

Allied Domecq was able to gain incremental floor displays for its brands without price promotion at a time when floor space is at a premium, says Joanne Kletecka, group brand director, adding, "We are constantly searching for innovative, yet strategic, ways to reach our consumer in a crowded marketplace."

"In-store promotion devices are becoming more brand-specific, aimed at changing behavior and attitudes, not just on rewarding a customer with a lower price that day," Mr. Kramer says. "The bottom line is that in-store displays matter more than ever, and every inch has to count for more, both for the marketer and the retailer."

Reprinted with permission from the February 9, 2004 issue of *Advertising Age.* Copyright, Crain Communications Inc. 2004.

69

Pizza people prepare Super Bowl blitz

Game faces are on for biggest day of the year

By Bruce Horovitz
USA TODAY

There's one thing that millions of Super Bowl viewers will do besides drink too much beer: gobble a slice of pizza.

Or four.

Don't think the nation's pizza giants aren't aware of the cosmic link between the Super Bowl and pizza. More pizza will be sold Feb. 1, Super Bowl Sunday, than any other day of 2004. Pizza has become to Super Bowl Sunday what eggs are to Easter. Or candy canes to Christmas.

Experts say that's no accident. It's not just because pizza marketers are pushing it so hard. It's also because pizza is the one food that seems to best meet three game-day criteria: It's cheap. It's easy. It's social.

"There are situations socially tied to food categories," says Jennifer Aaker, a consumer psychologist and marketing professor at Stanford University. "Just as you might go on an airplane and order a tomato juice, you watch the Super Bowl and eat pizza."

It's the one day many Atkins dieters will fall off the wagon and carb out. It's also the day pizza delivery drivers can expect $2 tips to rocket to $20.

For the pizza kingpins—who consider this their own Super Bowl in a box—this is as big as it gets. Some, particularly Pizza Hut, unleash their splashiest new products and ad campaigns. Others, such as Domino's and Papa John's, prefer to focus on the basics by opening hours earlier and doubling delivery staff.

Domino's will deliver about 1.2 million pizzas on Super Bowl Sunday—nearly twice as many as on a regular Sunday. Little Caesars will push its Party Pack promotion: four large pizzas for as little as $20 in some areas. And Papa John's expects its business will jump 70% in some areas—one reason CEO John Schnatter says he'll put on a smock and work in a shop that day.

But perhaps no one embraces the Super Bowl more than Pizza Hut, the world's most powerful and influential pizza seller. On Super Bowl Sunday, the company will unveil what it considers its biggest product idea in years: four square, topped-to-order pizzas in one large pizza box, which, at $11.99, costs about the same as a regular large pizza.

They've dubbed it the "4forAll," because Mom, Dad, brother and sister can each wolf down a topped-to-order personal pizza for the price of a single pizza. To display the family-friendliness of its new product, Pizza Hut is having the Muppets introduce it with the very blond, but rarely bland, singer and MTV reality star Jessica Simpson. "Of course, you can't watch football without pizza," says Simpson, of Newlyweds. Co-star and husband, singer Nick Lachey, "watches the game while I eat the pizza," she says.

Pizza Hut will spend $50 million to launch its newest offering. In the pizza world, this is huge. Some food industry consultants are predicting the newfangled pizza could change the way pizza is sold.

SUPER PIZZA PARTY

That is precisely why Pizza Hut is waiting for Super Bowl weekend—to put it in the world's brightest spotlight. It will co-sponsor the pregame Super Bowl show on CBS and fill the national airwaves with as many as 75 commercials throughout game day. "This is our Normandy landing," says Peter Hearl, president of Pizza Hut.

The $30 billion pizza industry's D-Day invasion takes months of planning. For its part, Pizza Hut has been planning the introduction of the 4forAll for almost two years. Never mind that hostile Pizza Hut franchisees, certain the new product would muck up their operations and damage sales, rallied to kill the product.

Pizza peaks

Like most big pizza chains, Domino's has its single-biggest sales day of the year on Super Bowl Sunday. It expects to sell 1.2 million pizzas in the USA on Feb. 1. The chain's biggest pizza-selling days of the year:

1. Super Bowl Sunday
2. New Year's Eve
3. Halloween
4. The night before Thanksgiving
5. New Year's Day

Source: Domino's

(Cont.)

At one contentious meeting, Jim Schwartz, Pizza Hut's largest franchisee, with 800 stores mostly in the Southeast, warned Hearl, "This is going to kill our restaurants."

But 4forAll is very much alive.

On Super Bowl Sunday, Pizza Hut's 4forAll will get more face time than CBS sports anchor Greg Gumbel, but well before the game.

At almost $2.3 million per 30-second ad slot, none of the pizza giants plans to buy an ad during the game. Besides, most figure that's too late to juice game-day sales, because most pizza-buying decisions are made before kickoff.

Even so, when there are breaks in the action—particularly at halftime—call volume picks up.

"There is no other day like this," says David Brandon, CEO of Domino's. Many Domino's locations will place TVs in the kitchen on Super Bowl Sunday—not to watch the game but to anticipate breaks in the action, when calls increase.

Sales will jump 42% at Domino's vs. an average Sunday, and its drivers will cover 4 million miles, the company says.

Super Bowl Sunday has evolved into a national party day: The average number of people at a Super Bowl party is 17, says Jeremy White, executive editor of *Pizza Today* magazine. "Any time you have large numbers of people together—and the TV on—pizza works because it's so easy to share."

And cheap. The typical large pizza feeds four adults for about $10.

"It's a belly filler," says Ron Paul, president of Technomic, a restaurant research and consulting firm. "If you have two or three beers and enough pizza, you're happy no matter who wins."

Even nutritionists have a tough time knocking pizza.

"Of all the junk foods, pizza is probably the best," says Marion Nestle, former chairwoman of the nutrition department at New York University and author of Food Politics. "As least it has some vegetables in the tomato sauce."

The key to healthy enjoyment, she says, is to eat a slice or two, not an entire pizza.

But it isn't just home-delivered pizza sales that soar on Super Bowl Sunday. So do sales of frozen and carry-out pizza, as well as hotel deliveries. Domino's is contacting hotel concierges in Houston—where the Super Bowl takes place this year—to coax them to recommend Domino's to pizza-craving guests, Brandon says. In exchange, he says, hot pizzas will be sent to

After rocky start, 4forAll rolls

Pizza Hut faced a number of obstacles in creating the 4forAll pizza, including intense opposition from some powerful franchisees. A look at what went on inside the company:

2002

May-July: New Product Team comes up with idea of four pizzas in one box.

August: Franchise Committee balks at idea, says it's too complex and costly.

September: Idea is tested in focus groups, scores exceptionally high.

November: Product team refines idea.

December: Leadership pushes for April 2003 test market against Franchise Committee opposition.

2003

January: Product team offers solutions; Franchise Committee reluctantly agrees to support April test. 4forAll chosen as product name.

February: Franchise Committee says 4forAll production will bog down restaurant kitchens and persuades leadership to halt test.

March-May: Product team invents new pans, tools and order-taking system to counter Franchise Committee concerns.

June: Product team presents solutions; August test market is reluctantly approved.

August: Test market begins in Jacksonville with strong sales results. Franchise Committee visits test stores, begins to embrace 4forAll.

October: Franchise Committee approves 4forAll for 2004 national launch, selects Super Bowl to time rollout.

2004

Jan. 26: National ad campaign kicks off for 4forAll.

Source: Pizza Hut

hotel staff on game day.

Delivery sales tend to spike most during close games, says Jeff Dufficy, a Domino's franchisee who owns 12 stores in the Boston area. And nothing is better for delivery sales than the home team playing in the big game. "If the (New England) Patriots are in it this year, our sales could be up 200%," he says.

The night before the Super Bowl is almost as big as Super Bowl Sunday at Little Caesars, says Michael Scruggs, senior vice president of global operations. "That's when the partying begins," he says.

Grocery store sales of Kraft's DiGiorno and Tombstone frozen pizzas typically jump 20% during Super

(Cont.)

Bowl week, says Renee Zahery, a Kraft spokeswoman. DiGiorno has an on-package Super Bowl promotion called: "Why Tip the Delivery Guy?" The grand prize winner gets $100,000.

And at Nick-N-Willy's World Famous Take-N-Bake Pizza, which sells made-to-order pizzas to be cooked at home, it's the biggest day of the year. The Colorado chain will sell four times as many pizzas on Super Bowl Sunday as on any other Sunday, CEO Scott Adams says.

ALMOST 4FORNONE

No one's anticipating a bigger bump on Super Bowl Sunday than Pizza Hut with its 4forAll.

But it hasn't been easy getting there. Nearly two years ago, a Pizza Hut franchisee in the United Kingdom raised corporate eyebrows by creating a round pizza called "The Quad," which was segmented into four quadrants with extra spaces of dough.

The Quad never took off. But executives liked the idea of a single pizza that could satisfy four people's tastes rather than those of one or two.

So Pizza Hut turned to its Explore Team, an in-house, super-secret group of research-and-development, marketing and consumer-behavior specialists, to improve The Quad.

Within a year, they had the pizza they wanted. But franchisees went ballistic. None more so than Schwartz, the biggest franchisee. "It was a product with way too many operational challenges," he says. It meant changing the way pizza was cooked and new equipment to cook it. And—since the 4forAll is four individual pizzas—each order appeared to require almost four times the labor of a conventional pizza. He feared it would be too costly to make, increase phone order time and stunt sales.

He orchestrated a mutiny. Just as Pizza Hut was ready to test the pizza, Schwartz stopped it by amassing angry franchisees.

Leah Evans, the chief food officer at Pizza Hut, who had overseen the development of 4forAll, dug in her heels. "If you want to kill it, it will be over my dead body," she recalls saying.

"We were at an impasse," Schwartz says.

Then, under pressure from headquarters, franchisees reluctantly agreed to try it—but only after R&D re-jiggered the ingredients to shrink the cooking time and reduced the cost of the cooking implements to hundreds from thousands of dollars per store.

A test was carried out in Jacksonville in August. Franchisees prepared for the worst. But the results stunned them. It has been such a wild success that Jacksonville franchisees refused to allow Pizza Hut to stop the test. Stores had to boost staff 20% to handle the additional business, Evans says.

Beginning Monday, Pizza Hut stores in various regions of the country will start to roll out the new pizza. But it won't be sold and marketed coast to coast until Super Bowl Sunday.

And Schwartz, the franchisee who fought so hard against it, says he expects it to be one of the chain's biggest hits.

> Dubbed the 4forAll, they're designed to please every member of the family, and they're arriving just in time for the Super Bowl.

"It's one of those products that will either make us or break us," he says. "I think it's gonna make us."

70

Conflict Issues Grow Murkier

Entertainment, talent agencies, media shops add to the confusion

By: Kate Fitzgerald

Although no one wants to talk about how many client conflicts are already lurking under agencies' roofs, several types are adding to existing headaches.

New challenges for shops include potential conflicts in branded entertainment, product placement and co-marketing ventures.

The growth of new international markets for automobiles and pharmaceuticals is also stretching conflict tolerance, as is the number of agencies that own minority stakes in shops that serve their accounts' rivals.

"Conflicts remain a big issue with clients, and it's spreading on several levels due to the complicated relationships among agencies and the growth of new types of marketing," says Judy Neer, exec VP-managing partner of agency consultancy Pile & Co., Boston. "It's less of an issue at the holding company level, but it can be a serious problem at the account planning level, where proprietary ideas might be shared."

ENTERTAINMENT ISSUES

Hollywood's growing role in creating branded media is creating some new puzzles over compensation and conflicts among talent agencies and entertainment management companies unfamiliar with advertising agencies' rules when dealing with a marketer's rival, say insiders.

"If you look carefully at major talent agencies such as CAA and William Morris, you will begin to see some interesting conflicts of interest in programming projects that might make some of their major clients squirm," says an executive at a major agency holding company with several entertainment shops under its wing. He would not identify the shops and marketers involved.

The pace of agency consolidation may have slowed, but agency holding companies' reach continues to extend, leaving few independents. Even those are at risk of being snapped up this year, says Lisa Colantuono, marketing director for agency consultancy AAR Partners,

New York. MDC Partners just bought a controlling interest in Kirshenbaum Bond & Partners.

Now it is almost impossible for a Fortune 500 marketer to avoid some crossover between their brands and the increasingly broad reach of ever-consolidating agency holding companies, especially in automobiles and pharmaceuticals.

Agency insiders are reluctant to identify simmering conflicts, while marketers claim to be content with current arrangements. But agency consultants predict this year will produce a few high-profile agency-marketer splits due to conflicts, and most of them will come without warning.

"Clients are getting increasingly sophisticated about analyzing conflict issues because they have to live with them, but they don't like them any more than they ever did," says Richard Roth, president of agency search consultancy Roth Associates, New York. "A situation that was never a conflict in the past suddenly becomes an issue because of different executives involved."

"We spend a great deal more time at the front end of an agency search, checking up and down the corporate ladder to

---

CROSSING OVER ON CARS

A wide array of relationships complicates how U.S. shops buy media and create advertising

HOLDING CO.	BRAND	SHOP	PARENT
Publicis Groupe	Toyota	Saatchi & Saatchi	Toyota
	Lexus	Team One	Toyota
	Cadillac, Pontiac	Chemistri	General Motors
	All GM marques	GM Planworks	GM
	BMW	Fallon	BMW Group
Interpublic Group of Cos.	Buick	McCann	GM
	Chevrolet, OnStar	Campbell-Ewald	GM
	Cert. Used Vehicles	Mullen	GM
	Mitsubishi	Deutsch	DaimlerChrysler*
	All GM marques	GM Mediaworks	GM
	Saab, GMC	Lowe	GM
Omnicom Group	Saturn	Goodby, Silverstein	GM
	Mercedes-Benz	Merkley & Partners	DaimlerChrysler
	Chrysler, Dodge, Jeep	BBDO	DaimlerChrysler
	Nissan, Infinity	TBWA	Nissan
WPP Group	Ford	J. Walter Thompson	Ford Motor Co.
	Jaguar, Land Rover, Lincoln, Mercury	Y&R Advertising	Ford
	All Ford marques	Ford Motor Media	Ford

*DaimlerChrysler owns a controlling interest in Mitsubishi.

(Cont.)

see what conflicts exist in a potential relationship, and who perceives it as a conflict," says Mr. Roth.

Examples of arrangements now being tolerated include WPP Group's purchase last year of Cordiant Communications Group, including Bates Advertising. WPP is a worldwide supplier for Ford Motor Co., but its Bates division also handles advertising for General Motors Corp. in China.

"There's hardly any large agency or marketer that doesn't have some tie-in somewhere that puts them at risk for a conflict," says John Bulcroft, president of the Advisory Group, Cresskill, N.J. "What's difficult for many automotive clients is that many of these relationships are long term, and to completely avoid conflicts, many would have to break up valuable agency connections, which will ultimately hurt them."

MIXING UP ACCOUNTS

Sorting through the car accounts shows rival brands frequently commingling under the same holding company (see chart above). For instance, Publicis Groupe agencies handle Toyota Motor Sales USA (Toyota at Saatchi & Saatchi), General Motors Corp. (Cadillac and Pontiac at Chemistri) and BMW of North America (BMW at Fallon Worldwide).

In many cases, imaginary walls within the agency are all that's keeping marketers' sensitive information secret.

LB Works, Chicago, was allowed to handle a Starbucks Coffee Co. account as long as the shop was considered a separate entity within the confines of its Leo Burnett USA parent. When LB Works was folded back into the parent agency last fall, it resigned the account to avoid conflict with Burnett client McDonald's Corp.

"Clients' trust is being put to the test as knowledge about two rivals' products and advertising may cross the same desks within an agency," says Ms. Colantuono. "In general, clients have to weigh the value of the relationship vs. the risk of information being shared somewhere along the line."

Other agencies will continue to handle business for rival conflicts under one roof, due to longstanding relationships.

Publicis' Starcom MediaVest handles several marketers whose business could be considered in conflict, but the marketers have chosen to trust the agency to keep its business separate. For instance, Starcom handles both Procter & Gamble Co.'s Folger's and Kraft Foods' rival Maxwell House coffee brand, but the arrangement is acceptable-for now-to both marketers.

The crossover is not a problem to either client, says the agency. At SMG offices in New York, the two marketers' brands are housed on different floors and staff members do not share information.

"Conflict's spreading due to complicated relationships and types of marketing"

"Conflicts have become almost a non-issue for many clients because of our internal firewalls, and the fact that our information technology people make sure client information is secure," says a Starcom spokeswoman.

P&G has explored consolidating its roster of shops, which number about 60 globally, but one factor that has prevented the company from doing so yet is a new kind of conflict that emerges in manufacturer-retailer co-marketing programs, says Qaisar Shareef, director of global shopper marketing at P&G. "When you work with these programs with individual retailers, there's a measure of confidentiality in the program until it becomes public," he says. "There's a tension between wanting to consolidate things to become more efficient and recognizing there's a need for different kinds of agency structures to keep things apart. We haven't cracked the code on this."

Of greater concern to agency advisers is the fact that the search to avoid conflicts may be costing agencies access to the best possible advertising resources, says Mr. Roth.

"The right match might involve a conflict, and in their eagerness to avoid conflicts, clients may be limited to choosing only among certain agencies and they may not get the best one for the job," he says.

Contributing: Jack Neff, Jean Halliday

Reprinted with permission from the February 9, 2004 issue of *Advertising Age.* Copyright, Crain Communications Inc. 2004.

71

What to Expect When You're Expecting a Mini-Cooper

BY FARA WARNER

When snow fell on Philadelphia last month, John P. Meyers, a local lawyer, posted a note on a Web message board for Mini Cooper owners, asking if his new car would handle slick and snowy roads. No problem, the owners told him.

But Mr. Meyers, 44, wasn't really an owner yet. His Mini Cooper S was being assembled thousands of miles away, at a factory near Oxford, England. In fact, it would be six more weeks before Mr. Meyers first set eyes on his car and tested it on a snowy January day.

To keep track of his purchase, he logged on at least once a day, if not two or three times, to the Owner's Lounge area of the Mini Cooper Web site (www.miniusa.com). Using his vehicle identification number, Mr. Meyers tracked his car's status from the day he ordered it, Nov. 11, to when it arrived at the port in Jersey City on Jan. 6. By the time he picked up his Mini at a local dealer on Jan. 15, he had already named it Chili Palmer, after John Travolta's character in the movie "Get Shorty."

"This car is definitely a guy," Mr. Meyers said of his Mini, which is chili red with a glossy white roof. He had also introduced Chili to other Mini owners by posting its specifications on the owners' section of the site. "I have become absolutely obsessed with my Mini," he said.

Many car makers must rely on big discounts to woo buyers, but some models are so popular that would-be owners face long waiting periods. They include the Mini, from **BMW;** the Maybach, from **Mercedes-Benz;** and, to a lesser extent, the **Mazda** RX-8 and the **Nissan** 350Z. The companies are aiming to make those delays, whether caused by high demand or custom orders, a bit more bearable for the consumer.

For many years, companies and their dealers did little for waiting customers. There seemed to be little advantage in doing so, given that the sales were already made. Sometimes, marketing campaigns tried to keep early enthusiasts in the loop until the cars were widely available. But after the initial excitement subsided, the programs were often discontinued.

The picture has changed as automakers find benefits in maintaining interest in their brands. Mini, for example, regularly sends out welcome kits to its new buyers as part of its "Make Waiting Fun" program. The kits include retro 1950's games like Interstate Highway Bingo and a stencil that can be used to spray-paint a "Mini Parking Only" sign in the garage.

The wait can be up to six months for the luxurious Maybach, which can cost more than \$350,000 depending on one's choice of wood, leather and other extras, including a golf bag. During that time, customers receive a replica of their radiator emblem and their car's blueprints in a brushed aluminum tube. Mazda allows buyers to track the progress of their RX-8 sports cars at the factory in Japan and has sent out miniature models and books.

Keeping up the enthusiasm has been the main goal for Kerri Martin, Mini's marketing communications manager in the United States, in its program. (Her business card calls her the "guardian of brand soul.")

"These people are super-excited for their cars, but they have a long way to go before they see them," Ms. Martin said. The wait for customized Minis, which make up 95 percent of sales, is now 8 to 12 weeks.

When BMW introduced the restyled Mini in early 2002, owners waited more than 10 months for their cars. Shortly after the introduction in the United States, Mini created the "Where's My Baby?" program on the Internet, so customers could check on their cars' progress. But that didn't seem enough for what were shaping up to be rabidly enthusiastic Mini owners. "It was a little impersonal to just be able to know the basics," Ms. Martin said.

So the company added online message boards, where owners can ask one another about maintenance and warranty issues or just swap stories about their cars. Owners, or soon-to-be-owners, can even write journals, some of which have become quite elaborate. The site has about 12,000 registered users.

Jerry Bradbury, 59, a retired technology executive from Berkeley, Calif., uses the name Siddhartha, after the character in the Herman Hesse novel, in his online journal. He wrote of his mission to find and take possession of Sad Arthur, as he called his red-and-white Mini Cooper S, to which he added the John Cooper Works supercharger package, pushing its horsepower to more than 200.

Instead of waiting up to 18 months to get his car through dealers in San Francisco, where Minis are in especially high demand, Mr. Bradbury ordered it from a dealer outside Chicago last October. When his car was ready, after about two months, he flew to Chicago and was met at the airport by his "motoring adviser," as Mini calls its dealers. He picked up his car the next day and drove 2,200 miles back to Berkeley, later chronicling his journey in detail online.

Chasing the Cars Everyone Wants

There are ways to get around the sometimes long wait for a popular car. Following are a few suggestions from auto experts:

• *Surf the Web.* The Internet has made researching cars easier, but it can also be invaluable for finding hard-to-get vehicles. AutoTrader.com may be a good place to start the search; more dealers are using the site to sell new cars. Many sites also let you search by ZIP code, so you can find dealers outside your area.

• *Get in line.* Before a car is even available, put your name on dealers' waiting lists. In some cases, you may have to put down a deposit. (Don't forget to get the deposit back if you change your mind, or have it deducted from the price after the sale is completed.)

• *Get to know the dealer.* By building a relationship with a dealer, you can find out when certain models will be delivered, or when waiting lists will be created.

• *Comb the lots.* If you're willing to compromise on the color and options, you may not have to wait.

• *Take a road trip.* Find out where the car you want is less popular. You may have to travel to a dealership in a faraway city or hire someone to deliver the car to you.

Fara Warner

(Cont.)

Some Mini owners say their experience was much better than their previous car-buying episodes.

"When my husband special-ordered his Acura, the dealer simply said, 'It'll be here in three months,' and that was it," recalled Angel Durham, 40, whose online name is Minimom.

By contrast, Mrs. Durham said, her entire neighborhood in suburban Atlanta knew about her car, which she named Maggie. Her family also became accustomed to all the gifts Mini sent while she waited more than two months for the car.

"My kids really like the bingo game," she said. She has five Mini mugs, and when she found out on the message board about the "Mini Parking Only" stencil, she called Mini to get one.

Mrs. Durham's customized car is blue with red-and-white stripes on the hood, and she added side-view mirrors with the Union Jack on them.

Mercedes-Benz takes customization further for its Maybach, as part of a "commissioning" procedure that is meant to turn the process of buying the car into a life event. It starts in special rooms at the dealership, where a potential buyer settles into a black leather chair in front of a giant plasma television screen.

Customers are offered Champagne or wine as they pick their way through the car's options. From black-lacquered drawers, the Maybach "relationship manager" pulls out heavy tiles in the 17 body and side panel colors, which have names like Himalayas Gray and Caspian Black. Leather and wood options run into the dozens. Customers then consider other extras, like sterling silver goblets, cigar humidors and luggage. They can also choose a glass roof, or even small flagpoles for the hood.

As options are chosen or rejected, the Maybach manager feeds the information into a computer modeling program through a wireless tablet. The options then appear on the plasma screen. Customers can virtually fly through their cars, inspecting their choices from almost any angle.

"It should be like a kid in a candy store," said Brian Bucholtz, the Maybach manager at Mercedes-Benz of Bloomfield Hills, Mich.

Ordering a Maybach requires a $50,000 deposit. During the four- to six-month wait that follows, the owners-to-be get the cell-phone numbers of their Maybach managers so they can contact them day or night.

"If I'm out on the golf course and they call, it's 'No problem, what can I do for you?'" Mr. Bucholtz said.

He has added some perks of his own. He gives customers Mont Blanc pens inscribed with their signatures and will deliver the new cars almost anywhere. Once, he picked up a new owner at the Detroit airport as onlookers gawked at the car.

Wayne Killen, a Maybach brand manager at Mercedes-Benz U.S.A., said he had not looked to other car companies for ideas about how to treat customers.

"We thought there was room for improvement even at the most luxurious levels in cars," he said. "Instead, we looked at the world of yachts and customized aircraft." What he found, he said, was that "you sim-ply can't spend too much time with these people."

"These people almost expect daily phone calls on what's happening as their cars are in production," he added.

Makers of more mainstream cars are not as likely to go to such lengths, but more are considering ways to ease the wait for popular or customized cars. Treating owners right can mean more revenue from repeat business, and even new business from word of mouth.

John Stramatos, a marketing manager at Nissan, led the product planning for the 350Z sports car when it was introduced in 2001. Before it was even on dealer lots, he said, 8,000 people were on the waiting list. His team stayed in contact with those on the list by sending out postcards and other direct mail. Recently, the company sent out coffee-table books about the "Z" to some customers.

Mr. Stramatos's work on the car taught him that keeping those early enthusiasts happy was crucial to the car's continuing success. "Those people bring in other customers," he said.

But they can just as easily make their complaints known. Mr. Stramatos said that when some dealers started charging premiums over the manufacturer's suggested retail price, "they were 'outed' pretty quickly on the Internet."

Price

72

Car-Rental Agencies Talk Of Realistic 'Total Pricing'

Obscure Fees and Surcharges Vex Drivers

BY CHRISTOPHER ELLIOTT

Nothing makes business travelers' blood boil quite like the unexpected fees and surcharges that car-rental companies tack onto their bills, from airport taxes to a $6-a-gallon charge for filling up the gas tank when the vehicle is returned.

A recent study by Travelocity, the online travel agency, found that the car-rental customer paid an average of 24.4 percent in taxes and surcharges over the base rate when renting at a major American airport. The list of these add-ons has been expanding steadily for the last decade, pushing many drivers to the point of revolt.

To blunt that anger, the car-rental industry and the online travel agencies recently began rolling out a program called total pricing, intended to quote a price that includes all taxes, fees and surcharges.

If this can actually produce a final bill that matches the advertised rate, it might just succeed in sidestepping a public relations disaster.

But that is a big if, industry insiders and business travelers say.

Travelocity.com, the first of the major online travel agencies to widely promote a complete price to its customers, guarantees that its estimate will be within 1 percent of the final bill.

A leading rival, **Orbitz,** promises that the price will be an exact match. And **Expedia** is expected to offer a similar warranty next month when it introduces a feature that will display an estimated rate at the end of each car-rental search.

Two other online travel sellers, Hotwire. com and **Priceline.com,** also guarantee all-inclusive rates in the form of prepaid vouchers.

But for business travelers, the road to a real, full price has been a bumpy one.

"I think rental customers are getting a more accurate idea of what a car rental will cost," said Neil Abrams, president of the Abrams Consulting Group. "But they aren't necessarily getting the whole picture. There are other optional charges, such as

fuel-purchase options, loss-damage waivers, that aren't included. And the systems that generate a total price are costly, complex and not yet perfected."

For example, Travelocity, one of the earliest converts to total pricing, still does not offer a complete rate when corporate travelers use its Travelocity Business booking service. The reservations technology used by Travelocity Business is different from the one used on Travelocity, and is not yet capable of calculating a total price, according to the company. That is expected to be fixed with upgrades this spring.

In the meantime, "total pricing is always available on Travelocity," said Phil Kennewell, who is Travelocity's director of car and rail products.

But even when an online service promises a full price, it sometimes leaves out important details that can affect the rate paid. Chuck Reagan booked a car through Travelocity in January and was quoted a "total" price of $135. But when an agent at **Enterprise Rent-A-Car** found that he planned to drive from Portland, Ore., into Idaho, she increased the four-day rate more than 60 percent, to $218.

"Nothing in Travelocity's total price mentioned charging extra for driving into Idaho," Mr. Reagan, a salesman from Logan,

From discount Web site to airport counter, often a road map of consumer frustration.

Utah, said. "But Enterprise said that it is its policy to charge more for Idaho. It was a classic bait-and-switch scam as far as I'm concerned."

Travelocity said Mr. Reagan failed to read the fine print in his rental agreement, which outlined the geographical restrictions.

But Mr. Kennewell acknowledged that the booking display "could have been clearer." Enterprise refunded the difference between what Mr. Reagan was first quoted and what he was billed. Travelocity has pledged to redesign its booking page.

At times, travelers are not sure if they are being quoted a total price. Warren Bell, a South San Francisco, Calif., market researcher who rented a car through Orbitz in August, said that the rate offered by **National Car Rental** in Las Vegas for a midsize vehicle came up as $18.95 a day, including all taxes and fees. But Orbitz failed to mention that the daily rate jumped to $50.96 over the weekend, leaving him with a bill of $211.

"When I returned the car and saw my bill, I honestly thought they had charged me for the wrong reservation," Mr. Bell said.

Orbitz, which asserts that it has never had to reimburse a car-rental customer under its rate guarantee, said the quote Mr. Bell received did not represent a total price.

Sam Fulton, its director of car rental operations, said National had not upgraded its systems to send a complete price to Orbitz last summer. Since Mr. Bell's rental, Orbitz has begun offering total prices for its National cars, and it plans to extend that to all its rentals by year's end.

Mr. Fulton acknowledges that the concept of total pricing is not without its flaws. "If a municipality imposed new taxes that weren't in the system at the time of the rental, then there wouldn't be much we could do about it," he said.

Rental vouchers like the ones offered on "opaque" Web sites like Hotwire and Priceline have not been problem-free.

Bonnie Schollianos, a manager for a resort in St. Thomas, in the Virgin Islands, booked a car through Priceline two years ago. A rental agent at the **Hertz** counter in Oakland, Calif., charged her a $5 airport fee, which was supposed to have been included in her rate. Priceline said that the agent misunderstood the terms of the rental voucher and refunded the $5.

Priceline later revised its display to calculate all taxes and fees at the beginning of the booking process, and since then there have been no misunderstandings at the counter, a spokesman, Brian Ek, said.

"The price you see," he added, "is the price you pay."

Car-rental companies are offering total pricing both to placate customers and to meet rate disclosure requirements from states like California and North Carolina.

"It's important that a consumer knows exactly what they will pay," a Hertz spokesman, Richard Broome, said. "The last thing you want is a surprise at the end of the rental."

The improvements have not come cheap to car-rental companies. The cost for a small

(Cont.)

company to upgrade so a total price can be sent through its reservations system runs "in the tens of thousands of dollars," according to Mr. Abrams, the rental analyst.

For one of the major companies, it can be a six-figure technology investment. None of the online agencies would disclose its exact investment in total-pricing technology. Expedia's director of car programs, Noah Tratt, said it had a team of 10 developers working on the system, adding, "We are very committed to total pricing."

There are further complications. Total pricing is far from complete. Mr. Broome said current total-pricing systems, while sophisticated, still had to make certain assumptions. For example, when an Internet user

The car-rental rate quoted Chuck Reagan of Logan, Utah, rose more than 60 percent because he had to drive across the state line to Idaho.

asks for a quote on a Hertz car in Boston and does not provide flight-arrival information, the system guesses that it is being rented at a location other than the one at the airport.

But if a car is picked up at the airport, certain airport fees would apply. "If you were flying into Boston, your car would be more expensive," he said.

There is also the matter of when the total price is displayed—at the start of the reservations process when an Internet user is shopping for a cheap rate, or at the end

when a purchase decision is all but made.

Car-rental companies have resisted listing a total price at the start—in part because it forces the system to make assumptions about the rental that may be erroneous, but largely for competitive reasons.

No company wants to show the real price until it absolutely has to, according to Marie Benz, who manages the Web site Autorental-guide.com.

"Base rates are still artificially low," she said. "You have to pay attention to the fine print in your rental contract, even with total pricing."

73

The New Drug War

Pharmaceutical companies need profits to develop new drugs. Patients need pills that they can afford. Their interests are colliding at the Canadian border. ■ *By Roger Parloff*

Four years ago, on the frozen prairies of Manitoba, two young pharmacists, working independently, founded a billion-dollar industry. In the process they created a quandary for global health-care policy, a hot-button issue for this year's U.S. presidential race, and a potential diplomatic crisis for Canada and the U.S

It all started in Minnedosa (pop. 2,426), about two hours west of Winnipeg and three hours north of the North Dakota line—when the roads are passable. Freshly graduated pharmacist Andrew Strempler, then 25, noticed that prices of Nicorette gum were much lower in Canada than in the U.S. So he began selling it to Americans over eBay. (Nicorette does not require a prescription.) Soon he set up a website. Within three months, Strempler recalls, his sales had gone from about one box a week to 150 per day. His distributor informed him that he was selling more Nicorette than any drugstore in Canada.

At just about the same time, Winnipeg pharmacist Daren Jorgenson began selling glucose-monitoring equipment over the Internet. Jorgenson had first checked with U.S. officials to make sure that the sales were legal, which they were. But while making his inquiries, Jorgenson says, he came across a U.S. Food and Drug Administration official, whom he identifies only as "Tom." Tom told Jorgenson that what he really ought to be selling over the Internet was prescription drugs, because that's where the price disparity was greatest—about 30% to 80% on brand-name drugs—and where the demand was most urgent

"I didn't think I could," says Jorgenson in an interview, alluding to U.S. laws generally forbidding the importation of pharmaceuticals except by manufacturers. But then Tom told him about the FDA's "personal use" policy. Jorgenson understood him to say that Americans were allowed to bring in a small supply of drugs (no more than three months' worth) for their own use.

Unquestionably, for many years busloads of American seniors lucky enough to live near the border have been crossing into Canada to buy cheap drugs with the tacit indulgence of

U.S. Customs and the FDA. Nevertheless, the FDA says today that its "personal importation" policy has never actually authorized those bus trips, let alone what Jorgenson was contemplating. (The written policy countenances only noncommercial importation under defined circumstances, such as when drugs are prescribed in another country and equivalent drugs are unavailable in the U.S.)

By March 2000, after consulting with lawyers who could find no *Canadian* laws against selling prescription drugs to American customers, Jorgenson launched CanadaMeds.com. Strempler followed suit with RxNorth.com.

The business idea worked. Over the next three years, RxNorth's sales multiplied 20-fold, from $3.2 million (all figures are in U.S. dollars) in 2001 to about $70 million in 2003. Strempler's Minnedosa facility now employs about 200 people. "We employ 10% of the population," he says. "The other 90% are unemployable, because they're retired." Though Strempler has a matter-of-fact, understated manner, he wears a gem-studded ring the size of a PDA.

Meanwhile, Jorgenson's CanadaMeds and a second Internet pharmacy he subsequently set up each sold about $70 million last year. Revenue for the whole industry—there are now 64 Internet pharmacies in Manitoba and maybe 75 more scattered across the rest of Canada—was about $800 million in 2003.

Strempler and Jorgenson are two brass knuckles on Adam Smith's invisible hand, which is now battering away at the fragile lattice of geographic price disparities that overlays the global pharmaceutical market. Though that structure evolved for complex reasons, the fundamentals are simple. Most Western nations other than the U.S. regulate the price of prescription drugs, either through direct price controls or through other government-driven cost-containment schemes. In Canada, for instance, a federal board effectively sets ceilings on the prices of patented drugs, while each province exerts further downward pressure by creating formularies and capping reimbursements under its social insurance plan. (It is only brand-name drugs

that are cheaper in Canada; generics actually cost less in the U.S. because of greater competition.) Though Canada's regulated prices exceed the manufacturers' rather trivial costs of making the pills, the companies claim that they do not begin to pay for the enormous R&D expenditures necessary to develop an innovative drug in the lab and see it through the years of animal testing and clinical trials needed to gain FDA approval. That process can often take as long as 12 years and cost as much as $802 million per drug that makes it to market, one academic study estimates. The manufacturers maintain that they must recover high returns where they can—i.e., the U.S.—to encourage the R&D that sustains the industry and benefits mankind. Greed might be a factor too.

The pressure is growing daily on U.S. politicians to alter that odd global price structure—in which the rest of the world seems to catch a free ride on the backs of American seniors. Expenditures on retail prescription drugs in America—$162 billion in 2002—now account for 10.5% of the nation's total health-care costs, which, in turn, consume 14.9% of the GDP. Prescription-drug expenditures are the fastest-growing piece of the health-care pie, having risen at a 15.6% annual rate from 2000 to 2002. As Americans live longer, as miracle drugs become an ever more crucial component of health care, as Medicare expands to encompass prescription-drug coverage, and as the baby-boom generation marches toward retirement, prognosticators can agree on only one proposition: Something's got to give.

You'll be hearing more about those issues in the coming weeks too, because Democrats believe President Bush is vulnerable on his pro-industry health-care stances. In the Democratic reply to the State of the Union address, Senator Tom Daschle urged legalization of Canadian drugs—as have all the Democratic presidential candidates.

But it's not just Democrats who are clamoring for legalization. For many of the 43 million Americans—including 40% of all seniors—who have no prescription-drug insurance, Canadian prices are a godsend.

(Cont.)

These Americans can't afford to heed safety warnings from FDA officials or lectures from economists about R&D incentivization. For them the new, gap-ridden Medicare prescription-drug benefit is unlikely to diminish the allure of Canadian drugs, even once it kicks in, in 2006. (No one knows yet if the government's discount drug card program, which launches in April, will afford greater benefits than existing discount cards, which have failed to deter seniors from exploring the Canadian option.)

More important, seniors aren't the only Americans who have come to see Canadian drugs as a quick fix. Elected state officials of both parties are looking north for relief from their own groaning budget crises. While Canadian Internet pharmacies currently account for a tiny percentage of the U.S. pharmaceutical market, that situation will change quickly if the officials have anything to say about it

"We pay about $600 million just through Medicaid for pharmaceutical products," says Minnesota attorney general Mike Hatch. "We can save $300 million by using a Canadian-style system. Then add in the state employees—which is huge. We're talking real dollars here." (The Pharmaceutical Research and Manufacturers Association—known as PhRMA—claims that Hatch's savings calculations are outlandishly inflated.) In late January, Minnesota's Republican governor, Tim Pawlenty, added a page to his official website telling Minnesotans how to order drugs from Canada and also recommending specific Canadian Internet pharmacies. Asked in the past about the FDA's safety concerns, Pawlenty has famously responded, "Show me the dead Canadians."

Notwithstanding PhRMA's notorious clout in Washington—the association and its members reportedly spent $139.1 million on lobbying during the first six months of 2003—national policymakers are also sharply split on the legalization issue. To be sure, most pro-corporate conservatives oppose importation, which they see as a way of importing foreign price controls into this country, undermining R&D. That is the view held by, for instance, the *Wall Street Journal* editorial board, certain American Enterprise Institute commentators, free-market icon Milton Friedman, and Republican Senators Bill Frist and Orrin Hatch.

But many libertarian conservatives come down in favor of legalization, which they see as a way of destroying foreign price controls and finally forcing other nations to shoulder their fair share of R&D costs. How would that happen? They theorize that once the manufacturers realize that they can no longer rely on American consumers to pay for R&D, they'll force Canada and Europe to relax the limits on prices—on pain of cutting

off those nations' drug supplies. Partisans of that theory include Cato Institute economists Roger Pilon and Edward Crane, and Republican Congressmen Dan Burton of Indiana, Jeff Flake of Arizona, and Gil Gutknecht of Minnesota. In fact, because Canada is so small a market, Cato types favor importation from other countries as well, including all the European Union countries. As sometimes happens, the libertarians are aligned with liberal Democrats on this issue. The day after President Bush signed the new Medicare law, Senators Daschle and Ted Kennedy each introduced bills that would, among other things, legalize importation from Canada.

What's most troubling about the drug-importation conundrum is that when you survey the chessboard and try to anticipate each player's future moves, most paths seem to lead to cataclysm. As ever more Americans turn to Canada for brand-name drugs, the manufacturers will limit Canada's supply—as at least six have already started doing. If the constriction in Canadian supply cuts off American seniors' lifeline to affordable drugs, state attorneys general may sue manufacturers alleging a collusive boycott—as Minnesota's Hatch is already threatening to do.

Meanwhile, manufacturers will start raising their Canadian prices—as at least four have done. Canadian price regulators will try to block those hikes—as Quebec is now trying to do. If manufacturers can't raise Canadian prices, they'll clamp down further on Canadian supply, creating shortages. If drug shortages threaten Canadians' health, Canada may cease honoring manufacturers' patents. And if Canada stops honoring U.S. patents, the U.S. might bring a complaint against Canada before the World Trade Organization. Or invade

But we're getting ahead of ourselves.

When he launched CanadaMeds, Jorgenson placed a small ad in the *Grand Forks* (North Dakota) *Herald*. "I got a lot of reaction from regulatory bodies," he recalls. "Yours called ours." The Manitoba Pharmaceutical Association was very dubious about what Jorgenson was doing. "Whereas historically the pharmaceutical association inspected once or twice a year, we were getting inspected on a daily basis, seven days a week," he says. "We had search warrants issued against our premises. They took up vanloads of stuff and scoured through it for months and months."

Internet pharmacies raise two obvious regulatory issues, one small and one big. The small one concerns the mechanics of prescription-filling. Jorgenson, Strempler, and all genuine, licensed Canadian pharmacies require U.S.

customers to provide short medical histories and to mail or fax a U.S. prescription for each drug sought. But Canadian law bars Canadian pharmacists from filling U.S. prescriptions. So the Internet pharmacies typically fax the U.S. patient's medical history and prescription to a Canadian doctor. The Canadian doctor reviews them, writes a Canadian prescription, and faxes that back to the pharmacy to fill. The problem is that the provincial regulatory bodies for doctors all take the position that it is a substandard practice for doctors to write prescriptions for patients they've never examined. Pharmaceutical regulators, in turn, are reluctant to let pharmacists run businesses predicated on substandard medical practices.

Then there is the bigger issue. Because

Seniors aren't the only ones who want Canadian drugs. State officials see them as a way to alleviate the pain of swelling budget crises.

pharmaceuticals are easy to counterfeit or dilute or sell past their expiration dates or damage through improper storage, Canada and the U.S. each use very similar "closed" systems of regulation. Deploying both federal and local authorities, each country oversees every step in the supply chain as a drug makes its way from manufacturer to wholesaler to retailer to patient. Though the manufacturing plants are often outside either the U.S. or Canada, each country's federal regulators—the FDA and Health Canada's equivalent agency—inspect those facilities and set up paper trails to ensure that the drugs pass through a seamless pipeline from that point forward. Regulators in each country get nervous when the pipeline is breached by an international transaction, since neither country has authority to inspect facilities or subpoena information across the border. Accordingly, the FDA and nearly every U.S. state board of pharmacy has denounced Canadian Internet pharmacies as unsafe; Health Canada has also acknowledged that it cannot guarantee the safety of drugs sent to America.

On the other hand, Health Canada has not tried to shut down the traffic, which it regards as fundamentally a U.S. issue. Moreover, its officials have taken offense at the FDA's sometimes broad-brush denigrations of Canadian pharmacies as a buyer-beware market. "We have no evidence at this time, in the

(Cont.)

context of Internet pharmacies, that there are unsafe products going to the United States," said assistant deputy health minister Diane Gorman last November, after a tense meeting with FDA commissioner Mark McClellan in Toronto. "It's very clear that Canada's safety record is second to none internationally," she pointedly added.

In fact, the FDA has hyped aspects of the safety threat. The agency periodically performs "blitz" inspections of drug packages entering the U.S. through the mail, for instance, and then reports that alarmingly high percentages of the packages seized—about 87% last November, for instance—contained drugs "unapproved" by the FDA. Photos are displayed of pills wrapped in baggies and bottles labeled in Chinese

The phrase "unapproved drug" may be a bit misleading. In FDA parlance, a drug is unapproved if it is improperly labeled, and Canadian drugs are, by definition, improperly labeled. A Canadian box of Lipitor may

be "unapproved" for no other reason than that it bears a Health Canada identification number instead of an FDA identification number. Canadian drugs also seldom carry precisely the same litany of small-print warnings that the FDA requires. In its public pronouncements the FDA doesn't distinguish between packages sent by licensed Canadian pharmacies—Manitoba's regulators require that return addresses be clearly displayed—and those sent, say, anonymously. The latter could come from any of the many illegitimate operators that advertise by spam, require no prescriptions, and claim to be Canadian but often aren't. Obviously, when people order VIAGR@ or VAL[I]UM from anonymous spammers, Lord knows what they receive in return. Licensed Canadian mail-order pharmacies cannot sell controlled substances like Valium at all. They primarily deal in long-term "maintenance" drugs—Plavix, Lipitor, and the like—rather than drugs that treat acute conditions. They typically send drugs to U.S. customers in the same sealed containers in which the manufacturers originally sent the drugs to Canadian wholesalers. In this respect, containers from licensed Canadian Internet pharmacies are arguably less likely to have counterfeit pills in them than ones from the U.S., where pills are often repackaged multiple times in their trek from the factory.

Notwithstanding serious misgivings, the Manitoba regulators have so far permitted the industry to survive—and, indeed, thrive. But as with many gray-market activities, thriving presents its own perils. If Canadian pharmacies were to begin selling too much of their supply to Americans, they could create shortages for Canadians. At that point Health Canada might abandon its neutrality toward the industry and shut it down—possibly overnight. Consequently, the industry is now divided against itself

"We need to be prudent and responsible so that we don't jeopardize the drug supply," says Dave MacKay, who represents one side of the schism. He heads the Canadian International Pharmacy Association, or CIPA, a group of about 35 of the largest Internet pharmacies. MacKay supports the creation of websites, like Governor Pawlenty's, that assuage Americans' safety concerns by effectively accrediting legitimate Canadian pharmacies. But MacKay believes that his industry should not start entering into contracts with American municipalities or states. "We just cannot sustain that kind of volume," he says. "It's not a problem for one state. But as soon as one state sets the precedent, it's going to be 20 or 30 states. And if it's California or New York, we're gonna be dead in the water, because there's more Californians than there are Canadians."

But not everyone shares MacKay's commitment to prudence.

When Tony Howard, who runs CanaRx.com, picks me up in a slush-encrusted Chevy van at the Detroit Metro airport in mid-January, I am surprised. I had assumed he'd send a chauffeur to take me to his office across the river in Windsor, Ontario. That's because I'd been told that Howard can't enter the U.S. any more for fear of being sued by the FDA—or maybe even arrested.

Howard received two warning letters from the FDA last fall advising him that CanaRx's operations violated the Federal Food, Drug, and Cosmetic Act and "present a significant risk to public health." Nevertheless, it is definitely Howard himself—cheerful, jokey, disheveled, logorrheic, intense— at the wheel. He immediately launches

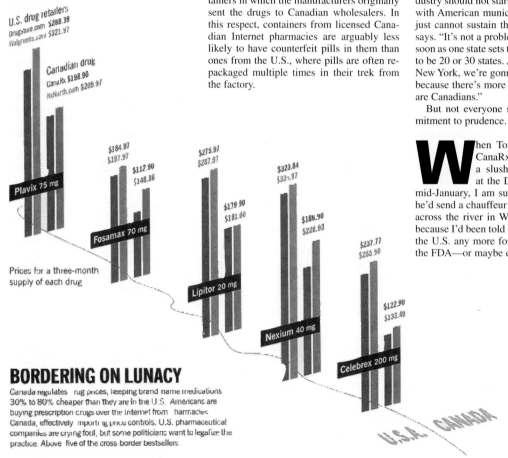

U.S. drug retailers
Drugstore.com $288.39
Walgreens.com $321.97

Canadian drug
CanaRx $198.90
RxNorth.com $209.97

Plavix 75 mg

Fosamax 70 mg
$184.97
$197.97
$112.90
$148.86

Prices for a three-month supply of each drug

Lipitor 20 mg
$275.97
$287.97
$179.90
$181.00

Nexium 40 mg
$323.84
$331.97
$186.90
$228.93

Celebrex 200 mg
$237.77
$265.98
$122.90
$133.49

BORDERING ON LUNACY

Canada regulates drug prices, keeping brand name medications 30% to 80% cheaper than they are in the U.S. Americans are buying prescription drugs over the Internet from pharmacies Canada, effectively importing price controls. U.S. pharmaceutical companies are crying foul, but some politicians want to legalize the practice. Above five of the cross border bestsellers

U.S.A.   CANADA

into a monologue without the formality of any questions having been posed. Just before entering the tunnel to Windsor, he stops at the Detroit post office and picks up a handful of prescription orders from a P.O. box he keeps there. He stopped listing this U.S. address on his website after the FDA sent its first warning letter last September, but some of Howard's longtime customers still don't know about the change

Though he presents like Buddy Hackett, Howard, 54, is a bit of a crusader. He grew up in Windsor but has had homes on both sides of the border and thinks of himself as a North American, he says. About ten years ago, after an early heart attack, he sold his Windsor insurance consulting firm and retired. He and his wife spent much of their time in Florida and Phoenix, and many of the people they befriended were much older. After one asked him to buy drugs for her in Canada, he found out about the enormous price disparities. Outraged by those inequities, he and what are now his partners—his wife, two doctors, and a pharmacist—decided to take action.

They're not in it for the money, Howard claims: "We're all well-off individuals. We want to change the laws, not build an empire." Their goal is to shame the U.S. government into forcing drug companies to lower their American prices. If he succeeds, of course, he'll put the whole Canadian Internet pharmacy industry out of business—including himself. He says he doesn't care. "I've put in all this time without any pay"—he claims to have recovered no profits for himself so far—"to be that one person who can say, 'I was there, and I helped.' It will affect so many Americans."

Accordingly, Howard, who is not a pharmacist, declines to play by MacKay's rules. Howard tries to sign up American towns, cities, states, unions, seniors' groups, and corporations, offering to supply Canadian drugs to their employees, retirees, prisoners—whomever! He has set up a network of Canadian pharmacies—mainly conventional brick-and-mortar types—that have agreed to sell through him at a single low price, which is often even lower than those of the Internet pharmacies. In 2002, Howard sold his house in Florida—"My lawyers told me to divest of all U.S. property," he explains—and in July 2003 he went operational with his first client: Springfield, Mass.

Springfield's then mayor, Michael Albano, had seen the town's prescription-drug bills double since he took office in 1996. When he heard about Howard's operation, he traveled to Windsor and visited several pharmacies in the CanaRx network. In March he tried out the service on his own family and, happy with the results, chose to offer it to all Springfield's municipal employees and

retirees. (The program is voluntary, in that nobody has to get his drugs through CanaRx; if an enrollee chooses to, however, the city agrees to cover his or her whole co-pay.) Albano says that about 3,300 Springfielders had used the program by the time his term as mayor expired in December, saving the city about $1 million. (Albano's successor has continued the program.)

Just as MacKay feared, once the Springfield precedent was set, Albano, Howard, and MacKay himself were deluged with inquiries. City officials from Miami, Seattle, Burlington, Vt., Boston, and Brockton, Mass., contacted them, as did state officials from Illinois, Minnesota, Iowa, Wisconsin, Michigan, North Dakota, Utah, West Virginia, New Hampshire, Rhode Island, and, yes, California. Illinois governor Rod Blagojevich's staff published an 85-page study last October setting forth a proposal that it claimed could safely provide Canadian drugs to state employees and retirees while saving the state as much as $56 million a year. He and Minnesota governor Pawlenty are hosting a national governors' summit on the topic in Washington, D.C., on Feb. 24.

So far, most officials have proved more cautious than Albano. Only Montgomery, Ala., and Westchester County, N.Y., are known to have actually followed Springfield's example, though Boston mayor Thomas Menino has vowed to launch a program by July. (Howard claims that he is already doing business with two other U.S. municipalities--as well as with two American unions and five corporations—but declines to name them, saying that they prefer to remain "under the radar.")

The FDA opposes the trade, but it hasn't filed suits against any mayors or retirees—guaranteed PR fiascoes

---

Since the arrival of Springfield-style operations, the FDA's rhetoric has grown more bellicose, and the agency has begun suing American intermediaries that try to profit from the trade. Last November the agency shut down Rx Depot—an Oklahoma chain of 85 storefronts that were connecting American seniors to Canadian pharmacies—and in January it sent a warning letter to Expedite-Rx, a Texas intermediary that helps the city of Montgomery get its supply.

Notwithstanding the earlier warnings to

CanaRx, Howard's ensconcement across the border appears to be sheltering him. To this point, the FDA has also shied away from the ugly spectacle of suits against American mayors, municipal employees, or retirees—guaranteed PR fiascoes.

With neither Health Canada nor the FDA shutting down the cross-border traffic, pharmaceutical companies have taken matters into their own hands. In January 2003, GlaxoSmithKline's Canadian unit advised distributors that they were contractually barred from selling to pharmacies that resell to U.S. customers, demanded to see their sales records, and warned that violators would be cut off from all future GSK products. Subsequently AstraZeneca, Wyeth, Eli Lilly, Pfizer, and Novartis have taken steps to clamp down on supply. GSK, Lilly, Pfizer, and Bayer have also begun raising their Canadian prices.

In press releases each company has usually stressed the FDA's safety concerns as the driving motivation for making certain that their drugs are not resold to Americans. But professor Richard Epstein, a law and economics professor at the University of Chicago Law School, speculates that the companies are also delivering a different message. The message is addressed to Canada, he says, and goes like this: "Look, this is your population. This is your utilization. We'll sell you enough to satisfy that population. You want to resell to the United States? Kill your own people."

Shortly after GSK began its crackdown, Minnesota attorney general Hatch issued civil subpoenas to the company, stating that he was launching an investigation into a possible collusive boycott by pharmaceutical manufacturers against Canadian pharmacies that sell to U.S. seniors. Hatch says he infers collusion from the close proximity in timing among the six companies' actions, and he claims that such a boycott would violate state antitrust laws.

If the reader is puzzled, so was GSK. Its lawyers protested to a Minnesota judge in October that Hatch's subpoenas were "predicated on the remarkable proposition that actions by GSK . . . to prevent the illegal importation of drugs from Canada into the United States can somehow give rise to liability under Minnesota's state antitrust laws." Hatch replies in an interview: "There are court cases that say you can't even boycott an *illegal* activity." In any event, he maintains, personal-use importation is legal, given the FDA's "long track record of permitting it."

Though Hatch's theories may sound aggressive, he's evidently not the only official propounding them. He's leading a multistate working group of 24 attorneys general focused on the issues, he says. In December the group submitted a letter to the Minnesota

(Cont.)

court urging enforcement of Hatch's subpoenas to GSK.

Will Hatch go after other drug companies too? "First, we want to get an order in this case," he says. "Probably nanoseconds after that order is issued, there will be [subpoenas] served on the others as well."

Though Strempler of RxNorth says he's been able to fill all his orders despite the supply crackdown, he's feeling the pinch financially. Suppliers that used to send him shipments on credit now require payment up-front, he says, and he has had to beef up inventory to ensure the continuity of his deliveries. MacKay admits that some Canadian pharmacists are even considering connecting their customers to pharmacies in other countries, like New Zealand, should the Canadian supply dry up. He hopes, he says, that CIPA members will be "transparent" with customers if they resort to such measures.

At one level the notion of legalizing the importation of prescription drugs is absurd on its face. If Canada's or any other nation's price regulations are a good idea, we should adopt such regulations here—not go through the Rube Goldberg mechanism of funneling

If helping those in need stalls delivery of new drugs to the next generation, have we acted morally?

all our drugs through a price-regulated foreign country.

But while importation may be an ideological dodge for some politicians—a way of getting the short-term benefits of price controls without admitting that's what they're doing—it's more than that. For other, more principled and more nervy people, importation is a high-stakes poker game. They hope it will force foreign countries to lift their price controls on pain of losing their drug supplies.

For most people, though, that's not what importation is about either. "It's a manifestation of an anger within the U.S.—almost like a temper tantrum," says Uwe Reinhardt, a health-care economist at Princeton University. "To my mind, the proper solution would

be for Congress to make sure that every American has financial access to the drugs that are beneficial to them, through either their own insurance or subsidized insurance. And once that has been achieved, you can then talk about what prices for drugs should be paid."

But the second step turns out to be exceedingly difficult, he acknowledges, especially for those patented drugs that have unique and indispensable therapeutic benefits. For such drugs, he observes, "the drug manufacturers can in theory charge whatever the hell they like."

And beyond that challenge lie more intractable enigmas. If our efforts to help those now in need end up stalling the delivery of new miracle drugs to the next generation, have we acted morally? What do we do when compassion in the short term causes suffering in the long term? Do we save one life today at the cost of two tomorrow?

The politicians will assure us that no such harsh choices are required. But what else would they say?

74

A Rare Chance to Take Back a Market

Johnson & Johnson's New Stent May Dominate Angioplasties

By REED ABELSON

Few companies ever get a second chance once they fall behind the competition on a pivotal product. Johnson & Johnson is about to become an exception to that rule.

Early this year, **Johnson & Johnson,** the giant health care conglomerate that sells everything from Band-Aids to birth control pills, is expected to receive regulatory approval in the United States for a new medical device—a drug-coated stent that promises drastic changes in the way that hundreds of thousands of patients with heart disease are treated.

The stent, called the Cypher, keeps coronary arteries open more successfully and much longer than the plain metal devices now used, sharply reducing the need for repeated angioplasties and for heart bypass surgery. Even at a price likely to be around $3,000 each—more than double the cost of current devices—the stents are expected to take over much of the market for angioplasties.

> "If you get a little complacent in the market, you're going to get hammered."
>
> **Robert W. Croce**

"It has the potential to change the landscape, not only for patients but also the economics," said Michael Dake, a professor at Stanford University School of Medicine. "It's a really big business."

Johnson & Johnson, in 1994, pioneered the stent, a meshlike device inserted in coronary arteries that serves as scaffolding to help overcome the constrictions that cause heart attacks. But the company squandered its lead. Failing to recognize just how important the device was, the company did not invest enough in developing better designs. It also alienated doctors and hospitals by charging $1,600 for each stent without making sure insurers would reimburse the cost. By the late 1990's, Johnson & Johnson's share of the market had fallen sharply.

Robert W. Croce, the chairman of Cordis, the unit at Johnson & Johnson responsible for making stents, vows not to make the same mistakes again. Even before the Food and Drug Administration approves the new stent, the company has been lining up insurance coverage and meeting with hospitals about the device's potential impact on their finances. Cordis is also already at work on new versions of the stent.

"We feel like we're staying ahead of our competitors and will be a moving target," Mr. Croce said. **Guidant** and **Boston Scientific** are already readying their own devices.

The market for the drug-coated stents is worth fighting for. Kurt Kruger, an analyst with Banc of America Securities, says the new stents could lead to a doubling of the existing American market, to $3.2 billion, in 2003. The overwhelming majority of those sales are expected to be of the drug-coated stent, with Johnson & Johnson capturing $2.8 billion of the total, compared with an estimated $415 million in stent sales in 2002.

"It's going to be an absolute gold mine for Johnson & Johnson," said Mr. Kruger, who estimates the market could reach nearly $4 billion by 2004.

While Johnson & Johnson is a huge company, expected to have $36 billion in sales this year, drug-coated stents are by far its most promising product. Recapturing the stent business will give the company a highly profitable franchise in cardiology devices, a rapidly growing market. Sales of the stents could approach those of Johnson & Johnson's most popular product, the Procrit/Eprex anemia drug.

If all goes as expected, Mr. Kruger said, the company's earnings growth in 2003 should reach the high double digits, largely because of the stents.

Because expectations are so high, however, if anything goes wrong Johnson & Johnson risks disappointing doctors and patients, not to mention the investors who have bid up its stock this year.

"Whenever there is a lot of hype surrounding a product launch, sometimes it's setting up for possible problems," said Michael Krensavage, an analyst for Raymond James.

Johnson & Johnson's original stent revolutionized angioplasty, a procedure that involves threading a catheter through a clogged artery and then inflating a balloon to unblock the vessel. The stents made angioplasty more effective, and Johnson & Johnson had the market to itself for about three years. But the company failed to anticipate how quickly the device would catch on, Mr. Croce said, and stumbled. Hospitals shouldered the extra cost of the new devices because Medicare was slow to reimburse them.

By the time competitors like Guidant entered the market in 1997, Johnson & Johnson was vulnerable. The company refused to drop the price of its stents, and the competing devices proved much more flexible and easier for doctors to use.

"If you get a little complacent in the market, you're going to get hammered," said Mr. Croce, who took over Cordis just as the company was losing its grip on the stent market.

Now, Johnson & Johnson is doing what it can to make sure the new device is paid for. Last year, Medicare took the highly unusual step of agreeing to pay for the drug-coated stent even before it received F.D.A. approval.

"I believe, and my staff believes, this is really a revolutionary new technology," said Thomas A. Scully, the head of Medicare, who said he had responded to concern from hospitals that they would lose significant sums if the new devices were not paid for.

While Johnson & Johnson has not yet said what it plans to charge for the new stent, analysts and others expect the price to be about $3,000. Company officials argue that

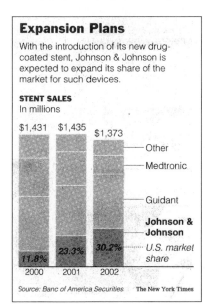

Expansion Plans

With the introduction of its new drug-coated stent, Johnson & Johnson is expected to expand its share of the market for such devices.

STENT SALES
In millions

$1,431 $1,435 $1,373

Other
Medtronic
Guidant
Johnson & Johnson
U.S. market share

11.8% 23.3% 30.2%

2000 2001 2002

Source: Banc of America Securities **The New York Times**

(Cont.)

the savings from fewer angioplasties and by-pass surgeries easily outweighs the device's costs. While the costs of these procedures vary widely, an average angioplasty with a stent costs some $8,000 and a bypass around $17,500 at the Health Alliance network of hospitals in Cincinnati, for example.

At Kaiser Permanente, the nation's largest not-for-profit health maintenance organization, the committee studying new procedures has recommended that its doctors consider using drug-coated stents, although it does not analyze the cost of new technologies.

Many private insurers are also deciding their reimbursement policies. **Aetna,** for example, is conducting an expedited review and should decide its reimbursement policy soon after the stent receives approval.

The new stent addresses a fundamental problem: 20 to 40 percent of patients who get the traditional stents experience reblock-age of their arteries because of scar tissue. Johnson & Johnson scientists discovered that the scarring could be prevented if stents were coated with a drug licensed from **Wyeth** called Sirolimus, now used in patients getting kidney transplants. The stent releases minute amounts of the drug for the first month or so, when the scarring tends to occur.

In the most recent clinical study, the drug-coated stent sharply reduced the need for a second procedure, and an F.D.A. advisory panel voted unanimously in late October to recommend its approval. The company is expected to get final clearance early this year, although regulators have expressed some concerns about the device.

Johnson & Johnson appears to have the market to itself for at least the first year, although any delay in regulatory approval will shorten that lead. Its competitors, Guidant and Boston Scientific, are scrambling to come up with their own versions of drug-coated stents, and the two have been wrangling over the rights to the drug they want to use, paclitaxel, licensed from **Angiotech Pharmaceuticals.**

'It's going to be an absolute gold mine,' one analyst says.

Boston Scientific is expected to come to the market at the end of this year. But Guidant, which reported disappointing preliminary results from a study yesterday, is now expected to enter the market sometime in 2005. The company is expected to cancel its plans to merge with the **Cook Group** and instead develop another kind of drug-coated stent.

But Johnson & Johnson may not be able to make too much of being first with the new devices. "It will be the best stent that captures the market, not the first," said Dr. William L. Hunter, Angiotech's chief executive.

And many of the factors that gave Johnson & Johnson a second chance also make its lead tenuous, said Gary P. Pisano, a Harvard University business professor who has studied the medical device market.

"The product cycles are very short," he said. "This is a very competitive market," and cardiologists, who tend to be quick to adopt a technology, are also likely to switch to a better device if it becomes available.

"They don't tend to be very brand-loyal," Mr. Pisano said.

While Mr. Croce says he is confident that Sirolimus is the best drug in keeping arteries open, paclitaxel also appears effective. "Neither Johnson & Johnson nor Boston Scientific has been able to deliver a knock-out blow" by producing studies that demonstrate significant superiority, Mr. Kruger of Banc of America said. In 2004, he estimates that Boston Scientific will sell about $1 billion of its drug-coated stents, compared with nearly $3 billion in sales for Johnson & Johnson.

Johnson & Johnson is also working to introduce other versions of its stent in the next few years. The last time around, "we didn't apply enough resources to develop the next generation," Mr. Croce said. Now, the compa-ny is planning to introduce an improved stent coated with the same drug in 2004 and another stent that is also coated with heparin, which reduces the chance of blood clots, in 2005.

But the hefty price tag of the Cypher may still prove a stumbling block. The device has already been approved in Europe, but doctors there have been slower than expected to embrace the new stent, and the device has so far captured only 10 percent of the market.

"It's all about reimbursement," said Mr. Croce, who predicted that as next year's budgets take into account more use of the drug-coated stent, more doctors will use it.

But some doctors also say they do not believe that every patient should get the new stent, even though they expect their colleagues to rush to use it. "There's a zeal for popping those things in," said Dean J. Kereiakes, a cardiologist who heads the Ohio Heart Health Center. But the stent may not prove as effective as hoped for in some patients, he said, including patients undergoing a heart attack or diabetics who take insulin.

"I'm an advocate," Dr. Kereiakes said of the new stents, "but I'm also cautious about extrapolating from limited data."

There are also concerns about the impact of the devices on hospitals, many of whom say they will still lose money because the reimbursement for the new stents is not likely to cover all their costs.

It will be years before anyone knows for sure just how lasting a breakthrough Johnson & Johnson's new stent turns out to be.

There will be "a ramp-up of clinical activity over the next few years," said Patrick O'Gara, the medical director of the cardiac service line for **Partners HealthCare,** which includes Brigham & Women's and Massachusetts General Hospitals in Boston, "to see what the limits of the new technology will be and what patients will most benefit."

75

Struggling With the Falling Dollar

It's Tough Bottom-Line Issue for Many Smaller Companies

BY MARK A. STEIN

Larry Lazin checks his computer regularly to see how the dollar is doing on the currency exchanges of London, New York and Tokyo. Every week, he calls his currency trader in California from his office in a New York suburb to buy euros, capitalizing on the later West Coast closing to search all day and into the evening for the best deal.

Mr. Lazin is not a banker, a hedge-fund manager or a day trader speculating from his spare room. He sells lighting fixtures to architects and interior designers, and like a lot of small-business owners he has become painfully aware of how the dollar's weakness resonates on his bottom line.

Since hitting its lowest point in October 2000, the euro has shot up by more than 50 percent against the dollar, effectively raising the prices that American businesses pay for European goods—from Portuguese cork and French oak barrels to English antiques or Italian machine tools—by about as much in dollars.

Similar gains have occurred with the currencies of America's other major trading partners, notably Canada and Britain. And with domestic inflation low, American businesses find it difficult to pass along the extra cost to their customers.

"For small little companies like us, that is a hard quest," Mr. Lazin said in a telephone interview from his business, Global Lighting Inc., in Irvington, N.Y. "You can't raise prices as much or as often as you need to."

He figures his profit will shrink at least 10 percent this year, even after he raised prices.

Small businesses that export their goods, meanwhile, are benefiting almost as much as importers are suffering because the dollar's weakness tends to make their goods significantly cheaper and more competitive abroad. That presents an opportunity not seen for decades, said Harvey D. Bronstein, senior international economist at the Small Business Administration.

"It's a great time to be an exporter," Mr. Bronstein said in a telephone interview. "If you're an exporter to Canada or Europe, you have had the effect of putting your goods for sale at a 40 percent discount without taking a hit on your profit."

More than 212,000 small businesses, with fewer than 100 employees, exported goods in 2001, the latest year for which the Commerce Department has data. Another 18,000 midsize companies—with 100 to 500 employees—also sent products abroad that year. Together, they accounted for $182 billion in trade, or 29 percent of all exports.

There are no comparable reports on importers, said Howard Schreier of the Office of Trade and Economic Analysis at the Commerce Department. The change has become more acute since last summer, with the euro and the British pound climbing 18 percent since September; since the end of July, the Japanese yen has risen 13 percent and the Canadian dollar 11 percent.

The cost of imports from China, the United States' fastest-growing trading partner, has not gone up significantly because Beijing pegs its currency, the yuan, to the dollar.

Yet that exchange parity has added to the pain of some American small-business owners who import goods from Europe and elsewhere that compete with Chinese-made products. Complicating matters, China has come under international pressure to revalue the yuan, and any relaxation of its policy could suddenly make its goods more expensive to Americans, too.

Small and midsize importers are scrambling to find a way to weather the weak dollar.

"Some of the little guys are stung pretty bad by it," said Paul W. Vierck, a vice president in the Oakland, Calif., office of Commonwealth Foreign Exchange. "They call and say, 'What can I do about the exchange rate?' I say, 'Not much. It's a trillion-dollar-a-day market.'"

One thing small businesses can do is lock in a rate now if they expect the dollar to weaken further. Companies like Commonwealth sell "dollar forward" contracts in which an importer agrees to buy a certain amount of euros, yen or some other currency at a specific date in the future—or over a specified period—for a price agreed upon now.

Such contracts are a gamble. If the dollar strengthens, buyers could lose money. But if the dollar continues to weaken, they can avoid a loss. Companies that buy forward contracts at least lock in an exchange rate, which makes it easier to see the profitability of a particular transaction.

Many small importers would welcome the chance to reduce the risk of the dollar weakening further, particularly if they were caught unprepared for the rapid swing of the last six months.

"Some are taking drastic measures—raising prices when they can, burning through inventory or delaying payment to their suppliers," said Mr. Vierck, whose company, based in Providence, R.I., specializes in trading currencies for software developers and other midsize companies as well as smaller businesses like art galleries, spice merchants and wine importers.

Often, he said, "suppliers overseas have been pretty sympathetic" to long-term customers who are delaying payment.

Mr. Lazin, who imports lamps and other lighting fixtures from three companies in Spain and one in Italy, said he had not postponed paying his suppliers. But he has had to innovate and act fast to stay in the black.

Like many small-business owners importing from Europe, Mr. Lazin made some assumptions about what the euro would be worth against the dollar after the European Union introduced the currency in 1999. Soon after the European Union began using the euro in banking transactions, its value

Currency Squeeze

The dollar's slide against major trading partners has made goods from abroad much more expensive.

Scale is inverted to show the falling value of the dollar

Source: Bloomberg Financial Markets

against the dollar fell, padding the profits of small-business exporters like Mr. Lazin.

After bottoming out toward the end of 2000, however, the euro flattened and then began to climb steadily against the dollar in 2002. It took a while for it to reach the value—the peg—that Mr. Lazin said he had assumed in 1999. "When it passed that peg," he said, "I knew I was in trouble."

Economists give several reasons for the dollar's weakness, but the chief ones are historically low American interest rates, which discourage foreign investments, and the country's ballooning trade deficits, which create unwanted dollar surpluses overseas.

"From a macroeconomic perspective, this country has been importing too much and exporting too little," Mr. Bronstein said. "People overseas are tired of taking pieces of paper with pictures of dead presidents in exchange for Lexus cars and mozzarella cheese."

Scrambling to stay ahead of the falling dollar, Mr. Lazin offered to pay suppliers sooner than was customary if they offered a discount, usually 2 percent; they agreed. That had the added benefit of letting him avoid some of the dollar's slide in the time between early payment and the usual invoice date.

He has also adjusted the volume discounts that he offers his clients, as well as the commissions he pays his representatives across the United States and Canada. Product lines with thin profit margins were weeded out, he added, and a year ago he widened the profit on the fixtures he kept. "It's a lot more work, a lot more confusing," he said of business today.

Customers have not always welcomed higher prices and narrower product lines. "Some of them don't understand" about exchange rates, he said, especially if they also buy goods from China, which had lower prices to begin with. "Not everyone can work with us on prices," he said.

Mr. Lazin has also developed his own approach to reducing his risk. Once a week, he buys a fraction of the total amount of euros he estimates he will need during the year. It is a form of cost averaging, of spreading out the risk of a price move in either direction.

The strategy has not completely insulated him from the weak dollar, he said, but "it makes it very easy at the end of the year to see what your costs were."

That, he added, has helped him plan better and take a longer view of his business.

"In importing," he said, "you have to look at how you do over three years because there is too much movement in the currency."

76

Value Positioning Becomes a Priority

By: Jack Neff

For most of its history, premium-brand giant Procter & Gamble Co. treated the poor much like well-off persons treat panhandlers—avoiding direct eye contact but handing over some spare change in the spirit of philanthropy.

But something happened in 2001 when Chairman-CEO A.G. Lafley started making his top global managers spend time with consumers in homes or stores once a quarter. Take Rob Steele, for instance. P&G's president-North America was standing in the checkout line one day with his research subject, and she asked him to come up with the participation fee right then and there so she could pay her grocery bill.

Due to experiences like this, top P&G executives began realizing how many poor people there really are in the world, what a big potential market they made up, and how seldom they could afford or wanted to buy high-price P&G products.

Pampers: To take the focus off price the Premium line was renamed Baby Stages of Development.

At the same time, private labels and such rivals as Unilever's Suave and Alberto-Culver Co.'s VO5 were snatching money from P&G's wallet more figuratively as their value brands took share from P&G's stable of premium ones.

Close encounters with the cash-strapped have helped change the way P&G thinks about brands and marketing as it launches more value brands, value versions of premium brands and other marketing initiatives geared toward lower-income consumers both in the U.S. and overseas.

"It's important just that they've acknowledged as they try to become a global company that 80% of the world can't afford their stuff," said an executive for one P&G competitor. "It's just part of the gale force of competition with Unilever and Colgate, which are already value companies. At the same time, advertising prices are going through the roof. At some point, their business model has to evolve."

CLOSING THE GAP

Just in North America, P&G could add $3 billion in sales overnight if it could close the gap with rivals among low-income, African-American, Hispanic and French-Canadian consumers, Mr. Lafley said at a December investor conference.

Symbolically, P&G's most dramatic shift toward value may be with Ivory, its oldest surviving brand. Dubbed "The House that Ivory Built" in a 1987 *Advertising Age* commemorative issue on P&G's 150th anniversary, the company 15 years later sold the house that built Ivory—its century-old

Cincinnati Ivorydale plant—to a Canadian contract manufacturer.

Following cost cuts derived in part from the outsourcing, P&G today markets Ivory as a "midtier" value brand, priced 10% to 15% lower-per-ounce than such rivals as Dial Corp.'s Dial or Unilever's Dove. Unlike most P&G brands, Ivory has no agency of record, but gets media support on a project basis from Benchmark Group, Cincinnati.

As P&G integrated its 2001 Clairol acquisition, it has similarly taken many of the lesser acquired brands, such as Daily Renewal 5x, Aussie and Infusium, down several price points. Most dramatically, Daily Defense, a failing premium brand Clairol had yanked in the U.S. as the deal was closing, came back last year priced at 99¢ or lower, positioned as what P&Gers called "a Suave killer."

The strategy hasn't immediately helped P&G's sales or share in U.S. hair care, both of which were down in 2003. But it did end several years of double-digit sales growth for Suave and helped ensure Unilever lost share in hair care despite its $100 million launch of Dove shampoo and conditioner.

DIFFERENT VENUES

Diana Shaheen, a hair-care marketing director whose portfolio spans Physique products priced north of $7 to Daily Defense, said having such a range "gives me more exposure to consumers in different venues. In shampoo, loyalty is not high, so learning their needs, having a lot of offerings and accelerating growth are really important."

Since the value strategy is global, P&G is sharing learning about appealing to low-income consumers among developing markets, lower-income European markets such as Poland and developed markets.

Mr. Lafley, in an interview with *Ad Age*, said he has been one of the chief drivers behind value brands, along with Kerry Clark, president-global market development, who oversees the units that handle local marketing and media buying efforts throughout the world.

Executives experienced in marketing to low-income consumers overseas are taking their knowledge to the U.S. and vice versa. Alex Tosolini, an Italian national who was marketing director for low-income consumers in P&G's U.S. fabric-care business, developing products for dollar stores, moved last year to become general manager for P&G's business in Poland. There, encroachment by German

(Cont.)

"hard discounters" like Aldi threaten to change the game in a market that had been one of the most favorable in Eastern Europe to premium brands, said Deutsche Bank analyst Andrew Shore.

DIFFERENT AUDIENCES

P&G's shift to value clearly won't mean heavy media advertising for these brands. Even if the thin-margin products could support the spending, it wouldn't necessarily be the right thing to do, said Dimitri Panayotopoulos, P&G's president-Central and Eastern Europe, Middle East, and Africa.

Value consumers "are very much different from the consumers who buy [premium] brands, which is good, because we don't cannibalize volume from the premium tier," he said. "Consumers who buy premium brands are more left-brained and pay for premium performance. [Value consumers] don't care so much about watching advertising and demonstrations and so on. They pride themselves on being savvy consumers who look for value."

After an initial ad push that included TV and print from Barefoot Advertising, Cincinnati, Daily Defense is now off the air, maybe for good, said an executive close to the company, though he added that the brand may remain on store shelves because it offers retailers a decent margin.

But the value focus isn't all about price, thin marketing budgets or even low-income consumers. Susan Arnold, president of P&G's global personal and feminine-care business, which markets some of the company's priciest products, last year had each of her top managers spend a month living on the median household budgets of their countries.

"The idea wasn't to think about price," she said. "It was to think about the value of our products compared with all the other things you could spend your money on with a limited budget."

Even well-off consumers often want value as they trade luxury in one area for thriftiness in another, said Paul Polman, P&G's president-Western Europe. "The Aldi consumer is not necessarily a low-income consumer," he noted. "You'll see plenty of Mercedes' in the parking lot."

77

DeBeers Is in Talks to Settle Price-Fixing Charge

Ending the Diamond Case Could Finally Give Cartel A Retail Presence in U.S.

BY JOHN R. WILKE

WASHINGTON—DeBeers SA, which built one of the richest and longest-reigning monopolies in history, is in talks to settle a criminal price-fixing charge and return to the U.S. market after nearly half a century of operating outside its borders.

The South Africa diamond giant pulled out of the U.S. shortly after World War II on the heels of a Justice Department suit alleging that it fixed the price of industrial diamonds. Federal antitrust enforcers filed another criminal charge in 1994 but again found DeBeers beyond their reach.

That hasn't stopped DeBeers from becoming one of the world's best-known brands and one of the biggest advertisers in the U.S., relentlessly linking diamonds to engagements, weddings and anniversaries with its "A Diamond is Forever" campaign. But DeBeers hasn't had a retail presence in America. It doesn't sell directly in the U.S.—only through intermediaries—and its executives are subject to being detained if they enter the country.

The 1994 charge is still pending in U.S. District Court in Columbus, Ohio, where the Justice Department alleges that a unit of DeBeers was part of a global conspiracy with General Electric Co. to fix prices in the industrial-diamond market, then valued at $500 million annually. The government lost its case against GE, which had denied the charge. Prosecutors said that they hadn't been given access to needed evidence overseas.

DeBeers's efforts to get the charge dropped were rebuffed by the Clinton administration and, initially, by the current Bush administration. But late last year, the company signaled that it might agree to plead guilty and pay a fine to settle the suit, and those discussions are now at an advanced stage, according to people close to the talks.

U.S. officials over the years haven't been eager to help DeBeers because of its history of harsh labor conditions and support for South Africa's apartheid regime. But Justice

Department officials apparently have concluded that—having lost their case against DeBeers's co-defendant GE in 1994—they have little leverage to continue to exclude the company from the U.S. if it is willing to plead guilty, unconditionally, to the 10-year-old charge. If the deal goes ahead, it is expected to be submitted for approval to Judge George S. Smith, who presided in the case. A Justice Department spokeswoman declined to comment.

A London spokeswoman for DeBeers wouldn't detail any possible U.S. settlement. "We have outstanding legal issues with the Department of Justice and the European Union, and we're working to resolve them," said Lynette Hori, the spokeswoman for De-Beers's diamond trading company. "The U.S. is the biggest market for diamond jewelry—accounting for 50% of global retail jewelry sales—and we would really, really like to resolve these issues."

DeBeers long controlled the market for both industrial and gem diamonds through a global cartel that includes many of the world's diamond producers in Africa and elsewhere. It hoarded vast stocks of rough diamonds, managing to maintain high prices despite relatively abundant supply, and parceled them out in small quantities to favored concerns that cut, polish and sell them.

In the past four years, though, DeBeers has changed the way it does business, including reducing its stockpile of diamonds. At the same time, Russia, Canada and Australia have emerged as significant diamond producers, gradually loosening the DeBeers cartel's grip on global diamond supply and pricing. Better techniques for making artificial diamonds also could become a factor in DeBeers's market.

DeBeers has pledged to relinquish some of its past practices intended to control the supply of rough diamonds coming to market, and embraced the so-called Kimberly Process, an industry effort to end trade in diamonds used to fuel bloody African conflicts.

DeBeers's efforts to transform itself began in the late 1990s after a strategic review by U.S. management consultants Bain & Co. With DeBeers's share of diamond production slipping, and the cost of maintaining its stockpile rising, Bain recommended that DeBeers abandon its role as industry enforcer and boost demand for diamonds by burnishing the DeBeers brand name, said people who were briefed on the review, which wasn't made public.

The review concluded that a transformation of DeBeers into a luxury-goods company would require a direct presence in the U.S. and a brand name unfettered by antitrust charges or "conflict" diamonds. Ms. Hori, the DeBeers spokeswoman, didn't comment on the Bain review, but said, "it was apparent by 2000 that diamonds were

beginning to lose out to other luxury goods. Our sales were flat, and other luxury goods were taking off."

DeBeers won't say what its plans might be for the U.S., but any changes are likely to come gradually. In 2002, it entered a venture with the premier luxury-goods group, LVMH Moet Hennessy Louis Vuitton SA of Paris, to establish a chain of retail stores. Outlets in Tokyo and London already are open. "Our store network will further expand into other major international markets," DeBeers LV, the joint venture, said last year.

DeBeers spent $183 million on advertising in 2003, much of it in the U.S. through its agency, J. Walter Thompson. The firm won the account in 1996 from N.W. Ayers, where copy writer Frances Gerety coined the "Diamond is Forever" slogan in 1947.

Dominant in Diamonds

Diamond production as of 2002

DeBeers, its partners and contract suppliers **62%** — **38%** Non-DeBeers producers

Production of uncut (or rough) diamonds, industrial and gems
By country in 2002, in millions of carats

Country	Carats
Australia	33.6
Botswana	28.4
Russia	23.0
Congo	18.2
South Africa	10.9
Angola	6.0
Canada	5.0
Other	6.6

Sources: Tacy Ltd., U.S. Geological Survey

Resolving the 1994 Justice Department case won't end DeBeers' legal problems. The company's "supplier of choice" plan, intended to reform diamond distribution, was cleared last year by European Commission antitrust enforcers. But officials vowed to "remain watchful of actual implementation to ensure the market remains competitive" and reserved the right to reopen the case.

More significantly, European authorities are investigating DeBeers's ties to Russia's Alrosa Co., a state-owned concern that is among the world's largest diamond producers and a potential competitor to DeBeers. Alrosa agreed in 2002 to sell half of its output to DeBeers over five years. In a statement in January 2003, the European Commission said the contract may violate European law

(Cont.)

and that DeBeers "abused its dominant position" in the market. DeBeers's Ms. Hori said the company is having "a productive dialogue" with Europe over Alrosa. DeBeers bought $634 million of rough diamonds from Alrosa in 2003, she said.

DeBeers also faces several private antitrust suits in the U.S., though some have been stalled by the concern's foreign status. A 2001 lawsuit in federal court in New York alleges that DeBeers "has controlled the supply, and set and managed the prices of diamonds in the U.S." The suit, brought as a class action by diamond buyers, was filed by Lovell & Stewart, a New York law firm. DeBeers hasn't responded to the claim or appeared in court.

If DeBeers returns to the U.S. market, it could face more private suits—and will again be directly subject to U.S. antitrust enforcement. The company has apparently decided that it is worth the legal risk to regain direct access to its largest market.

DeBeers changed its ownership structure in 2001, and became a private company. A consortium led by the controlling Oppenheimer family of South Africa holds 45% and Anglo American PLC, the London-based mining giant, holds another 45%. The remaining 10% is owned by Debswana, a joint venture with the nation of Botswana established to exploit that country's diamond deposits. DeBeers Trading Co., the company's London marketing arm, said the company's sales were $5.52 billion in 2003, up 7%.

From *The Wall Street Journal*, February 24, 2004. Reprinted by permission of Dow Jones & Co., Inc. via The Copyright Clearance Center.

78

Trade-Off

As China Surges, It Also Proves A Buttress to American Strength

Beijing Feeds a Giant Appetite In U.S. for Low-Cost Goods And Borrowed Capital

The Wood-Furniture Paradox

By Andrew Higgins

DONGGUAN, China—Frank Lin joined fellow Chinese furniture makers at a hotel here last summer to discuss some alarming news from America: U.S. furniture companies were asking Washington to investigate "illegal" Chinese trade practices and restrict Chinese sales to the U.S. Among the petitioners was one of Mr. Lin's longtime customers, Virginia-based Hooker Furniture Corp.

Mr. Lin's dismay turned to confusion days later when he received an e-mail from Hooker's chief executive. Hooker looked forward to an "exciting future" doing business with China, said the message, and wanted to "continue the extraordinary growth we have had in the last few years with Asian imports."

Indeed, thanks largely to the imports, Hooker has boomed. It closed a factory in North Carolina last summer but has boosted profits and dazzled investors with a stock that more than quadrupled in two years.

"I just don't understand what they are doing. It makes no sense," Mr. Lin said after receiving the e-mail in August. On his desk lay designs sent from America. Lining the wall, newly crafted chairs stood ready for inspection by U.S. buyers. "If they don't import, they die. They need us. So why do they want to hurt us?" Mr. Lin wondered.

His bewilderment flows from a much bigger tension besetting U.S. economic relations with China—and the economic forces that underpin America's global hegemony. China's rise both supports the American superpower and embodies some of its self-generated vulnerabilities.

Burgeoning business ties with China have become treacherous terrain. Anxious to calm workers' worries about jobs, and fearful of appearing unpatriotic, even some U.S. companies that rely on China are joining industry coalitions clamoring to curb the "China threat."

But there's another side to China's dynamism. China is slotting itself into the global economic order that America dominates and largely created. As a critical link in this capitalist chain, nominally communist China helps enrich companies such as Hooker. At the same time, it supports a central feature of America's superpower status: its gargantuan appetite for foreign goods and capital.

Though America is sometimes loosely called an empire, it defies the imperial economic script described by Lenin (who called imperialism "the highest form of capitalism"). The U.S. doesn't seek vassal states as outlets for surplus capital. In an anomaly for such a powerful nation, America sucks in money from abroad. With its large national debt and trade deficits, the U.S. binds not by lending but by borrowing and by importing.

Its status as a "hyper-debtor" makes this "hyper-power" oddly reliant on weaker partners, says Niall Ferguson, a professor at New York University and scholar of imperial history. "If you are dependent on the willingness of others to hold your assets, there is a limit to how unilaterally you can act."

For all their nation's power, many Americans feel an economic insecurity, for which China is a lightning rod. Its blitzkrieg thrust into U.S. markets over the past decade, many worry, reveals a soft economic core under the tough carapace of America's military might. From bed frames to circuit boards, the industrial bedrock of American power is crumbling, say some politicians and pundits. At stake, warns the American Furniture Manufacturers Committee for Legal Trade, which filed the complaint that upset Mr. Lin, "is our way of life, our culture and the competitiveness of America in the world."

China's emergence as a major economic power is beyond doubt. Its $1.2 trillion economy, while far smaller than the $10.4 trillion economy of America and Japan's $4 trillion output, is on track to catch up with Japan inside of two decades. Already, China's growing economic weight, including a voracious consumption of crude oil, is giving Beijing commensurate influence in geopolitics—another power center for America to contend with.

Also undeniable is a painful loss of U.S. manufacturing jobs to a country where the average plant worker earns around $80 a month, less than an American on minimum wage makes in two days. Cheap labor pushed China's trade surplus with the U.S. to $123 billion in a recent 12-month period, five times the gap a decade ago.

The figures, however, mask the many ways in which the world's two biggest continental economies complement each other. China's rests heavily on industry, with manufacturing, mining and related activities accounting for 51% of gross domestic product, by World Bank figures. America generates only a quarter of its GDP from industry and just 14% from manufacturing. Services contribute nearly three quarters.

Curbing Chinese imports through tariffs or a stronger yuan would only drive up imports from other countries, contends Stephen Roach, chief economist at Morgan Stanley. The only real alternative, he says, is for Americans to spend less and save more: "When Americans get frustrated with China, they should look in the mirror."

They could also look inside things they buy from China. Take the 20 million "made in China" computer mice shipped to the U.S. each year by Logitech International SA, a Swiss-American company with headquarters in California. The mice are put together in a six-floor building in Suzhou, a Chinese city once famous for its Confucian gardens but now better known as a frenetic manufacturing hub.

Mouse Called Wanda

Logitech's Suzhou parts warehouse is a microcosm of the global economy, and helps explain how China reinforces America's role as ringmaster. Piled to the ceiling on blue metal shelves are boxes marked with the logos of foreign companies, from big U.S. multinationals to a small Belgian billiard company that makes trackballs.

One of Logitech's big sellers is a wireless mouse called Wanda, which sells to Ameri-

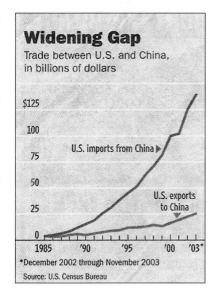

Widening Gap

Trade between U.S. and China, in billions of dollars

U.S. imports from China ▶

U.S. exports to China ▼

*December 2002 through November 2003

Source: U.S. Census Bureau

China's Changing Picture

The world confronting China, 25 years ago and today

THEN	AND	NOW
975 million	Population	1.3 billion
Deng Xiaoping	Leader	Hu Jintao
0	Number of private sedans	3 million
◄ Jiang Qing	Fashion icon	Gong Li ►
0	Oil imports	2 million barrels a day
$2.3 billion / $1.1 billion surplus for U.S.	Annual U.S.-China trade / Trade balance	$177 billion[1] / $123 billion deficit for U.S.[1]
Nonconvertible	Currency	Convertible in trade[2]
None	Stock trading	Two exchanges[3]
Hong Kong, Macao, Taiwan, Soviet border region, South China Sea islands	Unresolved territorial claims	Taiwan, South China Sea islands

Milestones

- 1979: Deng steers post-Mao China on "capitalist road"
- 1981: China convicts "Gang of Four" radicals, including Mao's widow, Jiang Qing
- 1989: China crushes pro-democracy protest in Tiananmen Square
- 1990: Reopens Shanghai Stock Exchange, closed since '49 revolution
- 1997: Deng dies; China regains Hong Kong from British
- 1999: Regains Macao, enclave Portugal had held since 16th century
- 1999: Protests as U.S. accidentally bombs Chinese embassy in Belgrade
- 2000: Cracks down on Falun Gong quasi-religious group
- 2001: Joins World Trade Organization
- 2001: Chinese jet collides with U.S. spy plane over South China Sea, prompting diplomatic standoff
- 2002: Communist Party says it will admit capitalists
- 2003: SARS outbreak (picture below)
- 2003: U.S., Japan urge China to float yuan; it declines
- 2003: Mass march for democracy in Hong Kong

[1] December 2002 through November 2003 [2] Beijing pegs yuan at 8.28 to a U.S. dollar [3] Shanghai and Shenzhen, listing 1,287 stocks in all   Source: WSJ research

can consumers for around $40. Of this, Logitech takes about $8, while distributors and retailers take $15. A further $14 goes to suppliers that provide Wanda's parts: A Motorola Inc. plant in Malaysia makes the mouse's chips, and America's Agilent Technologies Inc. supplies the optical sensor. Even the solder comes from a U.S. company, Cookson Electronics, which has a factory in China's Yunnan province next to Vietnam.

Marketing is led from Fremont, Calif., where a staff of 450 earns far more than 4,000 Chinese employed in Suzhou. China's take from each mouse comes to a meager $3, which covers wages, power, transport and other overhead costs.

Other Chinese-made products rely less on U.S. components and use Japanese, Korean or Taiwanese parts instead. But, in many cases, the upshot for China is the same: Foreigners get the bulk of the money. They supply many of the parts, often own the plants in China that assemble them, and get a markup on sales abroad. Foreign companies account for more than three-quarters of China's high-tech exports. The Chinese Ministry of Commerce's ranking of "China's" top 10 exporters includes two American companies—Motorola and hard-drive maker Seagate Technology.

Logitech, like most tech, toy and textile companies with plants in China, employs mostly young women such as Wang Yan, an 18-year-old from the impoverished rural province of Anhui. She is paid $75 a month to sit all day at a conveyor belt plugging three tiny bits of metal into circuit boards. She does this 2,000 times a day. To earn extra money, she gets up at 6 a.m. to tidy the dormitory space she shares with a dozen fellow workers.

This is her second stint in a factory. Before coming to Suzhou, she skipped school to become an underage worker at an electronics plant not far from Mr. Lin's furniture company in Dongguan. She complains about her salary but isn't going back to her village. That would mean only "eating bitterness," she says.

China's pivotal role in the global supply chain buttresses a pillar of foreign policy dating all the way back to 1899, when the U.S. pushed for an Open Door Policy making China's ports available to all. In turn, China's trade opening to the world in the past two decades softened its once-antagonistic foreign policy. Last year, as the U.S. prepared to invade Iraq, Beijing stood aloof from the Paris-Berlin-Moscow axis of outspoken opposition. It has offered the U.S. some help trying to curb North Korea's nuclear ambitions.

China's explosive growth as an exporter, though distressing for many American plants, prods the U.S. in a direction it has been moving for decades. Hooker furniture, which now imports more than 40% of the furniture it sells, mirrors this shift, scaling back on domestic manufacturing but expanding in services such as design, distribution and marketing. Meanwhile, other American companies, such as Intel Corp., focus on making high-end products, many of which end up in goods sold in America as "made in China."

China also does well out of an arrangement that provides millions of jobs, lets China steadily increase military spending and has created the biggest foreign-currency reserves after Japan's. Because of the U.S. debt habit, the arrangement also leaves China with leverage over America.

Borrowing Habit

The U.S. has been a net capital importer since at least the 1980s. This is in stark contrast to Britain at the height of its imperium before World War I, when the British had net foreign assets valued at 150% of their own GDP. America, though often described as Britain's successor as the world's dominant power, does the opposite. Recent figures from the Commerce Department's Bureau of Economic Analysis show that foreign holdings of U.S. stocks, bonds and other assets exceeded America's foreign assets to the tune of $2.3 trillion—or 22% of GDP—at the end of 2002.

"America is certainly a hegemon and may be occupying Iraq but, economically at least, it does the opposite of what Lenin described as imperialism," says Angus Maddison, a British economist whose many books include a survey of the world economy over the last millennium.

Tax cuts, spending in Iraq and other factors have stirred alarm among some economists that America's debt is getting out of control. A recent International Monetary Fund report said America's net foreign obligations could rise in a few years to 40% of GDP, and warned of an "unprecedented level of external debt for a large industrial country."

China didn't create this potentially unstable edifice, but it does, at least for the time being, help to keep it upright. China has loans outstanding to the U.S. government of more than $120 billion, in the form of Treasury debt that China owns. It holds probably that much again in Fannie Mae and other dollar-denominated debt securities.

Contrast that with what U.S. companies have invested in Chinese plants and equipment—not a direct comparison, by any means, but revealing nonetheless. This "foreign direct investment" stood at $10.2 billion at the end of 2002, according to the Bureau of Economic Analysis, about one-twenty-fifth the level of China's U.S.-securities holdings. The Chinese government offers a much higher figure for U.S. investment in China but still far below the value of Chinese holdings of U.S. debt.

America's addiction to foreign money hands China and other potential adversaries a weapon, some influential voices warn. Among them is Aaron Friedberg of Princeton University, an authority on Britain's imperial decline who is now a national security adviser to Vice President Dick Cheney. Mr. Friedberg wrote in a 2000 article in Commentary that China could one day dump its dollar assets to "trigger a run on the dollar, an increase in U.S. interest rates and perhaps a stock-market crash."

But China has reasons of its own to buy dollar assets—reasons that show how intricately the officially Marxist country fits into a U.S.-led world economic order. As China lends to the U.S. by buying U.S. government notes, it stows in a safe place the vast surplus cash its export economy generates.

Meanwhile, its buying of dollar assets buttresses another Chinese policy: keeping the yuan pegged at a low exchange rate against the greenback. Every time China buys a Treasury note it sells yuan. This selling helps stop the yuan from rising. By keeping its currency cheap, China keeps its exports especially inexpensive abroad—one of the

trade policies the U.S. complains about.

The Chip Trade

What worries some Americans most isn't the loss of menial jobs to tens of millions of Chinese such as Ms. Wang but a migration of white-collar work as China moves up the economic ladder. A Godzilla role once played by Japan is now assigned to China, and sometimes India. "When you hear that Intel, IBM and Goldman Sachs plan to move high-end jobs to China and India, what's going to be left here—restaurants?" asked Democratic Sen. Charles Schumer of New York at a Banking Committee hearing last year.

A study of the U.S. semiconductor industry's moves abroad, headed by Democratic Sen. Joseph Lieberman of Connecticut, said, "What is at stake here is our ability to be preeminent in the world of ideas."

Intel now produces more than 50 million chips a year in China. Most end up in computers and other goods for export.

Yet Intel's main facility, a $500 million plant in Shanghai, doesn't really make chips: It tests and assembles them from silicon wafers made in Intel plants abroad, mostly in the U.S. China adds less than 5% of the value. The U.S. generates the bulk of the value, and the profits.

Motorola, by contrast, does make chips in China, and has been far less successful. Its $1 billion plant in Tianjin has been plagued by problems. As part of a strategic rethink, Motorola has announced plans to transfer the facility to Semiconductor Manufacturing International Corp., a company based in China but partly owned by non-Chinese.

Attempts by domestic Chinese companies to make sophisticated semiconductors have a mixed record. Making high-end chips requires hugely expensive, imported equipment and does not play to China's natural strength in cheap labor. To try to overcome this, the government has been offering tax and other incentives in a big push reminiscent of an earlier drive to build up a large auto industry. This suggests the big competitive advantage China enjoys in labor-intensive manufacturing isn't easily transferred upward.

Whose Profits?

How much U.S. multinationals profit from their Chinese operations is hard to assess. Most book their earnings through Hong Kong or other offshore locations with low taxes. Bureau of Economic Analysis data, however, give a rough guide. American companies, after losing money in China in the 1980s and having minimal earnings for much of the 1990s, reported net income from their China affiliates of $755 million in 1999 and double that in the first three quarters of 2003. If income from Hong Kong affiliates is included, American corporate earnings from greater China totaled $5.16 billion in the first

three quarters of 2003, about the same as earnings from Japan.

"Americans are getting a great deal in China," says Huang Yasheng, a Massachusetts Institute of Technology professor and critic of a model he says benefits foreigners and state-owned Chinese concerns at the expense of Chinese entrepreneurs. China, he says, "produces zillions of low-value-added things, but this is a miracle of volume, not a miracle of value . . . . Americans get cheap goods and then get to borrow money from China at pathetic rates."

America's China deal looks pretty good from Frank Lin's furniture factory in Dongguan, operated by Glory Oceanic Co., a Taiwanese-owned company of which he is president. Mr. Lin makes low-cost, high-quality furniture that allows U.S. companies better margins than on their U.S.-made goods. He buys wood from America and coats it with lacquer from a Dongguan factory that is run by Americans, uses American chemicals and flies an American flag. (The lacquer factory, owned by Akzo Nobel of the Netherlands, briefly hoisted a Dutch flag at the start of the Iraq war.)

Also now benefiting is a group of Americans that Chinese furniture makers wish they didn't need: Washington trade lawyers. Mr. Lin and fellow factory bosses—most from Taiwan—have chipped in $2 million to defend their business against complaints of "dumping"—selling for less than fair-market value. After preliminary hearings, the U.S. International Trade Commission ruled this month that domestic furniture makers have been hurt by imports. The Commerce Department must now decide whether this is due to illegal pricing by the Chinese, and whether to impose duties, theoretically as high as 440%.

A Show of Hands

To plan strategy, a "defense committee" set up by Chinese furniture makers has been holding meetings in the ballroom of Dongguan's Fu Ying Hotel. At one gathering last year, the chairman read a list of U.S. companies that initiated the antidumping complaint and asked plant bosses to raise their hands if they made goods for any of them. Mr. Lin raised his hand four times. Many other hands also popped up, revealing that more than half of the U.S. furniture companies claiming concern about Chinese imports were themselves importers.

U.S. buyers, Mr. Lin said, "come here and go chop, chop, chop on our asking price and then complain that we are selling too cheaply." His warehouse was stacked with boxes full of furniture ordered by Hooker and marked with Hooker's corporate insignia.

Hooker's chief executive, Paul Toms, says he joined the antidumping petition to be "fair to our employees," and notes that it targets

(Cont.)

only bedroom furniture. Hooker and other supporters of the petition make most of their bedroom furniture in the U.S. "The last thing we want is to have the Chinese believe we are against them," Mr. Toms says, because imports from Asia "have been responsible for all our growth and a lot of the profit over the last few years." China, he says, is "both a threat and a great opportunity."

Mr. Lin and his colleagues said they were considering withholding shipments to U.S. companies that signed the petition. Scrambling to avoid a disaster for their businesses, Hooker and other importers rushed executives to China to try to calm tempers. In his e-mail, Mr. Toms assured Mr. Lin that, despite Hooker's joining the claims of illegal trade by China, he didn't think Mr. Lin had done anything "illegal or unethical."

Caught in the middle are scores of Americans working in Dongguan's furniture factories, lacquer-mixing plants and related enterprises. Smeared with sweat and sawdust after a day of supervising quality at a factory here, Karen Lanning and Bill Ward, both veteran furniture makers from North Carolina, swapped theories on what lay behind the importers' anti-import campaign.

"The whole thing is so goofy it must be politics," said Mr. Ward, aged 52. "It's a perfect platform: Wave the flag and whip up the crowd." Ms. Lanning, 49, who moved to China when factories back home began to close, blamed a failure to face economic reality by American furniture companies. "It breaks my heart to see workers lose their jobs at home, but we all picked up in our late 40s and 50s and came over here," she said. "This is evolution. You can't stop it."

From *The Wall Street Journal,* January 30, 2004. Reprinted by permission of Dow Jones & Co., Inc. via The Copyright Clearance Center.

79

P&G Adapts Attitude Toward Local Markets

Giant alters its approach in Asia by moving to tiered pricing model

By: Normandy Madden and Jack Neff

[Guangzhou, China] Procter & Gamble Co. likes to say it touches the lives of people around the world 2 billion times a day. Where it touches those lives increasingly is in developing countries like China, P&G's sixth-largest market.

Chairman-CEO A.G. Lafley says P&G's focus on such developing markets as China is one key difference between him and his predecessor, Durk Jager. P&G has been investing heavily in such countries as Russia and China since the mid-1980s, markets Mr. Lafley describes as favorites of Mr. Jager's predecessor, Chairman-CEO John Pepper. But now it's also increasingly looking to compete more effectively across a broader swath of the developing world, including such places as Vietnam and Iraq.

Mr. Jager "thought that the vast majority of the economic buying power is in Japan, the U.S. and Western Europe, and that's where all of our resources ought to go," said Mr. Lafley. "And I think we've decided in the past four years that there's a lot of opportunity" elsewhere.

NIMBLE COMPETITOR

Since P&G entered China in 1988, it has invested well over $1 billion and is by far the country's largest advertiser, spending an estimated $404 million in media in 2002, according to Nielsen Media Research. Olay is China's most advertised brand, said James Stengel, P&G's global marketing officer. China had been only the 10th-largest P&G market just three years ago, so the leap to sixth is significant.

It's taken more than a decade to evolve into a nimble competitor. In the past, P&G approached Asian markets by following the same pattern that made it a consumer goods giant in the U.S.—develop better products through innovation and research & development, then slightly raise the price for an enhanced product. It also charged nearly as much for a box of Tide or bottle of Pantene in Asia as it did in North America.

But most Asian consumers earn just a few dollars a day, limiting P&G's appeal to a sliver of the total population. Unilever, with more experience than P&G in developing markets, is peddling tiny packets of shampoo for a few cents to rural consumers through village fairs and street markets.

So P&G's Guangzhou-based managers took a hard look at their own marketing and production methods in China, and resolved to slash production costs, streamline distribution channels and expand market research. P&G also established an R&D center in Beijing to develop new products.

"We've spent a lot of time getting close to consumers. A one-size-fits-all approach won't work in China," said Austin Lally, P&G's general manager-greater China, in charge of fabric, home and feminine care.

Two-thirds of China's population earns less than $25 per month. So P&G developed a tiered pricing initiative in March 2003 to help compete against cheaper local brands while protecting the value of its global brands.

P&G introduced a 320-gram bag of Tide Clean White for 23¢, compared with 33¢ for 350 grams of Tide Triple Action. Clean White doesn't offer such benefits as stain removal and fragrance, and contains less advanced cleaning enzymes, but it costs less to make and, according to P&G, outperforms every other brand at that price level.

The results have in some cases been dramatic. P&G now sells more Crest toothpaste in China than in the U.S., Michael Kehoe, president-global oral care, said in an investor presentation last December, though dollar sales in China still are below those in the U.S.

Asia is a P&G testing ground for moving away from the low-margin detergent industry and toward beauty care, including hair care, skin care and personal cleansing brands. One of P&G's greatest success stories in this region is the emergence of SK-II, a popular Asian skin-care line. The brand is already available in the U.K., and P&G was to roll it into 11 Saks Fifth Avenue stores in the U.S. this month.

In a December talk with analysts, Mr. Lafley acknowledged P&G has had trouble invading the "walled cities," where competitors, often aided by colonial legacies, got a considerable head start. (Colonialism cuts both ways: P&G has a big edge in the Philippines, a former U.S. colony.) But Mr. Lafley said P&G has done well in such markets as China and Russia, where it entered the same time as competitors.

Closer to home, P&G has been behind competitors in much of Latin America, but without European colonialism as an excuse. U.S.-based rival Colgate-Palmolive Co. owns more than 80% of the Mexican toothpaste market, which in turn has helped it win more than 50% of the U.S. Hispanic market-more than 20 points ahead of its overall share.

(Cont.)

WALLED CITIES

Though much of its developing market progress has been limited to China, P&G is still trying to breach the walled cities of its competitors.

In India, where rival Unilever is bolstering its already huge lead by developing an Avon-style direct-sales force, P&G is countering with its own van sales program to reach rural areas, Mr. Stengel said. P&G also has followed Unilever by introducing low-cost single-use sachets of its laundry detergent brands.

P&G is finding new ways to compete in Latin America. In 2001, it launched in Mexico a new feminine protection brand, Naturella, with chamomile, alongside its existing Always and Tampax brands. Naturella allowed P&G to recapture share leadership in the country from Kimberly-Clark Corp. The brand specifically appeals to Latin women, many of whom prefer natural products, said Nancy Healey, VP-feminine care for P&G in North America.

These days, P&G also tries to be first in whenever new markets open. It was on the ground in June in Iraq, recruiting marketing executives for a new organization only three months after the U.S. armed forces landed.

"We say we have all the CNN countries in my region," said Dimitri Panayotopoulos, who became president-Central and Eastern Europe, Middle East, and Africa in 2001. "There's always a crisis somewhere. . . . It's good because from crisis comes opportunity. You can use that to build market share."

Marketing Strategies: Planning, Implementation, and Control

80

Reach Out and Upend an Industry

An Entrepreneur's Act II: Internet Calls

BY MATT RICHTEL

JEFFREY A. CITRON, the man who hopes to turn the telephone industry on its ear, works in a cubicle just down the hall from the "Tony Soprano" conference room. Nearby are the "Meadow" and "Uncle Jr." rooms, though if those are full, Mr. Citron's staff could gather in "Dr. Melfi."

The conference rooms at **Vonage,** an Internet telephone start-up in Edison, N.J., where Mr. Citron is chief executive, are named for characters from "The Sopranos." That hints at Mr. Citron's embrace of the unconventional, a trait that has made him a danger to some of America's most entrenched industries, but also at times to himself.

In the 1990's, he helped to pioneer computerized day-trading, putting a thumb in the eye of Wall Street's biggest companies. He amassed a fortune but wound up leaving the industry after he was charged with illegal trading by the Securities and Exchange Commission. Though admitting no wrongdoing, he agreed to pay a $22.5 million fine and was banned from the securities business.

Mr. Citron, the Sequel, is no less ambitious. Already one of the nation's wealthiest 30-somethings, he aims to use Vonage's Internet technology to bring fundamental change to the telephone industry, one of the most entrenched and tradition-bound economic sectors. "I'm going to change the world," Mr. Citron, 33, said in an interview last month over lunch at the New York Palace Hotel. "I did it before. Why not again?"

There are plenty of reasons. Mr. Citron's own investors acknowledge that Vonage may be zapped out of existence if it somehow misfires, its customer care problems persist, major rivals provide better service or regulators take steps like insisting that Internet phone companies pay the same fees as the rest of the industry.

Yet even skeptics credit Mr. Citron with helping to create an inflection point in the telephone industry by turning Internet telephony—which had long been just a great-sounding theory—into a viable product line.

In a little more than a year, he has signed up 100,000 customers who use his black box to connect their traditional telephone to the Internet. Customers pay a flat fee of around $35 for unlimited local and long-distance phone service, though that figure does not include the more than $40 a month that subscribers must also spend for the high-speed Internet access used to transmit the calls.

Industry analysts say Mr. Citron's success has hastened development of the technology by major telephone and cable companies, which are clearly following his lead. **AT&T** and **Time Warner Cable,** for instance, have recently announced their own voice-over-Internet strategies; **Verizon, Qwest, Cox Cable** and others have said they intend to deploy the technology, too.

Their efforts come not only in response to Vonage, but in the larger context of the upheaval in telecommunications. Since the deregulation of Ma Bell, a simmer of competition has turned into a boil. Companies deploying many technologies, from cable to wireless, are vying to create voice infrastructure that they hope will enable them to generate and capture billions of dollars in fees from subscribers.

So Vonage faces competition not just from big telecommunications companies but also from start-ups even tinier than itself. One of them, **Skype,** makes free software that lets people talk directly over computers—like a voice version of instant messaging—thus bypassing the telephone altogether. Another start-up, **Net2Phone,** offers Internet phone service directly to consumers (as does Vonage) and works with cable operators to help sell phone service over their lines.

Facing off against them all is a man who, by many accounts, is a study in extreme capitalism, not Harvard Business School niceties. Mr. Citron is not about polite cocktail conversation and low-carb diets; he leans more toward rolled-up sleeves, gut decisions and fast food. At the recent lunch at the Palace hotel, he ordered the salade nicoise, but mispronounced it nih-KO-see.

In other words, he is not the kind of guy who asks for permission slips. Just as he barreled into Wall Street seven years ago, breaking china along the way, he is now barging into the telecom fray. In doing so, he has put himself in position for a great entrepreneurial comeback.

"He's out for redemption; he wants to prove he can do this, and do this properly," said Harry R. Weller, a partner at **New Enterprise Associates,** a venture capital firm that invested $12 million last year in Vonage. After Mr. Weller's firm conducted extensive due diligence on Mr. Citron, it decided to forge ahead with the investment, despite what Mr. Weller described as the significant risk inherent in the technology and the man behind it.

That investment was followed last week by a $40 million round of financing from two other venture firms: **3i Group,** based in London, and **Meritech Capital Partners,** based in Palo Alto, Calif. As part of the deal, the investors have structured the board so that Mr. Citron does not have control over it—in part, Mr. Weller said, to make sure that Mr. Citron is kept within bounds.

Still, Mr. Weller said investors were convinced that it takes a personality like Mr. Citron's to shake the foundations of the telephone industry.

"You need somebody who knows how to disrupt an industry," he said. "You need to have a very, very aggressive entrepreneur. What we have to make sure to do is to take the best of Jeffrey Citron."

Mr. Citron grew up on Staten Island; his parents worked in the insurance business. As a boy, he says he did not know where his interests lay so much as where they did not: in school. He often skipped class, keeping mostly to himself, but he said he scored well enough on tests to offset his absences.

He made a quick transition from high school to Wall Street. In 1988, at the age of 17, he joined Datek Securities, where his father had close connections. By 20, he had made his first million as a trader.

Mr. Citron left Datek in 1991 to start his own firm, where, with a computer whiz named Josh Levine, he built the foundation of a computer-trading network called Island. It let individual traders swap shares inside the system—without help from the big Wall Street firms.

"Island was truly revolutionary," said Bill Burnham, who was an analyst at Piper Jaffray during the dot-com boom and is now a venture capitalist at Softbank Capital Partners. "It allowed individual investors to get direct access to the market to compete and get the same advantages that professional market makers do."

Mr. Citron returned to Datek Securities to create and become chief executive of Datek Online Holdings. Its technology allowed individuals to make their own trades automatically for $9.99, far less than the fees charged by full-service brokers. Datek Online became the nation's fourth-largest online trading firm.

But to regulators, Mr. Citron and his associates were involved in something far less upstanding. The Securities and Exchange

(Cont.)

Commission contended that from 1993 to 1998, he and others were involved in a scheme to use automated trading systems to manipulate Nasdaq, exploit loopholes and make millions of dollars.

In October 1999, amid the scrutiny, Mr. Citron agreed to resign as chief executive of Datek Online. The investigations into Mr. Citron and his associates led to the agreement in January 2003 in which seven former executives and traders at Datek paid a total of $70 million in fines. Regulators said they had created fictitious customer accounts, used them to place their own trades and filed false reports.

The $22.5 million fine Mr. Citron paid—one of the largest in S.E.C. history—only dented his wealth. In 2000, he sold his stake in Datek to private investors for $225 million. Today he lives in a mansion in Brielle, N.J., with his wife and two children.

But wealth isn't everything. There is also reputation. And Mr. Citron says he wants his back. What happened at Datek "was 100 percent about being young," he said.

"We were young, we were naive, we were inexperienced, and, yes, there were back-room dealings," he added. "But that is part of a lot of industries. This time, we are doing it differently." "This time" began with a helicopter ride. Mr. Citron flew from New Jersey to Melville on Long Island in the summer of 2000 to meet with Jeffrey Pulver and the other principals of a company called Min-X.com. Min-X was trying to create a market where companies could trade excess phone network capacity in blocks of minutes, in much the same way commodities like oil are traded. The principals approached Mr. Citron for financing.

He invested what he calls a "significant portion" of the $12 million raised in that first round of financing. But it was far from an arm's-length transaction. He took an active role in the company, immediately replacing Mr. Pulver as chief executive and then changing the concept for the business. Mr. Citron said that it was while flying from California to New Jersey in December 2000 that he decided to focus the company on offering Internet-based telephone calls, transforming it into Vonage.

The quick decision jibes with his overall philosophy that a good business idea does not require endless analysis. "If you can't figure it out in four months, you shouldn't do it," he said. "If you can't figure it out in a week, you shouldn't do it."

The concept of Internet-based calling was not new. It generated much buzz during the dot-com boom and was being pushed heavily by technology companies like **Cisco Systems,** which wanted to sell equipment that would be used to route calls as data.

The basic idea is to transmit telephone with the same technology used to handle e-mail and other Internet traffic. Calls are digitized and delivered as packets of data, rather than as traditional voice signals.

That may sound simple, but the reality was much more complex, particularly because the existing telecommunications giants had spent a century investing in a different type of technology, called circuit switch.

Mr. Citron was hardly the first person to understand that Internet calls were potentially less expensive than those made using circuit switch—for a variety of reasons. With circuit switch technology, a telephone line is dedicated to a single conversation. But when the packets are sent as data, that line can send many signals at once, making far more efficient use of the telecommunications infrastructure. In addition, Internet equipment is less expensive and gives operators and consumers more control over voice traffic—for instance, allowing people to get an e-mail reminder each time they receive a voice mail message.

But for all the advantages, and the hype, no one had figured out the basics: how to affordably hook a traditional phone into the

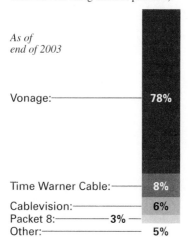

"Speaking In Ones And Zeros"

Share of U.S. residential Internet phone subscribers (local and long-distance service using Internet protocol).

As of end of 2003

Vonage:	78%
Time Warner Cable:	8%
Cablevision:	6%
Packet 8:	3%
Other:	5%

(Source by the Yankee Group)

Internet, then send a voice stream directly to another telephone. Mr. Citron and a small team spent the first half of 2001 working to solve the problem.

Louis Holder, a co-founder of Min-X who is now in charge of product development at Vonage, said it was a time of voracious fast-food consumption ("Everybody put on 10 pounds") and exhilaration. "Nobody had done this in the consumer space," he said.

The breakthrough came late on a Thursday night in June. Mr. Holder said he, Mr. Citron and two engineers figured out how to send a digitized call from one telephone to another through a firewall, a defense barrier between a computer or network and the wider Internet.

Initially, the company wanted to create partnerships with cable companies to help them in their assault on traditional telephone companies. But there was skepticism. Vonage was regarded by some executives as a leftover from the bubble. Besides, the cable companies were having their own problems, punctuated by the bankruptcy of @Home, which delivered Internet access over cable.

So in April 2002, Vonage started a consumer-based service. Secretly, the company hoped that if cable companies saw that Vonage was successful, they would consider signing partnerships, Mr. Holder said. But then Vonage took on a life of its own. Within 18 months, it has amassed 100,000 customers, and Mr. Holder said the company expects to have 250,000 by the end of this year, and 500,000 by the end of 2005. Vonage says it will be profitable this year.

Blair Levin, former chief of staff to Reed E. Hundt, chairman of the Federal Communications Commission during the Clinton administration, said that Vonage had proved that Internet calling could be done, and that it was forcing a giant industry to follow more quickly than it might have otherwise. "It's going to have a huge historical impact," Mr. Levin said. "Vonage was a match that was put on some pretty dry timber. But it was a match."

But Mr. Levin, like many others, said he wondered whether Vonage would be a historical footnote or a viable concern. "The question is: What is their defensible asset?" he said, noting that other companies can provide the same kind of service as Vonage, but with the added benefit of having well-known brand names and deep pockets. "They're playing in a world in which, traditionally, economies of scale and scope matter a huge amount."

An executive at a major telephone company, who requested anonymity, said Vonage was not seen as real competition. And the cable companies, which are vying to use their high-speed lines to deliver phone service, say they can do it far better than Vonage. Cox Communications, based in Atlanta, says that its version of Internet-based calling is more stable than Vonage's because it operates the data network, giving it more control. Even Mr. Citron conceded that this was a possibility. "Clearly, there might be some advantages," he said of the cable industry.

Indeed, Vonage acknowledges that it has two overriding challenges. One is the quality of calls made over its network. Customers often

(Cont.)

complain of having their calls dropped, or of hearing lags. Mr. Holder says that this happens because the high-speed Internet access in subscribers' homes can be spotty, and that when the lines falter, so does the call quality.

A related problem, Mr. Holder said, is insufficient customer service. The company is scrambling to hire and train qualified people to answer customer concerns. Vonage has 70 customer service employees and would like to have 110, he said.

Another major challenge is regulatory. So far, Vonage has been able to keep its costs low because it has been able to avoid the regulations that federal and state governments place on traditional telephone companies. But that may change: The F.C.C. said last Thursday that it intends to study the question of regulating Internet calling over the next year.

Mr. Citron said he hoped regulators would make the rules clear. He also said he did not intend to get into any gray areas, as he did in his first incarnation as a disruptive entrepreneur. But, in one way, he would like to see a similar outcome.

Internet calling, he said, "will be a large and transforming event."

RICK WAGONER'S GAME PLAN

CEO Rick Wagoner has fixed many of GM's problems. But he still has to deal with 30 years of management mistakes

It's a chief executive's nightmare. The better you execute, the more improvements you make—the more your stock drops. That was the position G. Richard Wagoner Jr. found himself in last October. A day after General Motors Corp. announced that it had lifted operating earnings 30% in a stagnant car market, Standard & Poor's downgraded the auto maker's debt with no warning. Surprised investors rushed to sell, and the stock dropped 8%. Credit analysts pointed to GM's $76 billion pension fund, which they estimated at the time to be underfunded by as much as $23 billion. GM will have to plow in billions of dollars for years to keep the fund flush, they said.

The earnings gain was no accounting fluke, either. GM finished the year just as strong, with an operating profit of $3.9 billion, nearly double what it earned in 2001, on 5% higher sales of $186.2 billion. GM clearly leads the rest of the U.S. Big Three car companies, reflecting real operational improvements that Wagoner, 49, helped make in the past decade, starting when he was chief financial officer and later as chief operating officer. After GM lost a staggering $30 billion during a single three-year stretch in the early '90s, Wagoner and Chairman John F. "Jack" Smith Jr. forced GM back to basics. They slashed costs, cut payroll, and overhauled aging plants. Once he took over the corner office in May, 2000, CEO Wagoner pulled the efficiency collar even tighter. Now, GM ranks close to Honda Motor Co. and Toyota Motor Corp. in productivity and has made strides in quality. GM also recaptured leadership of the truck business from rival Ford Motor Co., a coup that made the company billions. Last year, GM even nudged up its share of the U.S. market, to 28.3% from 28.1%.

But as good as those moves are, they pale next to the problems of GM's weak car brands and gargantuan pension payments. In essence, Rick Wagoner is battling 30 years of management mistakes that have left him with immense burdens and very little room to maneuver. Chief executives from Frederic Donner to Roger Smith built up a bloated bureaucracy that cranked out boring, low-quality cars. Turf battles at headquarters sapped resources and diverted attention from a rising threat out of Asia and Europe. Those competitors drove away with the U.S. car market. Now they're aiming to do the same in sport-utility vehicles and trucks—the last bastion of U.S. dominance. GM's most profitable segment is also under attack by environmentalists and safety regulators, and more and more buyers are flocking to smaller crossover SUVs.

Even worse for GM was the buildup of lavish health and retirement benefits for workers that it agreed to in fatter days as a way to buy peace with the United Auto Workers. The company says the gap between its pension funding and future liabilities is now $19.3 billion. That means GM will have to pump as much as $4 billion into the fund over this year and next. Providing health care to former and current workers will drain an additional $5 billion per year. The pension costs alone will cut projected 2003 net income from $4.2 billion to $2.8 billion. Providing for retirees saddles each car rolling off a GM assembly line with a $1,350 penalty vs. a Japanese car built in a new, nonunion U.S. plant, says analyst Scott Hill of Sanford C. Bernstein & Co. That's a daunting handicap in an industry that struggles to make an average operating profit of $800 per vehicle.

Those huge legacy costs explain why Wagoner has kept the heat on his competition with the 0% financing deals he unleashed after September 11, 2001. Closing plants and accepting a smaller chunk of the U.S. market—the route his rival, Ford, has taken—would give GM fewer vehicles over which to spread those big pension and health-care costs. And thanks to an onerous

Malibu on a Budget

One of Wagoner's biggest accomplishments has been reducing the time and money it takes to build vehicles. Here are some of the savings GM has wrung out of one mainstay car, the 2003 Chevy Malibu, compared with two other midsize sedans, the Oldsmobile Intrigue and Pontiac Grand Prix, that previously were built at the same Fairfax (Kan.) plant.

THE DESIGN — GM designed the Malibu so that fewer workers can assemble more cars. **PAYOFF** GM should be able to build the Malibu with 18 to 19 hours of labor instead of 24 hours.

THE PLATFORM — GM engineers in the U.S., Germany, and Sweden worked together to share the same platform and other parts for the company's Chevrolet Malibu, Opel Vectra, and Saab 9-3 midsize sedans. **PAYOFF** Engineering costs were cut by one-third.

THE INTERIOR — GM gave French interior supplier Faurecia the contract for seats for the Malibu, Vectra, and Saab 9-3. **PAYOFF** GM got seats made of more comfortable and durable materials for the price of cheaper seats.

THE GAS TANK — The Malibu and Saab 9-3 share the same gas tank, saving on engineering and safety tests. **PAYOFF** The tank's cost is 30% lower.

THE SUSPENSION — The Chevy Malibu and Opel Vectra share the same front and rear suspension. **PAYOFF** Development costs are 30% lower for those components.

deal it struck in 1990 with the UAW, GM has to pay furloughed workers about 70% of their salary for years after they're laid off. Says Wagoner: "We have a huge fixed-cost base. It's 30 years of downsizing and 30 years of increased health-care costs. It puts a premium on us running this business to

(Cont.)

generate cash. Our goal is to grow. We don't care who we take it from."

All that would make the outlook for GM pretty bleak, except for one thing: Eventually, those legacy costs start to diminish. Starting around 2008, the ranks of GM's elderly retirees will thin, relieving some of the burden. After that, more of the incremental gains Wagoner has been achieving will fall to the bottom line rather than to retirees. The results could be dramatic.

That makes Wagoner's imperative clear: He has to keep up cash flow to cover those costs until they start to shrink. At the same time, he must continue to rack up improvements in quality, efficiency, design, and brand appeal. If he can come anywhere close, he just might pull off an impressive turnaround. A stock market rebound would help immensely. GM's pension fund holds its own if it earns 9% a year on its investments. Each one-point rise above that is worth $700 million to the fund.

With much of the focus on GM's financial crunch, it's easy to lose sight of Wagoner's greatest achievement—and the best reason to believe that he might beat the legacy monster. Walk around GM's sprawling headquarters complex today and you soon realize that against all odds, Wagoner is making real progress in energizing GM's torpid culture. He broke with GM tradition by recruiting two respected outsiders for key positions—Robert A. Lutz as head of product development and John Devine as vice-chairman and chief financial officer. And he has given them extraordinary leeway to fix the company's problems.

To motivate his team, the self-effacing Wagoner leaves his ego at the door and lets his executives do their jobs. "Rick acts more like a coach than a boss," says David E. Cole, director of the Center for Automotive Research (CAR) in Ann Arbor, Mich. Thus it was Lutz who rolled out Cadillac's lavish Sixteen prototype luxury car at the Detroit auto show earlier this month as Wagoner sat in the background. Afterward, Wagoner chatted with a few reporters while Lutz held court beside the 16-cylinder vehicle, surrounded by a huge crowd, drinking a martini, and wearing someone's lipstick mark on his cheek.

That low-key style has helped Wagoner in tearing down GM's warring fiefdoms. Since giving the swaggering Lutz rule over product development, Wagoner has spiked the design-by-committee system and cut the time it takes to develop a new car to 20 months from nearly four years. GM used to have different studios for each division working on car designs that would get passed on to marketing, then engineering, then manufacturing. Lutz has one committee to cover the entire process. Every Thursday, he hashes out what vehicles should look like and which division will build them, along with a small group that includes Group Vice-President for Advanced Vehicle

Development Mark T. Hogan, GM North America President Gary L. Cowger, Design Chief Wayne K. Cherry, and Chief Engineer James E. Queen.

But low-key doesn't mean hands-off. Lutz may make the day-to-day decisions on car design, but Wagoner reserves final say. He meets monthly with top execs, who see car designs much earlier in the process. The ones they think are promising move ahead fast. Says retired executive Richard C. Nerod, who ran GM's Latin America operations: "Rick cut out a lot of the infighting and the bull – – – –."

GM is now the lowest-cost producer among the Big Three—and it's not far behind Toyota and Honda

---

Wagoner also exerts control by imposing tough performance standards. A legendary number-cruncher who rose up through GM's finance division, he holds top managers to strict measures. GM, like most big companies, always had performance goals. But they never went nearly as deep or into as much detail. Says Cowger: "Everything can be measured."

Everyone, too. Even Lutz, the larger-than-life product czar who flies his own fighter jet and sparked Chrysler's 1990s resurgence with cars such as the Dodge Viper and PT Cruiser, isn't exempt. Lutz was judged on 12 criteria last year, from how well he used existing parts to save money in new vehicles to how many engineering hours he cut from the development process.

Clearly, Wagoner's own ideas on how to fix GM have evolved. He seems to have learned from a brush with grand strategic vision back in the '90s, when, like now-deposed Ford CEO Jacques A. Nasser, he explored ways to grow outside of building cars. Wagoner was behind the decision to pump hundreds of millions into GM's OnStar Corp. telematics business and DirecTV satellite-TV service. Neither produced big revenues for GM. Now, with Devine applying a cold dose of realism to GM's finances, there's little illusion that such diversions can fix the cash crunch. "That was a dream a couple of years ago, but it's not reality," Devine says. "The math will tell you that the principal driver of revenue and profits is the car-and-truck business in North America and Europe."

If Wagoner has brought a new intensity to GM, he probably gets it from his mother, Martha, a onetime school teacher. Family members recall one Christmas several years ago when she doggedly kept baking cookies despite a broken arm. "My mom has a task orientation that you sometimes see in

my brother," says Judy Pahren, a financial-services manager who is one of Wagoner's two sisters. Rick had a Norman Rockwell upbringing in Richmond, Va. He picked up a rabid devotion to Duke University basketball from his father, George, an accountant at Eskimo Pie Co. Wagoner got a chance to play for the Blue Devils as a walk-on. He demonstrated a deft shot but learned the limits of his athletic ability. "The knock on Rick was that you couldn't slide a phone book under his jump," says roommate Charles H. McCreary III. The devotion to alma mater remains, though: A few years ago, he ordered a custom "Duke blue" Suburban SUV.

After Duke, Wagoner got his MBA at Harvard Business School, surprising some upon graduation when he chose GM over potentially more lucrative jobs on Wall Street. Wagoner's knack for crunching numbers propelled him through stints at GM units in Canada, Europe, and Brazil. His big break came in 1992, when then-CEO Smith tapped him to be CFO after a boardroom coup. Even as CEO, Wagoner is known for a low-key lifestyle. He prides himself on juggling his work schedule to attend games and other activities of his three sons. And when entertaining, Wagoner is more likely to cook on his backyard grill than hire a caterer.

Wagoner's willingness to let others shine is a classic trait of leaders who have boosted their companies to exceptional performance, says Jim Collins, author of Good to Great. As a longtime GM insider, Wagoner has other advantages: He knows what brutal facts need to be confronted, and he can assess which veterans can handle key jobs. Says Collins: "Wagoner has the opportunity to take it back to great." But the odds are stiff—only 11 of 1,435 companies Collins studied made such a lasting transformation. And those that did required an average of seven years to get breakthrough results.

Still, competitors are impressed with the progress Wagoner has made. "I'm a big admirer of his management style," says cross-town rival William C. Ford Jr., chairman and CEO of Ford. He should be—GM's operating profit may not match the $4.6 billion No. 3 Toyota made in just the six months through

---

To woo car buyers, GM uses incentives that cost $3,800 per car—twice what Toyota spends

---

September. And GM's stock, trading around 37, is down 26% from a year ago. But that performance sure beats Ford's $872 million operating profit and 36% lower stock price.

It's a testament to Wagoner's ability to cut costs that GM managed nearly to double margins in North America last year, to 2.6% of

(Cont.)

sales. Thanks to efficiency gains, GM is now one of the leanest car builders, with variable costs—labor, parts, outsourced production, etc.—amounting to 62% of revenues, according to UBS Warburg. That puts it ahead of Ford and Chrysler at 68%, and it isn't far behind leaders Toyota and Honda at 60%.

With lower costs than its domestic competition, GM is better able to withstand the price war it started with 0% financing. But Wagoner is betting that the cars he plans to launch in the next three years will be good enough to sell on merit, not price. A few "niche" vehicles, such as the hulking Hummer H2, are already out. But the assault begins in earnest later this year with the Chevy Malibu family sedan and Equinox car/SUV crossover, Cadillac SRX small SUV, and Pontiac Grand Prix sedan. "This is one major last-ditch effort to save themselves in the car market," says Joseph Phillippi, a former Wall Street analyst who consults for the industry.

Wagoner, who's not a classic Detroit "car guy," seems content to rely on Lutz and his team to fix the lineup. During one trip through the design studio last year, he spotted a sexy two-door version of the Cadillac CTS sports sedan. "I hope you guys figure out a way to build that," Wagoner said, but offered no solutions, recalls one senior designer. "Rick trusts my judgment implicitly," Lutz says, "but if I came up with some wacky product proposals, he'd pull me back."

The most dramatic gains won't come on a sketch pad anyway but in the way GM selects new car designs and then shepherds them through production. In the past, even if a bold design made it off a drawing board, it had little chance of surviving to the showroom. A concept would go from a designer to the marketing staff, which would try to tailor it to consumers. Then it would go to engineers, who would try to figure out how to build it, and so on. Separate teams worked with suppliers, factories, and parts suppliers on their individual slice of the process, with little interaction.

It was a recipe for mediocrity—and often disaster. The Aztek, which emerged in 2000 as a boxy, garish cross between an SUV and a minivan five years after designers first drew it up as a racy bid for younger drivers, is a prime example. Wagoner was determined to tear up that system by the roots. A few months after taking over, he ordered GM's product developers to ready the SSR concept vehicle for production. A combination of hot rod and pickup truck, it had been a big hit at the Detroit auto show. Wagoner thought its distinctive look, with chrome bars splitting the front grille and taillights, would be a great image builder. But the SSR still had to navigate the old GM system. Because it was announced before engineers had a precise blueprint to build it, the program quickly ran over budget. Today, its cost has ballooned way past the original $300 million projec-

tion, to almost $500 million. The $42,000 SSR will hit showrooms this summer, a quick turnaround for GM. But with only 5,000 sales projected per year, it makes for a very expensive showcase.

Since then, Wagoner and Lutz have smoothed things out a bit. Lutz, Cowger, Hogan, and the others decide what goes from the design studios into the funnel of cars that will be considered for funding by GM's Automotive Strategy Board, chaired monthly by Wagoner. Lutz says he and Wagoner have disagreed on some product decisions, but he hasn't been turned down yet. Now, 75% of the engineering work is finished when a program manager sits down to build a car.

That's how GM quickly green-lighted plans to resurrect the Pontiac GTO, its famous 1960s muscle car. For years, Pontiac and Chevrolet wanted a brawny car with rear-wheel drive, which is favored by driving enthusiasts. GM's Australian Holden Ltd. subsidiary had a promising candidate in its Monaro sports coupe, but the idea to bring it to the U.S. never made it out of committee. GM execs simply didn't want to spend what little money it would take to alter the Monaro to meet U.S. safety standards and American

---

To offset high health and pension costs, GM needs hot cars that bring in cash

---

styling. Says Lutz: "I just asked, 'Why not?'" GM got the program together in less than 18 months. Later this year, Pontiac will roll out the GTO as a 340-horsepower Americanized Monaro.

Wagoner has also streamlined GM's factories. GM is now the most productive domestic auto maker, having cut the time it takes to assemble a vehicle from an average of 32 hours in 1998 to 26 hours in 2001, according to Harbour & Associates. That compares with 27 for Ford, almost 31 at DaimlerChrysler, 22.5 at Toyota, and 17.9 at Nissan. A big factor was expanding parts shared across vehicles. The new Chevy Malibu, for instance, uses the same platform and many of the same parts as the Saab 9-3 sedan. GM's plants are also more flexible—each of seven full-size pickup and SUV plants can make any of the vehicles designed on that platform.

The cars rolling off GM's assembly lines today are undeniably better built than they used to be. Once ranked below the industry average, GM trails only Honda and Toyota in J.D. Power & Associates Inc.'s initial quality survey, which measures problems in the first 90 days of ownership. Some cars, such as the Chevrolet Impala, even beat the likes of the Toyota Camry. Last year, *Consumer Reports* recommended 13

GM vehicles—representing 41% of its sales volume—up from 5 last year. But one of GM's most stubborn woes is that many buyers still perceive the Chevy, Pontiac, and Buick brands as musty and second-rate. GM needs incentives averaging $3,800 a vehicle—more than twice what Toyota spends.

The biggest risk to GM's lineup is at the top. Its popular SUVs and pickups accounted for about 90% of profits last year but are under increasing assault from foreign competitors and safety regulators. Like his competitors, Wagoner is banking on crossover vehicles, which combine SUV-like space and looks with a carlike ride and better fuel economy, as a hedge against a big-truck backlash. Cadillac's luxury SRX hits the market this year as a viable rival to the Lexus RX 330 and Mercedes M-class, and Chevy will launch its Equinox as an all-wheel drive crossover. Next year, GM will start offering pickups and SUVs with hybrid gas/electric engines. New designs are also in the works. Lutz has tentatively approved a highly stylized 2007 replacement for the Chevy Silverado and GMC Sierra pickups, which hold a commanding 40% of the pickup market. It will be based on the slick Cheyenne concept truck that GM unveiled in January, which has improved driver and passenger room and doors on each side of the pickup bed to provide easier cargo access. But in small SUVs and gas mileage, GM is playing catch-up to the Japanese.

Wagoner and his team have little choice but to wait out their biggest mess—those massive health and pension costs. Wagoner is brutally realistic: "We'd be accused of a pipe dream if we said in 10 years these issues will go away." GM pays its UAW workers only slightly more per hour than Toyota, Honda, and Nissan pay their American factory workers. But the cost of pension and health-care benefits for current workers is huge—about $24 per hour at GM, vs. $12 at the foreign factories. Pension obligations swelled after the 1990 contract, when then-Chairman Robert Stempel practically guaranteed almost no layoffs. Underestimating the speed of its decline, GM agreed to pay workers for years after a furlough. As losses mounted, GM resorted to early-retirement offers—avoiding billions in unemployment benefits but adding thousands of retirees. Since GM was shrinking faster than Ford, its pension rolls grew more quickly, to 2.5 retirees per worker today, vs. Ford's 1-to-1 ratio. Last year, GM plowed almost $5 billion into the pension fund to shore it up as stock prices fell. But Carol Levenson, an analyst for bond research firm Gimme Credit, points out that GM had to take on $4.6 billion in debt to do it. Until the stock and bond markets spring back, it's three steps forward and two steps back.

That pressure should ease somewhat over the next decade. GM's average worker is 48 years old—five years older than those at

(Cont.)

Ford or Chrysler. GM's total number of retirees will drop below existing levels by 2010, says CAR's labor and manufacturing analyst, Sean McAlinden. Wagoner believes that even without another bull market to boost the pension fund, GM can handle the drain and maintain its $7 billion capital-spending budget. Meanwhile, to pay down the pension shortfall, Devine is working to sell Hughes Electronics' DirecTV business, possibly to News Corp.

Closing the gap on health-care costs will be tougher. This summer, GM and the UAW will start working on a new four-year labor agreement. GM is almost certain to ask for higher co-payments from its 138,000 UAW employees. The union is almost certain to balk. "We don't have an interest in cost-shifting," says Richard Shoemaker, head of the UAW's GM department. GM also is one of many companies pushing to have Medicare pick up a greater share of retiree drug costs. But even Wagoner admits: "I don't see that happening soon."

Can Wagoner return GM to dominance? He has made heroic gains. But he's taking nothing for granted. At a speech in Detroit last year, he told the story of William C. Durant, who pulled together such companies as Buick, Cadillac, and Olds to form GM in 1908. But Durant was more interested in cutting deals than managing, so he wound up running a bowling alley in Flint. "That fate has haunted GM chairmen for decades," Wagoner told his audience. He was joking, of course. But Wagoner will be the first to tell you that his own future is up in the air. It all depends on whether he can save GM from its past.

By David Welch, with Kathleen Kerwin, in Detroit

82

Under Renovation

A Hardware Chain Struggles to Adjust To a New Blueprint

Home Depot Chief Nardelli Tightens Central Control, And Employees Squawk

Today, He Reveals More Plans

BY DAN MORSE

ATLANTA — When Bernie Marcus ran Home Depot Inc., he fired up store managers inundated by paperwork from headquarters with this advice: "Get a rubber stamp that says 'Bulls—' on it, stamp it, and send it back to whatever bureaucrat sent it to you." The message: It's your store; do what's best.

Bob Nardelli came to the company from General Electric Co. two years ago with a very different approach: one that increasingly favors directives from headquarters in Atlanta. As chairman and chief executive, he has cut costs, centralized purchasing and tightened control of hiring and store displays. Performance is now measured by lingo that leaves many employees scratching their heads: receiving minutes per bill, percent of E-Velocity and SPR audits, to name a few.

By all accounts, the country's No. 1 home-improvement chain needed at least some tightening. But so far, Mr. Nardelli's swift, aggressive renovations have disrupted employees and spooked many shareholders. Home Depot's once-roaring stock has fallen close to its five-year low, having dropped 51% since Mr. Nardelli arrived.

Sales growth, which started to slacken the year before he took over, has slowed considerably. The company said earlier this month that sales in stores open at least a year will plunge as much as 10% in its fourth quarter, which ends Feb. 2. For the fiscal year, overall sales are expected to rise 10%, compared with 17% the year before.

At a company traditionally known for independent-minded managers and workers, some confusion and resentment have set in. After Mr. Nardelli arrived, "things weren't presented to you; they were told to you," says Tony Calveiro, a former store manager in Kansas City, Mo. He left in July 2001 to become an assistant manager for Costco Wholesale Corp.,

where he says he has more freedom.

Mr. Marcus says the company lost a lot of talented employees after Mr. Nardelli's arrival, although departures have tapered off. The company plays down the suggestion that it had sizable departures of talented employees because of the changed leadership.

Mr. Nardelli has emphasized hiring more part-timers to handle weekend crowds, but customers are complaining that the quality of service has lagged. The CEO's order to keep store inventory leaner made sense on paper, but in practice it has meant that homeowners and contractors couldn't always find what they were looking for.

Meanwhile, Home Depot is no longer cruising along as it did for nearly two decades, with strong sales and earnings quarter after quarter. Among other factors, the company has blamed cautious consumer spending and big promotions last winter that inflated sales in the same period a year ago. No. 2 Lowe's Cos.—a retailer known for its disciplined operations—has been chipping away at Home Depot's strong lead. (Because the housing market has remained strong, the overall slow economy hasn't hurt home improvement as much as it has other retailers, some industry executives say.)

Three big institutional investors—Fidelity Management & Research Co., Alliance Capital Management Inc. and Janus Capital Management LLC—have dumped Home Depot stock valued at a total of $4.2 billion in recent months, according to FactSet Research Systems Inc. This week, Gary Balter and Neel Gandhi, analysts at Credit Suisse First Boston who have issued a generally favorable rating on the stock, nevertheless fired a broadside at the CEO. Based on their own store visits, the analysts wrote, "Mr. Nardelli in two years at the helm has not yet shown the retail acumen that defines the winners." They cited a lack of skilled employees, poor store displays, missing products and poor purchasing decisions.

'Change Creates Fear'

Mr. Nardelli, 54 years old, is sticking to his strategy. "Change creates fear," he says. The only way for Home Depot to thrive, he adds, is for headquarters to know what's going on. "The naysayers could say, 'Well jeez, you're adding all these metrics.' Well, take all the gauges off the car. Why do you need a gas gauge? Why do you need a speedometer?"

Morale is holding up, he says, given all of the changes and the slumping stock price. "I love the entrepreneurial spirit. I just want to have some compliant entrepreneurial spirit at a certain time," he said in an interview last year.

Since he arrived, margins and cash on hand are up. The balance sheet is strong. The company continues to add stores, so overall sales are still climbing. Ken Langone, an influential board member who helped hire

Mr. Nardelli, says the CEO's strategy will pay off. "We think Bob is doing a superb job and is making the changes going forward that are necessary."

Today, the chief executive will spell out more improvement plans at the company's annual investor conference. On tap: continued programs to refurbish stores, more new merchandise and efforts to boost customer service.

A big part of Home Depot's success story has been the energy its managers customarily invested in taking command of their stores, ordering as many hammers and faucets as they thought their customers expected and hiring knowledgeable retired tradespeople and hungry newcomers to work the aisles. "You had these evangelists, if you will, who sold lumber," says consultant Robert Oxley. He used to train Home Depot employees and now teaches vendors trying to sell products to the company. These days, he says, "there's nowhere near the passion as there was under the old guard," saying that's one of the consequences of Mr. Nardelli's approach. "It's not manageable through a computer."

Mr. Marcus, who helped lead the company from its founding in 1978 through early 2001, acknowledges that the old ways sometimes got a little "loosey-goosey." And some of Mr. Nardelli's critics concede that a company that had grown to more than 1,000 stores needed to show more discipline, especially in light of increased competition.

Mr. Nardelli arrived in December 2000, after losing out in the race to replace Jack Welch atop GE. The new Home Depot chief, who lacked any retail experience, burrowed into the new job. Atlanta staffers remember him calling meetings for 8 p.m. on weekdays and 7:30 a.m. on weekends.

A number of executives left, some with strong encouragement, as Mr. Nardelli brought more subordinates under his direct control. He attacked labor costs, setting more structured "wage bands" for specific jobs and limiting merit raises, which he says were "out of control."

Home Depot's deflated stock has weighed on morale, because many employees have received bonuses in the form of stock options whose value has fallen. In break rooms and on the Internet, they grouse about their CEO's $13.8 million in total compensation last fiscal year, not including options.

Mr. Nardelli's challenges are compounded by the reverence with which many employees regard Mr. Marcus and Arthur Blank, the retired founders and longtime executives. Months after Mr. Nardelli arrived, workers who spotted Mr. Marcus in their store would beseech him to come back. But that is fading, says Mr. Marcus, who stresses that Mr. Nardelli is making needed changes that employees are starting to appreciate.

In a 1999 book, Messrs. Marcus and Blank wrote, "We hire people who couldn't

(Cont.)

work for anybody else, who might otherwise be well-suited to being self-employed or running their own shop, and many of them become store managers." The authors lauded employees for outlandish stunts. Larry Mercer, who would go on to become a top executive, once refunded money to a customer who showed up with a set of car tires, even though Home Depot hadn't sold them. After the customer left, Mr. Mercer hung his tires over the service desk to remind everyone that the customer is always right.

By the time Mr. Nardelli arrived, sales growth had started to slow. On Oct. 12, 2000, Mr. Blank, who was then the CEO, warned that profits would fall short of expectations for the remainder of the fiscal year. Investors bailed out, driving the stock down 28%, its biggest one-day decline ever. Home Depot's board accelerated the succession process that brought Mr. Nardelli aboard.

Purchasing Shift

One of the biggest changes he has pushed involves purchasing. Home Depot had nine regional buying offices, each one acquiring products independently. Mr. Blank had said that the structure helped boost sales 15% to 20%, because the people doing the buying understood so well what customers in their local markets wanted.

But the company's decentralized buying diluted its negotiating clout. And because each region would do things its own way, the company couldn't easily coordinate nationwide buys with nationwide store displays. Some vendors complained that the company was difficult to deal with. "It was like having nine different wives," says one Midwestern tool maker, who requests anonymity.

Mr. Nardelli's solution was to centralize buying in Atlanta. At the same time, he moved to clean out dead and redundant items from store shelves. The company, after all, didn't really need 13 different round-point shovels, he notes.

The buying changes, he says, have yielded better terms from vendors that have widened the company's gross margin, or gross profit as a percentage of sales, to 31.6% in the third quarter, from 30.2% for the same period the year before. Cutting inventory has helped Home Depot amass $4 billion in cash, up from $167 million two years ago.

Mr. Nardelli has forced stores to increase weekend staffing by hiring more part-time workers: college students, for example, and people who have other weekday jobs. Stores went from 30% part-time staffing in December 2001 to 50% just four months later.

But longtime employees say that some part-time workers aren't as committed to Home Depot as full-timers. Customers, meanwhile, have complained that they sometimes can't find knowledgeable sales help—or, in some instances, any help at all.

In Decatur, Ga., Don Schneider, owner of Old Timers Renovations, a residential-contracting business, spent 20 minutes one day, waiting for a forklift operator to arrive and pull out a stack of drywall. "They need to speed up their pit times," Mr. Schneider said, hefting the load into his pickup truck.

Mr. Nardelli has acknowledged he went too far with part-timers. The company has scaled back to a mix of 40% part-time and 60% full-time. He says customer service has had its "ups and downs" but is improving.

Managers also were directed to increase their "inventory velocity," or the speed at which merchandise flows through their stores. When some responded by ordering fewer products, customers couldn't find what they needed. "On paper, all these changes make sense," says Steve Mahurin, a former Atlanta merchandising executive at Home Depot who left voluntarily 14 months after Mr. Nardelli arrived. "Unfortunately, they don't work on the floor of the stores."

The company's buyers "in Atlanta truly do care," Mr. Mahurin says. "They just have 1,500 stores to deal with and it's impossible to give them the attention they need." Home Depot officials counter that they still have plenty of divisional merchants who, while they don't buy, keep tabs on local needs and communicate them to Atlanta.

Many on Wall Street have urged the company to imitate Lowe's, which caters strongly to women shoppers. But some Home Depot veterans chafe at new products purchased by Atlanta, such as crockpots, which don't have much appeal to the company's core customers. Mr. Nardelli also has pushed redesigned large-appliance sections in the stores but says Home Depot will always serve the contractor and serious do-it-yourselfer. And some of the new buys—cleaning products, for example—have been hits.

Mr. Nardelli also says centralized buying will work more smoothly once he gets new computer systems online. He acknowledges that some inventory directives have caused problems and that every buying decision hasn't been flawless.

"Has everything that's happened been perfect? No, this guy has made some errors," says Mr. Marcus, the co-founder. That said, "when he makes an error, he backs off of it, and he isn't ashamed to say, 'I made a mistake.' And he learns from it."

83

Flying With Panache, and at a Profit, Too

BY JOSEPH B. TREASTER

When Paul Austin, a British executive of a big construction company here on the Persian Gulf, travels by air, he no longer drives to the airport. His favorite airline, **Emirates Airlines,** sends a car to pick him up, as it does for all its business and first-class passengers in London, Paris, Hong Kong and 12 other cities.

In business class, he has a choice of 48 movie cassettes he can load when he wants, and a couple of dozen music and talk programs. Even in economy, passengers may choose from 17 movies and 18 video games available on personal screens.

Mr. Austin dines on meals set on pink linen and sips fine wines. In economy, settings are less plush, but the meals range from stir-fries and curries to lamb stew and Nile perch. Cocktails and wine are free—except for Champagne. When a passenger hesitates over the $5.50 charge for Champagne, flight attendants smile warmly and propose a mixed drink at no charge, easing gracefully out of an awkward situation.

"We want to make the customer feel comfortable," said Gary Chapman, who is in charge of personnel and training for the airline.

Since its start 18 years ago with two Boeing 727's in one of the world's politically explosive regions, Emirates Airlines has been trying to make flying enjoyable for its passengers and profitable for itself. It has been succeeding nicely, increasing passenger capacity about 20 percent annually, taking trade group awards away from distinguished carriers like **Singapore Airlines** and **Cathay Pacific** and winning the loyalty of business travelers like Mr. Austin.

"They make your entire journey stress-free," he said.

Dubai's location in the Middle East would be enough to stress out some people. To the northwest is Iraq; to the south is Yemen, the ancestral homeland of Osama bin Laden. Only 60 miles across the Strait of Hormuz is Iran. Just offshore in the Persian Gulf, American warships send fighter jets over Iraq every day; in a war, they would probably fire Tomahawk missiles as well.

Yet Dubai successfully promotes itself as a neutral haven, where business flourishes with little interference from government, and tourists from Europe and nearby Arab countries

flock to resorts along bone-white beaches. With about one million people and acres of glittering office and hotel towers rising from the desert, Dubai is the commercial and tourism center of the United Arab Emirates, a group of seven city-states set on a crescent of sand at the mouth of the Persian Gulf.

Though Dubai is an Islamic country, it permits drinking and dancing in hotels, creating a party atmosphere for Arabs from stricter regimes and making Dubai reminiscent of Beirut before the Lebanese and their neighbors reduced it to rubble in the 1970's and 80's. The city is also becoming something of a modern Casablanca, a place of international intrigue, spies and smugglers.

Unlike many Middle East airlines, Emirates makes alcoholic drinks an integral part of its service. But, following Islamic dietary practices, it keeps pork off the menu.

With many people still afraid of flying after the Sept. 11, 2001, attacks, and the likelihood of war rising in the Middle East, this is not a good time for airlines. But the little team of managers—from Britain, New Zealand, Ireland and other places—that runs the airline under the direction of Sheik Ahmed bin Saeed al-Maktoum, its chairman and a member of Dubai's ruling family, is pushing to make Emirates one of the world's major airlines. (It is already one of the most profitable, according to Airline Business magazine in England.)

The airline has sidestepped most of the ill effects of the industry's depression. Its plan to inaugurate service to the United States is in limbo because of tensions between Washington and the Arab world. Though it had an alliance with United Airlines, it faces no losses as a result of United's filing for bankruptcy. "We actually owe them money," said Dermot Mannion, the chief financial officer of Emirates, because Emirates carried more of United's passengers.

Fuel costs have risen for many airlines, but Mr. Mannion said "an aggressive hedging strategy" had kept fuel expenses for Emirates at about the same level as last year.

While other airlines have been cutting back on routes, Emirates, which already flies to 64 cities in Europe, Asia, Africa and the Middle East, continues to expand. It is graduating two classes of a dozen or so flight attendants, including some Americans, every

six weeks, and plans to put a new wide-body, long-haul jet into service nearly every month this year. Last fall, it opened a route to Osaka, its first destination in Japan. In the summer, it plans to begin flying to Moscow and Shanghai.

Plans to inaugurate service to the United States in June with a 13 1/2-hour nonstop flight from Dubai to New York had to be scrapped when delivery of a new-model Airbus for the route was delayed until next fall. Now Emirates executives say they are not sure when the New York flights will begin.

"One has to be reasonable," Mr. Chapman said. "Is the climate right? The timing has to be right."

In the past, Emirates executives have turned trouble to their advantage. During the Persian Gulf war in 1991, when most airlines grounded flights to the region, Emirates kept going. Its jets burned extra fuel skirting the combat zone, but the airline more than made up the difference in extra passengers and cargo. When some airlines refused to serve Pakistan and Afghanistan last year as American forces were hunting down members of Al Qaeda, Emirates again picked up the slack.

"We know our markets very well," Mr. Mannion said. "We won't go anywhere that is unsafe."

Sometimes, the airline seems to be going for shock effect. Two months after the World Trade Center attack, for example, when the entire airline industry was reeling, Emirates announced that it was buying $15 billion worth of long-haul, wide-body jets from **Boeing** and **Airbus.** The purchase, of about 50 jetliners, some at substantial discounts, was one of the biggest in aviation history.

The airline, said Mike Simon, the company's spokesman, wanted to send a message. "People would continue traveling," he said, "and we would continue expanding."

In an era of penny-pinching, no-frills flying, the experience in the Emirates' passenger cabins is stunning. Its female flight attendants wear elegantly cut jackets and skirts in the crisp tones of the desert, and crimson hats with trailing white gossamer scarves. The men wear double-breasted blazers.

On a mid-December flight from London to Dubai, one attendant paused at an economy passenger's armrest. "Good evening, sir," she said. "How are you feeling tonight? Sir, tonight we are offering a choice of chicken in tandoori paste or rack of lamb. Which would you prefer? Certainly, sir. Can I bring you another glass of wine?"

Compare that with the ambience on a Delta Air Lines flight a week later from Rome to New York, as a sullen flight attendant in a navy skirt and light blue blouse shuffled behind a food cart, barking, "Chicken or pasta? Chicken or pasta?"

Emirates Airlines was created to drive the economy of Dubai. As recently as 1971,

(Cont.)

when the British withdrew from the area and brokered the formation of the United Arab Emirates among the often warring families that ruled the city-states, Dubai was a dusty village of traders, pearl divers and fishermen. Huge amounts of oil had been discovered down the coast in Abu Dhabi, and as the wealthiest of the emirates, it became the capital of the new country.

In 1973, Abu Dhabi and three neighboring gulf states bought control of an airline, which became Gulf Air, but it offered limited service to Dubai. The rulers of Dubai, in control of much less oil, were determined to attract tourists and business, so they started Emirates Airlines. Emirates is now running circles around Gulf Air, which has been losing money for several years.

The Dubai government invites airlines from all over the world to fly to the emirate without restriction. As a result, more than 100 airlines now serve it, but Emirates dominates. In 2001, the last year for which full statistics are available, it carried more than half the 13.5 million passengers who moved through the Dubai airport terminal. The government said about 3.6 million people stayed over as tourists in 2001, and about 4 million

in 2002. By 2015, Dubai is hoping for airport traffic of 51 million passengers, including 15 million tourists.

In the first half of 2002, the airline's profit more than doubled over the period a year earlier, rising to $110 million on revenue of $1.17 billion. For all of 2001, profit rose 11 percent over those in 2000, to $127 million on revenue of $1.98 billion.

The airline's executives bristle at competitors' assertions that Emirates is heavily subsidized. But they acknowledge that it does not operate under the same rules as some rivals. Dubai has no income tax, unions or laws that ban age or sex discrimination. Emirates is free to recruit around the world for young, single and attractive flight attendants and to decide at the end of a three-year contract whether to keep them.

The airline is more efficient than many. Chris Tarry, an independent analyst in London, said that the major United States airlines, on average, were flying their planes about 74 percent full but that "they need to sell 90 percent of their seats to break even." Emirates, however, breaks even when its planes are 65 percent full. During the first

half of 2002, Mr. Mannion said, Emirates' planes operated at 78 percent of capacity.

Analysts say Emirates also benefits from a small, nimble group of top managers. "What it takes other airlines six months to do, they do in 24 hours," said Anne-Marie Siffroy-Pytlak, an aviation expert at the French bank Credit Agricole Indosuez, which has financed many of Emirates' aircraft deals.

Some executives in Dubai are skeptical about the airline's profitability, saying its financial reports do not have to be as detailed as those required of publicly traded companies. But Ms. Siffroy-Pytlak, who has analyzed the airline's finances, said, "The cash is there."

The decline of service on many airlines has played to Emirates' strengths. In business class on an Emirates flight from Dubai to Rome, Francois Berthier, a perfume maker from Grasse, France, said he preferred Air France's food, but "on this airline they really treat you like a human being, not just a number."

A BUMMER FOR THE HUMMER

Sales are way down. Can GM make its hulk less of a gas hog and comfier inside?

Last summer, the Hummer H2 was the hottest thing on four wheels. Buyers eager to get the hulking, militaristic sport-utility vehicle waited months to take delivery and even paid dealers as much as $10,000 on top of the $48,000 sticker price. With profits topping $20,000 per H2, General Motors Corp. looked downright clairvoyant for buying the Hummer brand from military contractor AM General Corp. in late 1999. The H2 was a bona fide hit.

Not anymore. Now it looks as if the big beast is starting to lose momentum just as GM is set to start production on its equally pricey pickup version, the H2 SUT, which is due out in June. Plagued by complaints about its abominable fuel economy, cheap interiors, and tiny cabin, the H2 saw sales tumble 33% in January over the previous year, the fifth straight month of declines. In October, GM even cut production. "Selling a Hummer was the easiest job in America," says Los Angeles dealer Howard Drake. "Now it's way harder."

Has Hummer lost its mojo? Not yet, but GM has its work cut out for it. Once on track to sell 40,000 units a year, the auto maker looks headed to move just 30,000 this year. Inventory has risen to 68 days' worth of vehicles—about average for the industry, but almost triple what dealers carried a year ago. GM is counting heavily on the launch of the smaller, $28,000 to $35,000 H3 next year to boost annual sales to 100,000. To get there, the H3—which debuted as a pickup concept in December at the Los Angeles auto show but will appear in '05 as an SUV—will have to trade on more than combat-truck styling and a macho image.

$50 EVERY 320 MILES

Taking the Hummer mainstream won't be easy. Even when sales were hot, customers had complaints. In a J.D. Power & Associates Initial Quality Survey taken last year, the H2 ranked near the bottom. The biggest gripe: While no one bought a Hummer for the sake of its thrifty gas mileage, its 11 to 13 miles per gallon was even worse than expected. Brian Walters, senior director of vehicle research for J.D. Power, said the firm spoke to owners who bought their Hummers in the fall of 2002. By the time the survey was taken in March, 2003, gas prices had spiked to $1.70 per gallon, forcing H2 owners to shell out more than $50 every 320 miles.

STUCK FOR SPACE

The Hummer's lack of creature comforts is another problem. In a Power study of vehicle appeal conducted last fall, the H2 ranked slightly below average among luxury SUVs. Owners dinged it for having poor rear-window visibility, cheap workmanship inside, and scarce passenger and cargo space. The H2 seats five comfortably, but fitting in a sixth person means squeezing into a jump seat next to the spare tire. And that takes up all of the storage space. Competing luxury SUVs such as the Range Rover, Lincoln Navigator, and Cadillac Escalade are nicer inside and usually have more room.

That's why, for GM, making future Hummers more practical is key. Hummer marketing director Michael C. DiGiovanni says the H2's interior will get a little sprucing up when the SUT comes out, and the H3 will be more plush, too. To improve gas mileage, next year's H3 will use a five-cylinder engine

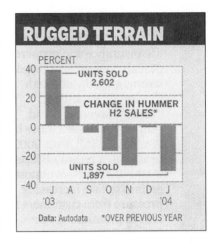

RUGGED TERRAIN

PERCENT

UNITS SOLD 2,602

CHANGE IN HUMMER H2 SALES*

UNITS SOLD 1,897

J A S O N D J
'03   '04

Data: Autodata   *OVER PREVIOUS YEAR

rather than a V8—though that will mean less power. As for the gas-guzzling H2, GM may around 2008 have in place a hybrid-electric system and a technology called displacement-on-demand, which saves gas by shutting down four of the engine's eight cylinders when it's cruising at highway speeds.

With sales falling, a year is a long time to wait for the new H3. In the meantime, Di-Giovanni is hoping the H2 SUT will provide a lift; the pickup version may seem smaller and a little less menacing to buyers turned off by the size of the H2 SUV. Then with the H3's rollout next year, GM is hoping to attract a whole new class of drivers, including those under 40 for whom the brand has special appeal. The trick will be to tame the Hummer without losing its rugged personality.

By David Welch in Detroit

Tough Trio

H2 Worse-than-expected gas mileage and cheap interiors have cooled buyer enthusiasm for the $48,000 Hummer

H2 SUT The $48,000 pickup spinoff of the existing H2, due out in June, could lift sales slightly, though it faces the same complaints

H3 The $28,000-$35,000 truck, an SUV version of this pickup concept, is designed for broader appeal. Due out in '05.

Linux Moves In On The Desktop

As more companies switch, Microsoft is hustling to protect its crown jewels

The doctors at Capital Cardiology Associates, with seven offices in New York and Massachusetts, pride themselves on latching on to the latest medical gizmos. But now they're pioneering in a different tech realm: computers. Employees at the 160-person company have traded in PCs running Microsoft Corp.'s Windows for machines using the up-and-coming Linux operating system. It spent more than $400,000 on a complete tech upgrade, but its president, Dr. Augustin DeLago, believes the investment will pay off handsomely over time in better security for patients' records and easier management of technology. "We're a small company, but I think we're out ahead on something," says Dr. DeLago.

Indeed, this could be the start of something big. After a long gestation period—and against all odds—Linux is finally gaining a toehold in Microsoft's backyard, office desktop computing. Market researcher IDC expects to announce within weeks that Linux' PC market share in 2003 hit 3.2%, overtaking Apple Computer Inc.'s Macintosh software. And the researcher expects Linux to capture 6% of this market by 2007. That's still tiny compared with Microsoft's 94% share. But it's clear now that Linux is becoming a viable alternative to Windows on desktop and laptop PCs for companies willing to put up with the trouble of switching.

Linux has made major strides in the past few months. In November, China declared it the operating system of choice. Starting on Jan. 1, the Israeli government plans gradually to replace desktop Windows with Linux. IBM CEO Samuel J. Palmisano late last year challenged his 319,000-employee company to move entirely to Linux PCs. And now, analysts say, dozens of major corporations in the U.S., Europe, and Japan are sizing up Linux. In a survey of corporate buyers by Merrill Lynch & Co., 43% said they would consider replacing Windows desktops with Linux. "I had expected governments to be interested, but now it's on the radar of corporate chief information officers," says analyst Steven Milunovich of Merrill Lynch.

FOREIGN FANS

Why the excitement now? Several factors are driving the growth. Linux, an open-source software package, has been steadily getting better and easier to use. It can be bought for moderate prices—or downloaded from the Net for free. Sun Microsystems Inc. in December introduced the Java Desktop System, which includes Linux, its StarOf-fice applications, a browser, and e-mail. The package sells for less than $100, while comparable Microsoft software for corporations costs more than $600. And corporations like to have alternatives to Microsoft software. What's more, unlike Windows, Linux has not been a big target of virus writers.

Even though Linux PCs are generating a lot of interest, don't expect them to bust Microsoft's monopoly anytime soon. That's because Windows is installed on 400 million PCs worldwide. Linux may have gained a 24% chunk of the market for server operating systems, but that's sold to techies. For Linux to chomp into Microsoft's PC lead, companies will have to make complicated transitions that might wipe out the initial cost advantages—switching not just operating systems but the applications that run on them. Tony Scott, chief technology officer for General Motors Corp.'s tech group, says GM will evaluate Linux, but "I'd be suspicious that it would be an easy swap in a large organization."

Clearly on edge, Microsoft is working overtime to protect its crown jewels. It has financed studies by market researchers that warn against switching to Linux, saying it could cost more over the long run. In high-profile cases, the software giant goes to great lengths to avoid losing out. When the city of Munich considered switching 14,000 PCs to Linux last year, Microsoft slashed its price by a third and dispatched CEO Steven A. Ballmer to woo the Bavarians. Munich went with Linux, but the city fathers may rue that day. *BusinessWeek* has learned that the project is behind schedule, bolstering Microsoft's message that Linux still isn't ready for prime time. "I haven't seen any of our customers use Linux in a mainstream way," says Martin Taylor, Microsoft's general manager for platform strategy.

Desktop Linux hasn't had any appreciable effect on Microsoft's finances yet, but it could do damage if Linux manages to grab a 10% share of the market, say analysts. IDC estimates that desktop Windows' share will shrink slightly, to 92% in 2007 as Linux' share doubles. Under that scenario, Microsoft would not only sell fewer copies of Windows than it might have otherwise, but it might feel pressure to lower prices, too, says IDC analyst Al Gillen.

If desktop Linux starts to hit Microsoft where it hurts, it will happen not so much among typical office employees but among specialized workers. These include stock traders, bank tellers, engineers, customer-service reps, and warehouse employees. They rely on just a few applications and need PCs that are simple to use and rarely crash—which Linux can handle. Cole National Corp. uses Linux desktops in 1,700 Pearle Vision and other optical stores. And Delta Air Lines Inc. says it's considering using Linux on its airport desktop terminals.

This market is potentially huge. Microsoft has estimated that while the number of typical knowledge workers in the U.S. is about 40 million, the broader market for desktop computing is potentially 117 million. So it's no wonder this is where Linux suppliers such as IBM, Hewlett-Packard, Sun, and Novell

Linux Why Now?

Several factors are making the Linux operating system a stronger contender in the office

THE PRICE IS RIGHT Organizations can buy Linux and Sun Microsystems' StarSuite of word-processing, spreadsheet, and other programs for less than $100—or even download free versions. Comparable Microsoft software for corporations costs more than $600.

TECHNOLOGY IS IMPROVING While Linux and the desktop applications designed to run on it don't have as many features as Microsoft's products, they offer the capabilities most people need.

THE COMPUTER INDUSTRY IS BEHIND IT Computer makers, including Hewlett-Packard and IBM, have gotten behind Linux on the desktop. Sun and software maker Novell have made Linux the lynchpin of their desktop strategies.

(Cont.)

are concentrating their efforts. While IBM previously focused on Linux server software, late last year its consulting unit started offering an array of Linux desktop services aimed at specialized workers.

Still, large corporations are reluctant to discuss their Linux plans publicly. That's partly because SCO Group, Inc., a tiny company in Linden, Utah, claims Linux violates its copyrights and has threatened to sue users. They also don't want to commit to something that they aren't completely sure of yet. One major European bank that requested it not be named says it's considering switching tens of thousands of its desktop computers to Linux. "We want to be close

Linux' spread could put pressure on Microsoft to lower its prices

to the front, but we don't want to be the pioneers with the arrows in our back," says one of the bank's CIOs.

In the short term, the best prospects for Linux on PCs are in governments and developing countries. Western governments are looking for ways to trim their budgets. At the same time, a number of governments, including Brazil and China, have adopted policies favoring the use of open-source technologies to help foster their own domestic software industries.

Think of this as the third lap of a 100-lap race. Desktop Linux could still spend a lot of time in the pits for repairs and tune-ups and continue to watch Microsoft zoom past. But if it gets up to speed, Microsoft better watch its behind.

By Steve Hamm in New York, with Spencer Ante in New York and David Fairlamb in Frankfurt

Puma Does Fancy Footwork to Stay Out of the Mainstream

BY SUSANNA RAY AND
MATTHEW KARNITSCHNIG

PUMA AG'S LOW-CUT sneakers and bowling-bag purses flew out the door for a couple years at "bruce," an upscale Vancouver fashion boutique. Then last summer, the shop's owner, Campbell McDougall, sensed that Puma and its retro athletic apparel was losing a little of its cachet. "I think it's cooling off. The brand has a reputation on the street as being mainstream," Mr. McDougall says. "One can only sit on re-issuing old styles for so long."

Stopping the slide from cutting edge to middle of the road is a challenge every trendy brand must face. It was only a couple of years ago that Puma's low-rise suede sneakers helped the company spring out of the shadow of athletic wear giants **Nike** Inc. and **Adidas-Salomon** AG, and its leaping-cat logo could be found on the feet of fashion plates like Madonna and Leonardo DiCaprio. Now, the popular brand is widely available and commonly spotted on folks far less glamorous.

And so Puma has had to grapple with keeping its cool while growing popular in the mass market. If the brand becomes too mainstream, it risks alienating the style-setters that fueled its comeback. Yet, if its sales don't grow, investors will flee.

It is up to Jochen Zeitz, Puma's 40-year-old chief executive, who guided the company back from the brink of collapse a decade ago, to manage the paradox. He wants Puma to stay hip by forging links with other hot icons.

Right now, Puma is rubbing elbows with the coolest name in cars—the BMW Mini. As part of a co-marketing agreement with **Bayerische Motoren Werke** AG, Puma has designed a black, two-piece driving shoe called the "Mini Motion 2 part shoe," which it is marketing as an accessory to the car. Puma says the shoe incorporates features of Formula 1 racing shoes. It consists of a flexible inner slipper, for comfort on long trips at the wheel or while puttering around the house, and a sturdier outer shoe, with ankle support and traction, to be worn outdoors and in city driving (to ease the strain of frequent gear-shifting).

Following a tried-and-true formula for maintaining an aura of exclusivity, Puma plans to limit production of the driving shoes to only about 2,000 pairs. They are expected

to sell for about $120 at Puma shops and Mini dealerships.

Puma also is limiting the availability of other shoes destined for stores. A new line created by Dutch designer Alexander van Slobbe (and there's nothing slobby about them) includes boots inspired by 1950s boxing shoes and black shoes stitched to look like old-time hockey skates. For the spring, Puma plans two apparel lines designed by the hipster label Vexed Generation Clothing of London, including a line of unisex garments inspired by martial-arts robes and a line with protective padding, for bike and scooter riders.

And later this year, Puma says, it will unveil a line of "modern, minimalist" shoes designed by French architect Philippe Starck. As it happens, Mr. Starck's credits straddle the divide between cool and mass market, encompassing avant-garde interiors for New York's Paramount and Royalton hotels and also a line of housewares for Target Corp. stores. "The fact that he's done so many different projects in different worlds is what made him interesting to us," says Puma spokeswoman Erin Cowhig.

Mr. Zeitz points to **Apple Computer** Inc. and **Porsche** AG as examples of brands that have maintained reputations for being cutting-edge while growing in mainstream popularity, Porsche with its Cayenne off-road vehicle and Apple with its iPod and iBook. "Puma is known for going its own way," Mr. Zeitz says. "It's a brand for individualists."

Puma's concentration on fashion contrasts with Nike and Adidas, which emphasize performance of their shoes and apparel and pay a stable of superstar athletes to wear them. Even when Puma does get into major sports, it still emphasizes style. For the national soccer team of Cameroon, which is known for its on-field flair, Puma recently created a striking one-piece uniform, with red shorts attached to a skin-tight green top. After the uniform's debut a month ago at the African Nations Cup tournament, soccer's ruling authority banned the suit because it violates the rule stating that uniforms must be in two pieces.

Puma says it was "shocked" by the ban, because it had received preliminary approval for the design from the soccer body. Of course, Puma also welcomes the free publicity: The

Puma's **'Mini Motion'** *driving shoe has an inner slipper for long trips and a sturdier outer shoe*

uproar, after all, bolsters the brand's rebellious image, especially since the team defied the ban and wore the bodysuits for the duration of the tournament.

Mr. Zeitz's reliance on design is a bet against expectations in the athletic-shoe industry: The style pendulum is expected to swing from fashion back to function with the approach of soccer's World Cup and the 2004 Olympics in Athens. Mr. Zeitz, however, says 80% of the athletic shoes bought in the U.S. are for casual wear, not sports. "We will see more technical looks, but that doesn't mean it's shifting away from fashion," Mr. Zeitz says.

The focus on looks, at least for now, is still paying off. According to preliminary figures reported last month, Puma rang up a 40% leap in 2003 sales to 1.3 billion euros, or $1.65 billion. Net profit more than doubled to $226.7 million. The order backlog—an important indicator of demand—was a record $914.4 million. Final figures for the year will be released today.

Still, with management predicting sales could hit the $2.5 billion mark by 2006, it may just be a matter of time before Puma becomes so popular as to be passe. That would be bad news for Jana Cipa, a 15-year-old who bought a Puma belt and her fourth pair of Puma sneakers on a recent visit to the brand's spartan Frankfurt store. "Puma is definitely the most popular brand," she says and offers her own prediction: "They're going to stay trendy for another decade."

Tough Shift

Lesson in India: Not Every Job Translates Overseas

ValiCert Learned Key Roles Must Remain in U.S. For Outsourcing to Work

---

E-Mails Across 14 Time Zones

By Scott Thurm

When sales of their security software slowed in 2001, executives at ValiCert Inc. began laying off engineers in Silicon Valley to hire replacements in India for $7,000 a year.

ValiCert expected to save millions annually while cranking out new software for banks, insurers and government agencies. Senior Vice President David Jevans recalls optimistic predictions that the company would "cut the budget by half here and hire twice as many people there." Colleagues would swap work across the globe every 12 hours, helping ValiCert "put more people on it and get it done sooner," he says.

The reality was different. The Indian engineers, who knew little about ValiCert's software or how it was used, omitted features Americans considered intuitive. U.S. programmers, accustomed to quick chats over cubicle walls, spent months writing detailed instructions for overseas assignments, delaying new products. Fear and distrust thrived as ValiCert's finances deteriorated, and co-workers, 14 times zones apart, traded curt e-mails. In the fall of 2002, executives brought back to the U.S. a key project that had been assigned to India, irritating some Indian employees.

"At times, we were thinking, 'What have we done here?'" recalls John Vigouroux, who joined ValiCert in July 2002 and became chief executive three months later.

Shifting work to India eventually did help cut ValiCert's engineering costs by two-thirds, keeping the company and its major products alive—and saving 65 positions which remained in the U.S. But not before ValiCert experienced a harrowing period of instability and doubt, and only after its ex-ecutives significantly refined the company's global division of labor.

The successful formula that emerged was to assign the India team bigger projects, rather than tasks requiring continual inter-action with U.S. counterparts. The crucial jobs of crafting new products and features stayed in Silicon Valley. In the end, exporting some jobs ultimately led to adding a small but important number of new, higher-level positions in the U.S.

In February 2003, ValiCert agreed to be acquired by Tumbleweed Communications Corp., a maker of antispam software with its own offshore operation in Bulgaria. Today, the combined Tumbleweed is growing, and again hiring software architects in Silicon Valley with six-figure salaries, as well as engineers overseas. Without India, Mr. Vigouroux says, "I don't know if we'd be around today."

ValiCert's experience offers important in-sights into the debate over the movement of service jobs to lower-cost countries, such as India. Such shifts can save companies money and hurt U.S. workers. But the process is difficult, and the savings typically aren't as great as a simple wage comparison sug-gests. Some jobs cannot easily or profitably be exported, and trying to do so can risk a customer backlash: In recent months, Dell Inc. and Lehman Brothers Holdings Inc., for example, moved several dozen call-center and help-desk jobs back to the U.S., after employee and customer complaints.

Founded in 1996, ValiCert specializes in software to securely exchange information over the Internet. Banks use ValiCert's software to safeguard electronic funds transfers, health insurers to protect patient medical records. Al-though still unprofitable, ValiCert conducted an initial public offering in July 2000, in the dying embers of the dot-com boom. In two months, the stock doubled to $25.25.

In 2001, however, sales growth slowed, as corporate customers reduced technol-ogy purchases. ValiCert had projected that it would break even with quarterly revenue of $18 million, according to Srinivasan "Chini" Krishnan, founder and then-chairman. Quar-terly expenses had grown to $14 million, but revenue was stalled at less than half that figure. Executives began considering shift-ing work to India. The "motivation was pure survival," says Mr. Krishnan, who left the company after the Tumbleweed merger.

India was a natural choice because of its large pool of software engineers. Moreover, both Mr. Krishnan and ValiCert's then-head of engineering grew up in India and were familiar with large tech-outsourcing firms.

Some, including Mr. Jevans, harbored doubts. The Apple Computer Inc. veteran says he preferred "small teams of awesome people" working closely together. Nonethe-less, that summer, ValiCert hired Infosys Technologies Ltd., an Indian specialist in contract software-programming, to supply about 15 people in India to review software for bugs, and to update two older products.

With no manager in India, ValiCert em-ployees in the U.S. managed the Infosys workers directly, often late at night or early in the morning because of the time differ-ence. ValiCert also frequently changed the tasks assigned to Infosys, prompting Info-sys to shuffle the employees and frustrating ValiCert's efforts to build a team there.

Within a few months, ValiCert abandoned Infosys and created its own Indian subsid-iary, with as many as 60 employees. Most employees would be paid less than $10,000 a year. Even after accounting for benefits, office operating costs and communications links back to the U.S., ValiCert estimated the annual cost of an Indian worker at roughly $30,000. That's about half what ValiCert was paying Infosys per worker, and less than one-sixth of the $200,000 comparable an-nual cost in Silicon Valley.

To run the new office in India, ValiCert hired Sridhar Vutukuri, an outspoken 38-year-old engineer who had headed a similar opera-tion for another Silicon Valley start-up. He set up shop in January 2002 in a ground-floor office in bustling Bangalore, the tech hub of southern India. The office looked much like ValiCert's California home, except for the smaller cubicles and Indian designs on the partitions. There were no savings on the rent. At $1 a square foot, it matched what ValiCert paid for its Mountain View, Calif., home of-fices, amid a Silicon Valley office glut.

Misunderstandings started right away. U.S. executives wanted programmers with eight to 10 years of experience, typical of ValiCert's U.S. employees. But such "career programmers" are rare in India, where the average age of engineers is 26. Most seek management jobs after four or five years. Expertise in security technology, key to Vali-Cert's products, was even rarer.

By contrast, Mr. Vutukuri quickly assem-bled a group to test ValiCert's software for bugs, tapping a large pool of Indian engineers that had long performed this mundane work.

But the Indian manager heading that group ran into resistance. It was ValiCert's first use of code-checkers who didn't report to the same managers who wrote the pro-grams. Those U.S. managers fumed when the team in India recommended in June 2002 delaying a new product's release because it had too many bugs.

By midsummer, when Mr. Vutukuri had enough programmers for ValiCert to begin sending bigger assignments to India, U.S. managers quickly overwhelmed the India team by sending a half-dozen projects at once.

Accustomed to working closely with veter-an engineers familiar with ValiCert's products, the U.S. managers offered only vague outlines for each assignment. The less-experienced

Indian engineers didn't include elements in the programs that were considered standard among U.S. customers. U.S. programmers rewrote the software, delaying its release by months.

In India, engineers grew frustrated with long silences, punctuated by rejection. Suresh Marur, the head of one programming team, worked on five projects during 2002. All were either cancelled or delayed. Programmers who had worked around the clock for days on one project quit for new jobs in Bangalore's vibrant market. Of nine people on Mr. Marur's team in mid-2002, only three still work for ValiCert. "The first time people understand," he says. "The second time people understand. The third time it gets to be more of a problem."

In the U.S., executives lurched from crisis to crisis, as ValiCert's revenue dipped further. Each quarter brought more layoffs. By year end, the California office, which once employed 75 engineers, was reduced to 17; the India office, meanwhile, swelled to 45. Engineers "felt the sword of Damocles was swinging above their cube," recalls John Thielens, a product manager.

Executives knew they could save more money by exporting more jobs. But they were developing a keener sense of how critical it was to keep core managers in the U.S. who knew ValiCert, its products, and how they were used by customers. "Even if you could find someone" with the right skills in India, says Mr. Krishnan, the ValiCert founder, "it wouldn't make business sense to move the job."

Frustrations came to a head in September 2002, when a prospective customer discovered problems with the log-on feature of a ValiCert program. The anticipated purchase was delayed, causing ValiCert to miss third-quarter financial targets. The India team had recently modified the program, and the glitch prompted U.S. managers to question ValiCert's entire offshore strategy.

Relations had long been strained between the U.S. and Indian product teams. John Hines, the Netscape Communications Corp. veteran who headed the tight-knit U.S. product team, thrives on quick responses to customer requests. As his team shrank to six engineers from 20, Mr. Hines was assigned three engineers in India. But he viewed the Indians' inexperience, and the communication delays, as more a hindrance than a help. "Things we could do in two days would take a week," he says.

Mr. Vigouroux, who became CEO in October 2002, admits to a touch of "panic" at this point. ValiCert's cash was running low. "We didn't have a lot of time," he says. He conferred with Mr. Hines, who said he wanted to be rid of India, even if it meant a smaller team. Mr. Vigouroux agreed to rehire one engineer in California. When he learned of the decision, Mr. Vutukuri says he felt as if he had failed.

By contrast, Matt Lourie, who heads ValiCert's other big programming group, welcomed additional help in India. He was struggling to keep pace with customer demands for new features on his product and new versions for different types of computers.

At the same time, ValiCert executives were streamlining operations and changing how they divided work between California and India. They gave the India team entire projects—such as creating a PC version of a program initially built for bigger workstations—rather than small pieces of larger projects. U.S. managers began writing more detailed specifications for each assignment to India.

ValiCert also killed its three smallest-selling products to focus resources on the remaining two. To improve morale in the U.S., Mr. Vigouroux crowded the remaining employees into one corner of the half-vacant office and installed a ship's bell that he rang each time ValiCert recorded $10,000 in revenue. He made sure the India employees received company-wide e-mails, and conducted multiple sessions of monthly employee meetings so the India group could listen at a convenient hour. Engineering-team leaders began conferring twice a week by telephone, shifting the time of the calls every six months so that it's early morning in one office and early evening in the other.

Toward the end of 2002, Mr. Vigouroux began to ring the bell daily, as customers such as Washington Mutual Inc. and MasterCard International Inc. purchased ValiCert's software.

By early the next year, ValiCert executives believed the company had stabilized. Revenue increased to $3 million in the fourth quarter of 2002, up 27% from the previous quarter. Expenses declined, and the company neared profitability. Investors detected a pulse, and the stock rose to 46 cents on the Nasdaq Stock Market at the end of January, from a low of 20 cents in August 2002.

But with just $3 million in cash, ValiCert remained precarious. Mr. Vigouroux started meeting with potential new investors and began talks with Tumbleweed CEO Jeffrey C. Smith.

Tumbleweed also had been through significant layoffs and retrenchment, and in February 2003, the companies agreed to merge. The combined Redwood City, Calif., company's 150 engineers today are almost evenly divided among California, the Tumbleweed operation in Bulgaria, and the India office started by ValiCert. In Bulgaria, engineers write and test software, and scan millions of e-mails daily for traces of spam. In India, engineers test software, fix bugs and create new versions of one product. Last September, Tumbleweed released its first product developed entirely in India, a program that lets two computers communicate automatically and securely. Mr. Marur's team had worked on it for over 18 months.

Core development for new products remains in California, where engineers are closer to marketing teams and Tumbleweed's customers. Since July, Mr. Lourie's U.S. team has grown to nine engineers, from six.

Tumbleweed's fourth-quarter revenue grew 69% from a year earlier, as its net loss shrank to $700,000, and cash increased by $2.4 million. Shares have risen five-fold in the past year.

Brent Haines, 36, is a new hire. He joined in October as a $120,000-a-year software architect, charged largely with coordinating the work of the U.S. and India teams. That often means exchanging e-mail from home with engineers in India between 11 p.m. and 3 a.m. California time, as Mr. Haines reviews programming code and suggests changes. Such collaboration requires extensive planning, he says, "something very unnatural to people in software."

"Nine months ago, people would have said [moving offshore] was the biggest . . . disaster," says Mr. Thielens, the product manager. "Now we're starting to understand how we can benefit."

88

A Radio Chip in Every Consumer Product

By CLAUDIA H. DEUTSCH AND BARNABY J. FEDER

Here's a tip to thieves: If you are bent on stealing packages of **Gillette** Mach3 razor blades, go someplace other than Tesco's Newmarket Road store in Cambridge, England. There, a "smart shelf" continuously queries tiny radio chips embedded in the packages it holds, and senses the silence when one is removed. The system may soon be programmed to alert security when several are taken at once, Greg Sage, a Tesco spokesman, said.

And, yes, **Procter & Gamble** will notice if a case of Pantene shampoo does not make it to the Wal-Mart Supercenter in Broken Arrow, Okla. Its truck is equipped to monitor signals continuously from chips hidden in each case. If any case stops sending its "Hi, I'm still here" signal, a monitor in the "smart truck" will record exactly when and where.

Such technology, known as radio-frequency identification—the same techniques that enable an electronic sensor to record data from an E-ZPass tag or an office door to open for people with chip-equipped cards in their pockets—could one day stymie pilferers. But it is also capable of doing much more for commerce. Beyond Gillette and Procter & Gamble, companies as diverse as **International Paper** and **Canon USA** are teaming up with retailers and customers to apply R.F.I.D., as it is known, to tracking products from the time they leave an assembly line to the time they leave the store.

The companies are tagging clothes, drugs, auto parts, copy machines and even mail with chips laden with information about content, origin and destination. They are also equipping shelves, doors and walls with sensors that can record that data when the products are near. "We want to track all of our merchandise, and that includes items that people are unlikely to steal," William C. Wertz, a spokesman for **Wal-Mart Stores,** said.

Chip manufacturers are busily spreading that gospel. "That need to have the right product on the right shelf in the right store at the right time—ultimately, that's what will drive our business," said Karsten Ottenberg, a senior vice president at Philips Semiconductor, the leading maker of radio frequency chips and a unit of **Royal Philips Electronics.**

Early tests are encouraging. For three months in 2001, Gap tested radio frequency tags on denim clothes at a store in Atlanta.

Sales jumped because the tags prevented the store from running out of popular items, and the tags made it quicker to find any items in stock.

Typically, 15 percent of shoppers leave clothing stores without getting what they want; during the test, fewer than 1 percent of Gap shoppers left empty-handed.

Radio frequency identification still has too many kinks, however, to be an immediate panacea for retailers. Cordless phones, two-way radios, local wireless networks and other communications devices that are widely deployed in factories, warehouses and stores can interfere with the signals. And, although radio tag readers can, under ideal conditions, identify well over 100 tagged items every second from quite a distance, radio waves have a hard time

> ### Tiny chips attached to packages of razor blades can send messages to store managers, alerting them when shelves are depleted.

penetrating metals and liquids—something that Procter & Gamble is addressing with the Pantene test.

And costs are still prohibitive. The electronic tags cost at least 30 cents apiece; most experts think anything above 5 cents is too expensive to be widely used for individual packaged goods. Prices would have to fall to less than a penny for virtually everything in stores to be tagged. Sensors, which can be either hand-held or built into walls, can cost $1,000 each.

But costs are coming down fast. **Alien Technology,** for one, says that it can now sell radio frequency identification tags profitably at 5 cents each for orders of a billion tags or more. Just last month, Gillette said it would buy up to 500 million tags over the next few years from Alien.

But Alien's manufacturing capacity is currently just a small fraction of what it would need to fill orders over a billion quickly. And experts warn that while the silicon chips continue to shrink in size and fall in price, making the attached antennas small enough and cheap enough is much harder.

Moreover, most retailers say they are reluctant to invest in the technology until product tags are universally readable, as bar codes are today. That means that every retailer, manufacturer and carrier must agree to standards, and use tags and sensors that speak the same language.

"It's one thing to say something is a great technology, but quite another to say that you're ready to scrap existing systems to accommodate it," said Daniel Butler, vice president for retail operations at the National Retail Federation, a trade association based in Washington.

Consumer privacy is also an issue. It would be easy to combine credit card data with information from the retail chips to know who bought what, and when—and, conceivably, track the product even after it left the store.

"I don't think the average consumer understands the threat to personal privacy that these kinds of technologies can present," said Alan N. Sutin, a partner specializing in information technology at the law firm of Greenberg Traurig.

William H. Steele, a consumer products analyst with Bank of America, doubts companies will "succumb to the temptation to keep tracking products in the consumers' hands," but he, too, stops short of calling the issue specious. "There should be a certain level of skepticism on the part of the U.S. consumer," he said.

Still, companies are increasingly viewing the identification technology as a potential savior. In 1999, Gillette, Procter & Gamble and the Uniform Code Council, which administers bar code standardization, founded the Auto-ID Center at the Massachusetts Institute of Technology to be a standards and research clearinghouse. The center has satellite labs at Cambridge University in England, and in Japan and Australia.

The technological limitations of bar codes makes the growing interest in R.F.I.D. easy to understand. Kevin Ashton, a P. & G. executive who directs the Auto-ID Center, estimates that on average 10 percent of stores are out of items the managers think are in stock—and as many as 40 percent do not realize they are out of a color or size.

The monetary impact of losing track of goods is huge. According to a survey by the University of Florida, shrinkage—the common retailing term for goods that disappear either through theft, misplacement, fraud or just bad record keeping—cost retailers a record $31.3 billion last year. Only a third was a result of shoplifting. Nearly half was employee theft, about 5 percent was vendor theft and 15 percent was paperwork errors.

Suppliers have as much at stake as retailers. Colin Peacock, the leader of a Gillette task force to study shelf availability, said that 73 percent of customers left a store if Mach3 blades were out of stock; 27 percent bought a competitor's blades. He said Mach3 sales had gone up 288 percent at the Cambridge Tesco store that had the smart shelf.

Stores often resort to putting frequently pilfered items behind glass or behind counters. That means customers must wait for a clerk to get the products. The practice drives away impatient shoppers and all but eliminates impulse buys.

Mr. Peacock suspects that sales are halved when products are hidden away. "The impact of such defensive merchandising can be worse than the problems it solves," he said.

Once it is perfected, radio frequency technology may solve not just those problems, but some that are unrelated to stocking issues. Because the tags, unlike bar codes, are programmable chips, a store like Wal-Mart that frequently changes prices can attach the price to the item and know exactly what a consumer paid if the item is returned—even if the customer lost the receipt.

And then there are product recalls to consider. Radio frequency technology could

---

Radio-frequency identification chips can track an item from the time it is assembled to the time it is sold. They now cost about 30 cents each, but prices are expected to fall sharply.

---

pinpoint a tainted batch, and—if customers paid with credit cards or used store discount cards—identify customers who purchased such items.

"It would be wonderful to be able to spot just those items that came from a plant that has a flaw, or those perishable items that took too long to arrive and thus might spoil sooner," Mr. Wertz of Wal-Mart said.

Canon USA wants to deploy radio frequency identification to track machines at locations that use dozens of printers and copiers. "It would help us schedule preventive maintenance, and alert us to get equipment back

when the lease expires," said James J. Gordon Jr., Canon's vice president for logistics.

Even the United States Postal Service has gotten into the act. Last month, it promoted Charles E. Bravo, until then its chief technology officer, to the new job of senior vice president for intelligent mail and address quality, and charged him with studying tracking technologies.

"We'd love to be able to tell a company that a customer's check is truly in the mail, or that its direct mail flier was just delivered to a customer's door," Mr. Bravo said.

And imagine if the company can also be sure that the item the flier is advertising will be available.

"Increasing productivity, lowering inventories, decreasing theft, all are important," said Paul J. Rieger, Procter & Gamble's associate director of supply chain innovation. "But ending out-of-stock situations, that is still our biggest goal."

89

The Annoying New Face of Customer Service

Virtual Phone Reps Replace The Old Touch-Tone Menus; Making Claire Less Irritating

By Jane Spencer

Meet the new face of customer service: perky, unflappable—and entirely virtual.

From Amtrak to Sprint PCS, a growing number of companies are ditching their automated service hotlines and replacing them with "virtual agents" that answer customer calls and emails. The phone characters are essentially talking computer programs with human voices—and, in some cases, names and personalities—that ask callers to speak rather than push buttons.

Using speech-recognition technology, the systems try to mimic the experience of talking with an enthusiastic human rep. Yahoo Inc.'s Jenni, who reads e-mails to customers through Yahoo by Phone, says, "Got it!" after nearly everything and quips, "Wow, you're popular!" to callers with crowded in-boxes. Julie, who books Amtrak tickets and offers schedule information, is designed to sound increasingly stressed out each time she misunderstands a customer's speech command.

But many callers aren't entertained by the anthropomorphizing gestures. "It's more annoying to talk to a computer pretending to be a person than just to talk to a computer," says Matthew Vogel, a Boston research analyst. One problem: The characters sometimes don't hear callers correctly. Since the software programs behind the characters match what callers say against a dictionary of possible responses, background noise or a spotty cellphone connection can throw off the entire conversation.

The virtual agents represent the latest push by companies to make customer service more efficient. For more than a decade, the touch-tone menu has ruled the call-center landscape. But the new technology allows companies to automate more-complex transactions. And the speech-recognition calls are 40% faster on average than touch-tone calls, according to Kelsey Group, because customers don't have to listen to lists of menu options. The latest systems understand hundreds of accents and recognize multiple synonyms for common words. (Simon at United Airlines, for example, responds to "mm-hmm" and "yeah, baby" as variations on yes.) And, while speech systems are more expensive than touch-tone automation, they still offer cheap labor. On average, a customer-service call handled by a speech system costs about $2.50, compared with $5 for a call taken by a human, says Gartner Research.

As the technology improves, companies from Aetna to Merrill Lynch are scrambling to replace their touch-tone menus. Total spending on speech-recognition technology in the U.S. topped $680 million in 2002, up 60% from the previous year, according to Kelsey Group.

But the virtual reps aren't popular with some customers, and already, some companies are starting to tweak their agents to make them less annoying. Sprint PCS's Claire has infuriated customers by sounding overly enthusiastic when they call with frustrations like billing or service disruptions. "She sounds completely and utterly thrilled to hear that I have a problem with Sprint," says Carrie Bancroft of New York City. In response to customer complaints, Sprint PCS President Len Lauer ordered phone rep Claire to undergo a personality upgrade, which included making it easier to reach human help through the system. In recent weeks, Claire has stopped introducing herself at the beginning of each conversation. "We're de-emphasizing her character," says a spokesman for Sprint PCS, the mobile unit of Sprint Corp.

Katie, the flirty "virtual skin-care assistant" on the Dove soap Web site, had to be reprogrammed after she was deemed "too aggressive" in her efforts to collect visitors' e-mail addresses, according to NativeMinds, the San Francisco company that built the system. Now, Katie requests an e-mail only if you ask her for free products or coupons.

Katie has plenty of company online. Customer-service "Verbots" or V-reps" now populate Web sites at companies including AT&T Corp., Ford Motor Co. and Coca-Cola Co. These tiny talking heads—usually represented by photos or digital cartoons—lurk in the corner of the Web sites, baiting site visitors with "ask me a question!" The faces front for computer programs that can scan the text of a typed question and generate a response from a dictionary of frequently asked questions. The resulting "chat" sessions mimic an

How to Talk to Your Verbot

The Web's virtual reps remain a work in progress. When we put them to the test, we found that we could stump each one with a seemingly easy question.

CHARACTER/COMPANY	WHAT WE ASKED	THEY SAID	STUMPED BY
Allie AT&T	Where is my remote control?	With your socks.	Can you explain the tax section of my bill.
Mama Ragu	Can you find me a man?	I think always the best place to meet a man is in the pasta section of the grocery store.	Do you use pesticides on your tomatoes?
Hank Coke	Do you ever drink Pepsi?	Never.	Where can I buy Diet Vanilla Coke?
Bill the Brewmaster Miller	Do you like your job?	Imagine working for a company where it's always MillerTime!	Is drinking and driving safe?
Kate Ford	Where do you live?	I live on a server at Ford Headquarters.	My Taurus is making a funny noise.
Katie Dove	Is Dove soap safe to eat?	Yes, Dove products do meet all safety and quality standards.	Is Dove good for dry skin?
Anne IAMS Pet Food	Would you like to go out sometime?	You might want to join a social club and meet some fellow humans.	My dog bites kids.

(Cont.)

instant message exchange.

Online V-Reps are often more cute than helpful. Some seem more knowledgeable about their personal histories than the company they work for. Hank, the V-rep at Coke.com, can answer questions about his sexual orientation but can't tell you where to buy New Vanilla Coke. But since the technology is new, companies are constantly adding new information to the character's answer dictionaries. Ford, for example, employs a small staff devoted to maintaining the online V-rep, Kate. Currently, she can answer at least 8,000 questions.

Some companies create extensive biographies for the characters that include everything from SAT scores to hobbies. Yahoo's Jenni is a free-lance artist who once played guitar in an all-girl rock band. Melinda, at the Internet provider Tiscali, is a British advertising assistant with a glittering Notting Hill social life.

Virtual customer-service agents are growing common. But some companies have already had to tweak their virtual reps to make them more customer-friendly.

Virtual reps—and the companies creating them—face a formidable challenge: Not all customers are seeking friendship when they call a customer-service line. "I don't want a relationship with a character," declares Sam Berkow, an acoustic designer in Manhattan. "I want an efficient system for buying a train ticket."

Jim DiCamillo, an Amtrak passenger, agrees. When Amtrak's Julie starts booking train tickets, unexpected itineraries some-times begin to unfold. "I say Philadelphia, Pennsylvania, she gives me Billings, Montana!" he says. "She almost convinced me to go there."

Despite the troubles, some customers seem to enjoy their interactions with some of the characters. Lourdes Ayala, a lawyer from Silver Springs, Md., frequently books train tickets through Julie and considers her a friend. "I know what she's going to say before she says it," says Ms. Ayala. "Julie asks all the right questions. She knows me better than my boyfriend."

Ethical Marketing in a Consumer-Oriented World: Appraisal and Challengers

90

Inside the Home of the Future

Houses that make your coffee, lock your doors and even measure your health are closer than you think

BY KELLY GREENE

As you pour the detergent into your last load of laundry, you realize the bottle is almost empty. But instead of making a mental note to add it to your grocery list, or running to the kitchen to scribble it down, you simply say out loud, "Remember: Buy laundry detergent." The word "remember" is picked up by a microphone in the wall and triggers a computer to transcribe your words to your to-do list.

It might sound like a sci-fi vision of the future. But it's actually a project called Audio Notes, currently in the works at the Georgia Institute of Technology's 5,000-square-foot Aware Home, a combination house and laboratory in Atlanta where scientists are dreaming up futuristic housing technology.

"I love that shopping list," says Eileen Lange, a 68-year-old retiree from Lithonia, Ga., who toured the house and tried out some of its projects last year.

Researchers and commercial labs around the country are building experimental homes to test technology that could make domestic life easier and extend the independence of older homeowners. Such efforts go beyond so-called universal design, a trend toward building houses with wider doorways, grab bars and adjustable kitchen cabinets that took off in the early 1990s.

"These are lifestyle services empowered by a new generation of technology," says Joseph Coughlin, director of the Massachusetts Institute of Technology's AgeLab in Cambridge.

In many cases, the mechanics for the gizmos already exist—mainly wireless sensors, cellphones, broadband access and home computers. What's been missing, and what researchers now are trying to develop, are ways to harness the hardware to run your entire house with little effort or technological savvy—letting you turn up the heat remotely, anticipating when you want the lights on, or

deciding automatically how long your food should cook.

And for the baby boomers who start remodeling and building houses for their retirement soon, the technology should be in place when they need it.

"If we can sneak these things into people's homes when they're young, for the convenience, they'll be there as we all get older and help us stay independent longer," says Beth Mynatt, an assistant professor of computing who directs Georgia Tech's project.

Here's a look at what's in store for your home in the future.

The Intelligent House

Would you like your home to "know" you better? Computer scientists at the University of Texas-Arlington are building a home with this scenario as the goal:

At 6:45 a.m., the house turns up the heat, without programming, because it has learned on its own that it needs 15 minutes to warm up before your alarm goes off. At 7 a.m., when your alarm sounds, it signals the bedroom light and kitchen coffee maker to turn on. When you step into the bathroom, the morning news pops up on a video screen, and the shower turns on automatically. While you shave, the house senses (through the floor) that you are two pounds over your ideal weight; it adjusts your suggested menu and displays it in the kitchen.

When you leave home after breakfast, the house locks itself. Later that morning, it notes that the refrigerator is low on milk and cheese, and it places a grocery order to be delivered just before you get home. When you arrive, the food is there—and the house has cranked up the hot tub for you.

What's powering all the automation is something called machine learning, which would enable the computer monitoring the house to observe a resident's habits for a while, and then anticipate individual needs and make decisions about what to turn on and off, says Diane Cook, the project's manager (see more at ranger.uta.edu/smarthome).

At the University of Florida in Gainesville, researchers are using a cellphone to run a home. (So far, the "home" is a simulated apartment inside a lab, but there's a real house under construction that should be finished in June.) When someone rings the doorbell, you either hear it or feel your cellphone vibrating. Then, you can open your phone and see a picture of the person at the door. (A video camera relays the picture.) If you recognize the visitor, you can push a button on your cellphone to unlatch the door. If it's dark and you can't see the visitor, you can push another button to turn on an outside light.

The project, started three years ago, has "evolved from focusing just on smart phones to the smart house," says William Mann, who heads Florida's Rehabilitation Engineering

Research Center on Technology for Successful Aging (rerc.ufl.edu).

The Walls are Watching

Other projects are aimed at installing eyes and ears in the woodwork and could help families keep an eye on aging relatives from a distance.

Home Guardian LLC, spun off from the University of Virginia's Medical Automation Research Center, is testing a wireless monitoring system at about two dozen independent-living and assisted-living apartments for senior citizens in Minneapolis. It takes only about 20 minutes to install, and it uses sensors, rather than cameras or microphones, to pinpoint "where you are in the home at any particular time," says Robin Felder, the company's head and center's director (smarthouse.med.virginia.edu). So far, the monitors have detected four residents' falls.

Another monitoring system, being developed by the University of Rochester's Center for Future Health in New York, uses both sensors and video cameras to track how people walk around in the house. Researchers are searching for ways to use data from the patterns for early detection of strokes, and to track changes in people with chronic conditions such as arthritis or Parkinson's disease.

"Our goal is active intervention, all the way to prevention, as much as possible," says Philippe Fauchet, the center's director.

A "Digital Family Portrait" being tested by a Georgia Tech alumnus and his mother, in her 70s, allows the adult child living far away from a parent to keep an eye out. The mother's house has sensors under the floorboards that track her level of activity, and her son's house has a digital screen where he can get a report at a glance.

The screen looks like a picture frame with her photo in the middle and is bordered by 28 digital butterflies of various sizes. The butterfly representing the current day is white (the rest are shaded pink). The larger the butterfly, the more active his mother has been that day. Touching the butterfly switches the screen to a report of the weather, indoor temperature and his mother's level of room-to-room movement for that day. (There's an example at www.cc.gatech.edu/fce/ecl/projects/dfp/index.html.) If the mother's level of activity changes sharply for no known reason, her son can give her a call to see what's up, says the school's Dr. Mynatt.

Interactive Living Room

Already, thousands of people have bought egg-shaped lamps that sit on coffee tables and change colors when the stock market or the outdoor temperature rises or falls. The information is transmitted over a wireless network, not phone lines or cable (see it at ambientdevices.com). The goal of David Rose, president of **Ambient Devices** Inc. in

(Cont.)

Cambridge, Mass., maker of these "orbs," was to provide information at a glance, much like an old-fashioned barometer.

"It's trying to be as simple as possible, and exist on your periphery and not be intrusive," he says.

Now, the company is expanding into other tabletop devices, starting with a three-needle display it calls a dashboard. And it's working with M.I.T.'s AgeLab to figure out how to use such gizmos to help people monitor their own health. One idea: You could keep a pedometer strapped on all day, then place it at night in a cradle that would transmit the day's record of your steps through the network to the device. The next day, you could compare the previous day's activity level with that of two earlier days.

Above the fireplace mantel in Georgia Tech's Aware Home, a large TV screen displays one researcher's effort to help people sift through their home videos to find specific clips, often a needle-in-a-haystack quest.

"It's important to help us treasure, organize and enjoy memories from the past," says Gregory Abowd, an associate computing professor. To do so, he's developing software to tag each scene based on the people involved, the occasion, and even the car in the background. Once tagged, he can group scenes together and export them to a computer file or DVD. A second project in the works: a video camera that can annotate images as they're being recorded, cutting down on the organizational work later.

Kicked-Up Kitchen

Scientists are devoting considerable attention to this room, where busy families can be distracted by caring for children, parents or both.

One tool on the drawing board, Georgia Tech's Cook's Collage, would use four cameras mounted under the kitchen cabinets to film your hands as you mix ingredients on the countertop below. The pictures, formatted like a filmstrip, would show what you've done most recently. That way, if you're interrupted by a phone call, or children needing help with homework, you can review what you've done to see whether you already had added the salt, for example, or to recall how many cups of flour you had sifted.

Since the cameras are focused on the counter, not on your face, study participants who have seen the tool haven't felt self-conscious about being filmed. "It avoids the bad-hair-day issue," says Dr. Mynatt. (There are pictures at www.cc.gatech.edu/fce/ecl/projects/cooking/index.html).

At the University of Florida, researchers are working on microwave ovens that can read a new kind of label, known as a radio-frequency identification tag. Such labels can store more information than bar codes and are expected to replace them eventually, says Dr. Mann, who heads the project.

For example: You might decide to make instant oatmeal for breakfast, which the computer screen in your kitchen might suggest as part of a menu that complies with your recommended diet. The microwave would recognize what you're preparing from the tag on the package and automatically set the appropriate time and power—whether or not you remember the cooking instructions. It also could tell if the food could cause you to have an allergic reaction.

A range at the LifeWise Home in Bowie, Md., built by the National Center for Seniors' Housing Research, first acts as a refrigerator, so you can pop in a casserole in the morning, then set it to bake later in the afternoon. If two hours pass after the cooking time has finished and you haven't removed the dish from the oven, it turns back into a refrigerator. (It's already commercially available through Whirlpool.)

"It's great for someone who's working, or [busy] during the day with volunteer work," says Charlotte Wade, the program director for the center, part of the National Association of Home Builders. It also could prevent people with memory loss from eating spoiled food.

Bedroom Checkup

Imagine a mattress that could flag early health problems while you sleep. Dr. Felder's lab in Virginia has come up with an inexpensive strip—much like the ones placed across the chest to work with heart-rate monitors—that goes under your mattress pad.

"By measuring your breathing and pulse all night long, we can test for sleep apnea," usually something that can be done only in a sleep laboratory, he says. "The measurements aren't as good, but they can indicate problems and lead to an earlier trip to the doctor."

The bed monitor will work with two people by installing one on each side of the bed. Most couples always sleep on their same side of the bed, Dr. Felder says, even when they stay in hotels, and thus one would get data on the same individual each night.

The bedroom might be the choice for another new device, as well. Georgia Tech has dreamed up what it calls Dude's Magic Box and Grandma's Lap Desk, with the idea of helping grandchildren interact with their grandparents through show-and-tell before they're old enough to do much through e-mail.

"When kids are four to eight years old, they like to say, 'Hey, look at this,'" explains Dr. Mynatt.

Here's how it works:

The grandchild puts something in the box, such as a pet turtle, then the box takes a photo of it. A cartoon character (called Dude in the prototype) pops up on a screen and says, "This is cool! Do you want to send it to Grandma?" At the grandparent's house,

a message pops up on a flat-panel screen or home computer. It sounds futuristic, but the main costs are simply a basic computer with a camera and a no-frills laptop (see more information at www.cc.gatech.edu/fce/ecl/projects/dude).

Bathroom Clinic

This room's getting a makeover, too. Researchers are working on ways to use toilets for instant urinalysis, which could provide data for tracking hypertension, diabetes and other chronic conditions.

"Smart toilets already exist—they cost $2,000 in Japan," says M.I.T.'s Dr. Coughlin. "You shave, you brush your teeth, then you use it to check your glucose. It's for the paranoid well."

If scientists find an efficient way to send that data to your physician, says Dr. Cook at Texas-Arlington, "we could integrate this information together to get a total health picture, then look for deviations from the norm. The nice thing is, this information could be given to the doctor without the person having to leave home."

Another toilet innovation could, to put it delicately, wipe out your need for toilet paper. The LifeWise home has a washing-and-drying toilet that provides a quick rinse with warm water, much like a bidet, then uses a built-in dryer to finish the job. Like many new home gadgets, this one often appeals to baby boomers as a luxury—but could provide needed help as they age as well, says Ms. Wade.

Your medicine cabinet might talk to you in the future, offering advice about interactions among multiple medications. At the University of Rochester, researchers have developed an interactive-computer system with a talking, cartoon pill on the screen that listens to your question, tries to figure out why you said what you said, and responds with an answer from its bank of drug data, which you customize by scanning the bar codes of your medications into it. (You can see a video of how it works at www.futurehealth.rochester.edu/smart_home).

The main thing holding the system back right now, says Dr. Fauchet, is that the natural-language interface needed to let you ask about drugs in your own words "is not to the level that we would like," but researchers are scrambling to improve it.

Tucked in the Closet

Looking for a way to save precious square feet as you downsize from a two-story colonial to a one-story villa? A new sort of water heater, demonstrated in the LifeWise home, heats the water quickly as it passes through, eliminating the need for a big storage tank and saving four square feet of closet space. It comes as a small box that can hang on the wall behind the washer and dryer.

"It's a little bit of cost upfront, but you

(Cont.)

get it back in energy savings," says Ms. Wade in Maryland.

Outside Work by Robot

Most of the research is indoors, but one effort by the Texas scientists could make a difference for people with big spreads: They are trying to control a robotic lawn mower (already commercially available) and sprinkler system through the Internet. So, during your month in Florida or Alaska or Europe, you could still get the lawn mowed regularly and turn the water on during a drought, or off during a tropical storm.

The research problem: "There isn't yet a really good standard for being able to interact with robot lawn mowers, vacuum cleaners" and other appliances, says Dr. Cook. "The market has really focused on these individual devices. There hasn't been an emphasis on how to use them as a whole."

But as researchers figure out how to link new appliances and toys with home-control systems through the Internet, and tie in more technology that absorbs homeowners' habits, that should change, she predicts.

"I can't wait to have a house that can learn my patterns and preferences—and have the hot tub waiting for me when I get home."

LET THEM EAT CAKE—IF THEY WANT TO

The U.S. take on obesity: "Personal responsibility"

How do you change the eating habits of several hundred million people? That's the daunting problem the World Health Organization (WHO) is trying to solve with a proposal for fighting obesity worldwide. It's a bold and necessary effort, but unfortunately, it may be undermined by the world's fattest nation: the U.S. The U.N. estimates that 300 million people worldwide are obese and a further 750 million are overweight, including 22 million children under 5. Health experts around the world are unanimous in saying that something must be done. And that's where the unanimity ends.

The WHO has spent the past year hammering out a series of nonbinding actions that governments could undertake to address their own citizens' weight problems. The initiative is slated for adoption in May, but the U.S., with backing from the powerful food lobby, is working furiously to water down the proposals. These include restrictions on advertising, changes in labeling, increased taxes on junk food, and the elimination of sugar subsidies.

The playbook for the Administration's attack is much the same as the one it used to block international action on global warming. It is charging that the WHO's conclusions are not supported by "sufficient scientific evidence" that fats and sugars cause obesity.

The effort is starting to pay off. The U.S. managed to delay the issuance of a final draft of the proposals for a month, until the end of February, to allow further comment. And now it has company: On Feb. 9, trade ministers from developing nations, many of them sugar producers, rejected the science behind the proposals.

INFURIATING

Technically, the U.S. has a point. William R. Steiger, the lead delegate to the WHO from the Health & Human Services Dept. (HHS), complained in a letter to the organization that the evidence linking sugar and fats to obesity comes from epidemiological studies rather than stringently controlled clinical trials. "In this country, you can't make a scientific claim unless you have the evidence to back it up," argues an HHS spokesman.

This argument infuriates nutrition experts. "The U.S. really isn't refuting the argument. It's saying it is not a tight enough case," says Shiriki Kumanyika, epidemiology professor at the University of Pennsylvania. It is, in fact, almost impossible to prove the cause of noninfectious diseases. For example, there is no absolute proof that smoking causes cancer. "Most major public health actions involve the best evidence available. Otherwise, we'd never do anything," she says.

Even the U.S. does not advocate doing nothing. The Centers for Disease Control estimates that one in every three adults in the U.S. is obese, and 15% of children are overweight—double the rate of 10 years ago. Steiger says in his letter that the U.S. favors guidance that "promotes the view that all foods can be part of a healthy and balanced diet, and supports personal responsibility to choose a diet."

"IMMORAL"

Poor self-control is only one aspect of the obesity problem, however. "Are we so much less responsible than we were 10 years ago?" asks Kelly D. Brownell, director of Yale University's Center for Eating & Weight Disorders. "There are huge obstacles to making healthier choices." Among them: larger portions, inadequate nutritional information on food labels, fast foods sold in schools, and cutbacks in physical education programs.

Health experts have not lined up en masse behind all the WHO's proposals. Some are uncomfortable with taxing food low in nutritional value, even though the tactic has worked against smoking. "Food is something we need to live," says Dr. C. Ronald Kahn, president of the Joslin Diabetes Center in Boston. "What we really need to do is eat less of it."

The idea of eating less is anathema to the food industry, however, and this suggestion is nowhere to be found in the proposals. The WHO, however, does recommend restrictions on advertisements that exhort us to eat more, particularly those aimed at children. "Advertising junk food to children is unethical and immoral," says Dr. Walter C. Willett, head of the department of nutrition at Harvard University's School of Public Health.

Ultimately, the WHO proposals form a multifaceted approach, combining education and regulations. With the same combination, the U.S. was able to cut the smoking rate in half, even though it took 40 years. "It will take at least that long to cut obesity rates by half," Willett predicts, and then only if the U.S. government gets serious about tackling the problem. So far, there is little scientific evidence proving that it is.

By Catherine Arnst

The Weight War

The World Health Organization's anti-obesity proposals:

	PROS	CONS
LABEL CHANGES Food labels should contain more nutrition and serving-size info	Would make it easier to identify healthy foods and plan accurate menus	Few consumers bother to read labels, and it's hard to police menus
"JUNK FOOD" TAX Levy a special tax on foods that are high in sugar and fat	As has been shown with cigarettes, higher prices decrease use	Food is a necessity; a tax penalizes thin and low-income people
ADVERTISING CHANGES Restrict advertising to children; require health warnings	Better to target kids before they grow up to be overweight adults	Marketing is so pervasive that it would be hard to regulate

Lost in Translation

A European Electronics Giant Races to Undo Mistakes in U.S.

Philips Is Big Name at Home, But American Unit Muffed Chances to Build Identity

Now, Get Profitable or Close

By Dan Bilefsky

NEW YORK—For years, every time the Dutch bosses of Philips Electronics NV came here for a visit, Terry Fassburg would take them to Union Square, an area blanketed with electronics stores.

Then Mr. Fassburg, the communications chief for the company's U.S. operations, would bet them $100 that they couldn't find three products made by Philips, Europe's biggest consumer-electronics company. He never lost. "It was my way of showing European executives we needed help," Mr. Fassburg says.

Despite its role in inventing hundreds of products, including the compact disc and the audio-cassette recorder, Philips's consumer-electronics division has lost money in the U.S. for the past 15 years. Meanwhile, through a long string of self-inflicted fiascoes, it has watched many of its inventions become blockbusters in the U.S.—for its rivals.

Now Philips's troubled North American consumer-electronics division is facing its toughest challenge yet. About two years ago headquarters in Amsterdam ordered the operation to show a yearly profit for 2004—or be shut down. The division seemed to be making progress toward that goal under a new U.S. chief executive, Larry Blanford. He introduced a host of marketing and distribution efforts and helped dramatically shrink the division's losses. But Mr. Blanford has announced his resignation, and Gerard Kleisterlee, Philips's CEO, hasn't backed down from his threat to jettison the U.S. division.

"We are in the business to make profits, and we can't support operations that continue to destroy value for shareholders," Mr. Kleisterlee said in a recent interview.

Selling off the division, which accounts for roughly 9% of the company's total sales of $41 billion, would leave one of the world's leading electronics companies without a foothold in the world's largest electronics market. And it might make other European companies, which are closely watching Philips's moves, question the extent of their investments in the U.S.

In Europe, the Philips name resonates with both history and contemporary cool. The Eiffel Tower is strung with Philips light bulbs, the product that launched the company in 1891, and today Philips gadgets mesmerize European teenagers at hip electronics stores. But in the U.S., Philips's consumer-electronics division has distinguished itself largely by its disasters: a mix of marketing and distribution problems that undermined some groundbreaking products.

That was partly because Philips since the 1970s had primarily been known as the low-end brand Philips-Magnavox. Philips executives had calculated that they needed the large scale of low-end sales to be profitable, so they focused their marketing on less-expensive items instead of the upmarket products that were a hit overseas. The move hurt Philips's profit margin and deprived it of upmarket European cachet in the U.S.

A recent study by Philips showed that only about 35% of Americans recognize that Philips is a consumer-electronics company. Though brand image and loyalty are everything in the U.S. consumer-electronics business, Philips until recently treated marketing in the U.S. as an afterthought. Meanwhile, throughout the industry, competition from brand names and knockoffs alike has grown fiercer and profit margins have fallen to less than 1% on some products. Sony Corp. was

forced to overhaul its consumer-electronics operation this autumn, shedding 20,000 jobs.

Reinier Jens, Philips's new U.S. CEO, acknowledges that a full turnaround—including a high U.S. profile for the Philips brand and big profits—is still a ways off. "You do not build a brand in one or two years," says Mr. Jens, a Dutchman who was until recently the London-based chief of Philips's Northern European consumer-electronics division. "It will take more time."

Cautionary Tale

Philips's history has been a cautionary tale. Though the company's engineers co-developed CD technology with Sony Corp., Philips lost out on U.S. profits because of its position as a low-end brand. Analysts estimate the company suffered $1 billion in losses between 1991 and 1996 with its CD-i machine, which let consumers play video games, listen to music CDs, watch movies and view digital photos. The product was chased from store shelves by Sony's PlayStation. Philips's version, which was pitched as a teaching device as much as a game machine, lacked its frenetic thrills. Even worse, the product was so complicated that it required a 30-minute demonstration.

In 1997, years before its competitors, Philips launched a $250 million U.S. advertising campaign for flat-screen TVs. But the company didn't get them into most stores until the market was overcrowded. "We ended up creating a buzz around the brand and then handed the flat television market to our rivals," says Mr. Blanford. One reason was the company's poor relations with upmarket retailers.

Matthew Foley, a manager at Provideo, an upmarket electronics retailer in Washington's

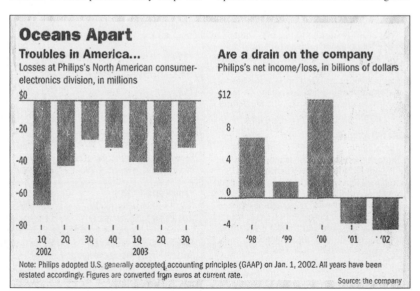

Oceans Apart

Troubles in America...
Losses at Philips's North American consumer-electronics division, in millions

Are a drain on the company
Philips's net income/loss, in billions of dollars

Note: Philips adopted U.S. generally accepted accounting principles (GAAP) on Jan. 1, 2002. All years have been restated accordingly. Figures are converted from euros at current rate.

Source: the company

(Cont.)

Georgetown neighborhood, says retailers like him didn't take the flat-screen TV because of Philips's low brand recognition and because the company priced the sets too high. Indeed, when potential customers could find the sets, they were stunned to discover that they cost $15,000. Philips's rivals quickly produced their own models, many at cheaper prices.

Attempts to capture the U.S. markets for digital cable boxes and cellphones also faltered. Philips was among the first to come up with mobile-phone technology but was beat to the market by rivals while Philips divisions debated their model's design.

Such ventures weren't a total drain for Philips. In 2002, its global royalty revenue on inventions it helped create, such as the CD player, was $340 million.

When Mr. Blanford took over as U.S. CEO in 2001, he emphasized improving distribution, particularly at high-end stores. By wooing U.S. retailers and placing Philips on shelves where it had never been, he helped shrink the division's losses from $372 million in 2001 to $250 million in 2002 and $88 million through the first three quarters of 2003. Philips doesn't release revenue numbers for the division.

Mr. Blanford says he was stunned to discover that Philips's 12 U.S. salespeople never visited upmarket electronics stores. Tweeter, one of the biggest electronics chains in the U.S., with 175 stores in 21 states across the country, didn't carry a single Philips television.

Mr. Blanford increased the sales force to 50, and ordered salespeople into retail stores at least three times a week. He also left his Atlanta headquarters to visit the CEOs of Tweeter and Best Buy. "Larry was relentless," says Sandy Bloomberg, chairman of Tweeter, which went from carrying no Philips products to carrying more than 70.

Mr. Blanford split the Philips-Magnavox brand in two, for high-end and low-end products. And he made an aggressive grab for the youth market, organizing a "brand-management team" of twenty- and thirty-somethings who trawl retailers across the country to check out Sony's latest offerings, test Philips prototypes and attend extreme-sports events in search of ideas. The team joined forces with MTV, Nike and makers of surfboards and snowboards to help make the Philips name resonate among young buyers. The company has sponsored concerts and competitions, and introduced "youth" products such as a Nike-branded sweat-resistant portable CD player, which the company says is selling well with sports enthusiasts.

Just eight months after Mr. Blanford took the job, Mr. Kleisterlee surprised him with his threat to get rid of the U.S. division if it didn't become profitable. The threat was delivered in a December 2001 interview with the Dutch current affairs magazine Elsevier. Mr. Blanford wouldn't say whether the deadline was also handed down to him personally by his Dutch bosses. But when the Elsevier article appeared, Mr. Blanford was forced into fast action. He called the CEOs of Tweeter and Best Buy to ensure no sales contracts were canceled and sent a letter to Philips's 960 U.S. consumer-electronics employees, assuring them they still had jobs.

Some industry analysts say they suspect Mr. Blanford was asked to leave his post because headquarters was growing impatient with progress. The company denies this. Mr. Blanford says his parting with Philips is amicable; he never intended to stay beyond three years, and both he and the company wanted to make a change before the big International Consumer Electronics Show in Las Vegas, which starts tomorrow. Mr. Blanford, a 50-year-old former Maytag executive from Dayton, Ohio, says he wants to be chief executive of a company, not just a division, so he's leaving Philips by the end of this week. He doesn't have a new post lined up.

Mr. Bloomberg, the chairman of Tweeter, says Mr. Blanford brought Philips a new understanding of the U.S. market. Some industry analysts questioned the wisdom of appointing a European with little U.S. experience to the top job. "It's baffling that they replaced him with a European, given that most of their past gaffes resulted from Europeans not understanding the U.S.," says Bert Siebrand, technology analyst at Bank Oyens & van Eeghen in Amsterdam.

Mr. Kleisterlee, the Philips global CEO, himself has lamented in the past that Philips has too many "boring, white Dutch guys." Mr. Jens, the new U.S. CEO, says he has worked in the industry across the globe, and holding a Dutch passport is no impediment to running a U.S. business.

A major part of Philips' problem now is its lack of a breakout product. Aside from a range of gear targeted at teens in the U.S. and other markets—such as a digital camera the size of a house key and a pocket-size "audio jukebox" that can record from any source of music—the company's main offerings are hard to distinguish from many of its competitors'.

Long Shots

Philips does have some expensive long shots in the pipeline. It plans to market a television screen that becomes a mirror when it's turned off—first aimed at boutique hotels, but then within two years at home consumers, likely at $4,000 to $5,000. More ambitiously, it's offering a set of products it dubs "the connected home," in which computerized appliances such as televisions, computers and DVD players can "talk" among themselves and download digital photographs, music and video games from the Internet.

It's so determined to get these gadgets into American living rooms that it's hiring European architects to build prefabricated homes, fitted with this gear, that can be assembled in two weeks and shipped anywhere in the U.S. But industry analysts say the technology could take up to a decade to become popular with customers. Meanwhile, rivals such as Samsung and others have similar concepts in the works.

In an effort to avoid the snafus of the past, Philips last year hired its first-ever world-wide marketing chief. At the direction of the CEO, Mr. Kleisterlee, Philips's marketing division is now involved in product launches from the beginning. Philips has created a model home in Eindhoven, the Netherlands, where American teenagers are being recruited to test out new products under video and audio surveillance.

Philips now is outspending some of its rivals on U.S. marketing, putting nearly $31 million into advertising last year, according to TNS Media Intelligence/CMR, a New York-based research firm. The company sponsored the U.S. Open snowboarding competition in Vermont and organized a California surfing event where local grunge bands played on a Philips-branded stage. Philips products are among the prizes on MTV's "Real World Challenge" reality show.

In the past, says Diego Olego, managing director of Philips's U.S. research-and-development operation, "All our engineers cared about was winning patents and hanging plaques on their walls. Now they also want to be able to take their kids to a store in New York or San Francisco, show them the latest blockbuster and say, 'Look, daddy made that.'"

For Philips, maintaining relations with retailers and salespeople is a top priority now. In New York, Philips is now the exclusive video-equipment supplier for a new consumer-electronics boutique at Macy's flagship department store. Located near a gourmet sushi stand and the designer-underwear section, the boutique carries only the most expensive Philips products. Philips also is pushing for prominent display space at stores such as Jordan's Furniture in suburban Boston, which has a 262-seat IMAX theatre and a replica of New Orleans's "Bourbon street" running through its entrance.

Mr. Fassburg, the U.S. communications chief, no longer makes his Union Square wager with visiting Dutch executives, for fear of losing his $100.

But there is work to be done. Neill Salamack, the Philips regional representative for New York, Connecticut and New Jersey, recently stopped by J&R Music World, an electronics megastore in lower Manhattan, and confronted the store manager, John Jensen: The store's main Philips display was barely visible, its sign hidden under a staircase. The Panasonic sign nearby was nearly triple the size. "I'm not happy about this," he said.

The New Public Service Ad: Just Say 'Deal With It'

BY SHAILA K. DEWAN

The image is lurid even by today's standards: a young woman kneels on a bathroom floor, head over the toilet, then stands, wiping her mouth with the back of her hand.

"Sound familiar?" asks a voice with muted Welsh vowels. "If so, you may have bulimia. You cannot flush away your problems. It won't go away until you stop gagging your pain and give it a voice."

The short animation, narrated by Catherine Zeta-Jones, is part of the "Face the Issue" campaign: seven public service announcements aimed primarily at adolescents and young adults, in which the voices of celebrities like Jennifer Lopez and Kate Hudson address eating disorders, domestic violence and drug abuse.

The campaign is different from those that have gone before it. It does not try to shame the viewer into action. There are no scare tactics that end in the coffins or graves. This is not your brain on drugs. Nor does it emphasize a positive message—snowboarding as the anti-drug, say—that might seem out of reach to its target audience.

Like its precursors in the squeamish 1950's, the wised-up 1970's, the fearful "Just Say No" and let's-hear-nothing-else-about-it 1980's, the "Face the Issue" campaign reflects its time. Brutally frank and uncomfortably intimate, it delves into a world in which young people grow up faster, are more sophisticated and, statistics show, are increasingly diagnosed as troubled. Perhaps more important, rather than appeal to parents, it asks young people to take action themselves. Each message ends with the words: "Your choice."

The 30-second spots, made at cost with the stars donating their time, have been shown on MTV, the WB and other networks. An important component is the corresponding Web site, www.facetheissue.com , a sort of online group therapy session whose users post messages about their problems. The day after the campaign began in late October, the site got 300,000 hits. As of last week, two million people had visited.

The postings lay bare the elaborate pathos of teenagedom today. A girl who says she cannot refrain from cutting herself wrote: "Everyone thinks that because I am a 'surgeon's daughter' and because we have money that my life is perfect. NEWSFLASH: MONEY DOES NOT BUY HAPPINESS."

Another user wrote of a disorder involving a compulsion to pluck one's eyebrows and lashes until only bloody clumps remain. "My parents say that I can stop anytime I want," she said.

Unlike most public service campaigns, "Face the Issue" was created without focus groups or market testing. It is the brainchild of two women, Jane B. Semel and Melanie Hall, with no experience producing such messages. Ms. Semel, the wife of Terry Semel, the chief executive of Yahoo, founded ijane inc., a nonprofit production company that promotes public health issues, and Ms. Hall is the company's president.

It gets high marks from mental health experts, particularly because the Web site offers teenagers, who may resist formal treatment, a way to seek support and information anonymously.

"These videos really represent the future rather than the past, because they use animation, they use the Internet, they're interactive," said Jay Winsten, who, as the director of the Center for Health Communication at Harvard, introduced the concept of the designated driver. "It's a model for what future communications with young people will look like."

Public service messages have long been driven by both the national mood and a continuing debate over effective strategy. In the 1950's, children were shown films like "Let's Be Clean and Neat," which emphasized conformity. As Ken Smith, a scholar of such films, writes in "Mental Hygiene," the

> **Stigma, shame and fear are out. Personal responsibility is in.**

narrators mocked hapless teens whose bobby socks sagged or who refused to get along.

Indifference toward the afflicted lingered into the 1970's, when one ad showed an addict crying and begging her father for money, then counting it the minute she was out. The "Face the Issue" ads do not ostracize or preach. But they do present reality: with unchecked anorexia, "you'll be dead before you're thin enough"; with abuse, "it will happen again."

"What I like about them is they portray the person in trouble as an active agent," said Sally Satel, a psychiatrist and a scholar at the conservative American Enterprise Institute. She said they served a different purpose than the "Just Say No" slogan. "They're aimed at different people," she said. "'Just Say No' is prevention. This is for people who really have a problem already."

It was AIDS that led to this plain speaking. In the 1980's, the Ad Council, the major producer of public service announcements, persuaded networks to broadcast the first commercials to use the word "condom."

When it came to effectiveness, celebrity competed against the tragic ending. But William J. Bennett, the first President Bush's drug policy adviser, argued in favor of the fear approach. "Kids need to see more burnout cases," he said in 1989.

Both strategies had pitfalls. Not everyone can identify with celebrities. Horror stories could scare people into inaction. If the peril were exaggerated, young people would smell a rat (or, as with "this is your brain on drugs," fodder for a joke).

A problem with public health campaigns is that they generally address a single issue, said Joseph A. Califano Jr., chairman of the National Center on Addiction and Substance Abuse at Columbia University. The reality, he said, is that people with eating disorders are more likely to abuse drugs and both must be treated to be effective. "It's all one ball of wax," he said.

In the 1990's, research showed that parents are far more effective messengers. New slogans urged parents to talk to their children about drugs and sex.

But an obstacle for teens with eating disorders or drug problems, several experts said, is their parents' denial. A child may not have anorexia but still have serious food-related problems, said Susan Smalley, a psychiatry professor at the University of California at Los Angeles who studies such disorders. "The site is tapping into that group of children and adolescents that aren't being identified," she said.

Peggy Conlon, the president of the Ad Council, said that one way to change behavior is to change what is considered normal. She points to the Legacy Foundation's antismoking ads, showing children ambushing tobacco executives with tough questions. "They're making kids appear smart if they resist smoking," she said.

"Face the Issue" grapples with another issue: what to do when low self-confidence and eating disorders seem to be the norm.

"There is no magic wand, 'Oh, do this and it's all going to be fine,'" said Ms. Semel. "The whole point was not to make the issues so negative. To take the stigma away from it and just make it like anything else in life, something you should deal with."

Nestlé Markets Baby Formula To Hispanic Mothers In U.S.

By Miriam Jordan

Anaheim, Calif.—By the dozens, mothers with strollers and protruding bellies approach the stand of the only infant-formula company exhibiting at an annual baby-products fair here. Like many others, Alicia Araujo leaves the booth clutching a free sample can. "They were very helpful," she says, pushing a carriage with her four-month-old, Danielle.

Nestlé SA is betting on Hispanic mothers like Mrs. Araujo to boost its share of the $3 billion U.S. infant-formula market—and some doctors and breast-feeding advocates are irate. The company has begun promoting Nan, a leading brand in Latin America, just as the U.S. government is poised to launch the first campaign in a century to persuade low-income, minority mothers to breast-feed.

At issue is whether companies should market baby formula to low-income immigrant mothers when health experts and government officials agree that breast-feeding is healthier, and saves in long-term health-care costs. Most health professionals say breast milk is superior to formula for infants, except in rare cases such as when a mother is HIV-positive. The American Academy of Pediatrics and the American College of Obstetricians and Gynecologists recommend that exclusive breast-feeding is ideal nutrition for the first six months after birth and that breast-feeding continue for at least 12 months, and thereafter for as long as mutually desired. An article on March 4 failed to state the entire recommendation, saying only that doctors recommend that all women breast-feed their babies for at least the first six months of life.

Nestlé came under fire in the 1970s for the way it marketed infant formula in the developing world to poor, illiterate women who often misused it. Health professionals at the time found bottle-fed babies sometimes became undernourished and suffered from chronic illnesses because their mothers were watering down the costly formula to make it go further or they were preparing it with contaminated water.

That prompted the World Health Organization, in 1981, to devise a voluntary code whereby countries and companies, particularly in the developing world, agreed to restrict the marketing of formula. And indeed, Nestlé doesn't advertise Nan in countries such as Mexico, which follows the WHO code.

The U.S. also signed the code, but never enacted laws to restrict marketing of formula here. The Swiss company takes care "to make sure that all advertising stays in the U.S.," says Kathy Mitsukawa, a marketing associate for Nestlé.

"We have launched Nestlé Nan in the U.S. with a fully bilingual label so that U.S. Hispanic moms, who choose not to or cannot breast-feed, can make an informed choice with regard to their child's nutrition," says Lisbeth Armentano, a spokeswoman for Nestlé's U.S. unit in Glendale, Calif. She adds that the company believes breast-feeding is better for babies and even says so in its advertising.

Nestlé entered the U.S. formula market in 1988 with Carnation's Good Start line. But the Swiss food titan has only a sliver of the market dominated by pharmaceutical companies. **Abbott Laboratories,** maker of Similac formula, and **Bristol-Myers Squibb** Co.'s Mead Johnson Nutritionals, which makes Enfamil, have long enjoyed an inside track in pushing their products because of their ties to the medical establishment. Many hospitals distribute free samples of Similac or Enfamil to mothers of newborns when they check out, a practice that breast-feeding activists and some doctors criticize. Research shows that many mothers end up using the formula they get for free at the hospital. While the two companies do some advertising, Nestlé alone markets with radio spots and promotions at baby fairs. However, the company also is trying to break into the maternity ward, Ms. Mitsukawa says.

The numbers help explain why Nestlé is focusing on the 38 million Hispanics in the U.S. They already make up 13% of the total population and that percentage is expected to grow to 20% of the U.S. population by 2020. "Hispanic households tend to be larger and have growing birth rates," Ms. Armentano says. In addition, Hispanic mothers in the

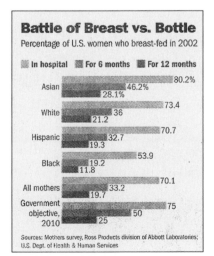

Battle of Breast vs. Bottle
Percentage of U.S. women who breast-fed in 2002

In hospital | For 6 months | For 12 months

Asian: 80.2% / 46.2% / 28.1%
White: 73.4 / 36 / 21.2
Hispanic: 70.7 / 32.7 / 19.3
Black: 53.9 / 19.2 / 11.8
All mothers: 70.1 / 33.2 / 19.7
Government objective, 2010: 75 / 50 / 25

Sources: Mothers survey, Ross Products division of Abbott Laboratories; U.S. Dept. of Health & Human Services

U.S. tend to be less educated, and research suggests that women with less education are more likely to bottle-feed their babies. That makes them a desirable marketing target for formula companies.

Critics say that also means Hispanic mothers, who lack fluency in English, won't get enough medical advice to make an informed choice between formula and breast-feeding their infants. And, for many immigrant women from deprived backgrounds, bottle feeding has an aura of acculturation and prosperity. "Nestlé is using a vulnerable population for a grab at market share," says Marsha Walker, executive director of the National Alliance for Breastfeeding Advocacy, an organization that works to make breast-feeding a public-health priority.

Doctors also voice concern. "I am very much opposed to any marketing at all of infant formula. It should not be regarded as a growth area for companies," says Larry Gartner, neonatologist and head of the American Academy of Pediatrics' breast-feeding division.

Still, the reality is that many Hispanic mothers must work and can't be with their babies all day, or some find their babies aren't thriving with breast-feeding and are receptive to the formula makers' pitches.

Nestlé posters at the "Yeah, Baby" Expo proclaim in Spanish that "women in Latin America have trusted Nan for more than 40 years." To cater to Hispanic moms, Nan puts instructions in Spanish right on the can; other formula brands in the U.S. require customers to snip off the label for Spanish directions on the inside.

"Hispanic moms in the U.S. are familiar with Nan . . . and asked us to carry it," says Nestlé's Ms. Armentano.

Some Hispanic mothers dispute the claim that breast-feeding is better. At the Anaheim hospital where she gave birth, Eva Hernandez said the nurses encouraged her to breast-feed, but she didn't see any health benefits for Marcos, her firstborn son. He "got colds, ear infections and sore throats," she says. She breast-fed her second child only four months, then switched to formula and "he was much healthier," she says. She didn't breast-feed her third child at all: "I simply don't have time to breast-feed."

Nestlé officials decline to disclose details of the marketing strategy for Nan, including how much it will invest in ads. The company first advertised the brand last year on billboards in Hispanic enclaves of Los Angeles and Houston. But recently it kicked off a national campaign, placing ads in Spanish-language parenting magazines and radio.

"I filled out the form to get coupons," says Michelle Hernandez, 29, of Garden Grove, who was at the Anaheim fair. At as much as $13 per twelve ounce can, "formula can get expensive," she says.

(Cont.)

The problem, critics say, is that a mother who supplements with formula is likely to wean her baby from the breast early. At six months of an infant's life, 36% of white mothers breast-fed, 32.7% of Hispanic mothers and 19.2% of black mothers, according to a 2002 study by Ross Products, a unit of **Abbott Laboratories.**

Breast milk helps prevent allergies, infections and other illnesses in infants. Studies also show that raising breast-feeding rates would save families, insurers and the U.S. government millions of dollars each year on health care.

In the face of such evidence, the U.S. government is launching a major campaign to promote breast milk with public-service announcements. Created by the Ad Council, the spots will target minorities and low-income women because they show the lowest rates of breast-feeding, said people familiar with the campaign.

Back at the Anaheim baby fair, Rosie Sanchez, who works as a clerk, has formula-fed her two American-born children, and plans to do the same with the third on the way. "Women only breastfeed in Latin America because they can't afford to buy formula," she says.

From *The Wall Street Journal,* March 4, 2004. Reprinted by permission of Dow Jones & Co., Inc. via The Copyright Clearance Center.

95

Behind Roses' Beauty, Poor and Ill Workers

By GINGER THOMPSON

Cayambe, Ecuador — In just five years, Ecuadorean roses, as big and red as the human heart, have become the new status flower in the United States, thanks to the volcanic soil, perfect temperatures and abundant sunlight that help generate $240 million a year and tens of thousands of jobs in this once-impoverished region north of Quito.

This St. Valentine's Day, hundreds of American florists and catalogs are offering the roses of this fertile valley. Calyx & Corolla, for instance, bills it as a place "where Andean mists and equatorial sun conspire to produce roses that quickly burst into extravagant bloom, then hold their glory long after lesser specimens have begun to droop."

But roses come with thorns, too. As Ecuador's colorful blooms radiate romance around the world, large growers here have been accused of misusing a toxic mixture of pesticides, fungicides and fumigants to grow and export unblemished pest-free flowers.

As in other industries like garment production, bananas and diamonds, the poor worry about eating first and labor conditions later. They toil here despite headaches and rashes here for the wealthier of the world, who in turn know little of the conditions in which their desires are met.

Doctors and scientists who have worked here say serious health problems have resulted for many of the industry's 50,000 workers, more than 70 percent of them women. Researchers say their work is hampered by lack of access to flower farms because of reluctant growers. But studies that the International Labor Organization published in 1999 and the Catholic University issued here last year showed that women in the industry had more miscarriages than average and that more than 60 percent of all workers suffered headaches, nausea, blurred vision or fatigue.

"No one can speak with conclusive facts in hand about the impact of this industry on the health of the workers, because we have not been able to do the necessary studies,"said Dr. Bolivar Vera, a health specialist at the Health Environment and Development Foundation in Quito. "So the companies have been able to wash their hands of the matter."

In the 20 years since the farms started here, Ecuador has out of nowhere become the fourth-largest producer of roses in the world, with customers from Kazakhstan to Kansas.

St. Valentine's Day is the biggest rose event in the United States, which buys more than 70 percent of its cut flowers from South America and is Ecuador's biggest trading partner. Roses retail for up to $6 a bloom. Last week, workers at RosaPrima, a plantation here, moved at a dizzying pace to cut, wrap and box 70,000 stems a day. Computers help supervisors track each stem and each worker's productivity.

The general manager, Ross Johnson, said he was proud of his business and especially his workers. He said that a doctor visited the farm several times a week and that all workers wore gloves and protective equipment, whether or not handling chemicals. Mr. Johnson said he had cracked down on contractors who hired children as temporary workers.

"We have made a lot of improvements over the years," said Mr. Johnson, who was born in Ecuador and who helped start the farm seven years ago. "I think this is a noble business that does noble things for people here and around the world."

He said roses were typically fumigated 24 hours before being cut. Then they are soaked overnight in a nontoxic chemical solution and shipped at near freezing temperatures.

Dr. Cesar Paz-y-Mino, a geneticist at the Catholic University, said several pesticides used on a farm that was the setting for his research in the late 1990's were restricted as health hazards in other countries, including the United States, and labeled as highly toxic by the World Health Organization.

Roses have become a major Ecuadorean export.

Among the most notorious are captan, aldicarb and fenamiphos. Dr. Paz-y-Mino refused to identify the flower farm under an agreement that he said he had with the owners.

He described the conditions as astonishing and recalled workers' fumigating in street clothes without protective equipment, pesticides stored in poorly sealed containers and fumes wafting over the workers' dining halls. When asked what government agencies monitor worker health and safety, Dr. Paz-y-Mino said, "There are no such checks."

Neither the Labor nor Health Ministries have occupational health departments. In an interview, Labor Minister Felipe Mantilla said he planned to visit flower and banana plantations in a few weeks. Human rights groups, including Human Rights Watch, have criticized Ecuadorean banana growers for using child labor. Mr. Mantilla said the government planned to set up "discussion tables" for workers and managers to discuss competitiveness and labor conditions.

"If there are violations," he said, "we will act firmly. We are drawing up a plan of action on the issue of workers' conditions and we are seeking help from international organizations. The ministry does not have funds to implement plans for progressive control. So that is why we look for international help."

Industry representatives denied that there was a health problem or that unacceptable risks were taken.

"The growers we know are very conscious of environmental issues," said Harrison Kennicott, the chief executive of Kennicott Brothers, a wholesaler in Chicago who is a former president of the Society of American Florists, a trade group.

"They go to lengths to get certified environmentally," Mr. Kennicott said. "The growers take care of the people. They provide housing and medical care.

"Our job is to satisfy our customers, who are the florists and retailers who deliver flowers to the public. Our interest is having the best quality product at a competitive price."

Yet it is hard to erase images of workers like Soledad, 32, and Petrona, 34, both mothers and both looking jaundiced and bony. In interviews after quitting time, they asked not to be fully identified out of fear that they would lose their $156-a-month jobs cutting flowers in greenhouses. The women said they had elementary school educations but did not need high-level science to tell them why their kidneys throbbed at night and heads throbbed in the day.

"There is no respect for the fumigation rules," said Petrona, who has worked on flower farms for four years. "They spray the chemicals even while we are working."

"My hair has begun to fall out," she added, running a hand from the top of her visibly receding hairline down a single scruffy braid. "I am young, but I feel very old."

Soledad, who has worked on flower farms for 12 years, slowly turned her head from side to side.

"If I move my head any faster, I feel nauseous," she said, and then pulled up her sleeve to show her skeletal limbs. "I have no appetite."

When asked whether the farm where they worked had a doctor on duty, the women rolled their eyes.

"He always tells us there is nothing wrong with us and sends us back to work,"

(Cont.)

Petrona said. "He works for the company. He does not help us."

The industry received a helping hand from the Andean Trade Preference Act of 1991. It gives tariff-free access to American markets for farmers in Bolivia, Colombia, Ecuador and Peru. The law was intended as part of Washington's fight against drug trafficking, offering incentives to abandon coca and poppy growing.

Roses have become one of the top five sources of export revenue for Ecuador. The bloom boom has transformed this once sleepy region of cattle ranches, inhabited primarily by Indians. Much of the heartland has been hollowed out by illegal immigration to Europe and the United States, but the population in the flower regions north and south of Quito has soared. In Cayambe, the population has increased in 10 years, from 5,000 to more than 70,000.

Flowers have helped pave roads and built sophisticated irrigation systems. This year, construction will begin on an international airport between Quito and Cayambe.

The average flower worker earns more than the $120-a-month minimum wage. By employing women, the industry has fostered a social revolution in which mothers and wives have more control over their families' spending, especially on schooling for their children.

As it has grown successful, the industry has come under fire from the green movement in Europe and was the subject of a recent article in Mother Jones magazine. European consumers have pressed for improvements and environmental safeguards, encouraging some growers to join a voluntary program aimed at helping customers identify responsible growers. The certification signifies that dozens of the 460 growers have distributed protective gear, given training in using chemicals and hired doctors to visit at least weekly.

"There are still farms that do not respect fumigation limits or give workers proper training and equipment for handling chemi-

---

The poor worry about eating first and labor conditions later.

---

cals," said Gonzalo Luzuriaga, chief executive officer of BellaRosa, another flower grower here. "But many of the farmers are very conscientious about these issues, and we are working to make improvements."

Still numerous signs remain that life for the workers, although better, is far from good. Looking over the town plaza from his second-floor office, Mayor Diego Bonifaz, who also operates a flower farm, said: "It's hard for me to get the wealth out of the plantations and into the community. The farms operate in the first world, selling flowers on the Internet. I am still struggling to pave streets."

Reliable health care, however, seems the most glaring need. Beds have been added to the local hospital, doctors said, but workers often cannot afford services there. The chief of the Red Cross clinic, Dr. Toribio Valladares, said he had seen growing numbers of people with respiratory problems, conjunctivitis, miscarriages and rashes, although he did not have firm numbers.

Like the two women who harvest greenhouse roses, Dr. Valladares voiced deep distrust of doctors who worked on the flower farms.

"When the workers go for help to the doctors on the plantations," he said, "the doctors treat the symptoms but do not examine the workers to try to determine their illnesses. And the doctors always tell them that their illnesses have nothing to do with their work."

In Miami, James Pagano, chief marketing officer of Calyx & Corolla, said he had not been to Ecuador and did not want to comment on environmental or worker conditions.

"We buy what we think consumers will perceive to be a high quality rose at a competitive price," he said. The environment "is not an issue we have any business being in."